Firm Innovation and Productivity in Latin America and the Caribbean

Matteo Grazzi • Carlo Pietrobelli
Editors

Firm Innovation and Productivity in Latin America and the Caribbean

The Engine of Economic Development

Inter-American Development Bank

palgrave
macmillan

Editors
Matteo Grazzi
Inter-American Development Bank
Washington, DC, USA

Carlo Pietrobelli
Inter-American Development Bank
Washington, DC, USA

ISBN 978-1-349-58150-4   ISBN 978-1-349-58151-1   (eBook)
DOI 10.1057/978-1-349-58151-1

Library of Congress Control Number: 2016941889

This Palgrave Macmillan imprint is published by Springer Nature
The registered company is Nature America Inc. New York

FOREWORD

After a decade of favorable international conditions, most Latin American and Caribbean countries are now confronting their reality. Despite the observed increases in growth rates, decline in unemployment, and spectacular figures in investment and saving, factors behind long-run growth and sustainability are still showing meager results. Total factor productivity has not changed in most countries in the region for more than a decade. This is alarming, since improvements on the inspirational side of economic growth are heavily correlated with movements in income per capita.

Most of the theoretical and empirical efforts have focused on analyzing the sources of this delay on a macro-level. By examining aggregate figures related to research and development (R&D), foreign direct investments (FDI), macro-regulations, and sometimes educational issues, it is possible to derive policy implications almost without considering several meso and micro-characteristics of the countries that may determine the success or failure of these recommendations.

We have recently learned that heterogeneity matters. In most of the countries in the region, not only do different sectors show dissimilar productivity performances but this phenomenon is also observed inside the sectors. To disentangle those macro-factors that are affecting the productive rhythm of the economies from those that are more sector or even firm-specific, we must use different lenses for different observation units. The mechanism behind those patterns may vary not only among countries but also among sectors and firms.

Thoughtfully considering the assumption that not only the level of productivity matters but also its variance, this book complies several empirical works that by using different lenses aims to reveal which variables may have a systematic effect on the productivity evolution observed at a firm and sectorial level in Latin American and Caribbean countries. The book emphasizes knowledge generation, diffusion, and implementation through innovation, while exploring the roles of human capital, financial resources, and linkages that also shape firms' inspiration.

Results provided throughout the book show that there are several dimensions that matter, including the ways that policy-makers design and implement public support that aim to enhance productivity. Some results were expected but others were not. Some variables are relevant in certain countries, others in certain productive sectors. The book is an invitation to a wider group of researchers and policy-makers to have a closer look at what is happening at a sectoral or even firm level. Understanding the challenges that most of these firms, sectors, and countries face and the way they surpass them is key for the design of public policies.

This is part of the role of the Inter-American Development Bank, and especially of the Competitiveness and Innovation Division. By producing knowledge products in a collaborative and effective manner, promoting a growing research community, and supporting our policy-makers in the areas of innovation, productivity, and human capital formation, we can help to increase economic performance and, in turn, improve the overall welfare of all citizens in the region.

José Miguel Benavente
Division Chief
Competitiveness and Innovation Division
Inter-American Development Bank

ACKNOWLEDGMENTS

This book was prepared by a team led by Matteo Grazzi and Carlo Pietrobelli of the Competitiveness and Innovation Division of the Inter-American Development Bank, who coordinated the research and edited the book. It is part of the research project on "Policies and Institutions for Productivity in Latin America and the Caribbean," financed by the Institutional Capacity Strengthening Fund (ICSF).

Eddy Szirmai acted as external scientific advisor and José Miguel Benavente provided guidance throughout the project. Leonardo Ortega and Siobhan Pangerl provided excellent research assistance. Sarah Schineller oversaw the editing and production of this volume, working closely with the editors and authors.

The construction of a book is a lengthy process during which the team was fortunate to receive valuable comments and advice from many people. We wish to thank Martin Chrisney, Jorge Rodriguez Meza, and Federica Saliola for launching the initial idea of a book on enterprise performance in Latin America and the Caribbean. In addition, we thank Rita Almeida, Leopoldo Avellan, Juan Blyde, Arturo Galindo, Juan Carlos Navarro, Jocelyn Olivari, Carmen Pages, Joan Prats, Graciana Rucci, Hong Tan, Sebastián Vergara, Christian Volpe Martincus, and Pluvia Zuñiga for their useful and insightful comments at various stages of the preparation of the book.

This volume has greatly benefited from participation and discussions at an IDB Workshop where preliminary drafts and ideas were discussed (Washington DC, USA, June 2014), and in many other seminars where preliminary drafts of the entire manuscript or individual chapters were presented. These include: Centro Rossi-Doria Workshop "Global Value Chains for Food and Nutrition Security" (University Roma Tre, Italy, September 2014); The European Trade Study Group—ETSG International Conference (Munich, Germany, September 2014); Universidad del Rosario Economics Seminar (Bogotá, Colombia, November 2014); ORT University Innovation Seminar (Montevideo, Uruguay, November 2014); UNU–MERIT Conference on "Future Perspectives on Innovation and Governance in Development" (Maastricht, the Netherlands, November 2014); AQR-IREA Seminar (Barcelona, Spain, February 2015); the Eighth Conference on Micro Evidence on Innovation and Development MEIDE (New Delhi, India, February 2015); VI Congreso de la Asociación de Economía para el Desarrollo de la Argentina (Buenos Aires, Argentina, May 2015); IDB Second Seminario Relampago IFD (Washington DC, USA, June 2015); XX Latin American Economic Association (LACEA) Annual Meeting (Santa Cruz de la Sierra, Bolivia, October 2015). The authors thank all colleagues that discussed their work on these occasions, greatly improving its quality.

The authors and editors are solely responsible for any errors in information and/or its analysis. Likewise, the opinions and policy recommendations stated in this book are those of the authors and do not represent the official position of the IDB, its President, or the Board of Directors.

Contents

EDITORS

Matteo Grazzi is a Specialist in the Competitiveness and Innovation Division of the Inter-American Development Bank (IDB). Before joining the IDB, Matteo worked as a consultant economist at the UN Economic Commission for Latin America and the Caribbean (ECLAC) in Santiago, Chile, and as a researcher at the Centre for Research on Latin American and Transition Economies Studies (ISLA) at Bocconi University in Milan, Italy. He holds a PhD in International Law and Economics from Bocconi University and an MA in Development Economics from the University of Sussex (Brighton, UK). His main research interests focus on international and development economics, economics of innovation, and ICT for development.

Carlo Pietrobelli is a Lead Specialist in the Competitiveness and Innovation Division of the Inter-American Development Bank (IDB). Prior to joining the IDB, he was Professor of Economics and Director of the Center for Studies on the Economics of Institutions (CREI) at the University of Roma Tre in Italy. He also served as Deputy Rector for University–Industry linkages at the same university. He holds a PhD in Economics from the University of Oxford in the UK and has worked as policy advisor for international organizations such as the European Commission, the World Bank, IFAD, UNIDO, UNCTAD, ECLAC, CAF, and OECD in many countries in Africa, Asia, and Latin America. His research interests include innovation and technological change, industrial policy, international trade, clusters, and value chains in developing countries. Currently, Carlo designs and manages programs to promote competitiveness and innovation in Latin America and the Caribbean.

EXTERNAL ADVISOR TO THE PROJECT

Adam (Eddy) Szirmai is Professorial Fellow at the UNU Maastricht Economic and Social Research Institute on Innovation and Technology (UNU–MERIT) and Professor of Development Economics at the Maastricht Graduate School of Governance of Maastricht University in the Netherlands. He holds a PhD in Economics from the University of Groningen and has published many books, including *Pathways to Industrialization in the 21st Century, New Challenges and Emerging Paradigms, Innovation in Theory and Practice, The Industrial Experience of Tanzania,* and *Entrepreneurship, Innovation and Development,* co-edited with Wim Naudé and Micheline Goedhuys. He is also currently working on a second edition of his textbook on development economics that was first published in 2005, *The Dynamics of Socio-Economic Development: An Introduction.* His research focuses on international comparisons of growth and productivity in manufacturing in developing countries, as well as, the relationships between innovation, technological change, and economic performance at sectoral level. He has been involved in research projects in manufacturing in Indonesia, China, South Korea, Tanzania, Zambia, South Africa, and Japan.

CONTRIBUTORS

Pablo Angelelli is a Lead Specialist in the Competitiveness and Innovation Division of the Inter-American Development Bank (IDB), where he has worked since 2000. His current duties include the design and supervision of projects that support science, technology, and business innovation in Argentina, Paraguay, and Uruguay. He holds a degree in economics from the National University of Cordoba, Argentina, and has completed two Masters degrees: one in Public Policy at George Washington University in the USA and another in Economics and Industrial Development at the National University of General Sarmiento in Argentina. He is the author of numerous articles and several books on issues of SMEs, innovation, and technology-based ventures.

Alison Cathles is a PhD candidate in the Economics and Policy Studies of Technical Change at UNU–MERIT at Maastricht University in the Netherlands. She holds a Master of Public Administration from Cornell University in the USA. Before beginning her PhD studies, Alison worked as a consultant in the Competitiveness and Innovation Division of the IDB.

Gustavo Crespi is a Principal Specialist in the Competitiveness and Innovation Division of the IDB. He holds a PhD in Public Policy (with a specialization in Science and Technology Policy) from Sussex University in the UK, a Masters in Economic Development and International Trade from the School of Economics and Business Administration of the University of Chile, and a BA in Economics from the National University of Cordoba, Argentina. His interests include industrial development, technological change, industrial structure and development of the firm, and management and technology policy evaluation, especially in developing countries.

Juan Federico is a Researcher and Lecturer at the Entrepreneurial Development Program at the National University of General Sarmiento in Argentina, where he holds a Masters in Economics and Industrial Development with a focus on SMEs. He is a PhD candidate in Entrepreneurship and Small Business Management at the Autonomous University of Barcelona in Spain. His areas of interest include new firms, clusters, industrial policy, industrial sectors, and entrepreneurship policy.

Roberto Flores Lima is an international specialist and consultant on employment services, job training, and labor competency. From September 2008 to May 2015, Roberto was a Lead Specialist at the Labor Markets and Social Security Unit of the IDB, where he created the Technical Support Network of Public Employment Services in Latin America and the Caribbean (RED SEALC) and collaborated with the design of projects and loans for labor market issues Colombia, the Dominica Republic, Honduras, Mexico, Panama, and Peru. He holds a BA and MA in Economics from the National Autonomous University of Mexico and has a diploma in foreign trade and international business at the Autonomous Technological Institute of Mexico.

Carolina González-Velosa is an Economist in the Labor Markets and Social Security Unit of the IDB. She specializes in labor markets in developing countries, particularly in the areas of skills, training, intermediation, and migration. Her work has been published in leading academic journals such as the Journal of International Economics. She obtained a PhD in Economics from the University of Maryland, an MA from New York University, and a BA from the University of los Andes in Colombia.

Sabrina Ibarra is a Research Assistant and Lecturer at Prodem since she joined in 2008. She has been involved in several research projects in quantitative data processing and analysis. She has a Bachelor's Degree in Economics from the University of Buenos Aires in Argentina, with postgraduate studies in Industrial Economics and Development with a concentration in SMEs. Her main research interests are the determinants of dynamic new ventures (especially in Latin America), the elaboration of composite indicators of entrepreneurship, and quantitative research methods.

Juan Jung is the Studies and Regulation Coordinator at the Latin American Association of Research Centers and Telecom Enterprises (AHCIET). He is concurrently a PhD candidate in Economics at the University of Barcelona; he holds an MA in Economics from the same University. His area of expertise is applied economics and has been involved in a variety of consultancy projects with multilateral institutions over the past few years.

Hugo Kantis is Director of the Entrepreneurial Development Program at the National University of General Sarmiento in Argentina, where he leads a seminar-workshop for Professionals in the Entrepreneurial Ecosystem in Latin America. He holds a PhD in Economics and Business Science and a Master of Research in

Entrepreneurship and Business Strategy from the Autonomous University of Barcelona in Spain. He has consulted with numerous international organizations including the World Bank, IDB, ECLAC, UNDP, and JICA. His research focuses on entrepreneurship and entrepreneurial innovation, policy design, implementation and evaluation, SME development, and best practices for business and institutional management.

Preeya Mohan is a Post-doctoral Research Fellow at the Sir Arthur Lewis Institute of Social and Economic Studies, Trinidad and Tobago, in the West Indies. She obtained her PhD in Economic Development Policy from the University of the West Indies, St. Augustine. Her thesis "Caribbean Development: The Role of Diversification and Hurricane Strikes" focuses on Caribbean growth and development primarily through diversification strategies and policies, and reducing vulnerability to climatic external shocks. She has worked on a wide range of topics including Caribbean economic history, natural disasters, financial economics, firm competitiveness and innovation, value chains, and clusters.

Pierluigi Montalbano is Associate Professor of International Economic Policy at the Sapienza University of Rome. His research interests include international economics and development, in particular the nexus between trade openness, instability and vulnerability in economies, multilateral and regional trade integration in emerging economies, and the theoretical and applied nexus between culture/creativity and local development.

Silvia Nenci is Assistant Professor in Economics at the University of Roma Tre in Rome, Italy. She holds a PhD in Economics from the Sapienza University of Rome. Her research focuses on international economics and economic policy. She has been consultant to several national and international institutions including the Italian Ministry of Foreign Affairs, the Global Development Network, and the Food and Agriculture Organization of the United Nations.

Siobhan Pangerl is a Consultant in the Multilateral Investment Fund of the IDB, where she works on youth employment and entrepreneurship projects. Before this she worked for two years in the IDB's Competitiveness and Innovation Division. She has experience working in various US government agencies including USAID and the State Department, and also spent two years as a Peace Corps volunteer in Peru. She has a Bachelor's Degree in Communications from the University of Miami in the USA and has a Master in Public Policy and a Master of Science in Foreign Service, both from Georgetown University in the USA.

Andrea Presbitero is an Economist at the International Monetary Fund. He obtained a PhD in Economics from the Università Politecnica delle Marche in Ancona, Italy, an MA in Development Economics from the University of Sussex, UK, and an MSc in Political Economy from the University of Ancona in Italy. His research interests include development economics, fiscal policy and debt sustainability, banking and SME financing, and international economics.

Roberta Rabellotti is Professor of Economics at the University of Pavia, Italy. She holds an MSc in Development Economics from the University of Oxford and a PhD from the Institute of Development Studies at the University of Sussex, both in the UK. She specializes in the analysis of the industrial sector in developing countries and has experience consulting with the IDB, EU, UNIDO, ILO, ECLAC, and UNCTAD. Her areas of interest are industrial policies, small business promotion, international trade policies, industrial districts and clusters, and global value chains.

David Rosas is a Lead Specialist in the Labor Markets and Social Security Unit of the IDB, where he specializes in labor training and labor intermediation, and in evaluating the impact of labor market interventions. He holds a PhD and an MA in Economics from the University of Paris Panthéon-Sorbonne.

Eric Strobl is Associate Professor at Ecole Polytechnique in Paris, France, and External Professor at the Sir Arthur Lewis Institute of Social and Economic Studies at the University of the West Indies in Trinidad and Tobago. He holds a PhD in Economics from the University of Dublin, Trinity College, Ireland. His main research interests are in applied labor economics in developing countries, foreign direct investment, and economic geography.

Ezequiel Tacsir is Coordinator of the Information, Monitoring and Evaluation Unit of the Interdisciplinary Center for Science and Technology Studies (CIECTI, Argentina) and researcher at CINVE (Uruguay). In the past he occupied positions at the Competitiveness and Innovation Division (previously Science and Technology) of the IDB, UNU–MERIT, ProsperAr, and served as consultant for the World Bank, the IDB, and different national governments in science, technology, and innovation policies and studies. He studied economics at the University of Buenos Aires in Argentina. Ezequiel has achieved postgraduate awards in Science, Technology and Innovation Management (UNGS) and completed doctorate studies at UNU–MERIT. His research interests include STI policies, impact evaluation, and the interlink between human capital and innovation.

Fernando Vargas is a PhD Fellow in Economics and Governance at UNU–MERIT, specializating in the economics and policy studies of technical change. He holds a Master of Science degree in Applied Economics from the University of Chile and a Bachelor degree in Industrial Engineering from the same university. Before joining UNU–MERIT, he worked at the Competitiveness and Innovation Division of the IDB, where he held advisory and research management responsibilities for Latin American public agencies in the design and implementation of innovation surveys. His field of interest is mainly focused on understanding the determinants of innovation, innovation strategies, and productivity in firms in Latin America, and their implications for public policy design.

Patrick Watson is Director of the Sir Arthur Lewis Institute of Social and Economic Studies (SALISES) at the University of the West Indies in Trinidad and Tobago. He holds a PhD in Mathematical Economics and Econometrics and an MSc in Economics from the Panthéon-Sorbonne in Paris, France. His areas of expertise include the econometric modeling of Caribbean phenomena (in particular monetary and fiscal policy), economic measurement, and statistical analysis. He has served on the board of directors of various state enterprises, as a government senator, and on government committees.

LIST OF FIGURES

LIST OF TABLES

OPEN

CHAPTER 1

Determinants of Enterprise Performance in Latin America and the Caribbean: What Does the Micro-Evidence Tell Us?

Matteo Grazzi, Carlo Pietrobelli, and Adam Szirmai

After a decade of relatively strong performance, growth in Latin America and the Caribbean (LAC) has begun to taper. This slowdown is even more worrisome considering the long-run economic performance of the region, where it is evident that there is difficulty in catching up with developed economies and even just keeping pace with other emerging regions. Over the last half-century, per capita income in Latin America has stagnated relative to the United States, while in East Asian countries[1] it has grown steadily since 1960, reaching a level that is almost half of current US levels. The expected fall in commodity prices may further hinder LAC's economic performance.

M. Grazzi
Inter-American Development Bank
e-mail: matteog@iadb.org

C. Pietrobelli
Inter-American Development Bank and University Roma Tre
e-mail: carlop@iadb.org

A. Szirmai
UNU-MERIT
e-mail: szirmai@merit.unu.edu

© Inter-American Development Bank 2016
M. Grazzi and C. Pietrobelli (eds.), *Firm Innovation and Productivity in Latin America and the Caribbean*,
DOI 10.1057/978-1-349-58151-1_1

1

Table 1.1   Growth accounting: LAC vs. comparison countries (1960–2011) (%)

Country/ region	Δ GDP per capita	Δ Factor accumulation	Δ TFP	% share
Average	(a)	(b)	(a – b = c)	(c/a)
Latin America and the Caribbean	1.79	1.80	–0.01	–0.6%
East Asia and Pacific	3.69	2.85	0.83	22.5%
United States	1.99	1.21	0.78	39.2%
China	6.04	4.21	1.83	30.3%
Finland	2.74	1.44	1.30	47.4%

Source: Authors' elaboration on data from Feenstra et al. (2015)

Notes: The LAC countries are Antigua and Barbuda, Argentina, Bahamas, Barbados, Belize, Bolivia, Brazil, Chile, Colombia, Costa Rica, Dominica, Dominican Republic, Ecuador, El Salvador, Grenada, Guatemala, Honduras, Jamaica, Mexico, Panama, Paraguay, Peru, St. Kitts & Nevis, St. Lucia, St. Vincent & the Grenadines, Suriname, Trinidad & Tobago, Uruguay, and Venezuela. The East Asia and Pacific countries are Australia, Brunei, Cambodia, China, Fiji, Hong Kong, Indonesia, Japan, Laos, Macao, Malaysia, Mongolia, New Zealand, Philippines, Singapore, South Korea, Thailand, and Vietnam. Physical capital and human capital are considered productive factors in the production function

This tapering raises various questions. For example, what is behind LAC's disappointing performance? And, why have other regions developed so much more rapidly than LAC? The central argument of this book is that answering such questions requires going beyond analyzing macroeconomic trends to analyzing the micro-dynamics of development. The chapters focus on firm-level sources of productivity growth. How are they related to the characteristics and strategies of firms? To what extent are productivity gains determined by better production methods, organizational improvements, firm-level innovation, learning, and capability development? Finally, what are the implications of microeconomic analysis for industrial and innovation policy?

Following the logic of the aggregate production function, factors of accumulation (capital and labor) and productivity (taken as a measure of technological progress) explain economic growth. A simple growth accounting exercise confirms recent economic research: despite years of rising factor accumulation, slow productivity growth is at the root of LAC's weak overall performance (Fernández-Arias 2014; Crespi et al. 2014; Pagés 2010). Between 1960 and 2011, GDP per capita in LAC grew at 1.79%, just below the rate for the United States over the same time period. The region was also able to outpace the United States in terms of factor accumulation. However, in the USA, total factor productivity (TFP) grew at 1.21%, while it stagnated in LAC, more than compensating for the lower factor accumulation. Thus, TFP can clearly be blamed for the LAC region's inability to catch up with US GDP per capita (Table 1.1).[2]

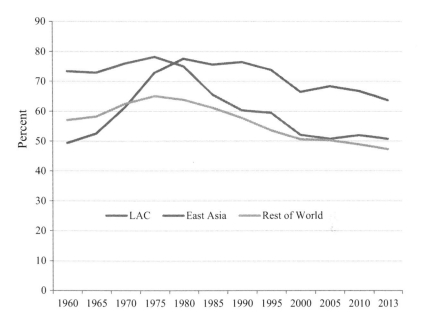

Fig. 1.1 TFP relative to the United States (1960–2013) (*Source*: Fernández-Arias 2014)

The LAC region's weak TFP performance is a stark contrast to other countries that were at similar development levels in 1960 but have since been able to converge toward US levels. For example, in Finland, TFP increased to 69 from 50% of the US level over the past 54 years, while in South Korea it went to 63 from 20% over the same period. In fact, the East Asian countries successfully boosted TFP relative to the United States from 49% in 1960 to 78% in 1980 and, after some decline, they were at 64% in 2013 (Fig. 1.1). The story for LAC is the opposite: between 1960 and 2011, GDP per capita growth in LAC was only sustained by factor accumulation, not by TFP growth, and productivity declined from 73% of US TFP in 1960 to only 51% in 2013.

While the aggregate picture of LAC reveals overall weak performance in terms of productivity, analysis by country shows remarkable heterogeneity. Figure 1.2 plots the annual TFP growth of LAC countries between 2000 and 2011 against the productivity (TFP) gap relative to the United States in 2011. On the whole, since 2000, average productivity growth in the LAC region has declined by 0.04 percent per year. However, not all LAC

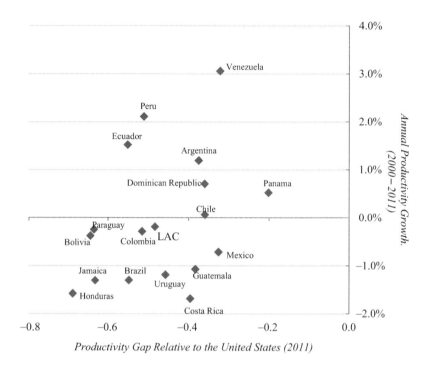

Fig. 1.2 Productivity performance by country (2000–2011) (*Source*: Fernández-Arias 2014)

countries have followed this pattern. Honduras, for example, has seen a dramatic decline in absolute productivity growth (1.6 percent per year) since 2000 relative to a high productivity gap with the United States (69 percent in 2011). Other Central American countries, such as Costa Rica and Guatemala, recorded similar negative productivity growth, although with much narrower productivity gaps (40 percent relative to the United States). In contrast, South American countries tended to see more positive productivity growth, with the exception of Brazil and Uruguay where productivity declines over 1 percent per year.

The macro-evidence presented so far clearly indicates that LAC countries have been growing at lower rates than some other emerging regions and that they are failing to efficiently combine production inputs. If economic growth based on factor accumulation is subject to diminishing returns and successful catch-up requires fast productivity growth (Easterly and Levine 2001; Hall and Jones 1999; Klenow and Rodriguez-Clare

1997), the fact that LAC countries have not been able to significantly increase their productivity is particularly worrisome. Indeed, this led us to investigate the reasons. In summary, what explains productivity and its evolution over time?

The research on this key issue is vast and has expanded in recent years (Syverson 2011). Many studies use macroeconomic data to estimate aggregate production functions and obtain the results we have described. However, the economic performance of a country or sector ultimately depends on decisions made at the firm level and this should explicitly be taken into account. Therefore, a disaggregated enterprise-level approach is necessary to obtain a deeper and more complete understanding of the dynamics of productivity growth (Foster et al. 2001). When the microeconomic dimension is introduced into the analysis, the economic literature has shown that firm productivity growth is essentially driven by two factors: reallocation of resources across firms; and within-firm efficiency improvements (Dollar et al. 2005; Bergoeing and Repetto 2006).[3]

The first factor, reallocation across firms, is only possible when resources can be easily allocated to different activities in the presence of smoothly functioning markets (Busso et al. 2013). In this context, the competition generates Schumpeterian creation and destruction processes, both within the same sector and across sectors. In the latter case, the process is expected to reshape economies toward more productive structures by shifting resources from less to more productive sectors. However, this shift does not appear to have happened in LAC in recent years, which led McMillan et al. (2014) to conclude that, during 1990–2005, the LAC region experienced significant productivity gains within the same sectors, but that displaced workers from the least productive firms ended up in less productive activities. "In other words, rationalization of manufacturing industries may have come at the expense of inducing growth-reducing structural change" (McMillan et al. 2014: 19).

The focus of this book is the second source of productivity growth: within-firm improvements that result from firm-specific characteristics, behaviors, and strategies. Here, efficiency gains can be explained as the result of improvements in management, internal organization, strategies, or technological capabilities as reactions to market incentives.

The interaction between firm-specific factors leads to high heterogeneity in firm productivity growth over time and, consequently, firms with disparate productivity levels can coexist, even within the same sectors.[4] For example, Syverson (2011) found that, within four-digit Standard Industrial Classification industries in the US manufacturing sector, the

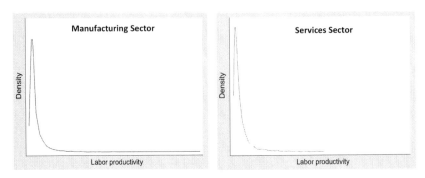

Fig. 1.3 LAC productivity distributions, 2010 (*Source*: Authors' elaboration using WBES data)

plant at the 90th percentile of productivity distribution had almost twice as much output as that at the 10th percentile with the same measured inputs. Even larger productivity differences were recorded in China and India, with average 90:10 TFP ratios over 5:1 (Hsieh and Klenow 2009).

Evidence from LAC confirms this situation: overall, the region is characterized by large disparities in productivity (Busso et al. 2013; Pagés 2010), with many low-productivity firms coexisting with few high-productivity firms (Lavopa 2015). Using World Bank Enterprise Survey (WBES) data for LAC, we found that the difference between the 90th and 10th percentiles of labor productivity distribution in the manufacturing sector is around 10:1. In Fig. 1.3, this trend is apparent for both the manufacturing and services sectors. Most firms are clustered at very low levels of productivity, but there are some highly productive firms. It is interesting to note that the distribution for the manufacturing sector appears to be more skewed than for the services sector,[5] extending much further to the right.

Dualism is a phenomenon that is frequently encountered in developing countries, and LAC is no exception. From a theoretical point of view, dualism has been explained differently by scholars belonging to various schools of thought. On the one hand, the neoclassical approach stresses the role of market incentives and generally the macroeconomic context that induces firms to behave differently in response to different prices. Heterogeneity is the upshot of market imperfections, as a result of which inefficient firms are not forced to exit the market (e.g. Busso et al. 2013). On the other hand, evolutionary and managerial approaches refer to: the intrinsic characteristics of firms; their internal organization, routines, and practices; and specific strategies to accumulate technological capabilities, learn, and innovate (Williamson

1973, 1985; Dosi 1988; Katz 1987; Lundvall 1992; Malerba 2002; Nelson and Winter 1982; Nelson 1991). Lall (1992) suggested, for example, that the development of firm capabilities is the result of the interplay between a "complex interaction of incentive structures with human resources, technological effort and institutional factors." Meanwhile, the dynamic capabilities approach advanced by Teece and Pisano (1994) argues that the strategic dimensions at the disposal of a firm range from managerial and organizational processes, their present position, and the paths available to them. These approaches attribute firm performance to the unique characteristics embedded within firm-specific decision-making, organization, and processes.

Foster et al. (2001) asserted that the magnitude of within-sector heterogeneity implies that firm-specific factors determine whether they achieve rapid productivity growth or suffer declines. They cited such factors as uncertainty of demand for the firm's products, managerial ability, the nature of installed capital, upgrading capabilities, location, and the diffusion of knowledge concerning new technologies. For example, uncertainty over market demand and profitability may lead firms to experiment to discover which technologies or processes best meet local market conditions (Jovanovic 1982; Ericson and A. Pakes 1989). Firm-level productivity will be affected by the success of such experimentation, and firms that have developed or acquired efficient technologies and know-how can put them to work, with immediate effects on productivity levels. Those firms still experimenting with how to most efficiently use their inputs may suffer from low productivity.

The substantial heterogeneity in firm performance provides the analytical foundation for this book, raising the question why some firms perform well while others fail. The core of the book seeks to empirically analyze the drivers of this heterogeneity, such as training, access to information and communication technologies (ICTs), international linkages, innovation, and access to finance. The heterogeneity present among firms in the region suggests the need to go beyond one-size-fits-all firm growth policies. There is an important challenge here for policymakers to devise policies that reflect the diverse nature of enterprises in LAC.

MOTIVATION FOR THIS BOOK

Depending on the objective of the intervention, policies to promote enterprise development can assume very different forms. Thus, for example, policies may address the two different sets of factors that in principle affect firm performance: (i) internal factors, which at least in principle are within a business's control, and (ii) external factors, which are aspects of the operating environment (Syverson 2011). Among the former are a host of elements that range from internal firm characteristics, technological capabilities, organizational structure, and linkages between firms and within networks, to sector-specific factors. Among the latter are the external pressures that influence firm behavior and success, including competition, the business environment, and the institutional framework.

Over the past 20 years in LAC, priority has been given to macroeconomic reforms that typically address the external factors, preventing an efficient allocation of resources across sectors and firms by improving the business and investment climate and market functioning. However, despite their relative success, these policies alone constitute a broad brush effort to address the needs of firms. In fact, although a sound institutional and regulatory framework is a necessary condition for sustained firm growth, once these barriers are reduced, firms respond to the same framework in different ways, depending on their characteristics and strategies. Once the basic framework is set in place, achieving efficiency improvements within firms requires detailed microeconomic policies that also address the internal factors that are hindering firm-level productivity.[6]

Moreover, macroeconomic reforms bring about once-and-for-all static gains. Once market flexibility is achieved (or restored) and the benefits from reallocation have materialized, these gains cannot be repeated. In contrast, the advantages from within-firm efficiency improvements can be pursued continuously through efforts and investments in innovation, human capital, and increasing credit access, among others. Despite this, macroeconomic conditions are often cited as playing the most significant role in shaping firms' trajectories. While important, these factors do not adequately take into account the specific characteristics, strategy, and behavior that are equally, if not more, responsible for sustained firm development. But the priority given to macroeconomic reforms has shifted interest away from the microeconomic dimension, leading many LAC governments to place microeconomic concerns further down the policy agenda (Solimano and Soto 2006).

This book contributes to bringing the microeconomic agenda back to the forefront by presenting and critically discussing new evidence about the drivers of within-firm productivity improvement across the region. A better understanding of the factors that foster or hinder firm performance is increasingly important from the perspective of economic policies. In fact, while there is widespread consensus on appropriate macroeconomic policies, the variety and ongoing experimentation with many different microeconomic policies in the region reveals that the policy debate is far from being settled.

As a consequence, this variety is not mirrored by volume, and the size and scope of government programs aimed at directly supporting enterprise

Table 1.2 LAC firms participating in publicly supported programs

	Participation in:		
	At least one program (%)	Only one program (%)	Two or more programs (%)
All firms	10.7	7.7	2.9
Micro firms	6.6	5.1	1.4
Small firms	9.4	6.6	2.8
Medium firms	14.4	10.4	4.0
Large firms	15.8	11.7	4.1

Source: World Bank (2010)

Notes: Includes both partially or entirely government funded programs

development across LAC remain limited. For example, Brazil, the Latin American country that devotes the largest amount of resources to firm development, is reported to use 0.085 % of its GDP to support small and medium-sized enterprises (SMEs). In the United States, this figure is nearly five times higher (ECLAC 2014). WBES data for LAC allow us to assess the diffusion of such instruments and the actual level of firm participation.[7]

Overall, approximately 10.7 % of all firms report having received some type of public support over the previous three years. But large differences emerge when the responses are broken down by firm size. Only 6.6 % of micro-firms and 9.4 % of small firms report receiving support, compared to 14.4 % of medium-sized firms and 15.8 % of large firms (Table 1.2). Most firms use only one publicly funded instrument and only a small fraction participate in two or more programs (2.9 %). Again, larger firms tend to participate more often in various programs at the same time, and evidence shows that it is often important to participate in different programs to obtain their full benefits (Álvarez et al. 2012). If we consider that many public programs in the region are designed to support SMEs, the fact that large firms are using them disproportionately raises some doubts about the targeting capacity of the institutions in charge of such programs in the region.

Disaggregating firm participation by typology of intervention, innovation support turns out to be the most frequently used instrument, with 5 % of firms using it. This is followed by quality certification and business development services (3.8 %) (Table 1.3). At the other extreme, only 1.5 % of the firms use instruments that facilitate business alliances with suppliers and clients, and 2.1 % participate in export promotion programs. In all these cases, participation rates increase with firm size. On the whole, this evidence alludes that firms in Latin America tend to participate very modestly in public programs In the Caribbean, this number is even lower, as public support for innova-

Table 1.3   LAC firms participating in publicly supported programs by firm size

In the last three years, firm used services to:	All firms (%)	Micro firms (%)	Small firms (%)	Medium firms (%)	Large firms (%)
Improve quality control/train to obtain quality certification	3.8	2.2	3.5	5.2	5.0
Make business alliances with other suppliers/clients	1.5	1.2	1.6	1.6	1.9
Support innovation	5.0	2.5	4.3	6.8	9.4
Support exports	2.1	1.1	1.9	3.2	2.7
Business development services (e.g., support training or technical assistance)	2.4	1.5	2.4	3.2	2.7

Source: World Bank (2010)

Notes: Includes both partially or entirely government funded programs

tion is still sporadic. According to WBES data, only 1.5% of Caribbean firms declared they had participated in innovation-related programs in 2010. This low percentage is confirmed by the data of the Productivity, Technology, and Innovation in the Caribbean (PROTEQin) Survey. In 2014, only 2.7% of firms received public support for innovation activities.

This book uses a series of econometric models with microeconomic data primarily from the WBES to address specific research questions. The questions were chosen based on their relevance for the region and the availability of the necessary data for the analysis. Each chapter is dedicated to analyzing a different factor affecting firm productivity in LAC: innovation, ICT usage, on-the-job-training, firm age, firm size, access to credit, and international linkages. Two chapters explicitly analyze Caribbean firms.

The cross-country comparability of the results provides first-hand evidence of how these factors affect firm performance, providing readers a richer understanding of firm dynamics in LAC. The findings update understanding of the business drivers in the region, which helps inform the design and development of policies to promote business performance.

DATA AND METHODOLOGY

The WBES are the primary datasets used in this book. WBES data is available for over 130,000 firms in 135 countries.[8] The World Bank collects survey information through face-to-face interviews with firm managers and owners regarding the business environment in their countries and the productivity of their firms, including questions relating to infrastructure, sales and supplies, competition, crime, finance, business development services, business–government relations, labor, and firm performance. Table 1.4 lists the countries and the number of companies surveyed in

Table 1.4 WBES: number of LAC firms surveyed

		2006	*2010*
1	Argentina	1063	1054
2	Bolivia	613	362
3	Brazil	—	1802
4	Chile	1017	1033
5	Colombia	1000	942
6	Costa Rica	—	538
7	Ecuador	658	366
8	El Salvador	693	360
9	Guatemala	522	590
10	Honduras	436	360
11	Mexico	1480	1480
12	Nicaragua	478	336
13	Panama	604	365
14	Paraguay	613	361
15	Peru	632	1000
16	Uruguay	621	607
17	Venezuela	500	320
Subtotal		**10,930**	**10,074**
18	Antigua and Barbuda	—	151
19	Bahamas	—	150
20	Barbados	—	150
21	Belize	—	150
22	Dominica	—	150
23	Dominican Republic	—	360
24	Grenada	—	153
25	Guyana	—	165
26	Jamaica	—	376
27	St. Kitts & Nevis	—	150
28	Saint Lucia	—	150
29	St. Vincent & the Grenadines	—	154
30	Suriname	—	152
31	Trinidad and Tobago	—	370
Subtotal		**—**	**2781**
Total		10,930	12,855

Source: Authors' elaboration based on WBES data

Note: Data for Brazil is from 2009

2006 and 2010 that are included in the dataset. The population of the survey is consistently defined in all countries as non-agricultural, non-extracting, formal, privately owned firms.[9] Both the manufacturing and services sectors are covered by the survey.

The Inter-American Development Bank (IDB) financed the 2010 WBES in 14 Caribbean countries, the first time it was conducted there. Furthermore, the IDB financed the inclusion of additional questions on key issues facing the firms of the region, including questions on innovation, business development services, and workforce training for human capital.[10]

The global methodology for most enterprise surveys implemented since 2006 is based on a core questionnaire with a uniform universe and methodology of implementation. The most recent survey in LAC was conducted in 2010 and, in some cases, the previous WBES conducted in Latin America in 2006 allows authors to create panel datasets for participating countries. The WBES uses stratified random sampling by location, size, and sector. This method guarantees that precise inferences can be made for each level of stratification. The standardization of enterprise surveys across all countries strengthens the level of external validity and provides a basis for comparisons across countries in the region and with other developing regions. This is especially crucial for the Caribbean, which had very little comparable firm-level data available before the 2010 surveys.

Despite the benefits of enterprise surveys, there are limitations that should be addressed. First and foremost, the surveys are administered to a representative sample of firms in the non-agricultural, formal, private economy. Consequently, by definition, the informal sector is excluded from the analysis. The effect of this limitation varies because the size of the informal economy differs by country. In countries like Paraguay and Nicaragua, the informal sector accounts for an estimated 70% of total GDP; in Caribbean economies like the Bahamas, Grenada, St. Kitts & Nevis, Trinidad and Tobago, and Barbados, the informal share is estimated to hover below 25% of GDP (Vuletin 2008). Regardless of the country, the exclusion of informal firms requires a cautious interpretation of the empirical results.

Another data limitation is the relatively low representation of services firms in the survey population. This is unfortunate given that services make up 60% of employment in the region. While both the manufacturing and services sectors are included, services firms were excluded from some of the key modules of the questionnaire, such as the innovation module in the 2010 survey and the labor module in the 2006 survey. When the data allow, the authors use observations from both sectors. However, this is not possible in those chapters where services firms are excluded from questionnaire modules, creating an unintended focus on manufacturing firms.

Other limitations of the data create some methodological issues that are addressed in a uniform way throughout the book. The first methodological decision was made in response to the low response rates in certain countries. The low number of observations for some of the key variables prohibits analysis at a country level. Therefore, the authors aggregate countries together for the empirical analyses, allowing for interpretations at a regional level only. All authors use country-level dummies to take into account cross-country heterogeneity.

The second issue is the conversion of financial variables. The WBES follow the World Bank methodology that first converts local currency variables to US dollars using market exchange rates and then subsequently deflates them to the reference year, 2009. An alternative methodology would be to use a measure of purchasing power parity (PPP) or the rate at which the currency of one country would have to be converted into that of another country to buy the same amount of goods and services in each country. Free of price and exchange rate distortions, the PPP methodology is often considered a better measure when making cross-country comparisons, especially for developing or emerging markets.[11] Despite these limitations, we follow the World Bank methodology, using market exchange rates for our analysis, for a number of reasons. First, to make accurate PPP comparisons, ideally, inputs and outputs need to be converted separately using different PPP converters; however, this was not feasible because of data limitations. Second, the greatest distortions between the two measures tend to occur when emerging country figures are converted into US dollars at market exchange rates and used for comparisons with developed countries. The LAC WBES are all developing economies within the same region, so we expected the distortions to be smaller than those found between LAC and other developing or advanced economies. Last, as already mentioned, country fixed effects are used in the regressions in all chapters to partly capture any persistent discrepancies between PPPs and exchange rates.

Another methodological issue is the decision about which measures of performance to use. Sales, employment, and productivity growth are just a few of the methods available to gauge firm performance. With the macroeconomic evidence of low productivity growth well established, this book uses firm-level productivity as the primary measurement of firm performance. It relies on labor productivity, calculated as sales per employee, as a measure of firm efficiency and performance. Where the data allows, authors also estimate the TFP. Both measures aim to proxy firm efficiency in using production inputs, thereby providing a basis to compare performance across firms.

Finally, while the main dataset is the WBES, the authors also use additional data sources to create another level of analysis when possible. Two relatively new micro-datasets are particularly interesting. Chapter 5 uses the IDB-financed Survey of Productivity and Human Resources in Establishments (Encuesta sobre Productividad y Formación de Recursos Humanos en Establecimientos, or EPFE), which includes detailed questions about on-the-job training that are not included in the WBES or other traditional business surveys.[12] For the Caribbean region, Chap. 7 uses the Productivity, Technology, and Innovation in the Caribbean (PROTEQin) Survey in tandem with the 2010 WBES. The PROTEQin expands the scope of WBES and incorporates more detailed questions related to labor, technology and innovation, commercial victimization, and productivity for 727 Caribbean firms.[13] Furthermore, Chap. 9 uses the new Organisation for Economic Co-operation and Development (OECD) and World Trade Organization (WTO) Trade in Value Added (TiVA) database.

OVERVIEW OF THE BOOK

The first three chapters of this book focus on innovation dynamics in LAC firms. They are followed by chapters dealing with specific factors affecting enterprise performance, such as on-the-job training, performance of young firms, access to credit, and international linkages. Two of the eight chapters—Chaps. 3 and 7—focus specifically on Caribbean economies, with new data sources for many of these small economies allowing for comparisons with larger mainland economies in Latin America.

INNOVATION DYNAMICS AND PRODUCTIVITY: EVIDENCE FOR LATIN AMERICA

Chapter 2, co-authored by Gustavo Crespi, Ezequiel Tacsir, and Fernando Vargas, focuses on the key relationships between innovation efforts, innovation outputs, and productivity. This chapter analyzes the links between firm characteristics and decisions about investments in innovation, between investment in innovation and innovative performance, and between innovative performance and economic performance. It also examines the role of spillovers between firms. All the empirical analyses use a cross-sectional dataset for 17 countries in Latin America, constructed from the 2010 round of WBES.

In a review of the firm-level literature on innovation, the chapter finds that, in general, innovation leads to more efficient use of resources and sustainable competitive advantage. Investment in research and development (R&D) tends to increase absorptive capacity, assimilation of knowledge, and catch up. Innovation and application of new ideas lead to the emergence of new sectors (structural change). In turn, changes in the production structure result in more complex chains of production, specialization, productivity growth, and a gradual expansion of more knowledge-intensive activities. At the macro-level, R&D, innovation, productivity growth, and per capita growth in GDP can reinforce each other in virtuous (or vicious) cycles.

The review also identifies some important differences between the findings of studies in Europe and studies in developing countries. First and foremost, the productivity gaps between innovative and non-innovative firms are much larger in developing (70%) than in advanced economies (20%). The productivity gaps highlight the shortcomings of ineffective innovation systems, where knowledge does not flow sufficiently easily from actor to actor. But they also indicate substantial potential for improvement through public policy measures intended to promote investment in innovation by lagging firms as well as more effective knowledge flow and improved conditions for knowledge absorption. A second important difference is that the strong links between innovation investment and innovation performance and between innovation performance and economic performance found in Europe are more ambiguous in Latin America, where the results of different studies have been inconclusive. According to the authors, the heterogeneity of findings may have to do with the very different circumstances in developing countries and emerging economies. Many firms are far from the technological frontier, incentives to invest in innovation are absent or weak, and it may take longer for effects to materialize (which makes the relationships more difficult to measure in a cross-section framework). Also, many innovations consist of incremental changes based on imitation and technology transfer, with little impact on competitiveness in international markets.

The authors build on a model first developed by Crépon et al. (1998), referred to as the Crépon–Duguet–Mairesse (CDM) model, that includes three steps. In the first step, the analysis focuses on the decision to spend on innovation. Next, an innovation function is estimated, relating subjective indicators of product and process innovation to innovation expenditures and other explanatory variables. Finally, the analysis focuses on the key relationship between innovation performance and labor productivity. This relationship is assessed in the context of a standard Cobb–Douglas production function with constant returns to scale, where innovation performance is added to capital and labor inputs, allowing the returns on innovation to be estimated.

In the various regression equations, five groups of variables are distinguished: (1) performance variables (e.g. labor productivity, employment, investment, and R&D); (2) innovation variables (e.g. product innovation, process innovation, innovative sales, and intellectual property rights); (3) firm capabilities (e.g. firm age, foreign ownership, human capital, knowledge stocks, and diversification); (4) degree of access to external knowledge (e.g. cooperation with other firms, urban location, use of licenses, and broadband access); and (5) market conditions (e.g. degree of competition and whether or not a firm exports to international markets). The variables on market conditions relate to policy, which includes the percentage of firms receiving public support for innovation activities by sector and country. Many of the variables described here are also used in subsequent chapters of this book.

The following summarizes the most striking findings in this chapter. The decision to invest in innovation (R&D) is strongly correlated with firm size and firm capabilities and is significantly and positively affected by public support. The intensity (amount) of investment is positively affected by firm capabilities (human capital and previous knowledge stock), access to external knowledge via licenses and connections, and public support. Surprisingly, the intensity of competition has no effect on the decision to invest and there are even significant negative effects of foreign control. Multinationals do not seem to invest in technology development locally.

What is the effect of R&D investment on innovative performance? Here the answer is straightforward and positive. A 10% increase in R&D spending results in a 1.7% increase in the probability of innovating. Most of the relationship between expenditure and innovation is through product innovation rather than process innovation. Some firm capabilities, such as size, diversification, and fixed investment, are important determinants of innovation outputs beyond their influence on R&D investment. Again there are some interesting results related to factors that negatively affect innovation. There are no significant effects on the stock of knowledge, but human capital is negatively correlated with innovative performance, and being a multinational has negative or non-significant effects. The effect of human capital is puzzling. Perhaps firms do not really require highly skilled workers because the product innovations are not very complex. But this still begs the question as to why the effect is negative.

One of the chapter's most powerful findings is that the effects of innovation on productivity are positive and large. Total factor productivity of innovative firms is 50% higher than that of non-innovative firms. In this respect, our research findings differ from the ambiguous findings for Latin America discussed in the literature review and the relationships are unambiguous.

The last two questions addressed in the chapter have to do with spillovers and heterogeneity. The authors conclude that there are positive and significant spillover relationships between R&D performed by other firms in the same sector and country, and a firm's economic performance. Unfortunately, a cross-sectional analysis does not provide enough information to discuss clearly the magnitude and importance of these spillover effects. In the final part of the chapter, the authors present some very interesting and quite novel findings about differences (heterogeneity) in the relationships between innovation performance and productivity across firms. On average, productivity increases when innovation occurs, shifting the whole productivity distribution to the right, but not equally. At the upper end of the productivity distribution, the increase in productivity is much higher than at the lower end.

The authors reflect on the policy implications of this heterogeneity. They argue that the lower returns on innovation in low-productivity firms suggest that the constraints on productivity improvement are not primarily financial since these firms are indeed innovating. The authors believe the lower returns have to do with some firm characteristics, such as the lack of complementary assets or the lack of appropriability of innovation. The importance of access to finance is discussed again in Chap. 8.

INNOVATIVE ACTIVITY IN THE CARIBBEAN: DRIVERS, BENEFITS, AND OBSTACLES

In Chap. 3, Preeya Mohan, Eric Strobl, and Patrick Watson examine the impact of innovation on firm productivity in the Caribbean, discussing questions and models similar to those in Chap. 2. So far, not much is known about firm performance in Caribbean countries and even less about their innovative behavior. This is mainly due to a lack of reliable data for the region, which is usually lumped together with Latin America. The availability of the 2010 WBES covering 14 Caribbean countries (and 2771 firms) for the first time makes it possible to address these issues empirically. Along similar lines as Chap. 2, the authors analyze the decision to invest in innovation, the impact of such investment on technological innovation (knowledge production), and the relationship between innovation and productivity. The few studies available for the Caribbean tend to use R&D expenditures as their measure of innovative activity and find that both innovation and productivity are low. However, excessive emphasis on R&D expenditures may underestimate the role of other forms of innovation that may be more important in small island developing states, where the cost of R&D is high and firms are too far from the technological frontier to have strong incentives to invest in R&D. This chapter uses a broader concept of innovation investment. In line with results obtained for many Latin American countries (Crespi and Zúñiga 2012; Chap. 2 of this book), innovative firms tend to be more productive than non-innovative firms; innovation matters for firm productivity performance.

The chapter starts with a descriptive analysis which reveals that in the manufacturing sector, the only one for which innovation data is available, innovative firms in the Caribbean tend to be medium-sized, domestic enterprises, half of which export a product. Moreover, there appear to be systematic differences in productivity between innovative and non-innovative firms (i.e. firms that do not spend any funds on R&D and/ or technological innovation activities). The results are robust to different non- and semi-parametric specifications of the estimates and to different measures of productivity (i.e. labor productivity and TFP). However, when analyzing the counterfactual—that is isolating the innovation behavior from other firm characteristics—the study suggests that differences in performance between the innovating and non-innovating firms are due more to underlying firm characteristics such as export status, foreign ownership, patent possession, government support, and size than to being or not being innovative.

The authors search for causality in the relationship between innovative performance and productivity. Firm innovation involves any action that aims to increase the firm's knowledge, including R&D expenditures, but also efforts to acquire external knowledge, such as expenditures on product design, marketing, staff training, new machinery, and patents and other trademark licensing.

The econometric estimates are run on a pooled dataset across countries and follow the CDM three-stage approach described above and in Chap. 2. The results show that firms that export and are larger are more likely to invest in innovation, while having patent protection or foreign ownership does not significantly predict the decision to invest in innovation. The positive effect of size and export status on the decision to innovate is not surprising. The lack of significance of the foreign ownership variable appears to signal that foreign firms develop their technologies abroad and only use Caribbean countries as an outlet for their products. This is a frequent finding in studies of foreign direct investment (FDI) in developing countries.

Public financial support is not a significant predictor of the intensity of investing in innovation, suggesting that, in contrast to mainland Latin America, public funds do not effectively promote innovation in the Caribbean. Having patents or cooperating with other firms also do not appear to encourage investment, perhaps indicating limited inter-firm knowledge spillover. Other results for the Caribbean countries are similar to those obtained for Latin America, but generally with larger effects. Caribbean firms are more likely to introduce product or process innovation if they spend more on innovation: the probability of innovation increases by 56% per unit increase in the log of innovation expenditure per employee.

The authors also estimate the causal impact of innovation on productivity in an econometric framework. The results suggest that product and process innovation increase productivity in the Caribbean with an estimated elasticity that is larger than for Latin America. Small firm size appears to be less of an obstacle for innovation to improve productivity.

ICT, Innovation, and Productivity: Evidence from Firms in Latin American and the Caribbean

In Chap. 4, Matteo Grazzi and Juan Jung single out ICTs as one of the important factors influencing firm performance. They analyze the determinants of broadband adoption in a large sample of LAC countries, and study their relationship with innovation and productivity.

Recently the economic literature has progressively recognized the role of ICTs as a key driver of economic growth. At the firm level, adopting ICTs can influence performance in various ways, such as faster communication and information processing, easier internal coordination, lower capital requirements, and better communication with suppliers and customers. However, in the absence of complementary investments in, for example, human capital or organizational improvements, simple diffusion of ICTs may not be sufficient to fully exploit their benefits. This chapter adds to the still limited evidence regarding these relationships for developing countries.

In the first part of the chapter, the authors empirically test the validity of various models of ICT diffusion, both at the inter-firm and the intra-firm levels. The latter part of the analysis is original because the processes by which ICTs diffuse within organizations have been little studied. In particular, the authors test propositions from rank and epidemic models. Rank models focus on the scores of firms on various characteristics, such as age, size, or human capital. Epidemic models predict that the greater the number of firms adopting broadband in a sector or a country, the greater the chance that a given firm will adopt broadband. The authors apply a probit model, and then a bivariate probit model, to control for multicollinearity. The results are robust to all the specifications and consistent with previous analyses in the literature. Firm size appears to affect the probability of broadband adoption, while the quality of human capital (percentage of workers with at least a bachelor's degree) and firm age affect adoption positively. These results hold for the entire sample, as well as separately for firms in the manufacturing and services sectors. Openness to foreign markets through participation in foreign trade—but not foreign ownership—increases the probability of broadband adoption.

The expected epidemic effects are confirmed. In non-technical language, firms operating in countries and sectors with larger shares of firms using ICTs have a higher probability of adopting them. Moreover, firms located in urban agglomerations with more than one million inhabitants are also more likely to adopt broadband.

To tackle the important issue of factors affecting ICT diffusion from firm to firm and within a firm itself, the authors construct an indicator based on the availability of broadband in a firm and the number of activities performed with it. The results show a similar pattern to those for inter-firm diffusion, with a significant positive effect of firm size. It appears, however, that there is a threshold, above which size no longer matters for intra-firm diffusion of ICTs. This threshold turns out to be lower for manufacturing firms than for services firms. Location in an urban agglomeration positively influences the decision to adopt broadband by the firm, but not how extensively it is used within the firm.

In the second part of the chapter, the authors empirically examine the effects of ICT adoption on innovation performance and labor productivity. The analysis shows that the impact of ICTs on innovation may be conditioned by several characteristics internal to the firm as well as external, such as the linkages with strong external organizations and network externalities. The authors show that using broadband is positively and significantly correlated with the probability of product and process innovation in firms. However, when they single out the different possible uses that a firm can make of broadband, the results begin to differ. First, using the internet to perform research is positively and significantly related to innovation, but no other uses are related to innovation. Second, the combined use of broadband for different activities matters and has a significant impact on innovation on top of the effects of using the internet for research. This is to say that simple access to ICTs is not enough to foster firm innovation. Technology needs to be used adequately to exploit its full potential. In addition, other variables are associated with a higher probability of innovation, such as firm size, human capital, and openness to export markets. This latter result confirms the evidence obtained in different contexts by Crespi et al. (Chap. 2) and Montalbano et al. (Chap. 9).

Using a Cobb–Douglas production function, the authors show that using broadband also has a positive effect on labor productivity, and that this result is robust when controlling for endogeneity. When testing for the effect of the different kinds of internet uses, research loses its significance, perhaps due to the time lags between investments in broadband and the related research and the ensuing productivity effects. However, the simultaneous use of the internet for various activities and overall broadband adoption retain their positive influence on productivity. The lesson to be derived from this chapter is that ICT adoption and diffusion should receive special attention within the broader perspective of innovation and innovation policy.

On-the-Job-Training in Latin America and the Caribbean: Recent Evidence

In Chap. 5, Carolina González-Velosa, David Rosas, and Roberto Flores focus on an important but neglected aspect of human capital formation: on-the-job training. The secondary literature indicates that up to a quarter of human capital is obtained after formal schooling has ended

(Heckman et al. 1998). Also, the type of training provided on the job may be more relevant to the production process than the skills learned in formal education.

The chapter opens with a brief review of theories of on-the-job training. Labor market theory assumes that, under perfect market conditions, the benefits of general training will accrue to the worker. As generalized training increases the productivity of workers, they will be able to increase their wages or leave the firm to work elsewhere. Therefore firms have no incentive to finance generalized training. Firm-specific training may increase a worker's productivity, but it does not increase the worker's employability. The benefits of productivity increases accrue to the firm, which thus has an incentive to invest in such training. The authors also provide a brief but useful overview of five barriers to investment in on-the-job training. The first is the lack of appropriability: if the firm cannot capture the benefits of training, it will have no incentive to invest in on-the-job training. The second is imperfect information about the advantages of training. The third is credit constraints. These three barriers affect the supply side. The last two barriers affect the demand side. If firms are facing limits to adopting skill-intensive technologies or modern managerial practices, there may simply be no demand for skilled labor and accordingly little incentive to invest in on-the-job training.

The chapter draws on two different data sources. The first is the WBES, which is the common source for all chapters of this book. The second is a Latin America-specific survey of human capital formation, the EPFE, which provides more detailed information about on-the-job training in five countries (the Bahamas, Colombia, Honduras, Panama, and Uruguay). The authors use a panel dataset of the WBES for 11 countries that participated in both the 2006 and 2010 waves of the survey for the regression analysis, though only for manufacturing.

Compared to other developing regions, firms in the 26 Latin American countries for which the authors have data offer quite a lot of on-the-job training, ranging from 26% of the firms in Jamaica to 60% in El Salvador (incidence of training). In the firms that offer training, the proportion of workers trained (intensity of training) is also quite high, ranging from 38% in Uruguay to 79% in Colombia. Skilled workers receive much more training than unskilled workers, so existing skill gaps tend to be amplified. Training is specific and does not involve general socio-emotional or behavioral skills.

The employers pay most of the training-related costs and provide most of the training themselves. Governments provide some training opportunities, but these are not used much, not even by small firms. When firms turn to external providers, they choose private companies. The authors speculate on the reasons for the unimportance of public funding and provision, and argue that this could be due to lack of coverage in rolling out programs or irrelevance of their content.

However, there are clear differences between more innovative and less innovative firms: more innovative firms (i.e. higher R&D expenditures, improved processes, ISO certificates, and new products) often decide to train their workers. The surveys provide some interesting information about the reasons why many firms do not choose to train their workers. The main reason is that they do not see it as necessary. Skills are not perceived as a major constraint to operations. This is consistent with the theoretical argument that absence of innovative skill-intensive technologies limits the demand for more training of skilled labor. Many firms find their workers to be adequately trained. The policy implication is that it does not make much sense to subsidize on-the-job training in the absence of demand.

The final section of the chapter provides estimates of the effects of on-the-job training on TFP. When country fixed effects and control variables are added, the effects of training are not significant in general. However, in large firms (with more than 100 workers) there is a clear, significant, and positive effect of training: a 1% increase in the proportion of trained employees would raise productivity by 0.7%.

The authors emphasize that the findings of this study should be treated with caution. However, what comes out rather clearly is that many firms do not see training their employees as a high priority. Only when firms become more innovative does demand for training emerge. As Crespi et al. show in Chap. 2, public policies have a significant effect on firms' investments in innovation. Thus, rather than subsidizing on-the-job training directly, public policy should promote increased innovativeness of firms. Indirectly this would result in greater demand for skilled labor and on-the-job training.

Business Performance in Young Latin American Firms

In the Schumpeterian literature, there are periods of economic development in which dynamic small firms are the agents of innovation and economic development. In other periods, referred to as Schumpeter II regimes, mature incumbent firms are much more important. In Chap. 6, Hugo Kantis, Juan Federico, Pablo Angelelli, and Sabrina Ibarra García discuss the performance and characteristics of small, young manufacturing firms in Latin America. While most of the literature on young firms focuses on startups, the authors examine the potential of young firms that have survived four years but are still younger than ten years. They study whether such young firms are a potential source of innovation, rejuvenation, and renewal of the economy. The analysis is based on a sample of 1074 young firms in 12 Latin American countries drawn from the WBES.

In the sample, almost 20% of all firms are young (i.e. four to ten years old), and in several countries young firms have a larger presence in knowledge-based sectors than mature companies (e.g. technology services and engineering-intensive manufacturing). They contribute to diversification of regional industrial structures by embarking on new activities. The entrepreneurs have previous experience as employees, often in managerial positions in mature companies, and only 3% of the entrepreneurs were previously unemployed. So there are few 'necessity entrepreneurs' in this category, although informal micro-enterprises are excluded from the surveys used in this book, and that is where survival entrepreneurship is generally found. Half of the young firms employ between 10 and 49 workers. They are mainly focused on domestic markets and only 16% export. Quite a few firms performed R&D (43%), a percentage similar to that for mature firms, and introduced new products or processes in the period analyzed. In terms of their growth performance, whether measured as sales growth or employment growth, young firms are quite dynamic. Most start as micro-enterprises with no more than five employees, but they can survive, grow, and develop into SMEs. Of course most startup failures occur in the first four years, and the firms in the sample are those that survived the so-called 'valley of death.' Sales growth slows down in the last two years but is still fairly high. The authors conclude that three-quarters of the young firms tend to achieve sales growth, 40% of them growing very rapidly at more than 20% per annum. One interesting feature of the high-growth SME segment is their stronger specialization in knowledge-intensive sectors, such as engineering-intensive manufacturing or technology sectors (29% of young firms and 21% of mature firms), suggesting their role is propelling a structural transformation.

Though young firms tend to have dynamic growth performance, their average labor productivity in 2009 was more than 20% lower than that of mature firms. However, young firms tended to catch up with mature firms, especially in services, during the short period studied (2007–2009) and their relative productivity increased from 72.0% in 2007 to 79.2% in 2009. High-growth SMEs show the biggest increase in productivity levels, especially in the manufacturing sector where young, growing SMEs outperform mature firms.

In the last section of the chapter, the authors analyze the determinants of sales growth, employment growth, productivity levels, productivity growth, and profitability using Ordinary Least Square regressions. The econometric analysis is restricted to manufacturing firms. The results are inconclusive, but some interesting findings stand out. There appears to be a positive and statistically significant relationship between the high-growth status of young manufacturing firms and their productivity levels, on average 32% higher.

Regulatory obstacles (e.g. tax rates, labor regulations, licenses, and permits) have a significant negative effect on sales growth. Financial constraints (lack of access to finance) have a negative impact on both employment growth and levels of productivity. Technical assistance (use of external technical services) has a significant and positive effect on sales growth and, with workforce training, on productivity levels. Though young firms are not less innovative than mature firms, the positive effects of innovation on productivity performance discussed in Chap. 2 do not seem to hold for young firms.

The general conclusion from this chapter is that, even though we do not know much about the determinants of performance for young firms, they are dynamic compared to mature firms, and therefore deserve special attention from researchers and policymakers. Their contribution to macroeconomic development should be studied in more detail.

DIFFERENT OBSTACLES FOR DIFFERENT PRODUCTIVITY LEVELS? AN ANALYSIS OF CARIBBEAN FIRMS

In Chap. 7, Alison Cathles and Siobhan Pangerl examine the implications of small country size in the island economies of the Caribbean. The chapter uses new firm-level data from the WBES and the PROTEQin Survey to better understand Caribbean firm dynamics and the differences among Caribbean countries.

The firms in the region tend to be micro or small, concentrated in the services sector, mature, and non-exporters. Comparing firms in different Caribbean countries, various differences emerge: smaller countries typically have a higher percentage of micro and small firms, the concentration in the services sector varies from 50 to 84%, and there are considerable differences in ICT penetration rates.

Then, the authors deepen the analysis and discuss the characteristics of human capital in Caribbean firms from two perspectives: entrepreneurs and workforce. Considering both firm owners and managers to be entrepreneurs, the authors find that previous experience varies widely throughout the region. In general, entrepreneurs tend to have previously been employed (either in managerial or non-managerial positions), but in some countries there is a significant percentage that transitioned directly from unemployment to being a top manager. This finding is consistent with the high percentage of firms in those countries that report that the business was started because of a lack of better employment opportunities. Moreover, the authors show that few Caribbean firms are created to introduce a new idea or product into the market. Rather they tend to replicate, imitate, or differentiate products or services that already exist. Thus, the capacity of a firm to absorb external technology and knowledge is key to good performance. But this capacity is strictly related to the availability of a sufficiently skilled workforce, a major concern in the region. In fact, over 35% of Caribbean firms report having unfilled vacancies, and the lack of an adequately educated workforce is one of the obstacles to firm operations most frequently mentioned in the surveys.

The next section of the chapter focuses on productivity. Larger, older, exporting, ICT-using, and foreign-owned firms are found to be more productive in the manufacturing and services sectors. As regards human capital, firms with more experienced managers on average show higher productivity, as do firms with a higher proportion of employees with at least a bachelor's degree.

Finally, the authors investigate the perception of Caribbean enterprises with respect to the main obstacles affecting their operations. In addition to scarcity of adequately educated workers, difficulties in getting access to finance, inefficient electricity, and high tax rates are consistently cited as the most relevant obstacles. Nevertheless, when the firms are classified by their productivity levels, by dividing the sample into labor productivity quintiles, it is clear that the perception about most relevant obstacles can change, possibly because more productive firms have different needs.

The descriptive analysis is complemented by an econometric estimation of the determinants of firm productivity in the region. Using quantile regression techniques, the authors differentiate the effect of various firm characteristics and perceived obstacles, depending on where the firms lie in the distribution of labor productivity. As for access to finance, the firms that report this as the main obstacle to their operations underperform only when they belong to either the lowest decile or the upper half of the productivity distribution. For firms in other parts of the distribution, there are no significant differences in performance between enterprises reporting access to finance as their main obstacle and enterprises not mentioning access to finance. This is an interesting result, as it opens the possibility for Caribbean policymakers to maximize the effectiveness of their interventions by designing different policies depending on the types of firms being targeted.

Credit Access in Latin American Enterprises One of the possible determinants of both innovation and productivity improvement is access to credit. In Chap. 8, Andrea Presbitero and Roberta Rabellotti single out this factor for special attention. Firms often mention lack of access to bank credit as one of the main constraints on growth, productivity, innovation, and export capacity, particularly regarding SMEs (Ayyagari et al. 2012).

Recent empirical studies find that the lack of adequate access to finance represents an important constraint to productivity growth at the firm level. Previous literature finds that the extent to which firms are financially constrained depends on micro-factors, as well as institutional frameworks and credit market structures. For example, firms that are more informationally opaque—it is harder to acquire reliable information about them—are more likely to be financially constrained. The degree of market concentration, the proximity between lenders and borrowers, the level of foreign bank penetration, the institutional setting, and the structure of the credit market all affect firms' access to credit. However, these results for advanced economies are not easily applicable to emerging and developing countries because of significant differences in firm size distributions and characteristics as well as in institutional, macroeconomic, and financial structures. This chapter aims to uncover the possible heterogeneities in financing constraints across firms and countries in LAC and to explain them according to differences in firm characteristics, as well as country-level institutional, macroeconomic, and financial settings.

The empirical analysis uses comprehensive data from the WBES for 31 countries in LAC and is matched with macroeconomic data on the credit market structure and the institutional settings in different countries. The data shows that, since 2006, there has been a general deepening of the domestic financial systems in LAC. However, there are still significant gaps and, in general, there has not been a convergence toward the measured levels of financial development observed in more developed countries. The region is characterized by a heavy presence of foreign banks, concentrated credit markets, and considerable variation in credit registry practices (in 2010, about half of all LAC countries had credit registries).

In the WBES, the use of bank credit is shown to be extremely limited for micro and young firms, while it is the second source of finance for large firms. More productive firms rely less on internal funding for working capital and tend to use more bank and trade credit. Access to bank credit is quite heterogeneous between countries. In Mexico, less than 30% of firms have an overdraft, a line of credit, or a loan, whereas in Brazil, Colombia, and Chile, the numbers are much higher and Argentinean firms are somewhere in the middle.

The empirical models measure demand for credit and credit availability across firms and countries on four binary indicators: loan demand, loan denial, constrained, and discouraged. Larger and older firms, as well as exporters, are more likely to demand bank credit. This pattern is reflected in a higher share of discouraged borrowers in smaller, younger, and more domestically oriented companies. As a result, these firms are more likely to be financially constrained. Foreign-owned firms are less likely to apply for bank credit than domestically oriented firms, but there is no robust evidence that they are more likely to be financially constrained.

Labor productivity is found to be statistically associated with better access to credit. High-productivity firms are significantly more likely to demand credit and less likely to be financially constrained than low-productivity firms. This finding suggests the presence of a financing constraint trap for low-productivity firms, as they are most likely to be financially constrained but do not have the resources to invest to improve their performance.

In terms of external characteristics, bank penetration, as measured by the number of branches per capita, is significantly correlated with a lower probability that borrowers are financially constrained and discouraged. This finding is consistent with the hypothesis that physical proximity to credit markets helps mitigate informational asymmetries between lenders and borrowers. When the authors control for degree of competition, a larger number of branches per capita reduces the average distance between firms and banks, which in turn reduces informational asymmetries and facilitates banks' screening and monitoring activities. Interestingly, the authors find that the presence of foreign banks can have both positive and negative effects on firms' financing constraints. Foreign bank penetration has a negative effect on access to credit in less developed and more concentrated markets, while it has a positive influence in more competitive and financially developed markets.

The results underline the importance of improving the functioning of domestic market structures. Policies to increase the degree of bank penetration and competition in financial markets can positively impact firms' access to credit and their productivity. Given this, the large heterogeneity in LAC financial markets provides ample opportunities for policies to increase productivity in countries across the region.

INTERNATIONAL LINKAGES, VALUE-ADDED TRADE, AND THE PRODUCTIVITY OF LAC FIRMS

The relationship between international linkages and firm productivity in LAC is an important topic. Though participation in international trade and the presence of inward foreign investment are often assumed to be a potential source of positive learning effects for local firms, there is no consensus in the literature on the existence of such effects and the factors that influence them. Moreover, the direction of causality between openness to trade and investment and firm performance is theoretically contested, while the empirical evidence is mixed.

Chapter 9, by Pierluigi Montalbano, Silvia Nenci, and Carlo Pietrobelli, contributes to this debate by investigating the issue in LAC, with a particular focus on the relationship between participation in global value chains (GVCs) and productivity. The authors claim that the increasing international fragmentation of production has made it necessary to rethink the concept of international trade, evaluating the value added in each step of production. This approach requires data beyond the standard trade statistics. So, the chapter uses the new OECD-WTO TiVA database to obtain indicators regarding the decomposition of the value added embodied in national exports and the participation and position of country industries in GVCs. Combining these indicators with the enterprise survey data, the authors provide a descriptive analysis of firms' international linkages in Argentina, Brazil, Chile, and Mexico, the only four LAC countries for which TiVA and WBES data are both available for the same fiscal year.

As for participation in GVCs, the picture differs from country to country. While it is substantial for Chile and to a lesser extent for Mexico, the involvement of Argentinean and Brazilian firms is limited. This can be explained by both a size effect—larger economies tend to be more self-sufficient in producing inputs for exports—and by different patterns of specialization: a relative specialization in manufacturing results in a higher degree of global participation than specialization in other sectors. Compared to their international counterparts, the Latin American countries under consideration are generally located upstream in GVCs (Brazil shows the highest GVC position in international comparison), with the relevant exception being Mexico. Again, differences are related to the countries' production structures.

Using a pooled dataset for the entire sample of LAC countries included in the enterprise surveys, the authors perform a three-step empirical exercise to investigate whether LAC firms characterized by stronger international linkages (in terms of trade and FDI) have higher productivity in comparison with LAC firms with weaker linkages. First, they perform a preliminary, static analysis of firm productivity premia for exporting and foreign-owned firms. As expected, there is a positive relationship between international linkages and firm productivity, in line with the theoretical predictions that low-productivity firms operate in the domestic market while firms with higher productivity export and compete in international markets.

Second, this result is tested using a Cobb–Douglas production function with labor, capital, and knowledge augmented by international linkages. As before, exporters and/or foreign-owned firms, on average and *ceteris paribus*, have higher productivity, with some heterogeneity by firm size. Third, in order to check for endogeneity bias, the authors perform instrumental variable (IV-2SLS) and control function (CF) estimations, confirming the existence of a causal relationship between exports and firm productivity.

Finally, the chapter focuses on the effect of GVC involvement (both participation and position) on firm productivity. This analysis is performed at the industry level, assuming firm performance in value added is heterogeneous across industries but homogeneous within them. Because of data availability, the sample is restricted to exporting firms from the four LAC countries for which TiVA data are available (Argentina, Brazil, Chile, and Mexico). The results show that there is no additional productivity effect in clustering firms by trade in value added, once the impact of gross exports is controlled for. This suggests that the effect of participation in international trade as such is more important than its specific value content. However, the position of the industry in the GVC is found to be important. Being upstream in a GVC has a positive impact on firm productivity performance. Thus resource production or processing is more productive than downstream assembly.

In conclusion, the results presented in the chapter support the hypothesis of a positive causal relationship between international activities and firm performance at the firm level in LAC. Moreover, this study constitutes a first attempt to explore the effects of participation in a GVC on industry performance in the region. Industries positioned more upstream in GVCs are more productive than more downstream ones. This is an interesting finding that confirms the impossibility of considering trade as a unitary concept and the necessity to differentiate it by its value added.

KEY QUESTIONS

Five groups of questions have guided the authors of the chapters of this book.

1. How important is innovation for firm-level performance? How innovative are firms in LAC? What are the empirical and theoretical connections between investment in innovation and innovation performance on the one hand, and innovation performance and productivity levels and productivity growth on the other? To what extent do firms profit from each other's knowledge and innovative activities?
2. How do differences in firm characteristics affect their innovation and productivity performance? What are the specific effects of factors such as broadband access, on-the-job training, and access to credit on firm performance? What are the differences between Latin American firms and Caribbean firms in terms of innovation and productivity dynamics? What are the implications of firm heterogeneity for economic policy design?
3. What role do young firms play in the dynamics of innovation, employment creation, and productivity growth? How do young firms differ from more mature firms?
4. How does globalization affect innovation and productivity in LAC firms? What is the role of FDI, participation in exports, and positions in GVCs on innovation and productivity growth?
5. What are the effects of public support for investment in innovation, and public policies to improve access to finance, human capital, and on-the-job training? What can we learn about the effects of policy through a better understanding of firm and country heterogeneity?

In the subsequent chapters these questions are discussed and analyzed in detail. In the concluding chapter, we revisit the questions and reflect on the lessons and policy implications of these studies.

Notes

1. East Asian countries considered in this analysis are Hong Kong, Malaysia, Singapore, South Korea, and Thailand (World Development Indicators, accessed November 2014).
2. Productivity is measured in multiple ways, with labor productivity and TFP being two of the most common measures. Labor productivity is a simple calculation of output (or value added) per hour, whereas TFP is slightly more complex and calculated by measuring the portion of output not explained by the amount of inputs used in production. In short, TFP measures how efficiently and intensely inputs are used in production. Which is the most appropriate measure remains a subject of debate among economists and policymakers. What is important to note is that performance across LAC remains consistently low across both measures in comparison to other regions worldwide. For example, labor productivity in Latin America grew by 0.9% annually between 1990 and 2014, compared to 1.6, 8.1, and 2.9% for the United States, China, and Developing Asia (Bangladesh, Cambodia, Indonesia, Malaysia, Pakistan, Philippines, Sri Lanka, Thailand, and Vietnam), respectively (The Conference Board 2015). The same trend emerges when using TFP, where Latin America had negative annual growth of 0.1%, compared to growth of 0.5, 2.9, and 0.4% for the United States, China, and Developing Asia, respectively (The Conference Board 2015).
3. The literature has acknowledged the importance of both factors (reallocation of resources across firms and within-firm efficiency improvements) in explaining productivity growth rates. Pagés (2010) found that both factors were key to explaining the productivity gains achieved over 1990–2005 in East Asian countries.
4. Bloom et al. (2014) concluded that the establishment-level dispersion in productivity remains high in apparently homogeneous product industries even after controlling for establishment-level output prices.
5. The skewness of a probability distribution measures its level of asymmetry. In this case, the distribution of labor productivity in the manufacturing sector is more asymmetric than that in the services sector.
6. Some authors argue that there is a likely time sequence, where within-firm effects occur only after inter-firm reallocation has been made possible. In their study on Chile, Bergoeing and Repetto (2006) concluded that the reallocation effects took place earlier, and that within-plant productivity growth driven by technology adoption and innovation only contributed

positively to aggregate productivity growth during the 1990s, after the macroeconomic reforms were consolidated. Some macroeconomic studies also appear to confirm this preliminary evidence, with between-sector and between-firm productivity effects prevailing during the early years of policy reform in LAC, during the 1970s and 1980s, and within-sector and within-firm effects prevailing later (Pagés 2010).

7. In the 2010 round of WBES surveys in LAC, the Inter-American Development Bank financed the inclusion of additional questions on participation in public support programs. These questions asked whether firms received public funding (either partial or full) for a range of business development services ranging from quality certification, creation of business alliances, innovation, export promotion, and training.

8. See www.enterprisesurveys.org/ for further information.

9. Public utilities, government services, health care, and financial services sectors are not included.

10. Some of the key IDB-financed variables are: product and process innovation; sales from innovative products and/or processes; R&D spending; cooperation on innovation activities; publicly financed training programs (1) to obtain quality certification, (2) to make business alliances, (3) to support innovation, (4) to support exports, or (5) on ICTs; publicly funded external and internal training; type of workers trained; average number of hours of training sessions; and the reason no training was carried out.

11. One of the main advantages of using PPP exchange rates is that they are fairly stable over time. Market exchange rates, in comparison, are more volatile and using them can produce large distortions.

12. At the time of writing, EPFE cross-sectional data was available for the Bahamas, Colombia, Honduras, Panama, and Uruguay from surveys collected between 2011 and 2013.

The PROTEQin was commissioned by the IDB with funding from the Compete Caribbean Program, a regional private sector development and technical assistance initiative financed by the IDB, the United Kingdom Department for International Development, and Canada's Department of Foreign Affairs, and Trade and Development, and executed in partnership with the Caribbean Development Bank. It was administered in 2013 and 2014. For more information, see www.competecaribbean.org

REFERENCES

Álvarez, R., G. Crespi, and C. Volpe Martincus. 2012. *Impact Evaluation in a Multiple Program World.*. Inter-American Development Bank.

Ayyagari, M., A. Demirgüç-Kunt, and V. Maksimovic. 2012. Financing of Firms in Developing Countries. World Bank Policy Research Working Paper, No. 6036. Washington, DC: The World Bank.

Bergoeing, R., and A. Repetto. 2006. Micro Efficiency and Aggregate Growth in Chile. *Cuadernos de Economía* 43(127): 169–191.

Bloom N., E. Brynjolfsson, L. Foster, R. Jarmin, M. Patnaik, I. Saporta-Eksten, and J. Van Reenen. 2014. IT and Management in America. Discussion Paper No. 1258. London, UK: Centre for Economic Performance.

Busso, M., L. Madrigal, and C. Pagés. 2013. Productivity and Resource Misallocation in Latin America. *The BE Journal of Macroeconomics* 13(1): 903–932.

Crépon, B., E. Duguet, and J. Mairesse. 1998. Research, Innovation and Productivity: An Econometric Analysis at the Firm Level. *Economics of Innovation and New Technology* 7(2): 115–158.

Crespi, G., E. Fernández-Arias, and E. Stein (eds.). 2014. *Rethinking Productive Development: Sound Policies and Institutions for Economic Transformation.* Washington, DC: Palgrave Macmillan for Inter-American Development Bank.

Crespi, G., and P. Zúñiga. 2012. Innovation and Productivity: Evidence from Six Latin American Countries. *World Development* 40(2): 273–290.

Dollar, D., M. Hallward-Driemeier, and T. Mengistae. 2005. Investment Climate and Firm Performance in Developing Economies. *Economic Development and Cultural Change* 54(1): 1–31.

Dosi, G. 1988. Sources, Procedures, and Microeconomic Effects of Innovation. *Journal of Economic Literature* 26(3): 1120–1171.

Easterly, W., and R. Levine. 2001. What Have we Learned from a Decade of Empirical Research on Growth? It's Not Factor Accumulation: Stylized Facts and Growth Models. *The World Bank Economic Review* 15(2): 177–219.

ECLAC. 2014. *International Trade and Inclusive Development: Building Synergies.* Santiago: United Nations.

Ericson, R., and A. Pakes. 1989. An Alternative Theory of Firm and Industry Dynamics. Discussion Paper 445. New York: Columbia University.

Feenstra, R.C., R. Inklaar, and M.P. Timmer. 2015. The Next Generation of the Penn World Table. *American Economic Review* 105(10): 3150–3182.

Fernández-Arias, E. 2014. Productivity and Factor Accumulation in Latin America and the Caribbean: A Database. Departamento de Investigación, Banco Interamericano de Desarrollo, Washington, DC. Available in: http://www.iadb.org/research/pub_desc.cfm?pub_id=DBA-015, accessed 31 August 2015.

Foster, L., J. Haltiwanger, and C.J. Krizan. 2001. Aggregate Productivity Growth: Lessons from Microeconomic Evidence. In *New Developments in Productivity Analysis,* ed. C.R. Hulten, E.R. Dean, and M.J. Harper. Chicago, IL: University of Chicago Press.

Hall, R.E., and C.I. Jones. 1999. Why Do Some Countries Produce So Much More Output Per Worker Than Others? Working Paper 6564. Cambridge, MA: The National Bureau of Economic Research.

Heckman, J.J., L. Lochner, and C. Taber, 1998. Tax Policy and Human Capital Formation. National Bureau of Economic Research.

Hsieh, C.T., and P.J. Klenow. 2009. Misallocation and Manufacturing TFP in China and India. *Quarterly Journal of Economics* 124(4): 1403–1448.

Jovanovic, B. 1982. Selection and the Evolution of Industry. *Econometrica* 50(3): 649–670.

Katz, J. (ed.). 1987. *Technology Generation in Latin American Manufacturing Industries*. London, UK: Macmillan Press.

Klenow, P., and Rodriguez-Clare, A. 1997. The Neoclassical Revival in Growth Economics: Has It Gone Too Far? In *NBER Macroeconomics Annual 1997*, Volume 12 (pp. 73–114). MIT Press.

Lall, S. 1992. Technological Capabilities and Industrialization. *World Development* 20: 165–186.

Lavopa, A. 2015. *Structural Transformation and Economic Development. Can Development Traps Be Avoided?* Doctoral Thesis. The Netherlands: Maastricht University.

Lundvall, B.Å. 1992. *National Systems of Innovation: Towards a Theory of Innovation and Interactive Learning*. London: Pinter.

Malerba, F. 2002. Sectoral Systems of Innovation and Production. *Research Policy* 31(2): 247–264.

McMillan, M., D. Rodrik, and Í. Verduzco-Gallo. 2014. Globalization, Structural Change, and Productivity Growth, With an Update on Africa. *World Development* 63: 11–32.

Nelson, R.R. 1991. Why Do Firms Differ, and How Does It Matter? *Strategic Management Journal* 12(S2): 61–74.

Nelson, R.R., and S.G. Winter. 1982. *An Evolutionary Theory of Economic Change*. Cambridge, MA: Harvard University Press.

Pagés, C. (ed.). 2010. *The Age of Productivity: Transforming Economies from the Bottom Up*. Washington, DC: Palgrave Macmillan for Inter-American Development Bank.

Solimano, A., and R. Soto. 2006. Economic Growth in Latin America in the Late Twentieth Century: Evidence and Interpretation. In *Vanishing Growth in Latin America*, ed. A. Solimano. Northampton, MA: Edward Elgar.

Syverson, C. 2011. What Determines Productivity? *Journal of Economic Literature* 49(2): 326–365.

Teece, D., and G. Pisano. 1994. The Dynamic Capabilities of Firms: An Introduction. *Industrial and corporate change* 3(3): 537–556.

The Conference Board. 2015. *Total Economy Database*, available at https://www.conference-board.org/data/economydatabase/, accessed 31 August 2015.

Vuletin, G.J. 2008. Measuring the Informal Economy in Latin America and the Caribbean. Working Paper 102. Washington, DC: International Monetary Fund.

Williamson, O.E. 1973. Markets and Hierarchies: Some Elementary Considerations. *American Economic Review* 63(2): 316–325.

Williamson, O.E. 1985. *The Economic Institutions of Capitalism: Firms, Markets, Relational Contracting.* New York: Free Press.

World Bank. 2010. *World Bank Enterprise Surveys (WBES).* Available at: http://www.enterprisesurveys.org. Washington, DC. The World Bank.

CHAPTER 2

Innovation Dynamics and Productivity: Evidence for Latin America

Gustavo Crespi, Ezequiel Tacsir, and Fernando Vargas

Although the GDP per capita of most Latin American countries has grown rapidly since 2003, it still significantly lags the levels of industrialized countries. Further, productivity, the main driver of long-term economic growth, has expanded at a lower rate than the world's technological frontier (IDB 2010). Thus, improving productivity is the main challenge for Latin America. But what creates productivity growth? Economies are becoming more knowledge based, and innovation is a key driver of national competitiveness, development, and long-term economic growth. At the firm level, innovation—the transformation of ideas into new products, services, and production processes—leads to a more efficient use of resources, creating sustainable competitive advantages. At the same time, innovation leads to

G. Crespi
Inter-American Development Bank
e-mail: gcrespi@iadb.org

E. Tacsir
CINVE (Montevideo, Uruguay), CIECTI (Buenos Aires, Argentina),
UNU-MERIT (Maastricht, Netherlands)
e-mail: etacsir@gmail.com

F. Vargas
UNU-MERIT
e-mail: fernando.e.vargas.c@gmail.com

© Inter-American Development Bank 2016
M. Grazzi and C. Pietrobelli (eds.), *Firm Innovation and Productivity in Latin America and the Caribbean,*
DOI 10.1057/978-1-349-58151-1_2

37

completely novel sectors, where new firms start operating and new production routines are generated. Change in the production structure is what increases specialization and productivity growth (Katz 2006) as well as the gradual expansion of more knowledge-intensive production activities. Hence, innovation is essential to spur economic growth and to raise living standards.[1] At the macro-level, research and development (R&D) spending, innovation, productivity, and per capita income reinforce each other and lead to sustained long-term growth (Hall and Jones 1999; Rouvinen 2002).

Evidence of the relationship between R&D, innovation, and productivity has been found in studies of industrialized countries (Griffith et al. 2004; Griffith et al. 2006; OECD 2009; Mairesse and Mohnen 2010). Investing in innovation can have substantial economic payoffs. Firms that invest in innovation are better equipped to introduce technological advances and tend to have higher labor productivity than those that do not. Crespi and Zuñiga (2012) reported that productivity gaps in the manufacturing sector between innovative and non-innovative firms are much higher in Latin America than in industrialized countries. For the typical country in the European Union, the productivity gap is 20%, while for the typical Latin American country it is 70%. Thus, Latin America has great potential to benefit from investment and policies that foster innovation.

One of the most important limitations of previous research on innovation in Latin America was the absence of harmonized and comparable indicators across the different countries, which seriously limited the possibility of inferring policy conclusions that were not affected by country specifics with respect to data quality and coverage.[2] Also, most of this research focuses on estimating firm-level correlations without attempting to identify market failures or other limitations that harm innovation investment. In this chapter, a wide range of innovation indicators are analyzed in order to describe the innovation behavior of manufacturing firms in Latin America using the World Bank Enterprise Survey (WBES) database.[3] The authors' objective is to understand the main characteristics of innovative firms in Latin America and to gather new evidence regarding the nature of the innovation process in the region. The next section of this chapter reviews the main findings in the literature on determinants of innovation in both industrialized and developing countries. Using various indicators, the third section presents statistics about the innovation performance of Latin American firms. The ways that innovation relates to firm characteristics in Latin America are explored using a structural model approach to untangle the determinants of innovation investment and performance and productivity at the firm level. The fourth section extends the model to gather some evidence regarding the prevalence of spillover effects and the extent to which there is an important heterogeneity regarding returns on innovation.

LITERATURE BACKGROUND

Innovation is fundamental to catching up economically and raising living standards. Evidence demonstrates a virtuous circle in which R&D spending, innovation, productivity, and per capita income mutually reinforce each other and lead to long-term, sustained growth rates (Hall and Jones 1999; Rouvinen 2002; Guloglu and Tekin 2012) and may foster job creation (Vivarelli 2013).[4] R&D is a source of direct and indirect advantages for firms. There is convincing evidence that shows positive linkages between R&D, innovation, and productivity at the firm level in industrialized countries (Griffith et al. 2004; Griffith et al. 2006; OECD 2009; Mairesse and Mohnen 2010; Mohnen and Hall 2013). In addition, R&D contributes to firms' absorptive capacity, a fundamental prerequisite for learning by doing. Internal R&D supports better identification of the value of external technology, its assimilation, and its use while expanding the stock of knowledge of firms (Cohen and Levinthal 1989; Griffith et al. 2004). Hence, strengthening in-house technological capabilities induces knowledge spillovers by acquiring machinery and equipment and interacting with other firms.

We note that an important strand of the literature deals with country- or sector-level information. However, considering the innovation results from the investment decisions made by individual firms, the microeconomic analysis has the potential to enlighten the foundations of the correlations found at the macro-level. Taking advantage of innovation surveys, Crépon et al. (1998) were the first to empirically integrate these relationships in a recursive model (Crépon–Duguet–Mairesse [CDM] model), allowing innovation inputs (R&D investment) to be estimated. Their findings for France corroborated the positive correlation between firm productivity and higher innovation output, even controlling for the skill composition of labor. They also confirmed that a firm's decision to invest in innovation (R&D) increases with its size, market share, and diversification, and with the demand-pull and technology-push forces.

Building on the CDM model, a new wave of studies that exploited innovation surveys emerged and reported similar results for other industrialized countries. Using different indicators of economic performance, such as labor productivity, multifactor productivity, sales, profit margins, and market value, studies repeatedly showed that technological innovations (product or process) lead to superior economic performance for the firm (Loof and Heshmati 2002; Loof et al. 2003; Janz et al. 2004; Van Leeuwen and Klomp 2006; Mohnen et al. 2006). This literature also highlights the fact that firm heterogeneity is important to explain innovation activities and their effects on firm performance, and must be controlled for in empirical estimations (Hall and Mairesse 2006; Mairesse and Mohnen 2010; and Chap. 1 of this book). Further, the correlation between product innovation and productivity is often higher for larger firms (Griffith et al. 2006; OECD 2009) and, as expected, in most countries the productivity effect of product innovation is larger in manufacturing than in services (OECD 2009). In addition, a positive association is consistently confirmed between R&D and innovation outcomes. Firms that invest more intensively in R&D are more likely to develop innovations, once endogeneity is corrected for and controlling is done for firm characteristics such as size, affiliation to group, or type of innovation strategy.

In contrast, evidence with regard to the ability of firms in developing economies to transform R&D into innovation is not as conclusive. This heterogeneity could be explained by the fact that firms in developing countries are too far from the technological frontier and incentives to invest in innovation are weak or absent (Acemoglu et al. 2006). In this vein, a positive association between R&D, innovation, and productivity was found for new industrialized countries such as South Korea (Lee and Kang 2007), Malaysia (Hegde and Shapira 2007), Taiwan (Aw et al. 2008), and China (Jefferson et al. 2006). By investing in R&D and human capital, these countries managed to narrow their distance from the best practices. However, in many Latin American economies, firms' innovations consist of incremental changes with little or no impact on international markets, and are mostly based on imitation and technology transfer, such as acquisition of machinery and equipment and disembodied technology (Anlló and Suárez 2009; Navarro et al. 2010). In many cases, R&D is prohibitive financially, and considering the human capital needed, its materialization could require long time horizons (Navarro et al. 2010).

There is evidence that higher levels of investment in innovation (notably in R&D) lead to a higher propensity to introduce technological innovation in firms in Argentina (Chudnovsky et al. 2006) and Brazil (Correa et al. 2005; Raffo et al. 2008), but research does not support this relationship for Chile (Benavente 2006) or Mexico (Perez et al. 2005). The results regarding the impact of innovation on labor productivity are equally inconclusive for Latin American firms. Raffo et al. (2008) found a significant impact of product innovation for Brazil and Mexico but not for Argentina, though

Perez et al. (2005), Chudnovsky et al. (2006), and Benavente (2006) failed to find any significant effect of innovation on firm productivity (measured as sales per employee) in Argentinean and Chilean firms. Hall and Mairesse (2006) suggested that the lack of significance of innovation in productivity in developing countries may reflect the very different circumstances surrounding innovation in these economies compared to Western Europe, and they suggested evaluating the effects over longer periods of time (for evidence from Chile, see Benavente and Bravo 2009).[5]

One important pitfall of previous research is related to the lack of homogeneous and comparable data across the different countries in the Latin American region, which may be a factor underlying this heterogeneity. Differences in sampling methodologies, questionnaire design, and data processing for the existing innovation surveys seriously affect the comparability of the results. Crespi and Zuñiga (2012) performed the first comparative study to examine the determinants of technological innovation and its impact on firm labor productivity in manufacturing firms across Latin American countries (Argentina, Chile, Colombia, Costa Rica, Panama, and Uruguay). The authors used micro-data from innovation surveys but the same specification and identification strategy. This exercise showed more consistent results. Specifically, firms that invested in knowledge were more able to introduce technological advances, and those who innovated exhibited superior labor productivity than those who did not. Yet, firm-level determinants of innovation investment are still more heterogeneous than in Organisation for Economic Co-operation and Development (OECD) countries: cooperation, foreign ownership, and exporting increase the propensity to invest in innovation in only half of the countries. At the same time, a firm's linkages and use of different sources of information for innovation activities (scientific and market) have little or no impact on innovation efforts. This illustrates the weak articulation that characterizes national innovation systems in the region. The results regarding productivity, however, highlight the importance of innovation for firms to improve economic performance and to catch up.

Taking these efforts a bit further, the contribution of this chapter is twofold. First, we make use of a homogeneous questionnaire and dataset, which allows us to make more easily generalizable conclusions. Second, most of the previous research on the micro-determinants of innovation and their impacts on productivity deal with structural determinants and, although these results are useful for policy design, they are insufficient in that they are not directly linked to market failures. Our research extends previous analyses by looking at the impacts of spillovers on the determinants of innovation investments.

RESEARCH QUESTIONS AND CONCEPTUAL FRAMEWORK

This chapter aims to gather new evidence regarding the determinants of innovation investments—in particular R&D—in LAC and their impacts on productivity at the firm level. More specifically, we address the following research questions:

1. What are the determinants of innovation investments in LAC?
2. What are the returns on innovation investments?
3. What are the impacts of innovation outputs on productivity?
4. Is there heterogeneity in the effects of investments in innovation on productivity?
5. Is there any evidence of spillovers that could guide policy design and analysis?

In this chapter, we apply the CDM model to estimate the determinants of innovation (R&D) and its impact on total factor productivity (TFP). The CDM model has three stages:

1. Firms decide whether or not to invest in R&D activities and how much to invest.
2. Knowledge (technology) is produced as a result of this investment ("knowledge production" function) (Griliches 1979; Pakes and Griliches 1980).
3. Output is produced using new knowledge (technological innovation) along with other inputs.

Thus knowledge is assumed to have a direct impact on firm economic performance, generally expressed by TFP. In addition to firm characteristics, the model includes external forces acting concurrently on the innovation decisions of firms and indicators of demand-driven innovation (i.e. environmental, health, and safety regulations), technological push (i.e. scientific opportunities), financing (i.e. R&D subsidies), and spillovers.

The CDM model is intended to deal with the problem of selectivity bias[6] and endogeneity in the functions of innovation and productivity.[7] The model can be written as follows.

Let $i = 1 \dots N$ index firms

Equation (2.1) accounts for firms' innovative efforts IE_i^*:

$$IE_i^* = z_i \beta + e_i \qquad (2.1)$$

where IE_i^* is an unobserved latent variable, z_i is a vector of determinants of innovation effort, β is a vector of parameters of interest, and e_i is an error term. We proxy firms' innovative effort IE_i^* by their (log) expenditures on R&D activities per worker denoted by IE_i only if firms make (and report) such expenditures. Thus we can only directly estimate equation (2.1) at the risk of selection bias (Griffith et al. 2006). Instead, we assume the following selection equation describing whether the firm decides to do (and/or report) innovation investment or not:

$$ID_i = \begin{cases} 1 \, if \, ID_i^* = w_i\alpha + \varepsilon_i > c, \\ 0 \, if \, ID_i^* = w_i\alpha + \varepsilon_i \leq c \end{cases} \qquad (2.2)$$

where ID_i is a binary endogenous variable for innovation decision that is equal to zero for firms that do not invest in innovation and one for firms investing in innovation activities; ID_i^* is a corresponding latent variable such that firms decide to do (and/or report) innovation investment if it is above a certain threshold level c, and where w is a vector of variables explaining the innovation investment decision, α is a vector of parameters of interest, and ε is an error term. Conditional on firm i doing innovation activities, we can observe the amount of resources invested in innovation (IE) activities, and write:

$$IE_i = \begin{cases} IE_i^* = z_i\beta + e_i \, if \, ID_i = 1 \\ 0 \, if \, D_i = 0 \end{cases} \qquad (2.3)$$

Assuming the error terms e_i and ε_i are bivariate normal with zero mean, variances $\sigma_\varepsilon^2 = 1$ and σ_e^2 and correlation coefficient ρ_e, we estimate the system of equations (2.2) and (2.3) as a generalized Tobit model by maximum likelihood.

The next equation (2.4) in the model is the knowledge or innovation production function:

$$TI_i = IE_i^*\gamma + x_i\delta + u_i \qquad (2.4)$$

where TI_i is knowledge outputs by technological innovation (introduction of a new product or process at the firm level), and where the latent innovation effort, IE_i^*, enters as an explanatory variable, x_i is a vector of other determinants of knowledge production, γ and δ are vectors of parameters of interest, and u_i is an error term. The last equation (2.5) relates innovation to productivity. Firms produce output using a technology represented by a Cobb–Douglas function with labor, capital, raw materials, and knowledge as inputs as follows:

$$y_i = \pi_1 k_i + \pi_2 m_i + \pi_3 TI_i + v_i \qquad (2.5)$$

where output y_i is labor productivity (log of sales per worker), k_i is the log of physical capital per worker (measured by physical investment per worker), m_i is the log of raw materials and intermediate goods per worker, and TI_i is an explanatory variable that refers to the impact of technological innovation on productivity levels.[8]

In all equations, we control for unobserved industry characteristics by including a full set of two-digit ISIC code dummies. We control for idiosyncratic characteristics of each national innovation system by including a full set of country dummies. We also control for firm size in all equations but the R&D investment equation (2.2), because R&D investment intensity is already implicitly scaled for size. As this recursive model does not allow for feedback effects between equations, we implement a three-step estimation routine. First, we estimate the generalized Tobit model (equations 2.2 and 2.3). Second, we estimate the innovation function as a probit equation using the predicted value of (log) innovation expenditure as the main explanatory variable instead of reported innovation efforts, thus correcting for potential endogeneity in the knowledge production equation. Last, we estimate the productivity equation using the predicted values from the second step to take care of the endogeneity of TI_i in equation 2.5.

As in other studies using innovation survey data, our estimation of the CDM model suffers from several measurement shortcomings. First, both Griliches (1979) and Crépon et al. (1998) used patent data as indicators of technological innovation; however, patent information is almost irrelevant in developing countries where only a very small set of firms innovate at the frontier level. Instead, we use a self-reported innovation output variable, which is qualitative information and much noisier than patent statistics. This type of innovation measurement is very subjective because firms are asked to declare whether they innovated or not (introduced a product or a process), and what one firm considers an innovation may not be the same as what other firms consider innovation. Second, the original knowledge production models relate knowledge production to knowledge capital, or the stock of R&D (or innovation investment). As we have cross-sectional information, we can only use the investment in knowledge in the previous year(s), inducing a measurement error in knowledge capital.[9] These are typical limitations encountered when analyzing R&D or innovation activities using innovation survey data; many previous studies share these limitations.

Consistent with evidence from developed countries, we also use R&D as the main dependent variable in equations 2.2 and 2.3. This decision is mostly data driven. According to Crespi and Zuñiga (2012), a better dependent variable could have been total innovation investment, which also includes training and investment in know-how and technology transfer. Unfortunately, the data is not detailed enough to be able to produce information on these additional sources of innovation investment. However, R&D plays a privileged role as part of the mechanism that leads to creating, adapting, and absorbing new ideas and technological applications (Griffith et al. 2004). Including R&D as the main dependent variable enables a better identification, assimilation, adaptation, and exploitation of external know-how (Cohen and Levinthal 1989), augmenting the impact of innovation on productivity. From a policy perspective, R&D consists of an intangible investment and, as such, the most likely to be affected by market failures such as externalities or coordination failures.

In line with previous studies, we not only use technological innovation as a dependent variable but we also estimate separate versions of equation 2.4 for each type of innovation output (product or process). This allows us to explore whether there are different returns for each different class of innovation investment. Lastly, in line with Griffith et al. (2006) and Crespi and Zuñiga (2012), we estimate the CDM model not only for innovative firms but for all firms. Accordingly, we estimate steps (1) and (2) based on reported innovation investment activities. Then, we use the relationship between observable characteristics and innovation spending to predict the likelihood of investing for all firms as a proxy for innovation effort in the knowledge production function. In turn, equation 2.4 (technological innovation) and equation 2.5 (productivity) are estimated for all firms. In equation 2.5, we include the predicted value of technological innovation. There are two reasons for using this estimation strategy.

First, the survey does not have a filter and most of the questions are asked to all firms. Second, the model assumes that all firms exert some kind of innovative effort but that not all firms report this activity. The output of these efforts produces knowledge and, thus, enables us to have an estimate of innovation efforts for all firms.[10] Of course, this strategy is debatable because the approach assumes that innovation efforts and innovation output for firms that do not report innovation activities is the same as for reporting firms. Given that we use estimated independent variables, we need to correct for the standard errors in equations 2.4 and 2.5, which we do by bootstrapping.

DATASET AND EMPIRICAL IMPLEMENTATION

For this study, we use the WBES, which are firm-level surveys of a representative sample of the private sector of an economy. The World Bank has been conducting these surveys since 2000 for key manufacturing and services sectors in every region of the world. In each country, businesses in the cities or regions of major economic activities are interviewed. The WBES surveys formal (registered) companies with five or more employees, but excludes firms that are wholly government owned. The sampling methodology is stratified random sampling, where firm size, business sector, and geographic region within a country are used as strata. Typically 1200 to 1800 interviews are conducted in larger economies, 360 interviews in medium-sized economies, and 150 interviews in smaller economies.

We use the data from the innovation module of the WBES 2010, which excluded the service sector. As a result, our analysis only covers manufacturing firms for 17 Latin American countries.[11] In addition to descriptive and performance variables, the surveys include data on a range of innovation activities, such as developing technological products, processes, and non-technological innovation (e.g. managerial, organizational, and marketing practices). A firm is considered an innovator if it has introduced a product or a process innovation in the previous three years (2007–2009). These innovations could be new to the firm or new to the market.

Following Mohnen et al. (2006), we eliminate all firms with sales growth over 250% and lower than 60% in the 2007–2009 period, and firms that reported a ratio of R&D spending to sales higher than 50%. To maintain consistency with the sample design of the survey, we drop firms that reported less than five employees, and we only consider sectors in countries that have at least five firms surveyed. After we apply this data cleaning procedure, we ensure that we have enough observations, setting a threshold of at least 50 observations in each country (a third of the minimum sample size).

Table 2.1 summarizes the definitions of the main dependent variables and introduces the main control variables. Overall, 70% of the firms in our dataset are innovators, and product innovators are more pervasive than process innovators (57 vs 50%). However, successful product innovations are quite limited, on average representing only 14% of total firm sales. Moreover, only 26% of firms reported having filed an intellectual property rights (IPR) application, significantly lower than the percentage of firms that innovated. If an IPR application is a signal of novelty, then more than half of the innovators did not protect their innovations or mostly used and adopted already protected technologies. With regards to innovation efforts, the R&D investment by a typical Latin American firm was about US$386 per employee.[12] This small amount of investment would only support hiring a few engineers for a short period of time, which is consistent with adaptive R&D rather than with highly novel activities.

The main determinants of innovation are divided into four groups: internal capabilities, access to external knowledge, demand pull, and access to financing. The first variable listed under internal capabilities is firm age, which is intended to capture the tacit knowledge accumulated at the firm level through processes such as learning by doing (Arrow 1962). The average firm in the sample is almost 30 years old. The second variable related to capabilities is human capital, which captures the degree of cognitive skills needed to absorb new knowledge and to develop new technologies (Acemoglu et al. 2006). Another indicator of internal capabilities is whether the company is part of an economic group or subsidiary of a multinational corporation. In principle, the economic superiority of multinational firms can be associated with more sophisticated knowledge assets (Girma and Gorg 2007) and easier access to human capital (Kumar and Aggarwal 2005).

Sales diversification is also an indicator of the scope of the productive capabilities of a firm. It provides a sense of the extent to which the firm's knowledge base is specialized in narrowly defined sectors or if it can be used in different sectors. A diversified knowledge base is likely to allow a firm to jump more easily into other sectors, thereby improving the expected returns on its R&D investments. The final two indicators of internal capabilities are manager experience and previous knowledge stock. We approximate managerial experience using the manager's years

Table 2.1   Main variables used in the analysis

	Definition	Observations	Mean	Minimum	Maximum
Innovation					
Innovation	(0/1) if firm introduced a product or process innovation	4376	0.7	0	1
Product innovation	(0/1) if firm introduced a product innovation	4376	0.57	0	1
Process innovation	(0/1) if firm introduced a process innovation	4376	0.5	0	1
Innovative sales	% of sales of innovated products	4376	14.22	0	100
IPRs	(0/1) if firm has filed for a IPR application	4376	0.26	0	1
Performance					
Labor productivity	(US$ of 2009) sales per worker	4376	166,373	151	437MM
R&D per worker	(US$ of 2009) R&D expenditures per worker	4376	386	0	40,700
R&D dummy	(0/1) if firm has invested in R&D	4376	0.43	0	1
Fixed investment	(US$ of 2009) fixed investment per worker	4376	2510	0	780,556
Employment	(headcount) full-time employment	4376	158	5	21,955
Determinants of Innovation					
Internal capabilities					
Age	(years) firm age	4376	28.73	2	183
Human capital	% of workers with bachelor degree	4376	0.14	0	1
Group	(0/1) if firm is part of a large group	4376	0.16	0	1
FDI	(0/1) if firm has 10% or more of foreign ownership	4376	0.12	0	1
Diversification	Diversification Index (100% of sales of main product)	4376	32.77	0	99
Manager experience	(years) experience of the manager in the sector of the firm	4376	24.63	1	70
Knowledge stock	(0/1) if firm has any patents abroad	4376	0.11	0	1

(continued)

Table 2.1 (continued)

	Definition	Observations	Mean	Minimum	Maximum
Access to External Knowledge					
Cooperation	% of firms that cooperate for innovation activities in same sector and country	4376	0.20	0	0.55
Large city	(0/1) if firm is located in a city with more than 1 million population	4376	0.76	0	1
Licenses	(0/1) if firm uses technology licensed from a foreign owned company	4376	0.15	0	1
Internet	(0/1) if firm has broadband access	4376	0.90	0	1
Demand pull					
Competitors 1	(0/1) if firm faces 0 competitors in main market	4376	0.03	0	1
Competitors 2	(0/1) if firm faces 1 competitor in main market	4376	0.03	0	1
Competitors 3	(0/1) if firm faces 2 to 5 competitors in main market	4376	0.32	0	1
Competitors 4	(0/1) if firm faces more than 5 competitors in main market	4376	0.62	0	1
International market	% of firms whose main market for their main product is international in same sector and country	4376	0.09	0	0.6
Access to financing					
Public support	% of firms that receive public support for innovation activities in same sector and country	4376	0.12	0	0.5

Source: Authors' elaboration based on WBES data

of experience in the same sector. Previous research (Barker and Mueller 2002; Balsmeier and Czarnitzki 2014; Galasso and Simcoe 2011) identified a robust positive relationship between the industry-specific experience of the top manager and the decision to innovate, as well as the share of new product-related sales. These effects were particularly pronounced for small firms in countries with relatively weak institutions. Results suggest that managerial experience affects firm innovations predominately indirectly; for example, by reducing uncertainty about future returns on innovations (Balsmeier and Czarnitzki 2014). With regard to knowledge stock, we include a variable that measures whether the firm has any patents abroad. The patent indicator measures (i) the capacity of the firm to manage intellectual property to protect the results of innovation investments and (ii) the degree of novelty of a firm's innovations, both of which are positively correlated with innovation efforts. Although potentially interesting, unfortunately we do not have enough information to untangle these two effects. We assume that having these patents is exogenous to the decision to invest and the level of investment in innovation. As the process of examination is quite long in patent offices (it usually takes around two years), patents that are granted during the period of inquiry for surveys probably concern inventions that occurred much earlier (for knowledge investment, at least two years before the date surveyed).

Access to external knowledge is normally an important determinant of innovation decisions. We explore this issue by using several variables. First, we use an indicator that measures whether a firm is collaborating with others on innovation activities. In principle, collaboration has ambiguous effects on innovation investment. On the one hand, by allowing firms to share costs and internalize spillovers, collaboration enhances productivity of internal innovation activities, which stimulates further innovation investment (Kamien et al. 1992). On the other hand, collaboration might allow research resources to be pooled, increasing access to effective R&D (internal plus external), while perhaps saving costs on internal innovation activities (Irwin and Klenow 1996). To deal with the potential endogeneity problem, instead of collaboration activities reported by the firm, we use the average of firms in the same sector and in the same country that collaborated with other organizations pursuing innovation activities.

The second variable measures whether the firm was located in a large city. Previous research has shown the importance of agglomeration economies as key determinants of innovation investments. Agglomeration allows a firm to get access to a pool of specialized resources (mostly human capital) and service providers (Moretti 2004). Moreover, knowledge spillovers are normally geographically bounded due to the limits of tacit knowledge (Jaffe et al. 1993). So, in principle, agglomeration economies increase the expected returns on R&D and innovation-related investments.

Third, acquiring technology through licenses is a potentially important means of accelerating productivity growth, especially in late starter developing countries that are trying to catch up. Yet, the literature has tended to focus on the potential benefits to the seller, overlooking those to the purchaser. Álvarez et al. (2002) found that expenditures on licensing showed exceptionally high rates of return, in the order of twice those of investment in physical capital. This investment significantly improved firms' performance and productivity in Chilean industry during the 1990s. Therefore, we expect that licensing could be a powerful complementary asset to endogenously generated knowledge, in particular for economies that are catching up.

Fourth, the information and communication technologies (ICT) revolution has allowed exponential growth in the volume and circulation of information. Indeed, given that ICTs substantially decrease the costs of information storage and transmission, their diffusion across economies reduces the uncertainty and costs associated with economic interactions. This, in turn, leads to an increase in the volume of transactions, generating higher levels of production for the same set of inputs. In other words, ICTs become a trigger for higher productivity (Chen and Dahlman 2005). Furthermore, ICTs increase organizational capabilities to codify knowledge that otherwise would have remained tacit, accelerating learning processes and productivity growth (Foray 2007), thereby increasing the returns on innovation investment.[13]

Innovation investments are not only the result of internal capabilities or access to external knowledge, they are also the result of incentives. One long-standing issue about innovation concerns the relationship between it and competition. Some researchers argue that innovation is at odds with competition because the need to generate innovation rents to reward innovators typically implies accepting the existence of a market distortion (e.g. by granting IPRs) as the price to pay to gain more innovation. Recent research on this subject has re-evaluated this view, finding that the relationship between these two variables is more complex than previously thought. Aghion et al. (2002) argued that the decision to invest in innovation depends on the degree of competition among firms: the more competitive the sector, the more firms in the sector will be encouraged to innovate in order to *escape competition*. In other words, competition is a key trigger for investment. As a measure of competition faced by the firm, we use a self-reported categorical variable indicating the number of competitors in the main market for the main product.[14] An additional key component of demand pull is exposure to international markets. Regarding exports, we expect the competition and learning effects from exporting to enhance innovation efforts by firms, notably when local firms have a certain level of technological skills. Braga and Willmore (1991), for Brazilian firms, and Álvarez (2001)), for Chilean firms, reported that exporting firms invested more in innovation (R&D in these cases).[15] We use the average exposure of the sector and country, rather than specific firm exposure.[16]

A key variable is the extent to which the firm had access to public support programs for innovation. Public financial support has frequently been found to boost R&D investment. Most studies conclude that government R&D support leads to additional private R&D, innovation expenditures, or innovation outputs, and not to the crowding out of private R&D by public financial support (Mairesse and Mohnen 2010; Hall and Maffioli 2008). For Latin American firms, public support for R&D investment is essential (Navarro et al. 2010; Anlló and Suárez 2009). Constraints in securing financing for innovation (high costs of innovation and risks) and the inability of firms to wait for long periods of time (rates of return) are among the most important obstacles to innovation as perceived by firms in Latin America. Although we do not aim to do a full impact evaluation of public funding, we think that it is an important control variable for capturing the costs of financing and as such it should be included in the analysis.[17] To address the issue of reverse causality related to the costs of financing, we use the proportion of firms that claimed to receive support from government by sector and country as the explanatory variable rather than whether a particular firm had access. We think that this average better captures the generosity of the public support system, which is likely to be more exogenous than the alternative of using a dummy variable for whether the firm has used a particular innovation instrument. It is worth noting that we do not include this variable in the innovation equation, mainly because we think the availability of public support for innovation does not affect the effectiveness of the firm's innovation process. The same argument is valid for excluding the number of competitors and the exposure to international markets of the local industry in this equation. Therefore, while public support and competition may trigger innovation investments, they likely do not affect how these efforts (eventually) become innovations.

Finally, in all our regressions we control for the size of the firm, as this characteristic has been proven to be a significant determinant of innovation-related activities. The claimed advantages of large-size firms are numerous: a larger spread of R&D fixed costs over greater output (Cohen and Levinthal 1989), economies of scope relating to R&D production and diversification, as well as a better appropriation of external knowledge spillovers.[18] However, here it is important to differentiate between the effects of size on the decision to invest from the impacts of size on investment expenditures. The empirical evidence suggests that there is a positive and proportional relationship between R&D investment and the size of the firm. That is, large firms invest more in R&D, but not proportionally more, once the decision to invest has been taken into account (Cohen and Klepper 1996). Based on this finding, for the generalized Tobit model, we assume the size of the firm affects the decision to invest in innovation but does not affect the intensity of that investment when the decision to invest has been taken into account. For Latin American firms, a positive association between size and the propensity to invest has been systematically reported for many countries (Benavente 2006; Crespi and Peirano 2007; Crespi and Zuñiga 2012). Yet, results regarding the innovation intensity equation, mostly done with R&D intensity, point out that larger firms are not necessarily the ones who invest the most (for Colombia see Alvarado 2000; for Brazil see De Negri et al. 2007), so we are confident our identification assumption is appropriate. Furthermore, this is the same identification assumption used by many of the empirical implementations of the CDM model reviewed above. In summary, we assume that the decision to invest depends on the size of the firm measured by the (log) employment, but that this variable will not affect the intensity of innovation investments.

THE RESULTS

The Decision to Invest in Innovation and the Intensity of Innovation Expenditure

Table 2.2 summarizes the findings regarding R&D investment. In general, the decision to invest in R&D is strongly correlated with the size of the firm, with larger firms more likely to invest. The firm's level of knowledge stock, human capital, and diversification also positively influence this decision. Age, however, is negatively correlated with the decision to invest in R&D, suggesting that new firms are more likely to invest than

Table 2.2 The determinants of R&D investment

	R&D per worker	Decision to invest
Age	-0.0034	-0.0049***
	(0.0017)	(0.0011)
Human capital	1.7087***	0.5291***
	(0.2078)	(0.1239)
Group	0.0595	-0.0145
	(0.0945)	(0.0585)
FDI	-0.1336	-0.3300***
	(0.1134)	(0.0707)
Diversification	-0.0002	0.0026***
	(0.0013)	(0.0008)
Manager experience	-0.0008	0.0014
	(0.0029)	(0.0017)
Knowledge stock	0.3960***	0.1984***
	(0.1077)	(0.0685)
Cooperation	-0.1231	0.0187
	(0.4864)	(0.2955)
Large city	0.1253	-0.0674
	(0.0964)	(0.0533)
License	0.2385***	0.1832***
	(0.0914)	(0.0589)
Broadband	0.4003***	0.4952***
	(0.1561)	(0.0783)
Competitor 2	0.3323	0.0251
	(0.3012)	(0.1685)
Competitors 3	-0.0013	0.0226
	(0.2333)	(0.1246)
Competitors 4	-0.1134	-0.0755
	(0.2296)	(0.1225)
International markets	-0.1231	-0.0201
	(0.4864)	(0.3007)
Public support	1.7068***	1.4029***
	(0.7340)	(0.4257)
Employment	—	0.2121***
		(0.0157)
N	4376	
Ll	-5797.2963	
chi2	556.1525	
p	0.0000	
rho	0.7530	
chi2_c	149.7066	

Source: Authors' elaboration based on WBES data

Notes: Coefficients reported are marginal effects, meaning they predict the likelihood of introducing product or process innovation. Standard errors in parentheses

*Coefficient is statistically significant at the 10% level; ** at the 5% level; *** at the 1% level; no asterisk means the coefficient is not different from zero with statistical significance

old firms. Access to external knowledge seems to be very relevant, as the acquisition of licenses and broadband access are positively related with the decision to invest. In contrast, firms that operate in sectors with higher levels of cooperation for innovation do not show a higher propensity to invest in R&D. Neither the intensity of competition faced by the firm nor the degree of exposure to international markets within the sector in which the firm operates are relevant to the decision to invest. However, firms in sectors that have relatively greater public support for innovation are more likely to engage in R&D activities.

With regards to the determinants of the intensity of investment, we again found that the internal capabilities of firms are very relevant, in particular the presence of qualified workers and previous knowledge stock. Access to external knowledge, licensing, and connectivity are also important and positive determinants of R&D investment. However, this does not seem to be the case for cooperation, suggesting that the incentives for increasing innovation investments and the benefits of saving costs in collaborative innovation activities noted above are also present in Latin American firms. Competition and exposure to international markets remains insignificant. Finally, public support systems for innovation have a positive influence on the intensity of R&D expenditures.

Being in a large city and being a foreign controlled firm produced some unexpected results. First, the absence of significance for city size suggests that there are no relevant agglomeration economies. Foreign direct investment (FDI) presents a negative and highly statistical relationship with the decision to invest in R&D. These results, as in Crespi and Zuñiga (2012), confirm that the FDI that the region has managed to attract does not develop technology locally. One plausible interpretation of this result is that, generally speaking, in technologically lagging countries, multinational firms rarely invest in local R&D units if the market size is not large enough to justify fixed costs for R&D or if there is not a specific national academic attractiveness (Raffo et al. 2008).[19] This result could also mean that multinational firms do not invest in innovation in LAC at all, given that their activity is more focused on exploiting comparative advantages in terms of, for instance, access to natural resources, distribution costs, or labor savings; and they also use technological assets from their headquarters (Navarro et al. 2010). If foreign firms conduct technological activities, they frequently focus on adapting and tailoring products to local markets (with low needs for R&D investment).

From Innovation Effort to Innovation Outputs

Next we consider the estimates of the knowledge production functions (equation 2.4) in Table 2.3, where the reported coefficients are marginal effects. We consider five different outputs: innovation (product or process), product innovation, process innovation, innovative sales (defined as the share of sales from new products), and filing for IPRs. The results for innovation suggest that there is a positive and significant correlation between R&D investment and the likelihood a firm will innovate. Indeed, a 10% increase in R&D spending translates into a 1.7% increase in the probability of innovation. According to the results reported in Table 2.3, this is mostly due to the impacts of R&D spending on product rather than process innovation. Furthermore, R&D spending increases the likelihood that a firm will apply for IPRs and that it has a positive impact on innovative sales (an increase of 10% in R&D spending translates into an increase of 1.6% in innovative sales).

Of the remaining control variables, some internal capabilities are important determinants of innovation outputs beyond their influence through R&D. Indeed, highly diversified firms are more likely to introduce any type of innovation. In the same vein, a firm's stock of knowledge, although not significantly correlated with product innovation (and only slightly with process innovation), has a strong effect on the likelihood of the firm applying for IPR protection. Although mostly not significant, human capital is negatively correlated with the likelihood of introducing innovations. This effect is mainly driven by the relationship with product innovation, and remarkably noticeable in estimating innovative sales. We do not have a clear explanation for this unexpected relationship, but we speculate that, if the firms with a higher share of skilled workers are competing in more complex markets, there may be a lack of the required innovation capabilities to develop new successful products in these types of markets. Although potentially interesting, the data available do not allow us to probe this hypothesis.

On the one hand, being part of a group correlates positively with the probability of introducing a product innovation. On the other hand, multinationals are less likely to introduce innovations, particularly process innovations, or file for IPRs. This result could be capturing the sector orientation of most of the subsidiaries in the region, which tend to operate in non-innovation driven sectors.

External knowledge is also an important determinant of innovation results. In particular, licensing is an important channel to acquire

Table 2.3   The determinants of innovation outputs

	Innovation	Product	Process	Innovative sales	IPRs
	(1)	(2)	(3)	(4)	(5)
R&D per worker	0.1677**	0.1481**	0.1029	0.1579***	0.1305***
	(0.0655)	(0.0712)	(0.0671)	(0.0441)	(0.0450)
Age	−0.0000	0.0001	−0.0003	−0.0005	0.0013***
	(0.0004)	(0.0005)	(0.0005)	(0.0003)	(0.0004)
Human capital	−0.1958	−0.2068	−0.0758	−0.2709***	−0.1255
	(0.1223)	(0.1311)	(0.1250)	(0.0857)	(0.0846)
Group	0.0206	0.0543**	0.0091	0.0192	−0.0174
	(0.0219)	(0.0253)	(0.0237)	(0.0157)	(0.0204)
FDI	−0.0441	−0.0141	−0.0919***	−0.0186	−0.0967***
	(0.0282)	(0.0312)	(0.0323)	(0.0175)	(0.0210)
Diversification	0.0021***	0.0031***	0.0006*	0.0009***	0.0006**
	(0.0003)	(0.0003)	(0.0004)	(0.0002)	(0.0003)
Manager experience	−0.0003	0.0001	−0.0000	0.0007	−0.0010*
	(0.0006)	(0.0007)	(0.0007)	(0.0005)	(0.0006)
Knowledge stock	0.0471	0.0128	0.0663*	−0.0164	0.2395***
	(0.0341)	(0.0361)	(0.0386)	(0.0260)	(0.0372)
Cooperation	0.0939	0.0750	0.1179	−0.0263	0.1420
	(0.0930)	(0.1098)	(0.1123)	(0.0670)	(0.1042)
Large city	−0.0042	−0.008	−0.0135	−0.0142	−0.0047
	(0.0205)	(0.0248)	(0.0254)	(0.0148)	(0.0195)
License	0.0613**	0.0667**	0.0496*	0.0318*	0.0258
	(0.0280)	(0.0282)	(0.0300)	(0.0191)	(0.0239)
Broadband	0.0362	0.0964**	0.0351	0.0631**	0.0369
	(0.0388)	(0.0420)	(0.0370)	(0.0272)	(0.0259)
Fixed investment	0.0174***	0.0156***	0.0244***	0.0107***	0.0120***
	(0.0022)	(0.0020)	(0.0020)	(0.0016)	(0.0019)
Employment	0.0229***	0.0179***	0.0247***	−0.0022	0.0497***
	(0.0062)	(0.0068)	(0.0069)	(0.0052)	(0.0058)
N	4376	4376	4376	4376	4376
Ll	−2394.0886	−2718.2569	−2818.4319	−2197.7553	−2116.7052
chi2	695.0068	850.4943	652.4171	526.3368	1163.1858
P	0.0000	0.0000	0.0000	0.0000	0.0000

Source: Authors' elaboration based on WBES data

Notes: Coefficients reported are marginal effects. Bootstrapped standard errors in parentheses

*Coefficient is statistically significant at the 10% level; ** at the 5% level; *** at the 1% level; no asterisk means the coefficient is not different from zero with statistical significance

technological knowledge for product and process innovations, but this effect is not significant for new IPR applications. Broadband, in contrast, is a significant variable for both the product innovation and the innovative sales models. The size of the firm and the level of fixed investments, as expected, are also important factors affecting results for all classes of innovation, particularly for filing for IPRs in the case of size, and process innovation in the case of fixed investments.

From Innovation Outputs to Productivity

Given that firm capabilities, connectivity, and innovation efforts have some effect on innovation results, the next step is to explore the extent to which these changes translate into higher productivity levels. This is done by estimating equation 2.5, a traditional Cobb–Douglas production function, which we expand by including a measure of quality of labor input (labor and managerial skills) and the predicted innovation results. The findings summarized in Table 2.4 suggest that innovation has a strong impact on labor productivity, even when controlling for intermediate inputs and capital stock per worker, employment, and human capital. The coefficients reported in this table are elasticities or semi-elasticities, since the dependent variable is the log of sales per employee. Consistent with evidence for industrialized countries, our results confirm a positive impact of technological innovation on productivity. The coefficients are large. Innovative firms are 50 % more productive than non-innovative firms (column 1). In column 2, innovation is split among product and process innovation. Productivity impacts on product innovation seem to be higher, and more significant, than on process innovation (36 vs 19 %). These results remain when using innovative sales rather than the product innovation categorical dummy (column 3). Finally, firms that managed to file for an IPR application strongly increased productivity (35 %, column 4).

From Innovation Spillovers to Productivity

Although in general it is very tricky to assess for the presence of spillovers in the context of cross-sectional data, it is worth a preliminary exploration. Since the seminal works by Nelson (1959) and Arrow (1962), knowledge has been regarded as a non-rival[20] and non-excludable[21] good. If knowledge does indeed have these properties, then rivals may be able to free-ride

Table 2.4   The impacts of innovation on productivity

	Ln (Q/L)	Ln (Q/L)	Ln (Q/L)	Ln (Q/L)
	(1)	(2)	(3)	(4)
Materials	0.5025***	0.5028***	0.5028***	0.5070***
	(0.0208)	(0.0191)	(0.0190)	(0.0174)
Capital	0.0919***	0.0914***	0.0918***	0.0903***
	(0.0075)	(0.0078)	(0.0089)	(0.0080)
Human capital	0.4821***	0.4915***	0.5170***	0.4957***
	(0.0557)	(0.0548)	(0.0556)	(0.0637)
Employment	0.0777***	0.0783***	0.0909***	0.0766***
	(0.0110)	(0.0099)	(0.0093)	(0.0112)
Manager experience	−0.0003	−0.0005	−0.0007	−0.0004
	(0.0007)	(0.0006)	(0.0006)	(0.0007)
Innovation	0.5543***	—	—	—
	(0.0879)			
Product innovation	—	0.3635***	—	—
		(0.1195)		
Process innovation	—	0.1860	0.0636	—
		(0.1307)	(0.1746)	
Innovative sales	—	—	0.5225**	—
			(0.2113)	
IPRs	—	—	—	0.3477***
				(0.0865)
N	4376	4376	4376	4376
Ll	−3596.6234	−3596.8416	−3597.4046	−3607.396
chi2	14787.2106	9124.5645	13287.8438	17278.7706
P	0.0000	0.0000	0.0000	0.0000

Source: Authors' elaboration based on WBES data

Notes: Coefficients reported are marginal effects. Bootstrapped standard errors in parentheses

*Coefficient is statistically significant at the 10% level; ** at the 5% level; *** at the 1% level; no asterisk means the coefficient is not different from zero with statistical significance

on a firm's investments. Spillovers may create a wedge between private and social returns and a disincentive to private investment in knowledge production. However, spillovers are not automatic and should not be taken for granted in every circumstance because not all knowledge enjoys the properties of a public good with the same intensity. Certainly, the public good rationale of knowledge applies more strongly to *generic* or *scientific* knowledge than to *technological* knowledge, which is more applicable and specific to a firm.[22] Furthermore, for the public good rationale to be valid, there should be some possibility of free-riding. If the originator can protect the results of the knowledge generated (e.g. through barriers to entry or strategic mechanisms), then the potential for market failure declines. Conversely, knowledge generated through collaboration might be more difficult to protect and therefore more prone to spillovers than knowledge generated by individual entities. So, in principle, not all types of innovation lead to the same degree of spillover and thus the intensity of focus for innovation policy varies.

To explore this issue, we assume that a firm will benefit from spillovers if its productivity increases as a result of the innovations introduced by other firms. In this context, we compute innovation by other firms as the average of the innovation propensities at sector and country levels (i.e. we assume that spillovers are mostly the result of within-sector and within-country knowledge flows). In sum, we expand the standard Cobb–Douglas production function to include these sector-level indicators of innovation intensity. The results are summarized in Table 2.5. In general, within the limitations of the dataset, it is possible to say that there are spillovers of technological innovation, and that these are more related to product than process innovation. Indeed, column 2 shows that the coefficient of sector product innovation is positive and strongly significant, while it is negative and far from significant for sector process innovation. The findings stay the same when IPRs are used as a proxy for innovation (column 4). However, when sector innovative sales are used as a measure of product innovation, the positive correlation remains but is not significant (column 3).

Not All Are the Same: Exploring the Heterogeneous Impacts of Innovation

To some extent the previous results refer to the typical or representative LAC firm, which is somehow at odds with the tremendous heterogeneity that exists in the region in terms of productivity (IDB 2010). One way to assess whether these impacts are heterogeneous is by simulating the productivity distribution in two scenarios: with and without innovation. This exercise, which is summarized in Fig. 2.1, infers two results. First, the shift to the right of the whole distribution of productivity with innovation is consistent with a positive average impact. Second, the spread of the distribution is larger with innovation, suggesting that the productivity impacts of innovation are not uniform across firms but instead vary according to where the firm is within the productivity distribution.

Table 2.5 The impacts of innovation on productivity: the search for spillovers

	$Ln(Q/L)$	$Ln(Q/L)$	$Ln(Q/L)$	$Ln(Q/L)$
	(1)	(2)	(3)	(4)
Material	0.5020***	0.5021***	0.5026***	0.5067***
	(0.0172)	(0.0188)	(0.0178)	(0.0181)
Capital	0.0922***	0.0916***	0.0920***	0.0902***
	(0.0069)	(0.0076)	(0.0084)	(0.0079)
Human capital	0.4874***	0.4927***	0.5205***	0.4977***
	(0.0557)	(0.0549)	(0.0588)	(0.0559)
Employment	0.0781***	0.0785***	0.0912***	0.0767***
	(0.0087)	(0.0107)	(0.0101)	(0.0114)
Manager experience	−0.0003	−0.0005	−0.0007	−0.0004
	(0.0007)	(0.0007)	(0.0007)	(0.0007)
Innovation	0.4999***	—	—	—
	(0.0875)			
Innovation spillovers	0.9817***	—	—	—
	(0.2762)			
Product innovation	—	0.3242***	—	—
		(0.1188)		
Product spillovers	—	1.1456***	—	—
		(0.4180)		
Process innovation	—	0.1854	0.0389	—
		(0.1403)	(0.2014)	
Process spillovers	—	−0.2052	0.445	—
		(0.3846)	(0.3224)	
Innovative sales	—	—	0.5099***	—
			(0.2310)	
Spillovers sales	—	—	0.1687	—
			(0.5415)	
IPRs	—	—	—	0.3269***
				(0.0716)
Spillover IPRs	—	—	—	0.5050**
				(0.2406)
N	4376	4376	4376	4376
Ll	−3589.6525	−3590.1052	−3595.0157	−3605.3952
chi2	10070.4587	17809.6335	11512.1608	9047.2573
P	0.0000	0.0000	0.0000	0.0000

Source: Authors' elaboration based on WBES data

Notes: Coefficients reported are marginal effects. Bootstrapped standard errors in parentheses

*Coefficient is statistically significant at the 10% level; ** at the 5% level; *** at the 1% level; no asterisk means the coefficient is not different from zero with statistical significance

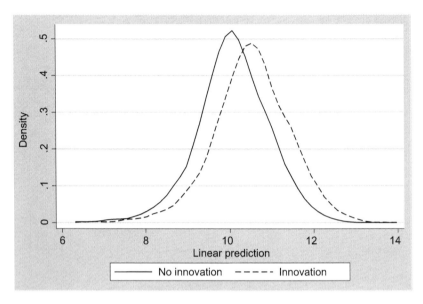

Fig. 2.1   The heterogeneous productivity impacts of innovation (*Source*: Authors)

To explore this issue further, we use a regression quartile approach to estimate the impacts of innovation on productivity according to the productivity levels of the firms. The results of this exercise are presented in Table 2.6. In general, the returns on innovation depend on the position of the firm within the productivity distribution. For companies at the bottom of the distribution, private returns are not higher than 35 %; however, returns increase to more than 65 % for companies at the top of the distribution. It is also worth noting that private returns on innovation are not that different between the first three quartiles of the productivity distribution (between 30 and 40 %). The big leap is observed between this group and the top 10 % of firms. Interestingly the gap between the bottom and the top of the distribution is also observed in the human capital premium. In fact, while this premium is 17 % for firms at the bottom end of the distribution, it grows to almost the 77 % for firms at the top.

Although these results require further exploration, they could have important consequences for policy design. For example, if low productivity is due to firms that cannot innovate because of financial constraints, returns at the bottom of the distribution would be higher than returns at

Table 2.6 The heterogeneous impacts of innovation

	Q10	Q25	Q50	Q75	Q90
	(1)	(2)	(3)	(4)	(5)
Innovation	0.3328***	0.2980***	0.3005***	0.3845***	0.6559***
	(0.0657)	(0.0658)	(0.0609)	(0.1178)	(0.1600)
Materials	0.7445***	0.7010***	0.6429***	0.5415***	0.4229***
	(0.0122)	(0.0108)	(0.0092)	(0.0140)	(0.0204)
Capital	0.0562***	0.0631***	0.0667***	0.0804***	0.1020***
	(0.0058)	(0.0052)	(0.0056)	(0.0074)	(0.0105)
Human capital	0.1708***	0.2500***	0.3970***	0.6177***	0.7661***
	(0.0427)	(0.0323)	(0.0479)	(0.0794)	(0.1043)
Employment	0.0305***	0.0400***	0.0436***	0.0535***	0.0768***
	(0.0065)	(0.0050)	(0.0067)	(0.0085)	(0.0185)
Manager experience	0.0003	0.0004	-0.0001	-0.0011	-0.0027*
	(0.0006)	(0.0004)	(0.0005)	(0.0008)	(0.0014)
N	4376	4376	4376	4376	4376

Source: Authors' elaboration based on WBES data

Notes: Coefficients reported are marginal effects. Bootstrapped standard errors in parentheses

*Coefficient is statistically significant at the 10% level; ** at the 5% level; *** at the 1% level; no asterisk means the coefficient is not different from zero with statistical significance

the top. However, the opposite is found to be true (i.e. firms at the bottom of the distribution face lower private returns on innovation than firms at the top), which suggests that there are constraints that affect the resources of the firm related either to the lack of complementary assets (which leads to low private and social returns) or the lack of appropriability (which leads to low private but not necessarily low social returns). Untangling these two situations is important because, if it is the lack opportunities, it does not seem reasonable to focus innovation policy on low productivity firms. If, on the other hand, it is due to appropriability, it is reasonable to focus on low productivity firms. Identifying which constraints dominate is the focus of a future research agenda.

CONCLUSIONS

This chapter has presented an econometric comparison using micro-level data. We investigated drivers of technological innovation and how they feed into productivity at the regional level in Latin America. We estimated a common structural model that described the relationships between knowledge investment, innovation outputs, and firm productivity.

We found strong evidence concerning the relationships between innovation input and output, and innovation output and productivity. In line with the literature, firms that invest in knowledge are more able to introduce new technological advances, and those who innovate have superior labor productivity. The consistency in these two results provides solid evidence for Latin American countries. With these results, we hope to fill in some of the gaps in the literature and alleviate the inconclusiveness of previous studies.

Our findings have important repercussions. Firms that invest in knowledge combine internal capacities with innovations. However, internal capacities are not enough, requiring absorption of technology from abroad. We found that the typical multinational firm operating in Latin America is both less prone to invest locally in R&D and also less likely to innovate. These results contradict previous positive effects found in Argentina, Panama, and Uruguay (Crespi and Zuñiga 2012); however, particular market conditions or policies to attract FDI could be driving those results. Our results reveal that public support for innovation is a key factor in facilitating investments in innovation by Latin American manufacturing firms, different from Crespi and Zuñiga (2012), who did not find a consistent positive impact of governmental support.

We have provided evidence that the private returns on innovation depend on the type of innovation, with larger effects for product than for process innovation. Similarly, we found evidence that spillovers are stronger for product than process innovation, suggesting that the wedge between private and social returns could be higher for product innovation. This finding could guide policy focus on such innovations. Furthermore, we found the returns on innovation to be higher for the most productive firms. This increasing relationship between returns and productivity is not consistent with the interpretation that financial constraints cause more harm to low productivity firms. However, it is consistent with alternative interpretations related to the lack of innovation opportunities in the case of low productivity firms or that low private returns are the result of poor appropriability. In this case there could still be some hope for policy intervention for these types of firms. These weaknesses seem common among firms in the first three quartiles of the productivity distribution. Clearly, this is an important topic for further research.

NOTES

1. Hall (2011) presents a short discussion about how the productivity of individual firms aggregate with the economy as a whole.
2. The IDB, together with regional agencies such as the Network of Indicators of Science and Technology (known by its Spanish acronym RICYT for Red de Indicadores de Ciencia y Tecnología), has emphasized the need to develop comparable innovation surveys and has developed suggestions for sample design, data collection, and harmonization of questionnaires based on existing manuals. Anlló et al. (2014) summarize these recommendations.
3. The WBES defines innovation rates as the share of firms introducing product or process innovations. In this chapter, the term 'product innovation' refers strictly to firms that introduced a new or significantly improved product that is new to the firm or the establishment's market between 2007 and 2009. 'Process innovation' refers strictly to firms that introduced new or significantly improved processes that are new to the firm or to the industry in the 2007 to 2009 period. Mohnen and Hall (2013) present the notions of different types of innovation and discuss the way they are measured.
4. Crespi and Tacsir (2011) present empirical evidence of the impact of process and product innovation on employment growth and composition in a sample of Latin American countries.
5. Accordingly, if adjustment costs emerging from weaker innovation systems are higher in developing countries, they may be more important to specific dynamic linkages than in Western economies, for which it is more likely that the cross-sectional estimates of the CDM model can reflect long-run relationships.
6. The problem of selectivity is due to the fact that only a handful of firms report positive investment in R&D at any particular time. Deleting firms with zero activity would bias the sample.
7. Innovation indicators are noisy (in part because they are subjective measures) and need to correct for errors in variable measurement. Hence, non-observable factors that affect the probability of innovation may lead companies to invest more in innovation activities. Likewise, there are unobservable factors that explain productivity that may also affect the choice of inputs (which implies correlation between the error in the productivity equation and explanatory variables).
8. It is worth mentioning that the relative significance of product and process innovation on TFP is debatable, especially when sales per worker are used as a proxy. To the extent that product innovation may imply superior quality in production systems and more inputs, we may not see any change in productivity levels. In contrast, we would expect process innovation to directly affect the average cost of production and indirectly impact output and profit

margins. For France, Mairesse et al. (2005) found that process innovation yields higher returns than product innovation, using TFP as a dependent variable. Yet, this is not always the case in other countries (Griffith et al. (2006) for Germany, Spain, and the UK; Roper et al. (2008) for Ireland).

9. For further discussion on using innovation surveys for economic analysis of innovation see Hall and Mairesse (2006) and Mairesse and Mohnen (2010).
10. As explained by Griffith et al. (2006), workers in firms engage in innovation related tasks not officially recorded as innovation activity (below a certain threshold activities are not recorded) to improve efficiency in production systems or to develop new products.
11. We do not include Brazil in the analysis because innovation variables are not available for this group of firms.
12. Only 43% of the firms reported some investment in R&D.
13. In this respect, this chapter considers broadband connectivity a factor behind the decision to invest and the likelihood of obtaining innovation outputs from which productivity effects might be derived.
14. There was a significant amount of missing data across countries for this variable. To maintain the number of observations in the sample, we imputed missing values with the median of the competitors reported by the firms with the same main market in the same sector and country.
15. See Chap. 9 in this book, where a causal relationship between trade and higher productivity is found.
16. Before calculating sector-country averages, firms that did not report their main market in the survey were assumed to focus on local/national markets if they reported exports equal to zero.
17. To properly correct for and evaluate the impact of public support, we would need to model its determinants or, as it is usually done, compare the difference in innovation performance between matched pairs of supported and unsupported firms (give each treated firm a counter-factual).
18. Yet it is also argued that small firms have more flexibility and adaptability (and less complex organizational structures), which favor innovation and the development of new projects (Acs and Audretsch 1988).
19. Recent exemptions are China, India, and some South East Asian countries where technology hotspots are emerging and increasingly attracting R&D investment and new labs from foreign firms.
20. Once produced, new knowledge can be used simultaneously by many different firms because the new blueprints are not normally associated with physical constraints. This characteristic is an extreme form of decreasing marginal costs as the scale of use increases: although the costs of the first use of new knowledge may be large in that it includes the costs of its generation, further use can be done at negligible small incremental costs (Aghion et al. 2009).
21. The non-excludable nature of knowledge refers to the difficulty and cost of trying to retain exclusive possession of it while, at the same time, putting it to use.

22. Technological knowledge is also more likely to be protected by IPRs, which provide innovating firms the right to temporarily exclude others from using a new idea commercially so the originators can appropriate the rents of their investments in innovation. In exchange for this, the owner must disclose the invention so anyone can improve upon it. However, IPRs can also generate unintended consequences, as they cause a static market distortion in the form of monopoly power and slower technology diffusion for producers that must pay a higher cost to transfer protected technology. In other words, IPRs also create market distortions that might or might not be compensated by the increased incentives to innovate (De Ferranti 2003).

REFERENCES

Acemoglu, D., P. Aghion, and F. Zilibotti. 2006. Distance to Frontier, Selection, and Economic Growth. *Journal of the European Economic Association* 41: 37–74.

Acs, Z.J., and D.B. Audretsch. 1988. Innovation in Large Firms: An Empirical Analysis. *American Economic Review* 78(4): 678–690.

Aghion, P., N. Bloom, R. Blundell, R. Griffith, and P. Howitt. 2002. Competition and Innovation: An Inverted U Relationship. Working Paper No. W9269. Cambridge, MA: National Bureau of Economic Research (NBER).

Aghion, P., P.A. David, and D. Foray. 2009. Science, Technology and Innovation for Economic Growth: Linking Policy Research and Practice in 'STIG Systems.'. *Research Policy* 38(4): 681–693.

Alvarado, A. 2000. Dinámica de la Estrategia de Innovación: El Caso de Colombia. *Coyuntura Económica* 30(3): 61–119.

Álvarez, R. 2001. External Sources of Technological Innovation in Chilean Manufacturing Industry. *Estudios de Economía* 28(1): 53–68.

Álvarez, R., G. Crespi, and J. Ramos. 2002. The Impact of Licenses on a "Late Starter" LDC: Chile in the 1990s. *World Development* 30(8): 1445–1460.

Anlló, G., G. Crespi, G. Lugones, D. Suárez, E. Tacsir, and F. Vargas. 2014. Manual para la implementación de encuestas de innovación. IDB-BR-143. Washington, DC: IDB.

Anlló, G., and D. Suárez. 2009. Innovación: Algo más que I+D. Evidencias Ibeoramericanas a partir de las encuestas de innovación: Construyendo las estrategias empresarias competitivas. Unpublished. Buenos Aires: CEPAL-REDES.

Arrow, K.J. 1962. The Economic Implications of Learning By Doing. *The Review of Economic Studies* 29(3): 155–173.

Aw, B.Y., M.J. Roberts, and D. Yi Xu. 2008. R&D Investment, Exporting, and Productivity Dynamics. Mimeographed document. Cambridge, MA: NBER.

Balsmeier, B., and D. Czarnitzki. 2014. How Important Is Industry-Specific Managerial Experience for Innovative Firm Performance? Discussion Paper 14-011. Mannheim, Germany: Center for European Economic Research (Zentrum für Europäische Wirtschaftsforschung, or ZEW).

Barker, V.L., and G.C. Mueller. 2002. CEO Characteristics and Firm R&D Spending. *Management Science* 48: 782–801.

Benavente, J.M. 2006. The Role of Research and Innovation in Promoting Productivity in Chile. *Economics of Innovation and New Technology* 154(5): 301–315.

Benavente, J.M., and C. Bravo. 2009. Innovation, R&D Investment and Productivity in Latin American and Caribbean Firms: The Chilean Case. Unpublished. Washington, DC: Latin American and Caribbean Research Network, IDB.

Braga, H., and L. Willmore. 1991. Technological Imports and Technological Effort. *Journal of Industrial Economics* 39(4): 421–432.

Chen, D.H., and C.J. Dahlman. 2005. The Knowledge Economy: The KAM Methodology and World Bank Operations. Working Paper 37256. Washington, DC: World Bank Institute.

Chudnovsky, D., A. Lopez, and G. Pupato. 2006. Innovation and Productivity in Developing Countries: A Study of Argentine Manufacturing Firms Behavior 1992–2001. *Research Policy* 35: 266–288.

Cohen, W.M., and S. Klepper. 1996. Firm Size and the Nature of Innovation within Industries: The Case of Process and Product R&D. *The Review of Economics and Statistics* 782: 232–243.

Cohen, W., and D. Levinthal. 1989. Innovation and Learning: The Two Faces of R&D. *The Economic Journal* 99(397): 569–596.

Correa, P., I.G. Sanchez, and H. Singh. 2005. Research, Innovation and Productivity: Firm Level Analysis for Brazil. Mimeographed document. Washington, DC: World Bank.

Crépon, B., E. Duguet, and J. Mairesse. 1998. Research, Innovation and Productivity: An Econometric Analysis at the Firm Level. *Economics of Innovation and New Technology* 7(2): 115–158.

Crespi, G., and F. Peirano. 2007. Measuring Innovation in Latin America: What We Did, Where We Are and What We Want to Do. Paper presented at the *Conference on Micro Evidence on Innovation in Developing Countries UNU-MERIT*. Maastricht.

Crespi, G., and E. Tacsir. 2011. Effects of Innovation on Employment in Latin America. Paper presented at *The Atlanta Conference on Science and Innovation Policy*. Atlanta.

Crespi, G., and P. Zuñiga. 2012. Innovation and Productivity: Evidence from Six Latin American Countries. *World Development* 40(2): 273–290.

De Ferranti, D.M. (ed.). 2003. *Closing the Gap in Education and Technology*. Washington, DC: World Bank Publications.

De Negri, J.A., L. Esteves, and F. Freitas. 2007. Knowledge Production and Firm Growth in Brazil. Working Paper 21. Brazil: Institute for Applied Economic Research (Instituto de Pesquisa Econômica Aplicada [IPEA]).

Foray, D. 2007. Tacit and Codified Knowledge. In *Elgar Companion to Neo-Schumpeterian Economics*, ed. H. Hanush and A. Pyka. Northampton, MA: Edward Elgar.

Galasso, A., and T. Simcoe. 2011. CEO Overconfidence and Innovation. *Management Science* 57: 1469–1484.

Girma, S.A., and H.B. Gorg. 2007. Multinationals Productivity Advantage: Scale or Technology? *Economic Inquiry* 45(2): 350–362.

Griffith, R., E. Huergo, J. Mairesse, and B. Peters. 2006. Innovation and Productivity Across Four European Countries. *Oxford Review of Economic Policy* 22(4): 483–498.

Griffith, R., S. Redding, and J. Van Reenen. 2004. Mapping the Two Faces of R&D: Productivity Growth in a Panel of OECD Industries. *The Review of Economics and Statistics* 864: 883–895.

Griliches, Z. 1979. Issues in Assessing the Contribution of Research and Development to Productivity Growth. *Bell Journal of Economics* 101: 92–116.

Guloglu, B., and R.B. Tekin. 2012. A Panel Causality Analysis of the Relationship Among Research and Development, Innovation, and Economic Growth in High-Income OECD Countries. *Eurasian Economic Review* 2(1): 32–47.

Hall, B. 2011. Using Productivity Growth as an Innovation Indicator. Report for the High Level Panel on Measuring Innovation. Brussels: European Commission, DG Research and Innovation.

Hall, B., and A. Maffioli. 2008. Evaluating the Impact of Technology Development Funds in Emerging Economies: Evidence from Latin America. *European Journal of Development Research* 202: 172–198.

Hall, B., and J. Mairesse. 2006. Empirical Studies of Innovation in the Knowledge Driven Economy: An Introduction, Economics of Innovation and New Technology. *Economics of Innovation and New Technology* 15(4/5): 289–299.

Hall, R., and C. Jones. 1999. Why Do Some Countries Produce so Much More Output Per Worker Than Others? *The Quarterly Journal of Economics* 114(1): 83–116.

Hegde, D., and P. Shapira. 2007. Knowledge, Technology Trajectories, and Innovation in a Developing Country Context: Evidence from a Survey of Malaysian Firms. *International Journal of Technology Management* 40(4): 349–370.

IDB. 2010. *The Age of Productivity: Transforming Economies from the Bottom Up*. Development in the Americas. Washington, DC: IDB and Palgrave Macmillan.

Irwin, D.A., and P.J. Klenow. 1996. High-Tech R&D Subsidies Estimating the Effects of Sematech. *Journal of International Economics*, 40(3–4): 323–344.

Jaffe, A.B., M. Trajtenberg, and R. Henderson. 1993. Geographic Localization of Knowledge Spillovers as Evidenced By Patent Citations. *Quarterly Journal of Economics* 108: 577–598.

Janz, N., H. Loof, and B. Peters. 2004. Innovation and Productivity in German and Swedish Manufacturing Firms: Is There a Common Story? *Problems and Perspectives in Management* 2: 184–204.

Jefferson, G.H., B. Huamao, G. Xiaojing, and Y. Xiaoyun. 2006. R&D Performance in Chinese Industry. *Economics of Innovation and New Technologies* 15(4–5): 345–366.

Kamien, M., S. Oren, and Y. Tauman. 1992. Optimal Licensing of Cost-Reducing Innovation. *Journal of Mathematical Economics* 21: 483–508.

Katz, J. 2006. Structural Change and Domestic Technological Capabilities. *CEPAL Review* 89: 55–68.

Kumar, N., and A. Aggarwal. 2005. Liberalization, Outward Orientation and In-House R&D Activity of Multinational and Local Firms: A Quantitative Exploration for Indian Manufacturing. *Research Policy* 344: 441–460.

Lee, K., and S.M. Kang. 2007. Innovation Types and Productivity Growth: Evidence from Korean Manufacturing Firms. *Global Economic Review* 36: 343–359.

Loof, H., and A. Heshmati. 2002. Knowledge Capital and Performance Heterogeneity: A Firm-Level Innovation Study. *International Journal of Production Economics* 761: 61–85.

Loof, H., A. Heshmati, R. Asplund, and S.O. Nas. 2003. Innovation and Performance in Manufacturing Industries: A Comparison of the Nordic Countries. *The Icfaian Journal of Management Research* 2: 5–35.

Mairesse, J., P. Mohnen, and E. Kremp. 2005. The Importance of R&D and Innovation for Productivity: A Reexamination in Light of the 2000 French Innovation Survey. *Annales d'Économie et de Statistique* 79(80): 487–527.

Mairesse, J., and P. Mohnen. 2010. Using Innovation Surveys for Econometric Analysis. Working Paper 15857. Cambridge, MA: NBER.

Mohnen, P., and B. Hall. 2013. Innovation and Productivity: An Update. *Eurasian Business Review* 3(1): 47–65.

Mohnen, P., J. Mairesse, and M. Dagenais. 2006. Innovativity: A Comparison across Seven European Countries. *Economics of Innovation and New Technology* 15(4–5): 391–413.

Moretti, E. 2004. Workers' Education, Spillovers and Productivity: Evidence from Plant-Level Production Functions. *American Economic Review* 94(3): 656–690.

Navarro, J.C., J.J. Llisterri, and P. Zuñiga. 2010. The Importance of Ideas: Innovation and Productivity in Latin America. In *The Age of Productivity: Transforming Economies from the Bottom Up*, ed. C. Pages. Development in the Americas. Washington, DC: IDB and Palgrave Macmillan.

Nelson, R.R. 1959. The Simple Economics of Basic Scientific Research. *Journal of Political Economy* 67: 297.

OECD. 2009. *Innovation in Firms: A Microeconomic Perspective*. Paris: OECD.

Pakes, A., and Z. Griliches. 1980. Patents and R and D at the Firm Level: A First Look. Working Paper No. 0561. Cambridge, MA: NBER.

Perez, P., G. Dutrenit, and F. Barceinas. 2005. Actividad Innovadora y Desempeno Economico: un analisis econometrico del caso mexicano. In *Indicadores de Ciencia y Tecnología en Iberoamerica*. Buenos Aires, Argentina: RICYT.

Raffo, J., S. Lhuillery, and L. Miotti. 2008. Northern and Southern Innovativity: A Comparison Across European and Latin American Countries. *The European Journal of Development Research* 20(2): 219–239.

Roper, S., J. Du, and J.H. Love. 2008. Modelling the Innovation Value Chain. *Research Policy* 376(7): 961–977.

Rouvinen, P. 2002. R&D-Productivity Dynamics: Causality, Lags, and Dry Holes. *Journal of Applied Economics* 1: 123–156.

Van Leeuwen, G., and L. Klomp. 2006. On the Contribution of Innovation to Multi-Factor Productivity Growth. *Economics of Innovation and New Technologies* 15(4–5): 367–390.

Vivarelli, M. 2013. Technology, Employment and Skills: An Interpretative Framework. *Eurasian Business Review* 3(1): 66–89.

CHAPTER 3

Innovative Activity in the Caribbean: Drivers, Benefits, and Obstacles

Preeya Mohan, Eric Strobl, and Patrick Watson

Innovation has long been associated with productivity growth in that, hypothetically, it results in more effective use of a firm's resources and improved productivity. There is ample empirical evidence that firms that engage in innovation-type activities—such as spending on research and development (R&D) and obtaining intellectual property rights through patents and copyrights—are more technologically advanced and have higher labor productivity, enabling them to compete better internationally (Schumpeter 1939; Griliches 1986; Freeman 1994; Griffith et al. 2006; Mairesse and Mohnen 2010). Furthermore, there is evidence that investment in innovation-type activities results in sustainable long-run growth and development (Hall and Jones 1999; OECD 2009; Rouvinen 2002).

In view of the potential benefits, policymakers in the Caribbean have acknowledged the role that innovation may play in increasing productivity, as well as economic growth and development. For instance, in 1988,

P. Mohan (✉) • P. Watson
Sir Arthur Lewis Institute of Social and Economic Studies (SALISES),
University of the West Indies
email: Preeya.Mohan@sta.uwi.edu •
patrick.watson@sta.uwi.edu

E. Strobl
Ecole Polytechnique
email: eric.strobl@polytechnique.edu

© Inter-American Development Bank 2016
M. Grazzi and C. Pietrobelli (eds.), *Firm Innovation and Productivity in Latin America and the Caribbean*,
DOI 10.1057/978-1-349-58151-1_3

the Caribbean Community Secretariat (CARICOM) adopted a regional science and technology policy (Nurse 2007); in 2000, it established the Caribbean Council for Science and Technology to coordinate and implement this policy; and, in 2007, it formulated a regional framework for action (Nurse 2007). More recently, Jamaica's National Council for Science and Technology (NCST) introduced a strategic plan entitled "Science and Technology for Socio-Economic Development: A Policy for Jamaica" for 2005–2010, using foresighting techniques to develop a five-year master strategy and implementation plan for information communication technologies (ICTs) called "E-Powering Jamaica 2012" (NCST 2005). In other countries in the region, while there are institutions responsible for establishing and implementing national innovation systems, for the most part no formal strategic plans exist.

It is not clear how much benefit will accrue to the Caribbean because of innovation, largely because there is a paucity of studies on innovation and its impact on productivity in small island developing states like those in the Caribbean. The few studies tend to group the Caribbean with Latin America, and findings suggest that innovation and productivity are quite low and, indeed, constrain growth (Lederman et al. 2014; Ortiz et al. 2012; Daude and Fernández-Arias 2010; IDB 2010). Further, we note that most of these studies use spending on R&D to measure innovation activity though, as argued by Crespi and Zuñiga (2012), in developing countries the link between innovation and productivity is not well established since imitation and technology acquisition may play a more important role than R&D investment.

In this chapter we examine the impact of innovation on firm productivity in the Caribbean, hoping to fill existing gaps in the literature. We use cross-sectional firm-level data for the manufacturing sector from the World Bank Enterprise Surveys (WBES) for 14 Caribbean countries. Using non- and semi-parametric tests, and a set of productivity measures, we find evidence that innovative firms exhibit higher productivity than non-innovative firms. To identify any causal effect of innovation on productivity, we follow Crespi and Zuñiga (2012) and Griffith et al. (2006) and use a structural recursive model that takes into account firms' decision to invest in innovative activities rather than simply R&D expenditures. This approach models a knowledge-production function based on how much knowledge output is generated from the innovation investment, then estimates an output-production function in which labor productivity is determined by innovative activity together with other inputs. In using this approach, we experiment with other measures of productivity.

The next section of this chapter provides a brief overview of the literature on the productivity effects of innovative activities. Then we describe the data we used in our study, followed by non- and semi-parametric tests of productivity differences between innovative and non-innovative firms. We next outline our econometric model, and then present and discuss the results of our estimations. We then provide conclusions.

LITERATURE REVIEW

Traditionally, a firm's R&D expenditures were considered a direct determinant of innovation activity and increased productivity. Moreover, since data on the amount firms spend on R&D are widely and readily available (they are routinely recorded by firms), they are a convenient proxy to measure innovation activity. It is generally assumed that the more a firm spends on R&D the more innovative it is. In other words, increased R&D expenditures help boost process and product innovation by reducing the production cost of existing goods and helping increase the number of new goods produced. The relationship between innovation and productivity can then be modeled using a knowledge-production function, and the contribution of innovation to productivity measured using an output-production function, where the production of new knowledge is determined by the amount firms spent on R&D (Griliches 1979; Griliches and Pakes 1980; Cohen and Levinthal 1989).

Crépon et al. (1998) were the first to investigate the relationship between innovation and productivity with innovation inputs measured using the R&D expenditures of French manufacturing firms. The CDM model is a system of recursive equations linking a firm's R&D expenditures to its innovation output which, in turn, is linked to productivity. Their findings provided evidence that firm productivity increased with higher innovation as measured by R&D investment. Further, they showed that R&D spending increased with firm size, market share, diversification, and demand-pull and technology-push forces.

Later studies by Hall and Mairesse (2006) and Mairesse and Mohnen (2010) confirmed the results obtained by Crépon et al. (1998) but emphasized the importance of firm heterogeneity in explaining innovation activities and the need to control for their effects on firm performance in empirical work. Further, the correlation between product innovation and productivity is often higher for larger firms (Griffith et al. 2006; OECD 2009) and, in most countries, the productivity effect of product innovation is larger in the manufacturing sector than in the services sector

(OECD 2009). These studies showed that, in developed countries, the more a firm spent on R&D, the more likely it was to be innovative when controlling for firm characteristics such as size, market, and diversification.

The empirical evidence on innovation and productivity in developing countries is, however, not as straightforward. For instance, a positive relationship between R&D, innovation, and productivity has been found in newly industrialized Asian countries (Lee and Kang 2007; Hegde and Shapira 2007; Aw et al. 2008; Jefferson et al. 2006 and some Latin American countries (Chudnovsky et al. 2006; Arza and Lópezez 2010; Correa et al. 2005), but other studies in Latin America found no significant relationship (Raffo et al. 2008; Pérez et al. 2005; Chudnovsky et al. 2006; Hall and Mairesse 2006). The failure of R&D expenditure to correlate positively with innovation and productivity may be explained by the fact that firms in developing countries are too far from the technological frontier and that incentives to invest in innovation are weak or absent (Acemoglu et al. 2006). Moreover, in developing countries, R&D costs are high and may require a longer time to produce results (Navarro et al. 2010).

Later studies identified several weaknesses in using R&D expenditures alone to measure innovation. First, not all R&D expenditures necessarily lead to successful innovation and productivity growth: rather, they are simply an input into the innovation process and not a measure of innovation output. Using R&D, therefore, does not prove how successful a firm is at introducing new and improved products and services or production processes.

Second, innovation is a multi-dimensional and complex process, and R&D expenditures is but one component of innovation expenses. R&D expenditures alone, therefore, may not accurately measure innovation and may, on the contrary, be an underestimation of the true cost of innovation, which may include financing product design and training. In a study of German manufacturing firms, Felder et al. (1996) highlighted the importance of non-R&D innovation expenditures. Calvo (2003), in a study of Spanish manufacturing firms, found that more than half of the innovative firms did not spend on R&D.

It is clear, therefore, that approximating innovation using R&D expenditures may underestimate a firm's innovative capacity. More recently, innovation surveys provide data for studies that introduce a broader set of variables to measure innovative activity. In this regard, Griffith et al. (2006) and Crespi and Zuñiga (2012) extended the recursive system approach developed by Crépon et al. (1998) to incorporate broader measures of innovation. More precisely, they took into account firms' decisions to invest in innovative activity rather than simply R&D expenditures, along with other inputs related to labor productivity, in creating the knowledge-production function from which the output-production function was then created. A firm's innovation decision then included any action that aimed to increase its knowledge, such as new concepts, ideas, processes, and methods. This included R&D expenditures, but also other expenditures, such as product design, marketing, staff training, new machinery, patents, and other trademark licensing.

The model used by Griffith et al. (2006) and Crespi and Zuñiga (2012) was also different because it distinguished between process and product innovation by estimating them separately, since there is likely to be a high collinearity between these factors as the majority of the firms undertook both simultaneously. Empirically, it is hard to separate product and process innovation, which results in identification problems when using the two variables in the productivity equation. In addition to firm characteristics, the model also included external forces that affected a firm's innovation decision, such as: demand-driven innovation, including environmental, health, and safety regulation; technological-push innovation (scientific opportunities); and innovation policy. Ultimately, their frameworks also allowed selectivity bias and endogeneity in the innovation and productivity function to be controlled in the same manner as the original CDM framework. We use a similar approach in this study.

DATA AND DESCRIPTIVE ANALYSIS

Data

We use data from the WBES, which consists of firm-level surveys of a representative sample of an economy's private sector. The surveys cover a wide range of topics and are not limited to innovation, technology, and performance measures.[1] Private contractors administer the surveys face-to-face with business owners and top managers. The stratification factors are firm size, business sector, and geographic region within a country. These data provide rich firm-level data on 2771 firms from 14 Caribbean countries, all interviewed in 2010 (see Table 3.1). Unfortunately, the innovation module of the 2010 surveys was limited to manufacturing firms, thus limiting our analysis to that sector.

Descriptive Analysis

Table 3.1 shows the number of firms interviewed in each country: the number ranges from 376 (Jamaica) to 150 (Bahamas, Barbados, Belize,

Table 3.1   Summary statistics, WBES data

Country	ISO code	No. of firms	No. of innovative firms	No. of firms (sample)	No. innovative firms (sample)
Antigua and Barbuda	ATG	151	8	29	5
Bahamas	BHS	150	12	35	11
Barbados	BRB	150	27	64	20
Belize	BLZ	150	15	69	14
Dominica	DMA	150	4	23	1
Dominican Republic	DOM	350	81	109	42
Grenada	GRD	153	7	22	7
Guyana	GUY	165	35	59	27
Jamaica	JAM	376	62	105	23
St. Kitts & Nevis	KNA	150	10	23	6
Saint Lucia	LCA	150	7	56	6
St. Vincent & the Grenadines	VCT	154	15	45	11
Suriname	SUR	152	12	71	12
Trinidad and Tobago	TTO	370	20	102	16
Total		**2771**	**315**	**814**	**201**

Source: Authors' calculations based on WBES data

Note: All surveys were conducted in 2010

Dominica, St. Kitts & Nevis, and Saint Lucia). Among the 2771 firms interviewed, only 315 are innovative. The country with the largest number of innovative firms is the Dominican Republic (81 firms) and the country with the lowest is Dominica (four firms). Moreover, there is considerable variation in ownership (foreign versus domestic), export activity, size, and industry (manufacturing versus services). The left side of Table 3.2 provides the percentage of all firms interviewed by country, broken down by descriptive categories. As seen, the majority of firms interviewed are domestic, non-exporting, small service providers. Very importantly, therefore, we are missing information on innovative activity for a large proportion of Caribbean firms. In contrast, Table 3.3 displays the percentage of innovative manufacturing firms in each country, broken down by descriptive categories. Innovative firms in the Caribbean are domestic, medium-sized manufacturers, and about half export.

We also examine innovation by type of activity. Table 3.4 shows that innovation expenditures in Caribbean manufacturing occurs mainly through R&D expenditures: 8% of firms in the region are innovative on

Table 3.2 Innovation activity (%)

	Research and development	Cooperate on innovation	Receive public support for innovation	Patents abroad	Patents locally	Purchases of licenses for intellectual property
Antigua and Barbuda	5	0	1	0	0	2
Bahamas	8	3	0	0	0	6
Barbados	18	5	6	0	0	6
Belize	4	1	0	0	0	10
Dominica	2	0	0	0	0	3
Dominican Republic	11	10	4	8	23	13
Grenada	5	3	1	0	0	3
Guyana	21	16	2	0	0	7
Jamaica	9	5	1	7	16	7
St. Kitts & Nevis	7	5	1	0	0	1
Saint Lucia	5	0	0	0	0	2
St. Vincent & the Grenadines	10	6	3	0	0	3
Suriname	2	5	3	0	0	8
Trinidad and Tobago	5	4	0.2	2	5	3
Total	**8**	**5**	**2**	**2**	**6**	**6**

Source: Authors' calculations based on WBES data

the basis of R&D spending, followed by 6% of firms that innovate through local patents and license purchases of intellectual property. Furthermore, only 2% of firms innovate through public support and patents abroad. The country with the highest percentage of firms spending on R&D and cooperating on innovation is Guyana, followed by Barbados and the Dominican Republic. Barbados, however, has the highest percentage of firms that receive public support for innovation (6%) while, in many other countries, firms receive very little or none (Bahamas, Belize, Dominica, Saint Lucia, and Trinidad and Tobago).

In Table 3.5, innovative activity in manufacturing is broken down by type of innovation (product or process). Product occurs more frequently than process innovation: 15% of firms in the region introduced new or improved products, while only 9% introduced new or improved processes. Suriname has the largest percentage of firms undertaking product

Table 3.3   Product versus process innovation (%)

	New/significantly improved products introduced	New/significantly improved products new to establishment market	New/significantly improved process for producing/supplying products	New/significantly improved processes also new to your industry
Antigua and Barbuda	7	1	1	0
Bahamas	17	12	7	3
Barbados	28	16	16	9
Belize	14	3	3	2
Dominica	3	0	0	0
Dominican Republic	17	10	14	8
Grenada	11	7	5	3
Guyana	17	12	22	9
Jamaica	12	6	9	5
St. Kitts & Nevis	9	6	5	3
Saint Lucia	7	0	1	0
St. Vincent & the Grenadines	15	10	13	9
Suriname	34	16	7	1
Trinidad and Tobago	15	5	9	4
Total	**15**	**7**	**9**	**4**

Source: Authors' calculations based on WBES data

innovation (34%), followed by Barbados, the Bahamas, the Dominican Republic, and Guyana. Countries with the lowest percentage of firms undertaking product innovation are Dominica (3%), Saint Lucia (7%), and St. Kitts & Nevis (9%). Guyana has the highest percentage of firms undertaking process innovation (22%) followed by Barbados and Suriname (16%), while countries with the lowest percentage are Dominica (0%), Antigua and Barbuda, and Saint Lucia (1%).

NON AND SEMI-PARAMETRIC ANALYSIS OF PRODUCTIVITY DIFFERENCES

All of the variables used in this section are listed in Table 3.6. Since the techniques we use do not accommodate missing values, the sample size is substantially reduced, to 814 firms. The country and innovation

Table 3.4 Summary statistics, regression variables

	Mean	Standard deviation	Mean	Standard deviation	Difference-in-means test
	INNOV=1	INNOV=1	INNOV=0	INNOV=0	
TFP (stochastic)	12.3	1.6	12.5	1.5	6.21***
TFP (deterministic)	12.4	1.7	12.5	1.6	6.97***
Labor productivity	1.8	0.7	1.6	0.7	4.17***
Firm size	12.6	1.5	12	1.4	5.78***
Public finance	0.1	0.3	0.02	0.2	3.34***
Patent protection	0.2	0.3	0.05	0.1	2.67***
Exporter	0.4	0.5	0.2	0.4	6.36***
Cooperation	0.3	0.5	0.1	0.3	8.74***
Foreign ownership	0.2	0.4	0.2	0.4	2.59***

Source: Authors' calculations based on WBES data

Notes: *Coefficient is statistically significant at the 10% level, ** at the 5% level, *** at the 1% level; no asterisk means the coefficient is not different from zero with statistical significance. Difference-in-means test reports the t-statistic. TFP = total factor productivity

Table 3.5 Kolmogorov–Smirnov test of productivity, innovative versus non-innovative

Productivity measure	F = G	F ≤ G
Stochastic TFP	0.267***	0.000
Deterministic TFP	0.265***	0.000
Labor productivity	0.148***	0.020

Source: Authors' calculations based on WBES data

Notes: *Coefficient is statistically significant at the 10% level, **at the 5% level, ***at the 1% level; no asterisk means the coefficient is not different from zero with statistical significance. F is the distribution of the innovative and G the distribution of the non-innovative firms

breakdown of these firms is shown in Table 3.1 and, while the country breakdown remains relatively unaffected, the percentage of innovative firms appearing in the reduced sample is about 5 percentage points larger than the corresponding figure in the total sample.

Employing both non- and semi-parametric methods, we determine whether firms investing in innovation in the Caribbean are indeed more productive than non-innovative firms.[2] The latter group does not spend any funds on R&D or technological innovation activities.

Table 3.6   Probability of investing in innovation (ID) and intensity of innovation expenditure per employee (IE)

ID (probability of investing in innovation IE>0)	
Exporter	0.1320***
	(0.0370)
Foreign ownership	0.0100
	(0.0350)
Patent protection	0.0080
	(0.0480)
Firm size	0.0340***
	(0.0090)
IE (log innovation expenditure per employee)	
Exporter	−0.8530***
	(0.3020)
Foreign ownership	−0.1820
	(0.3350)
Patent protection	0.1590
	(0.4560)
Cooperation	0.3840
	(0.2500)
Public finance	0.4380
	(0.4260)
Observations	812
Wald test	142.13***
Wald test of independence (ρ=0)	20.81***
Log pseudo likelihood	−737.541

Source: Author's calculations based on WBES data

Notes: Coefficients reported are marginal effects.

* Coefficient is statistically significant at the 10% level, ** at the 5% level, *** at the 1% level

Non-Parametric Test

The simplest measure of productivity available from our data is labor productivity. The difference-in-means test, shown in Table 3.7, confirms that, in the Caribbean, the mean value of labor productivity for innovative firms is larger than that of non-innovative firms. Non-parametric kernel density graphs of each firm type's labor productivity distribution, shown in Fig. 3.1, provide evidence that innovative firms are also characterized by more productivity dispersion than their non-innovative counterparts.

Table 3.7 Probability of technological innovation (TI: introduction of product or process innovation)

IE_p (predicted innovation expenditure per employee)	0.557*** (0.119)
Firm size	0.045*** (0.016)
Exporter	0.477*** (0.075)
Foreign ownership	0.178*** (0.055)
Observations	812
Wald test	151.69***
Log psuedo likelihood	−476.63
Psuedo R²	0.153
Observed probability	0.502
Predicted probability (values at means)	0.506

Source: Authors' calculations based on WBES data

Notes: Coefficients reported are marginal effects. Robust standard errors in parentheses.

*Coefficient is statistically significant at the 10% level; ** at the 5% level; *** at the 1% level

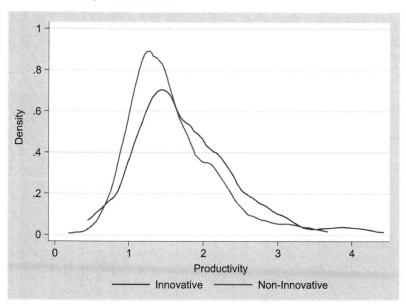

Fig. 3.1 Productivity distribution—labor productivity

Source: Authors' calculations based on WBES data

To test differences across firm types by taking into account moments of order higher than 2, we resort to the concept of first-order stochastic dominance. More precisely, let F be the cumulative distribution of innovative and G be the same for non-innovative firms' productivity (*prod*). First-order stochastic dominance is defined as $F(prod) - G(prod)$ uniformly in $prod \in \Re$, with strict equality for some. In contrast to a means test, first-order stochastic dominance thus considers all moments of the productivity distribution of firms.

We use the non-parametric one-sided and two-sided Kolmogorov–Smirnov tests (Delgado et al. 2002) to establish or refute first-order stochastic dominance of the productivity of innovative firms over non-innovative firms. The two-sided test investigates the hypothesis that both the innovative and non-innovative firms' productivity distributions are identical. The null (H_0) and alternative (H_1) hypotheses are:

$$H_0 : F(prod) - G(prod) = 0 \, \forall prod \in$$
$$H_1 : F(prod) - G(prod) \neq 0 \text{ for some } prod \in \qquad (3.1)$$

In contrast, the null and alternative hypotheses of the one-sided test of first-order stochastic dominance are:

$$H_0 : F(prod) - G(prod) \leq 0 \; \forall \, prod \in$$
$$H_1 : F(prod) - G(prod) > 0 \text{ for some } prod \in \Re \qquad (3.2)$$

In order to conclude that the distribution of innovative firms, F, dominates that of non-innovative firms, G, we need to reject the null hypothesis for the two-sided test but not for the one-sided test.

The Kolmogorov–Smirnov test statistics for the one-sided (equation 3.1) and two-sided (equation 3.3) tests are:

$$KS_1 = \sqrt{\frac{n.m}{N} \max_{1 \leq i \leq N} \left| F_n(prod_i) - G_m(prod_i) \right|} \qquad (3.3)$$

$$KS_2 = \sqrt{\frac{n.m}{N} \max_{1 \leq i \leq N} \left\{ F_n(prod_i) - G_m(prod_i) \right\}} \qquad (3.4)$$

Table 3.8   The impact of innovation on labor productivity
(Y: log sales per employee)

IE_p (predicted innovation expenditure per employee)	0.625***
	(0.243)
Firm size	0.019
	(0.021)
Non-technological innovation	0.266**
	(0.127)
Capital per employee	0.006
	(0.073)
Observations	812
Wald test	346.470***
R^2	0.314

Source: Authors' calculations based on WBES data

Notes: Bootstrapped standard errors in parentheses (100 replications). The
variable used as a proxy for physical capital is investment made during the
period considered the stock of physical capital

*Coefficient is statistically significant at the 10% level, ** at the 5% level, ***
at the 1% level

where n and m are the sample sizes from the empirical distributions of
F and G, respectively, and their sum is N. We report the Kolmogorov–
Smirnov statistic for the one- and two-sided tests for labor productivity in Table 3.8. The test statistics provide evidence that labor
productivity in innovating firms stochastically dominates productivity in
non-innovative firms. Thus, innovative firms in the Caribbean exhibit
higher productivity across all moments of the distribution, not just
around the mean.

Semi-Parametric Test

The non-parametric test has the advantage that it does not require any
(possibly restrictive) distributional assumptions. On the other hand,
it does not allow the investigator to account for the possibility that
innovative firms may differ from non-innovative firms in characteristics
that are correlated with productivity. For instance, a cursory glance at the
difference-in-means of the control variables across firm type in Table 3.7

shows that non-innovative firms are smaller, are less likely to obtain public financial support for innovation, are less likely to have patents, are less likely to export, are less likely to cooperate with other firms or institutions in terms of innovative activity, and are less likely to be foreign-owned. Thus, conclusions about the relationship between productivity and innovation spending, based on non-parametric testing, may be, at least in part, driven by differences in other firm characteristics.

To account for differences in characteristics when comparing distributions, DiNardo et al. (1996) developed an approach that allows for graphical assessment of the difference in distributions of an outcome variable of interest between two groups by disentangling what is due to differences in characteristics and what remains unexplained. In essence, their approach is a semi-parametric method based on the construction of counterfactual densities obtained by reweighting observations according to differences in the underlying characteristics. In our context, this means calculating the distribution of productivity of non-innovative firms if they had the characteristics of innovative firms. More specifically, each individual observation may be considered a vector ($PROD$, Z, $INNOV$), where Z is the vector of firm attributes other than innovation that are correlated with productivity. The joint distribution of productivity and characteristics conditional on innovation status may be defined as $F(PROD, Z|INNOV=0,1)$. The density of productivity for innovative firms, $f_{INNOV=0,1}(PROD)$, may then be expressed as the integral of the density of productivity, conditional on some firm characteristics and on innovative activity, $f(PROD|Z, INNOV=0)$, over the distribution of firm characteristics $F(Z|INNOV=1)$:

$$f(PROD; INNOV = 0,1) = \int_Z dF(PROD, Z \mid INNOV = 0,1) \qquad (3.5)$$

where the set of productivities comes from innovative firms and the set of characteristics from non-innovative firms. In like manner, the counterfactual for Z from innovative firms, $f(PROD; PROD_{INNOV=0}, Z_{INNOV=1})$, may be expressed in terms of reweighting the actual distribution as:

$$f(PROD; PROD_{INNOV=0}, Z_{INNOV=1})$$
$$= \int_Z f(PROD \mid Z, PROD_{INNOV=0}) \Psi_Z(Z) dF(Z \mid INNOV = 1)) \qquad (3.6)$$

where

$$\Psi(Z) = \frac{dF(Z \mid INNOV = 1)}{dF(Z \mid INNOV = 0)}$$
$$= \frac{\operatorname{Prob}(Z_{INNOV=1} \mid Z)\operatorname{Prob}(INNOV = 0)}{\operatorname{Prob}(Z_{INNOV=0} \mid Z)\operatorname{Prob}(INNOV = 1)} \qquad (3.7)$$

To estimate this counterfactual, the weight $\Psi_z(Z)$ (i.e. the probability of being innovative or not given firms' characteristics Z) is estimated using logit or probit methods, which predicts the probability $Prob(INNOV = 1|Z)$ and $Prob(INNOV = 0|Z)$ for each firm in the sample.

We employ the DiNardo et al. (1996) method to explore distributional differences in labor productivity between innovating and non-innovating firms using a firm's export status, foreign ownership, patent possession, government support, size, non-technological innovation, and innovation cooperation status as other productivity determinants. We estimate equation 3.6 using the probit model.[3] In Fig. 3.2, we depict the

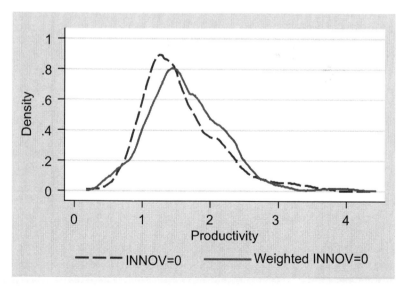

Fig. 3.2 Non-innovative and weighted non-innovative firms—labor productivity
Source: Authors' calculations based on WBES data

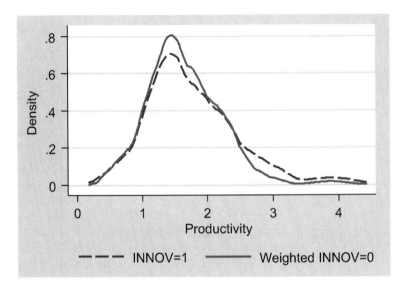

Fig. 3.3 Innovative and weighted non-innovative firms—labor productivity
Source: Authors' calculations based on WBES data

counterfactual distribution of equation 3.5, the distribution of productivity of non-innovative firms but with innovative firm type characteristics relative to their true distribution. Accordingly, the counterfactual has a higher mean and higher dispersion, implying that, if non-innovative firms were similar in characteristics to innovative firms, they would have higher mean productivity as well as greater inequality in productivity across that group.

In Fig. 3.3, we compare the counterfactual non-innovative firm productivity distribution to the true innovative firm productivity distribution. Relative to the raw difference in distribution, these graphs show that the difference in distributions in labor productivity between innovative and non-innovative firms is less marked. This implies that some non-negligible part of the difference in the distributions of productivity between the two types of firms was due to differences in their other characteristics. Moreover, the counterfactual non-innovative distribution also appears to be somewhat closer to that of the innovative firms rather than that of the actual non-innovative distribution, suggesting that differences between innovative and non-innovative firms are due more to differences in characteristics than to being innovative. Nevertheless, it remains clear that, even after adjusting for differences in characteristics, non-innovative firms have a lower mean and more dispersion in productivity than innovative firms.

Alternative Productivity Measures

Thus far we have focused simply on labor productivity as a measure of a firm's efficiency. However, the data also allow us to obtain, relatively simply, more sophisticated measures of productivity. As a starting point, we assume that there is some efficient production frontier where output is at its maximum and where a firm, if it is operating at that frontier, is regarded as technically efficient. Consider, for example, a firm with a Cobb–Douglas production function with two inputs, labor (L) and capital (K):

$$Y_i = A_i K_i^{\beta_k} L_i^{\beta_L} \tag{3.8}$$

Given that A is unobservable, it is estimated. In natural logarithms, an empirical equivalent of equation 3.7 is:

$$y_i = \beta_0 + \beta_k k + \beta_l l + \varepsilon_i \tag{3.9}$$

where β_0 measures the mean efficiency across firms and ε is the producer-specific deviation from that mean, which can be further decomposed into observable (i.e. predictable) and unobservable components:

$$y_i = \beta_0 + \beta_k k + \beta_l l + v_i + u_i \tag{3.10}$$

where firm-level productivity is just $\beta_0 + v_i$, which can easily be estimated with data on a firm's output, capital stock, and labor using simple regression analysis.

The logic underlying this one-sided error component specification is that differences in firm productivity are due to differences in management ability, and thus any firm not operating at the frontier is less efficiently managed. However, more realistically, sometimes maximum output itself may be higher or lower due to exogenous shocks, meaning the frontier may be different across firms. Moreover, not all firms share a common family of production, cost, and profit functions, and thus some measurement error will inevitably be introduced in estimating productivity from equation 3.11. Aigner et al. (1977) extended the deterministic frontier analysis approach to allow for these factors. More specifically, they assumed that u_i can be decomposed as:

$$u_i = \pi_i + \eta_i \qquad (3.11)$$

where π is the symmetric disturbance from the frontier and $\eta < 0$ is the true error component, which is assumed to be distributed independently of π. The normally distributed π captures the possibility that the frontier may vary for each firm due to measurement errors and uncertainty regarding external events, and not necessarily due to managerial inefficiency. Aigner et al. (1977) demonstrated how incorporating equation 3.11 into equation 3.12 can be estimated using maximum likelihood methods.

Both the deterministic and stochastic frontier-derived productivities for all firms are estimated using equations 3.10 and 3.11.[4, 5] The mean and standard deviation for these alternative productivity measures are shown in Table 3.7. As is the case with the labor productivity results, average productivity is higher for innovative firms for these proxies as well, which is confirmed by a simple difference-in-means test.[6]

In order to check for robustness we computed the raw distributions, and the difference is even more pronounced for the two total factor productivity (TFP) measures than for simple labor productivity (details available from the authors). The relevant Kolmogorov–Smirnov test statistic is shown in Table 3.8. Again, the conclusion holds: innovative firms exhibit higher productivity across all moments of the distribution. Similarly, the conclusions with regard to the semi-parametric distributional method also hold, meaning the non-negligible part of the difference in the distributions of productivity between the two types of firms appears to be due to differences in their other characteristics. Differences between innovative and non-innovative firms are due more to differences in characteristics than to being innovative, although the latter aspect appears to be less so for the two TFP measures than for labor productivity.

ECONOMETRIC MODEL

The non- and semi-parametric tests suggest that firms that spend on innovation are more productive than ones that do not, even after controlling for differences in characteristics. However, this does not imply causality.

Moreover, given the dichotomous nature of these tests, we can only focus on whether a firm spends money or not, not how much it spends. In order to gain further insight into causality and amount of spending, we follow Crespi and Zuñiga (2012) and explicitly model the innovative decision process to determine its causal impact on productivity.

In their analysis of the impact of innovation on productivity in several Latin American countries, Crespi and Zuñiga (2012) extended the structural recursive model of Crépon et al. (1998) as follows. Let $i = 1,...,N$ represent an index of firms. The first equation of the model accounts for the firm's innovative effort IE_i^*:

$$IE_i^* = zi'\beta + e_i \qquad (3.12)$$

where IE_i^* is an unobserved latent variable and is measured by the log of expenditures on innovation activities divided by the number of employees, z_i is a vector of determinants of the firm's innovation decision, β is a vector of parameters, and e_i is the error term.

A firm's decision to undertake innovative activity is then modeled as follows:

$$ID_i = 1 \text{ if } ID_i^* = w_i'\alpha + e_i > c,$$
$$= 0 \text{ if } ID_i^* = w_i'\alpha + e_i \leq c \qquad (3.13)$$

where ID_i is a binary endogenous variable equal to 1 if the firm invests in innovative activity above a certain threshold level c, and 0 if it does not; w is a vector of variables explaining the innovation investment decision; α is a vector of parameters of interest; and e_i is an error term.

Conditional on firm i engaging in innovation activities, we can observe the amount of resources invested in innovation (IE) activities:

$$IE_i = IE_i^* = z_i'\beta + \varepsilon_i \text{ if } ID_i = 1$$
$$0 \text{ if } D_i = 0 \qquad (3.14)$$

Assuming the error terms e and ε are bivariate normal with zero mean and variances, respectively, $\sigma_\varepsilon^2 = 1$ and σ_c^2 and correlation coefficient $\rho_{\varepsilon e}$, the system of equations 3.14 and 3.15 can be viewed as a generalized Tobit model, estimable by maximum likelihood.

To model the knowledge/innovation production function, consider:

$$TI_i = IE_i^* \gamma + x_i' \delta + u_i \qquad (3.15)$$

where TI_i is knowledge outputs by technological innovation (introduction of a new product or process at the firm level) and the latent innovation effort, IE, enters as an explanatory variable, x is a vector of other determinants of knowledge production, γ and δ are vectors of parameters of interest, and u is an error term.

The final equation of the model sets out the relationship between innovation and labor productivity. Firms produce output using constant returns to scale with labor, capital, and knowledge inputs as follows:

$$y_i = \theta_1 k_i + \theta_2 TI_i + v_i \qquad (3.16)$$

where output y is labor productivity (log of sales per worker), k is the log of physical capital per worker (measured as physical investment per worker), and TI enters as an explanatory variable that refers to the impact of technological innovation on productivity levels.

To estimate the full set of equations, we use a three-step estimation procedure since the model does not allow for feedback effects. First, we estimate the generalized Tobit model in equations 3.14 and 3.15. Next, we estimate the innovation function in equation 3.16 using a probit model, where the predicted value of (log) innovation expenditures is the main explanatory variable rather than reporting innovation efforts. Importantly, this corrects for potential endogeneity in the knowledge-production equation. Finally, we estimate the productivity equation using the predicted values from the second step to take care of the endogeneity of TI_i in equation 3.16.

Given the small sample sizes of individual countries, data across countries are pooled prior to applying the Crespi and Zuñiga (2012) procedure. In this regard, we control for unobserved country characteristics as well as sector differences by including a full set of two-digit ISIC code and country dummies in all specifications. The remaining explanatory variables are in line with Crespi and Zuñiga (2012), except for their controls "the importance of market sources of information," "scientific sources of information," and "public sources of information." We eliminate these controls because there are too many missing values for these variables in the dataset. The model is estimated for all firms—not for innovative firms only—since most surveys do not have a filter and most of the questions are asked of all firms. Also, the model assumes that all firms exert some kind of innovative effort, but not all report this activity. The output of these efforts produces knowledge, and we can then estimate innovation efforts for all firms.

ECONOMETRIC RESULTS

The Decision to Invest in Innovation and the Intensity of Innovation Expenditures

Table 3.9 presents the results for the estimation of equations 3.14 and 3.15, which specify the determinants of the likelihood to engage in innovation activities within the firm and the intensity of these expenditures (log of innovation expenditure per worker) for the Caribbean. The reported estimates are the marginal effects of the generalized Tobit model. The identification of our model rests on the assumption that firm size affects the decision to invest but not how much a firm will invest (Crespi and Zuñiga 2012).

The results show that firms that export and those that are larger are more likely to invest in innovation, while having patent protection or foreign ownership does not significantly predict the decision to invest in innovation. The effect of the "size" variable is not surprising given that it is generally believed that there are economies to scope resulting from investing in innovation (Cohen and Levinthal 1989). Similarly, the finding that exporting firms are more likely to invest is expected, as this is consistent with the findings of Aw et al. (2008) that the decision to export and the decision to invest in R&D are intrinsically linked. The insignificance of "foreign ownership" may signal that foreign firms are using Caribbean countries as an outlet for their products rather than as a testing ground to improve production.

In terms of the size of the coefficients, an exporting firm is 13% more likely to invest in innovation, while a one unit increase in logged employment increases the probability of investment by 3.4 percentage points. With regard to the latter, for example, the largest firm in our estimation sample is nearly 50% more likely to invest in innovation than the smallest firm, all else being equal. Crespi and Zuñiga (2012) also found that "exporting" is a significant predictor of innovation expenditures in Argentina, Chile, and

Table 3.9 Main characteristics of Caribbean firms (%)

	Ownership		Exporter		Size			Industry	
	Foreign	Domestic	Exporter	Non-exporter	Small	Medium	Large	Manufacturing	Services
Antigua and Barbuda	10	90	19	81	62	34	4	23	77
Bahamas	22	78	14	86	47	37	17	28	72
Barbados	19	81	32	68	33	41	26	47	53
Belize	13	87	21	79	53	41	6	48	52
Dominica	23	77	27	73	69	29	3	19	81
Dominican Republic	16	84	11	89	30	38	32	32	68
Grenada	17	83	7	93	65	27	8	16	84
Guyana	25	75	23	77	31	44	25	44	56
Jamaica	14	86	10	90	37	45	18	32	68
St. Kitts & Nevis	21	79	17	83	55	40	5	19	81
Saint Lucia	19	81	34	66	49	40	11	42	58
St. Vincent & the Grenadines	16	84	17	83	71	25	4	32	68
Suriname	6	94	13	87	43	51	6	49	51
Trinidad and Tobago	13	87	17	83	55	28	27	33	67
Total	**16**	**84**	**17**	**83**	**47**	**37**	**16**	**33**	**67**

Source: Authors' calculations based on WBES data

Columbia. Our results are similar in size to those of Crespi and Zuñiga (2012) for Argentina and Chile but larger for Colombia. Our result for employment is also similar to the Crespi and Zuñiga results for all countries in their study, although for none of these was the coefficient smaller than 0.08. Thus, in the Caribbean, size seems to be a better predictor of a firm's willingness to invest in innovation. In contrast to our results, foreign ownership did not seem to matter in Crespi and Zuñiga's (2012) Latin American sample, except Argentina, and patent protection was important for all countries, again except Argentina. The fact that patent protection does not matter in our results suggests that it is less credible and/or less effective in the Caribbean compared to Latin America (see Chap. 2). Only the "exporter" variable is significant in the innovation expenditure equation. The fact that public financial support is not a significant predictor may be a worry, as it suggests that public funds to promote innovation are not efficiently spent in the Caribbean. Similarly, the insignificance of the "cooperation" variable suggests that spillovers between firms are minimal. In the Crespi–Zuñiga study, exporting was a significant determinant only for Argentina and Colombia. Somewhat surprisingly, in our study, exporting decreases spending on innovation.

The Impact of Innovation Investment on Technological Innovation

Table 3.10, which presents the estimates of equation 3.16 (the knowledge-production functions), shows marginal effects. The results show that the variables "exporter" and "foreign ownership" increase the probability of technological innovation. More specifically, an exporting firm is 48 % more likely to be undertaking innovation, while being foreign-owned increases the probability by 18 percentage points. The fact that foreign firms undertake more innovation, without investing it in the Caribbean, indicates that innovation is probably taking place in the firms' countries of origin. Crespi and Zuñiga (2012) found a similar result only for Chile, where the effect was around 22 %. In contrast, to the Crespi–Zuñiga sample, only Colombian exporters were more likely to undertake technological innovation, where the effect is only about a third of what is found for the Caribbean sample.

Caribbean firms, like their Latin American counterparts, are more likely to introduce product or process innovation if they spend more on innovation. More specifically, a unit increase in logged innovation expenditure per employee increases the probability of innovation by

Table 3.10   Main characteristics of innovative Caribbean firms (%)

	Ownership		Exporter		Size			Industry
	Foreign	Domestic	Exporter	Non-exporter	Small	Medium	Large	Manufacturing
Antigua and Barbuda	13	87	25	75	50	50	0	100
Bahamas	33	67	42	58	42	50	8	100
Barbados	19	81	59	41	30	40	30	89
Belize	20	80	60	40	27	53	20	100
Dominica	75	25	50	50	0	75	25	100
Dominican Republic	15	85	30	70	19	30	41	100
Grenada	29	71	43	57	43	43	14	100
Guyana	20	80	46	54	5	46	49	100
Jamaica	19	81	31	69	23	35	42	100
St. Kitts & Nevis	30	70	50	50	20	50	30	100
Saint Lucia	14	86	29	71	71	29	0	100
St. Vincent & the Grenadines	27	73	53	47	47	40	13	100
Suriname	0	100	33	67	33	58	9	100
Trinidad and Tobago	20	80	60	40	20	65	15	100
Total	**25**	**75**	**45**	**55**	**30**	**47**	**23**	**99**

Source: Authors' calculations based on WBES data

56 %. The size of the effect is thus higher than that found for all Latin American countries in Crespi and Zuñiga (2012), except for Chile. It appears that spending on innovation has a higher return in terms of product innovation in the Caribbean than most of the countries in Latin America.

The Impact of Innovation on Productivity

Table 3.11 depicts the results of equation 3.4 (productivity), where the coefficients reported are elasticities or semi-elasticities since the dependent variable is the log of sales per employee. Non-technological innovation has a positive and significant impact on labor productivity, similar to the Crespi–Zuñiga result for Argentina and Colombia, although smaller for the former and somewhat larger for the latter. Caution should be exercised

Table 3.11 Table of variables

Variable	Abbreviation	Definition	Mean	St. Dev.
Technological innovation	TI	Dummy equal to 1 if the firm introduced product or process innovation	0.50	0.50
Expenditures on innovation activities per employee	IE	Log of firm innovation expenditure divided by number of employees	8.38	2.11
Productivity	Y	Log of total sales divided by number of employees	1.61	0.61
Firm size	EM	Log of number of employees	12.10	1.40
Exporter/non-exporter	EX	Dummy variable equal to 1 if firm exports	0.26	0.44
Non-technological innovation	NTI	Log of capital investment divided by number of employees	1.05	0.69
Foreign ownership	FO	Dummy variable equal to 1 if foreign capital above 10%	0.17	0.34
Patent protection	PA	Dummy variable equal to 1 if firm has or filed for patent	0.17	0.37
Cooperation	CO	Dummy variable equal to 1 if firm collaborated on innovation	0.14	0.34
Public finance	FIN	Dummy variable equal to 1 if firm received public finance for innovation	0.04	0.20
Capital per employee	INV	Log of capital divided by number of employees	0.40	1.16

Source: Authors' calculations based on WBES data

in reading too much into this result, as we assume that there is no selection bias and no endogeneity for non-technical innovation. Innovation expenditures have a positive and significant impact on labor productivity. The estimated elasticity, 0.63, is larger than for Costa Rica (no effect), Chile (0.60), and Argentina (0.24), but substantially smaller than for Columbia (1.92), Panama (0.8), and Uruguay (0.80).

CONCLUDING REMARKS

In this study we have examined the determinants of spending on innovation and its impact on productivity in the Caribbean. We used a rich cross-sectional enterprise survey covering 14 Caribbean countries with detailed information on innovative activity for manufacturing firms. Our analysis showed that there are indeed productivity differences, regardless of the definition of productivity, between innovative and non-innovative manufacturing firms in the Caribbean, although a significant proportion is due to differences in other observable characteristics. More precisely, those firms not spending money on innovation tend to be less productive, although they are also more heterogeneous in their productivity.

We also estimated the determinants of innovation and the causal impact of innovation on productivity in an econometric framework, and compared our results to a previous study done for several Latin American countries. This unearthed a number of interesting results. Specifically, we found that, while there are economies of scope, size appears to be less of an obstacle to undertaking innovation in the Caribbean than in Latin America. The fact that neither having patents nor cooperating with other firms appears to encourage investment is worrisome. Maybe the current legislative framework in the Caribbean does not effectively encourage innovation.

We also discovered that foreign-owned firms are not more inclined than domestically owned firms to invest more in innovation, probably in part because their innovative activities generally take place in their country of origin. Fortunately, it appears that, in the Caribbean, foreign-owned firms nevertheless introduce more innovative techniques than domestically owned ones, thus probably creating the opportunity of spillovers to local firms. Reassuringly, investment in innovation appears to be as successful in the Caribbean as in Latin America in the sense that it translates into introducing new products and processes, not necessarily less than in Latin American countries. Most importantly, we found that new products and processes increase productivity in the region, and that the change may be larger than in some Latin American nations.

More generally, our study showed that the benefits of investing in innovation are not too different than those found for Latin America. Given this, further analysis should investigate what Caribbean firms perceive specifically as obstacles to devoting funds to innovation. Possibilities include insufficient or inefficient legal protection, government support, or inability to compete with foreign firms.

Notes

1. Other topics include access to finance, gender participation, business–government relations, bribery, trade, capacity utilization, corruption, infrastructure, crime, and competition.

2. Following Griffith et al. (2006) and Crespi and Zuñiga (2012), an innovative firm is defined as any firm that has taken action to increase its knowledge (i.e. new concepts, ideas, processes, and methods). This includes R&D expenditures but also spending on other activities related to technological innovation, such as cooperation on innovation activities, receipt of public support for innovation, securing patents, or the purchase of licenses for intellectual property.

3. We chose the other determinants based on data availability and to be in line with our parametric analysis in the "Econometric Model" section of this chapter.

4. For the stochastic productivity component, we assume a half-normal distribution. However, using an exponential distribution instead did not noticeably change our results.

5. We estimate the returns on capital and labor to be 0.18 and 0.89, respectively, and statistically significant at the 1% level.

6. The test statistics were 6.97, 6.21, and 4.17 for deterministic productivity, stochastic productivity, and logged labor productivity, respectively.

References

Acemoglu, D., P. Aghion, and F. Zilibotti. 2006. Distance to Frontier, Selection, and Economic Growth. *Journal of the European Economic Association* 4(1): 37–74.

Aigner, D., C.A.K. Lovell, and P. Schmidt. 1977. Formulation and Estimation of Stochastic Frontier Production Function Models. *Journal of Econometrics* 6: 21–37.

Arza, V., and A. López. 2010. Innovation and Productivity in the Argentine Manufacturing Sector. Working Paper Series no. IDB-WP-187. Washington, DC: The Inter-American Development Bank (IDB).

Aw, B.Y., M. Roberts, and D. Xu. 2008. R&D Investments, Exporting, and the Evolution of Firm Productivity. *American Economic Review* 98(2): 451–456.

Calvo, J. 2003. The Export Activity of Spanish Manufacturing Firms: Does Innovation Matter? *Proceedings of the 43th Congress of European Regional Science Association. August 2003.* Finland.

Chudnovsky, D., A. López, and G. Pupato. 2006. Innovation and Productivity in Developing Countries: A Study of Argentine Manufacturing Firms' Behavior (1992–2001). *Research Policy* 35(2): 266–288.

Cohen, W., and D. Levinthal. 1989. Innovation and Learning: The Two Faces of R&D. *Economic Journal* 99(397): 569–596.

Correa, P.I., G. Sánchez, and H. Singh. 2005. *Research, Innovation and Productivity: Firm Level Analysis for Brazil.* Washington, DC: The World Bank.

Crépon, B., E. Duguet, and J. Mairesse. 1998. Research, Innovation and Productivity: An Econometric Analysis at the Firm Level. *Economics of Innovation and New Technology* 7(2): 115–158.

Crespi, G., and P. Zuñiga. 2012. Innovation and Productivity: Evidence from Six Latin American Countries. *World Development* 40(2): 273–290.

Daude, C., and E. Fernández-Arias. 2010. The Importance of Ideas: Innovation and Productivity in Latin America. In *The Age of Productivity: Transforming Economies from the Bottom Up*, ed. C. Pages. Washington, DC: Palgrave Macmillan.

Delgado, M., J.C. Fariñas, and S. Ruano. 2002. Firm Productivity and Export Markets: A Non-Parametric Approach. *Journal of International Economics* 57(2002): 397–422.

DiNardo, J., N. Fortin, and T. Lemieux. 1996. Labor Market Institutions and the Distribution of Wages, 1973–1993: A Semi-Parametric Approach. *Econometrica* 64(5): 1001–1045.

Felder, J., G. Licht, E. Nerlinger, and H. Stahl. 1996. Factors Determining R&D and Innovation Expenditure in German Manufacturing Industries. In *Determinants of Innovation: The Message from New Indicators*, ed. A. Kleinknecht. London: Macmillan.

Freeman, C. 1994. The Economics of Technical Change. *Cambridge Journal of Economics* 18(5): 463–514.

Griffith, R., E. Huergo, J. Mairesse, and B. Peters. 2006. Innovation and Productivity Across Four European Countries. *Oxford Review of Economic Policy* 22(4): 483–498.

Griliches, Z. 1979. Issues in Assessing the Contribution of Research and Development to Productivity Growth. *Bell Journal of Economics* 10(1): 92–116.

Griliches, Z. 1986. Productivity, R&D, and Basic Research at the Firm Level in the 1970s. *American Economic Review* 76(1): 141–154.

Griliches, Z., and A. Pakes. 1980. Patents and R&D at the Firm Level: A First Look. NBER Working Paper no. 561. Cambridge, MA: National Bureau of Economic Research.

Hall, R., and C. Jones. 1999. Why do Some Countries Produce so Much More Output per Worker Than Others? *The Quarterly Journal of Economics* 114(1): 83–116.

Hall, B., and J. Mairesse. 2006. Empirical Studies of Innovation in the Knowledge-Driven Economy. *Economics of Innovation and New Technology* 15(4–5): 289–299.

Hegde, D., and P. Shapira. 2007. Knowledge, Technology Trajectories, and Innovation in a Developing Country Context: Evidence from a Survey of Malaysian Firms. *International Journal of Technology Management* 40(4): 349–370.

IDB. 2010. *Science, Technology and Innovation in Latin America and the Caribbean: A Statistical Compendium of Indicators*. Washington, DC: IDB.

Jefferson, G., B. Huamao, G. Xiaojing, and Y. Xiaoyun. 2006. R&D Performance in Chinese Industry. *Economics of Innovation and New Technologies* 15(40–45): 345–366.

Lederman, D., J. Messina, S. Pienknagura, and J. Rigolini. 2014. *Latin American Entrepreneurs: Many Firms but Little Innovation.* Washington, DC: The World Bank.

Lee, K., and S. Kang. 2007. Innovation Types and Productivity Growth: Evidence from Korean Manufacturing Firms. *Global Economic Review* 36(4): 343–359.

Mairesse, J., and P. Mohnen. 2010. Using Innovation Surveys for Econometric Analysis. NBER Working Paper no. 15857. Cambridge, MA: National Bureau of Economic Research.

Navarro, J.C., J.J. Llisterri, and P. Zuñiga. 2010. The Importance of Ideas: Innovation and Productivity in Latin America. In *The Age of Productivity: Transforming Economies from the Bottom Up*, ed. Carmen Pages. Washington, DC: IDB and Palgrave Macmillan.

NCST. 2005. Science and Technology for Socio-Economic Development a Policy for Jamaica. Kingston, Jamaica: National Commission on Science and Technology (NCST). Available at http://www.eclac.cl/iyd/noticias/pais/7/31467/Jamaica_Doc_2.pdf

Nurse, K. 2007. Science, Technology, and Innovation in the Caribbean. Paper presented at Technology Policy and Development in Latin America UNECLAC, Santiago, Chile.

OECD. 2009. *Innovation in Firms: A Microeconomic Perspective.* Paris, France: Organization for Economic Cooperation and Development (OECD).

Ortiz, E.A., G. Crespi, E. Tacsir, F. Vargas, and P. Zuñiga. 2012. Innovation for Economic Performance: The Case of Latin American and Caribbean Firms. Technical note IDB-TN-494. Washington, DC: IDB.

Pérez, P., G. Dutrenit, and F. Barceinas. 2005. *Innovation Activity and Economic Performance: An Econometric Analysis of the Mexican Case.* Buenos Aires, Argentina: Indicators of Science and Technology in Latin America. M. Albornoz and D. Ratto (eds.), Indicadores de Ciencia y Tecnología en Iberoamerica. Agenda 2005, 299–318.

Raffo, J., S. Lhuillery, and L. Miotti. 2008. Northern and Southern Innovativity: A Comparison Across European and Latin American Countries. *European Journal of Development Research* 20(2): 219–239.

Rouvinen, P. 2002. R&D-Productivity Dynamics: Causality, Lags, and Dry Holes. *Journal of Applied Economics* 5(1): 123–156.

Schumpeter, J. 1939. *Business Cycles: A Theoretical, Historical, and Statistical Analysis of the Capitalist Process.* New York: McGraw-Hill.

CHAPTER 4

Information and Communication Technologies, Innovation, and Productivity: Evidence from Firms in Latin America and the Caribbean

Matteo Grazzi and Juan Jung

Over recent decades, the economic literature has progressively recognized the role of information and communication technologies (ICTs) as a key driver of economic growth. In particular, a large body of research has clearly shown the link between accelerating productivity growth and ICT diffusion in the context of growth accounting (Oliner and Sichel 1994, 2002; Jorgenson 2001).

At the firm level, ICT adoption can improve business performance in various ways: ICTs speed up communication and information processing, decrease internal coordination costs, and facilitate decision-making (Cardona et al. 2013; Arvanitis and Loukis 2009; Atrostic et al. 2004; Gilchrist et al.

M. Grazzi
Inter-American Development Bank
e-mail: matteog@iadb.org

J. Jung
IASIET, Universidad de la República,
Centro de Estudios de Telecomunicaciones de Latinoamerica
e-mail: juanjung@gmail.com

© Inter-American Development Bank 2016
M. Grazzi and C. Pietrobelli (eds.), *Firm Innovation and Productivity in Latin America and the Caribbean*,
DOI 10.1057/978-1-349-58151-1_4

2001). ICTs may also promote substantial firm restructuring, making internal processes more flexible and rational, and reducing capital requirements, by improving equipment utilization and reducing inventory. Moreover, the possibility of developing better communication channels with suppliers, clients, knowledge providers, and competitors may increase innovation capacity.

Nevertheless, ICT-driven productivity gains vary largely among countries and sectors, suggesting that simple diffusion may be not sufficient to take full advantage of the potential of ICTs. Empirical evidence indicates that firm-specific operational and organizational characteristics determine not only the expected benefit of ICT adoption, but also the impact once adopted. Therefore, complementary investment in areas such as organizational change and human capital appear necessary both to increase absorptive capacity and to maximize the real impact of new technologies (Brynjolfsson and Hitt 2000). As a result, ICTs seem to function as an enabling factor that allows firms to use new processes and business practices, which, in turn, improve performance.

A complete understanding of these dynamics is central to designing effective public policies to promote ICT adoption and increase firm productivity. However, the bulk of the literature has focused on developed countries, while evidence from emerging economies is still scarce and fragmented. This chapter aims to fill this knowledge gap by exploring the determinants of broadband adoption and assessing their relationship with innovation and productivity in Latin America and the Caribbean (LAC).

The rest of the chapter is organized as follows. First we describe the main patterns of diffusion of the internet in LAC and the data we use in our empirical analysis. Then we discuss determinants of ICT adoption and explore the relationship between broadband, innovation, and productivity. We review the relevant theoretical and empirical literature, specifying the empirical model employed and discussing the main results. Finally, we provide concluding remarks.

DATA AND MAIN PATTERNS OF INTERNET DIFFUSION IN LAC

The diffusion and use of ICT is still relatively low in LAC. In fact, although ICTs have significantly increased in the region, there is still a notable divide between LAC and developed countries, especially in the most advanced technologies.[1] Using data from the International Telecommunications Union (ITU) for 2014, Fig. 4.1 displays an international comparison for fixed broadband penetration. Western Europe (EUR) and USA–Canada (US-

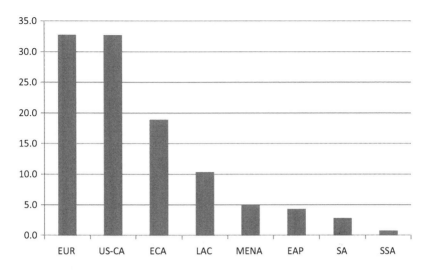

Fig. 4.1 Fixed broadband subscriptions by region (2014)

Source: Authors' elaboration using data from the ITU

Notes: Simple average of available countries in each region. **EUR**: (*Western Europe*) Austria, Belgium, Croatia, Cyprus, Denmark, Finland, France, Germany, Greece, Ireland, Italy, Luxembourg, Malta, Netherlands, Portugal, Spain, Sweden, United Kingdom, Norway, and Switzerland; **US-CA**: The United States and Canada; **ECA**: (*Eastern Europe and Central Asia*) Bosnia and Herzegovina, Bulgaria, Czech Republic, Estonia, Hungary, Kazakhstan, Kyrgyz Republic, Latvia, Lithuania, Moldova, Mongolia, Montenegro, Poland, Romania, Russia, Serbia, Slovak Republic, Slovenia, and Ukraine; **LAC**: Argentina, Bahamas, Barbados, Belize, Bolivia, Brazil, Chile, Colombia, Costa Rica, Dominica, Dominican Republic, Ecuador, El Salvador, Grenada, Guatemala, Guyana, Honduras, Jamaica, Mexico, Nicaragua, Panama, Paraguay, Peru, Saint Lucia, St. Kitts & Nevis, St. Vincent & the Grenadines, Suriname, Trinidad and Tobago, Uruguay, and Venezuela; **MENA**: *Middle East and North Africa*) Algeria, Djibouti, Egypt, Arab Republic, Jordan, Lebanon, Libya, Morocco, Syrian Arab Republic, Tunisia, and Yemen; **EAP**: (*East Asia and Pacific*) Indonesia, Lao PDR, Micronesia, Philippines, Samoa, Timor Leste, Tonga, Vanuatu, and Vietnam; **SA**: (*South Asia*) Afghanistan, Bangladesh, Bhutan, India, Iran, Maldives, Nepal, Pakistan, and Sri Lanka; **SSA**: (*Sub-Saharan Africa*) Angola, Benin, Botswana, Burkina Faso, Burundi, Cabo Verde, Cameroon, Chad, Comoros, Congo, Cote d'Ivoire, Eritrea, Ethiopia, Gabon, Gambia, Ghana, Guinea, Guinea-Bissau, Kenya, Lesotho, Liberia, Madagascar, Malawi, Mali, Mauritania, Mauritius, Mozambique, Namibia, Niger, Nigeria, Rwanda, Sao Tome and Principe, Senegal, Somalia, South Africa, South Sudan, Sudan, Swaziland, Tanzania, Togo, Uganda, Zambia, and Zimbabwe

CA) appear at the top, with 32 connections per 100 people. Eastern Europe and Central Asia (ECA) and LAC are far behind, with 19 and 10 connections per 100 people, respectively. Middle East and North Africa (MENA), East Asia and the Pacific (EAP), South Asia (SA), and Sub-Saharan Africa (SSA) report 5, 4, 3, and 1 connections per 100 habitants, respectively.

With respect to ICT diffusion in firms, an international comparison is much more complicated because it requires precise and comparable data, which is not easy to find. Nevertheless, a first approximation can be made using data from the World Bank Enterprise Surveys (WBES). The WBES have been conducted in various waves across 135 developing countries since 2002, using face-to-face interviews with top managers, covering a broad range of topics relevant to business, including innovation, ICT, access to finance, corruption, infrastructure, crime, competition, and performance measures. However, a full set of ICT-related questions was only introduced in the 2010 round and not in all the surveyed countries.[2]

For this reason, a comparison is possible only among those regions that have enough countries reporting data on ICT access. Fig. 4.2 shows the level of broadband diffusion, email use, and website availability for the surveyed firms, by region.

LAC emerges as the region among the developing countries with the highest level of ICT penetration, with almost 85% of its firms indicating that they have a high-speed internet connection, 90% using email to communicate with clients or suppliers,[3] and 60% having their own website. This analysis shows that, overall, ICT diffusion among firms in LAC appears generally to be higher than in other developing regions, though we are cautious in our assessment of these results. First, the WBES does not provide information about adopting and using more advanced ICTs, only basic technologies that firms in advanced economies take for granted, and thus the resulting picture could be too optimistic. Second, WBES data on ICT diffusion in firms are not always consistent with ITU data on diffusion in society, raising some concerns about data reliability. For example, Fig. 4.3 shows the correlation between the percentage of households with a fixed broadband connection (ITU data) and the percentage of firms with broadband on their premises (WBES data) in LAC. It is clear that in some cases the two indicators substantially differ. For example, Panama shows a high level of household connection (31.6%), much higher than most Central American countries (with the exception of Costa Rica), but has the lowest percentage of firms with a broadband connection, even lower than Nicaragua and Honduras.

Even considering these caveats, the WBES provide excellent observations to empirically study ICT dynamics in LAC firms because they are the first attempt to collect related data with the same questionnaire and sampling across all countries. After data cleaning, the analysis included in this chapter is based on a 2010 cross-section dataset of 10,477 enterprises from 19 LAC countries,[4] with Mexico (13.7%), Argentina (9.6%), and

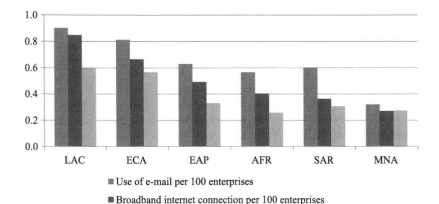

Fig. 4.2 ICT diffusion in enterprises (2009–2010)

Source: Authors' elaboration based on WBES data

Notes: Simple average of available countries in each region. **LAC**: Antigua and Barbuda, Argentina, Bahamas, Barbados, Belize, Bolivia, Brazil, Chile, Colombia, Costa Rica, Dominica, Dominican Republic, Ecuador, El Salvador, Grenada, Guatemala, Guyana, Honduras, Jamaica, Mexico, Nicaragua, Panama, Paraguay, Peru, Saint Lucia, St. Kitts & Nevis, St. Vincent & the Grenadines, Suriname, Trinidad and Tobago, Uruguay, and Venezuela; **ECA**: (*Eastern Europe and Central Asia*) Armenia, Azerbaijan, Bosnia and Herzegovina, Bulgaria, Czech Republic, Estonia, Fyr Macedonia, Hungary, Kazakhstan, Kosovo, Kyrgyz Republic, Latvia, Lithuania, Moldova, Mongolia, Montenegro, Poland, Romania, Russia, Serbia, Slovak Republic, and Slovenia; **EAP**: (*East Asia and Pacific*) Fiji, Indonesia, Lao PDR, Micronesia, Philippines, Samoa, Timor Leste, Tonga, Vanuatu, and Vietnam; **AFR**: (*Africa*) Angola, Benin, Botswana, Burkina Faso, Cameroon, Cape Verde, Chad, Congo, Democratic Republic of the Congo, Eritrea, Gabon, Ivory Coast, Lesotho, Liberia, Madagascar, Malawi, Mali, Mauritius, Niger, Sierra Leone, and Togo

Chile (8.6%) being the most represented in terms of observations. The resulting sample includes enterprises of various sizes[5] from both the manufacturing and services sectors. In Table 4.1, we provide the sample's main descriptive statistics.

ICT ADOPTION

From a theoretical point of view, several models have been developed to explain patterns of ICT adoption among firms, building on the existing body of research on technology diffusion. Karshenas and Stoneman (1995) proposed a general conceptual framework, distinguishing four sub-models: Epidemic, rank (probit), stock, and order.

Table 4.1 Descriptive statistics

Variables	Mean	Standard deviation	Minimum	Maximum	Observations
Broadband	0.848	0.359	0	1	10,440
E-mail	0.904	0.295	0	1	10,462
Website	0.630	0.483	0	1	10,460
Internet use for purchases	0.626	0.484	0	1	10,440
Internet use to deliver services	0.605	0.489	0	1	10,440
Internet use for research	0.674	0.469	0	1	10,440
Internet for purchases, to deliver services, and for research	0.429	0.495	0	1	10,440
Broadband intensity (scale)	2.752	1.426	0	4	10,440
Log (productivity)	10.426	1.200	4.06	16.34	8431
New product	0.574	0.495	0	1	6155
New process	0.483	0.500	0	1	6147
Log (capital per worker)	8.706	1.546	1.09	14.95	4293
Micro firm	0.219	0.414	0	1	10,440
Small firm	0.394	0.489	0	1	10,440
Medium firm	0.277	0.448	0	1	10,440
Skilled human capital	16.864	21.635	0	100	10,165
Age of firm	25.898	20.036	1	185	10,330
Foreign direct investment (FDI)	0.129	0.336	0	1	10,477
Exporter	0.162	0.369	0	1	10,477
Investment	0.555	0.497	0	1	10,415
Capital city	0.497	0.500	0	1	10,477

Source: Authors' elaboration based on WBES data.

Early research introduced epidemic models based on the concept that the diffusion of a technology depends on information about its availability (Mansfield 1963). These models predict that the diffusion of new technology gradually increases over time, as adoption costs and risks decline, based on learning effects among firms. The process is similar to the spread of epidemics: early adopters disseminate information, then other firms adopt the technology and release further information, and so on until the saturation point. While epidemic models are traditionally based on information spillovers from users to non-users, for ICT another dimension is very relevant: network effects. In fact, the gains that derive from ICT adoption—as well as the opportunity costs of not adopting—increase with the number of users of the technology, causing a snowball effect.

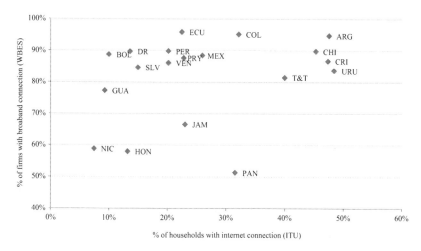

Fig. 4.3 ICT diffusion in LAC (latest available year)

Source: Authors' elaboration based on ITU and WBES data

However, without considering firm heterogeneity, these models are not sufficient to explain fully variations in adoption rates among firms. Another group of theoretical models (rank or probit models) was developed with increasing emphasis on the link between different firm characteristics, differentials in expected or potential returns, and adoption decisions.

Finally, two game theory approaches model the returns on adoption depending on the number of previous adopters and the order of adoption. Stock models are based on the assumption that the benefit of adoption decreases as the number of previous adopters increases. Then, for any given adoption cost there is a number of adopters beyond which adoption is not profitable. On the other hand, order models reflect the advantages of early adopters, assuming that returns on adoption depend on the position of a firm in the order of adoption because of advantages such as obtaining better skilled labor or geographic locations.

It is important to stress that, even if the majority of the literature has focused on the demand side, technology diffusion dynamics are the result of the interaction between demand-side and supply-side factors. The models usually assume declining prices over time, but do not relate it to supply-side forces. Moreover, and quite surprisingly, empirical research has mainly focused on inter-firm diffusion—the access a firm has to a new technology—and has neglected intra-firm diffusion—the extent of technology usage in the firm.

Model Specification and Results

In this chapter, in line with recent literature, we empirically test the validity of the rank and epidemic[6] models in LAC firms, focusing on inter- and intra-firm ICT diffusion. To identify determinants of inter-firm diffusion, we estimate the following equation to model the probability a firm will adopt ICT:

$$\Pr(\text{ICTADOPTION} = 1) =$$
$$\text{F}(\alpha + \beta_0 * RankEffects + \beta_1 * LocationEffects$$
$$+ \beta_2 * \text{EpidemicEffects} + \beta_3 * \text{CountryEffects}$$
$$+ \beta_4 * \text{SectorEffects}) \tag{4.1}$$

To measure inter-firm ICT adoption, we consider two dichotomic indicators: broadband, using the value 1 if a firm has a high-speed internet connection on its premises, and website, using the value 1 if a firm has its own website. Then, we estimate two equations where broadband and website are the dependent variables.

As for rank effects, we first consider the size of the firm, grouping them into four categories: micro (10 or less employees), small (11–50 employees), medium (51–250), and large (251 or more). Size is generally considered relevant to the adoption of new technologies. Given that larger firms have fewer financial constraints and are usually less risk adverse, supposedly they are in a better position to withstand the costs and risks associated with new technologies.[7] Empirical evidence generally supports this hypothesis (Teo and Tan 1998; Fabiani et al. 2005; Haller and Siedschlag 2011; Giunta and Trivieri 2007).[8] We use large firms as our reference group.

We then consider the firm's age as a proxy for its technological experience (age of firm), and we look at the percentage of workers with at least a bachelor's degree as a proxy for human capital (skilled human capital). The relationship between a skilled workforce and ICT adoption is relatively clear in the literature,[9] which shows that a more educated workforce facilitates the early adoption of technologies (Chun 2003) and that the demand for skilled workers increases with the use of new technologies (Bartel and Sicherman 1999); however, the role of firm age is not theoretically straightforward. In fact, on the one hand, older firms are better equipped to assess the risks and benefits of introducing new technologies, while, on the other hand, younger enterprises are believed to be more flexible in dealing with the organizational changes that come with adopting ICTs. The empirical evidence is inconclusive, in general finding either a non-significant (Bayo-Moriones and Lera-Lopez 2007; Giunta and Trivieri 2007) or negative impact (Haller and Siedschlag 2011; Gambardella and Torrisi 2001) of age on ICT diffusion.

The next two variables we consider are exposure to international competition (exporter) and the need to be early adopters of ICT to maintain fluid communication with foreign partners (foreign direct investment, or FDI). Exporter is a dummy variable, taking the value 1 if at least 10% of the firm's sales are exported. FDI is also a dummy variable, taking the value 1 if at least 10% of the firm's capital is foreign-owned. In general, empirical evidence shows that firms that engage in foreign trade are more likely to adopt new technologies (Hollenstein 2004; Lucchetti and Sterlacchini 2004; Haller and Siedschlag 2011), and that those foreign-owned tend to be early adopters, contributing to technology diffusion in the country where they operate (Keller 2004; Narula and Zanfei 2005).

Capital city, a dummy variable that takes the value 1 if the firm is located in a capital or in a city with more than one million inhabitants, controls for location effects. The empirical literature demonstrates the influence of an urban or densely populated location on ICT adoption. Many arguments support this hypothesis, such as the proximity of suppliers, technology prices, and the availability of a qualified labor force (Galliano et al. 2001; Karlsson 1995).

The epidemic variable calculates the percentage of other firms that have adopted a technology (broadband or website) in the same country and sector. This variable tests for the existence of network effects for ICT diffusion, following the hypothesis that existing technology adopters have positive spillover effects on firms considering adoption. In other words, firms operating in more digitally advanced countries and sectors may face reduced costs and increased benefits. Finally, in all estimations we include country and three-digit sector dummy variables to control for unobserved industry- and region-specific effects.

To estimate equation 4.1 for the two indicators (broadband and website), we use a sequential approach. First we apply a probit model, which is a common econometric approach that uses maximum likelihood estimation. This approach is not always fully efficient because it does not consider the correlation between firm choices in adopting broadband and having a website. Therefore, to consider this possible correlation, we complement the probit analysis with a bivariate probit (biprobit) model (Greene 2003).

We show the marginal effects resulting from our estimations with pro-bit in Table 4.2. Columns 1 and 2 present results for broadband connec-tion, while columns 3 and 4 refer to having a website. Columns 1 and 3 correspond to the basic model, while columns 2 and 4 add the capital city and epidemic variables.

Table 4.2 Determinants of broadband connection and using firm website: probit estimations

Variables	Broadband connection		Website	
	Basic	Inclusive	Basic	Inclusive
	(1)	(2)	(3)	(4)
Micro firm	−0.2718***	−0.2666***	−0.4782***	−0.4697***
	(0.0182)	(0.0182)	(0.0198)	(0.0198)
Small firm	−0.1433***	−0.1403***	−0.3084***	−0.3040***
	(0.0181)	(0.0180)	(0.0195)	(0.0194)
Medium firm	−0.0609***	−0.0588***	−0.1172***	−0.1155***
	(0.0188)	(0.0186)	(0.0203)	(0.0203)
Skilled human capital	0.0022***	0.0022***	0.0023***	0.0023***
	(0.0002)	(0.0002)	(0.0002)	(0.0002)
Age of firm	0.0007***	0.0007***	0.0014***	0.0014***
	(0.0002)	(0.0002)	(0.0002)	(0.0002)
FDI	0.0138	0.0126	0.0612***	0.0594***
	(0.0122)	(0.0122)	(0.0155)	(0.0155)
Exporter	0.0868***	0.0876***	0.1115***	0.1120***
	(0.0146)	(0.0145)	(0.0148)	(0.0148)
Capital city	n.a.	0.0233***	n.a.	0.0458***
		(0.0070)		(0.0094)
Epidemic (broadband)	n.a.	0.1193***	n.a.	n.a.
		(0.0326)		
Epidemic (website)	n.a.	n.a.	n.a.	0.1517***
				(0.0365)
Country dummies	Yes	Yes	Yes	Yes
Sector dummies	Yes	Yes	Yes	Yes
Log likelihood	−3010	−2999	−4880	−4859
Pseudo R-squared	0.278	0.281	0.232	0.236
Observations	9583	9583	9583	9583

Source: Authors' elaboration based on WBES data

Notes: "Inclusive" includes the capital city and epidemic variables. Estimated marginal effects from the probit regression. Delta-method standard errors are in parentheses. * Coefficient is statistically significant at the 10% level, ** at the 5% level, *** at the 1% level; no asterisk means the coefficient is not different from zero with statistical significance. n.a. = not applicable.

We present the biprobit estimates in Table 4.3, with the basic estimations displayed on the left side and those with capital city and epidemic variables included on the right side.

Table 4.3 Determinants of broadband connection and using firm website: biprobit estimations

Variables	Basic estimations		Incl. capital city and epidemic variables	
	Broadband	Website	Broadband	Website
	(1)	(2)	(3)	(4)
Micro firm	-0.2656***	-0.4708***	-0.2605***	-0.4625***
	(0.0175)	(0.0192)	(0.0175)	(0.0192)
Small firm	-0.1409***	-0.3041***	-0.1381***	-0.2998***
	(0.0174)	(0.0189)	(0.0174)	(0.0188)
Medium firm	-0.0621***	-0.1161***	-0.0598***	-0.1143***
	(0.0181)	(0.0197)	(0.0180)	(0.0196)
Skilled human capital	0.0021***	0.0024***	0.0020***	0.0024***
	(0.0002)	(0.0002)	(0.0002)	(0.0002)
Age of firm	0.0007***	0.0013***	0.0007***	0.0013***
	(0.0002)	(0.0002)	(0.0002)	(0.0002)
FDI	0.0121	0.0557***	0.0109	0.0538***
	(0.0117)	(0.0150)	(0.0117)	(0.0150)
Exporter	0.0818***	0.1057***	0.0822***	0.1064***
	(0.0141)	(0.0141)	(0.0140)	(0.0141)
Capital city	n.a.	n.a.	0.0226***	0.0454***
			(0.0068)	(0.0092)
Epidemic (broadband)	n.a.	n.a.	0.1073***	n.a.
			(0.0303)	
Epidemic (website)	n.a.	n.a.	n.a.	0.1487***
				(0.0341)
Country dummies	Yes	Yes	Yes	Yes
Sector dummies	Yes	Yes	Yes	Yes
Log likelihood	-7825		-7796	
Rho	0.4448		0.4435	
	(0.0206)		(0.0207)	
/Athrho	0.4779***		0.4766***	
	(0.0257)		(0.0257)	
Observations	9950		9950	

Source: Authors' elaboration based on WBES data

Notes: Estimated marginal effects from the biprobit regression. Delta-method standard errors in parentheses. * Coefficient is statistically significant at the 10% level, ** at the 5% level, *** at the 1% level; no asterisk means the coefficient is not different from zero with statistical significance. n.a. = not applicable

Additionally, to check for sectoral differences, we split the sample between manufacturing and services. In Table 4.4, we report the marginal effects from these disaggregated biprobit estimations.

Overall, the results appear robust for all the specifications and are generally in line with the findings of previous studies. The smaller the

Table 4.4 Determinants of broadband connection and using firm website: biprobit estimations by sector

Variables	Manufacturing		Services	
	Broadband	Website	Broadband	Website
	(1)	(2)	(3)	(4)
Micro firm	−0.2545***	−0.4702***	−0.2673***	−0.4496***
	(0.0229)	(0.0247)	(0.0271)	(0.0310)
Small firm	−0.1447***	−0.3021***	−0.1233***	−0.2990***
	(0.0227)	(0.0240)	(0.0269)	(0.0307)
Medium firm	−0.0490**	−0.1264***	−0.0699**	−0.0928***
	(0.0240)	(0.0246)	(0.0274)	(0.0325)
Skilled human capital	0.0017***	0.0030***	0.0022***	0.0019***
	(0.0003)	(0.0004)	(0.0003)	(0.0003)
Age of firm	0.0005**	0.0015***	0.0009***	0.0008**
	(0.0002)	(0.0003)	(0.0003)	(0.0004)
FDI	0.0047	0.0141	0.0225	0.1047***
	(0.0166)	(0.0199)	(0.0171)	(0.0225)
Exporter	0.0871***	0.0957***	0.0446	0.1637***
	(0.0151)	(0.0150)	(0.0332)	(0.0408)
Capital city	0.0278***	0.0336***	0.0161	0.0647***
	(0.0087)	(0.0119)	(0.0110)	(0.0148)
Epidemic (broadband)	0.0148	n.a.	0.1586***	n.a.
	(0.0364)		(0.0604)	
Epidemic (website)	n.a.	0.0544	n.a.	0.1576**
		(0.0429)		(0.0612)
Country dummies	Yes	Yes	Yes	Yes
Sector dummies	Yes	Yes	Yes	Yes
Log likelihood	−4645		−3092	
Rho	0.407		0.51	
Observations	6147		3803	

Source: Authors' elaboration based on WBES data

Notes: Estimated marginal effects from the biprobit regression. Delta-method standard errors in parentheses. * Coefficient is statistically significant at the 10% level, ** at the 5% level, *** at the 1% level; no asterisk means the coefficient is not different from zero with statistical significance. n.a. = not applicable

firm, the less likely it is to have a broadband connection or a functioning website. The level of skilled human capital appears to be an important determinant of adoption, confirming the importance of having a skilled workforce to increase a firm's capacity to absorb technology. Interestingly, firm age showed a positive and significant—although small—coefficient. This result seems to demonstrate that previous technological experience is more important for ICT adoption by LAC firms than flexibility to organizational changes. These results hold for the entire sample, as well as for both the manufacturing and services sub-samples.

Also, in general, exposure to competition in foreign markets, as measured by the exporter dummy, has a positive impact on the probability a firm will adopt ICTs, with the only exception of broadband adoption in the case of exporters in the services sector. On the contrary, we do not find any significant effect of foreign ownership on broadband connection, although it seemed to be important for having a website, especially in the services sector.

Finally, the estimations show the key role that location and epidemic effects play in ICT adoption. In all the specifications using the entire sample, a firm operating in a country and sector where there is a larger share of firms using ICTs has a bigger probability of adopting them. However, when the sample is split by sector, the epidemic variable loses significance for manufacturing firms, suggesting that epidemic effects can be particularly important for firms in the services sector. Moreover, the firms that are located in a capital or in a city with more than one million inhabitants are, in general, more likely to have both a broadband connection and a website.[10] This may reflect lower technology costs, higher availability of trained human capital, and potential partners (i.e. suppliers and clients) having a higher level of connectivity. If we adopt an extended concept of epidemic effects, not limited to firms operating in the same sector, this result complements the importance of the level of technological assimilation of the environment in which a firm is operating in order to determine its pace of adoption.

The basic model of intra-firm diffusion does not differ substantially from the inter-firm one, given that the level of penetration is supposed to depend on epidemic and rank effects. The first major difference is related to the form of the dependent variables. The WBES collect data on three different categories of internet use: (i) making purchases, (ii) delivering services, and (iii) researching or developing ideas for new products and services. In order to measure intra-firm diffusion, we build an indicator related to the availability of broadband and the number of internet activities performed by a firm. Our dependent variable, intra-firm, is an indicator using values 0, 1, 2, 3, and 4. And, we use an ordered probit model, which is appropriate if the dependent variables are measured on an ordinal scale.

However, this approach fails to take into account the correlation between broadband adoption and intensity of internet use. In fact, broadband adoption entirely determines the extent of use, selecting firms that have the capabilities to perform activities. Therefore, in order to disentangle the determinants of inter- and intra-firm adoption, it is necessary first to complement the analysis with alternative econometric approaches, taking into account this sample selection. Then, we generalize the Heckman sample selection model (Heckman 1979; Van de Ven and Van Praag 1981), specifying an ordered probit with sample selection, where the first stage equation is the broadband inter-firm diffusion equation, including both location and epidemic effects.

Table 4.5 reports the estimated coefficients resulting from the ordered probit model and the ordered probit with sample selection, for the whole sample and disaggregated by sector. In general, the estimates show a similar pattern to those for inter-firm diffusion. Skilled human capital, age of firm, and being an exporter remain important drivers of ICT diffusion in most specifications. However, there are some interesting differences. First, in the ordered probit, firm size is negative and significant only for small and micro-firms, while the coefficient for medium firms is significant only for the services sector. Once we control for the sample selection, for manufacturing, all the size coefficients become smaller and not significant; for services, the coefficients also become smaller, but they lose significance only for medium firms. For manufacturing, size does not seem to matter for intensity of use once broadband is adopted. For services, the result seems to indicate a dimension threshold, above which size does not matter for intra-firm diffusion. Furthermore, we do not find any strong statistical evidence related to being located in a capital city, which suggests that location affects the decision to adopt broadband but not how extensively it is used. Finally, there is some evidence of a negative correlation between foreign ownership and intra-firm diffusion, but only in the manufacturing sector. This result is stronger in the ordered probit with sample selection model, which may be related to the fact that foreign investments in manufacturing in LAC are concentrated in low value-added activities. Therefore, ICTs are especially important for communication with headquarters, but not for research and relationships with providers and clients, the activities used to build the intensity index.

Table 4.5 Determinants of broadband intensity of use: ordered probit and ordered probit with sample selection estimations

Variables	Ordered probit			Ordered probit with sample selection		
	Whole sample	Manufacturing	Services	Whole sample	Manufacturing	Services
Micro firm	-0.8623***	-0.8576***	-0.8756***	-0.1545***	-0.1183	-0.2527**
	(0.0476)	(0.0617)	(0.0773)	(0.0596)	(0.0744)	(0.1212)
Small firm	-0.3081***	-0.2928***	-0.3312***	-0.1101**	-0.0565	-0.1993**
	(0.0424)	(0.0543)	(0.0699)	(0.0470)	(0.0600)	(0.0818)
Medium firm	-0.0683	-0.0081	-0.1667**	-0.0368	0.0005	-0.1076
	(0.0418)	(0.0523)	(0.0703)	(0.0456)	(0.0570)	(0.0791)
Skilled human capital	0.0069***	0.0067***	0.0071***	0.0021***	0.0031***	0.0018
	(0.0007)	(0.0010)	(0.0009)	(0.0007)	(0.0010)	(0.0011)
Age of firm	0.0026***	0.0021***	0.0035***	0.0016**	0.0016*	0.0018
	(0.0006)	(0.0008)	(0.0011)	(0.0007)	(0.0008)	(0.0012)
FDI	-0.0649*	-0.1146**	0.0102	-0.0771*	-0.1154**	-0.0194
	(0.0374)	(0.0498)	(0.0570)	(0.0394)	(0.0513)	(0.0621)
Exporter	0.2291***	0.2322***	0.2115**	0.1069***	0.0872**	0.1999***
	(0.0356)	(0.0396)	(0.0913)	(0.0375)	(0.0421)	(0.0947)
Capital city	0.0377	0.0172	0.0644	-0.0385	-0.0852**	0.0307
	(0.0261)	(0.0343)	(0.0412)	(0.0283)	(0.0369)	(0.0455)
Country dummies	Yes	Yes	Yes	Yes	Yes	Yes
Sector dummies	Yes	Yes	Yes	Yes	Yes	Yes

(continued)

Table 4.5 (continued)

Variables	Ordered probit			Ordered probit with sample selection		
	Whole sample	Manufacturing	Services	Whole sample	Manufacturing	Services
Thresholds						
	-1.3715***	-1.3274***	-1.9148***	-1.5240***	-1.4638***	-2.0654***
	(0.1029)	(0.1096)	(0.1730)	(0.1291)	(0.1396)	(0.1851)
	-1.1731***	-1.1381***	-1.7011***	-0.6470***	-0.5941***	-1.1625***
	(0.1034)	(0.1105)	(0.1730)	(0.1276)	(0.1376)	(0.1807)
	-0.6678***	-0.6387***	-1.1819***	0.1701	0.214	-0.3148*
	(0.1033)	(0.1104)	(0.1726)	(0.1283)	(0.1387)	(0.1800)
	0.0346	0.0607	-0.4672***	n.a	n.a	n.a
	(0.1032)	(0.1104)	(0.1721)			
Log likelihood	-12,736	-7718	-4984	-12,533	-7613	-4880
Rho	n.a.	n.a.	n.a.	-0.513	-0.571	-0.324
				(0.0783)	(0.0876)	(0.2138)
/Athrho	n.a.	n.a.	n.a.	-0.5669***	-0.6488***	-0.3358
				(0.1063)	(0.1299)	(0.2388)
Observations	9958	6148	3810	9958	6148	3810
Observation censored	n.a.	n.a.	n.a.	1514	865	649
Observation uncensored	n.a.	n.a.	n.a.	8444	5283	3161

Source: Authors' elaboration based on WBES data

Notes: Estimated coefficients from ordered probit regression and ordered probit with sample selection. Robust standard errors in parentheses. * Coefficient is statistically significant at the 10% level, ** at the 5% level, *** at the 1% level; no asterisk means the coefficient is not different from zero with statistical significance. n.a. = not applicable

BROADBAND, INNOVATION, AND PRODUCTIVITY

The economic impact of ICT has received considerable attention in the literature, and many firm-level empirical studies have identified multiple ways ICT can have a positive effect on performance. For example, Mack and Faggian (2013) stated that ICTs have dramatically changed every aspect of modern life, including business management, which has been revolutionized by the new capacity of finding, sharing, and storing information.

In fact, ICTs have the potential to have substantial impact on the internal communication processes of a firm. For example, it is usually argued that ICTs can help reduce internal communication costs (Jorgenson 2001), allowing quicker information processing, lower coordination costs, fewer supervisors (reduction in labor costs), and easier decision-making (Cardona et al. 2013; Arvanitis and Loukis 2009; Atrostic et al. 2004; Gilchrist et al. 2001). In turn, reduced communication costs can spur additional investments (Colecchia and Schreyer 2002).

Moreover, ICTs may enable development of new processes and new work practices (Mack and Faggian 2013), and facilitate substantial firm restructuring (Brynjolfsson and Hitt 2000), making internal processes more flexible and rational, and reducing capital requirements through better equipment utilization and inventory reduction. These improvements may also allow firms to improve the quality of their outputs.

Also, adopting ICTs opens the possibility of better external communication channels with suppliers, clients, and other firms, facilitating innovation processes, arranging new distribution systems, and prompting knowledge spillovers across firms and regions (Czernich et al. 2011). Cheaper information dissemination can facilitate the adoption of new technologies devised elsewhere. As knowledge is increasingly becoming crucial for economic activity, ICTs have the potential to generate more efficient external collaboration and promote the creation of new knowledge (Forman and van Zeebroeck 2012). From a market perspective, ICT development can contribute to lower entry barriers and promote transparency, fostering competition and development of new products, processes, and business models (Czernich et al. 2011).

ICTs have become a substantial part of the modern business environment (Cardona et al. 2013), allowing factor productivity gains in industries that are ICT intensive. Recent empirical research has found extensive evidence about the impact of ICTs on innovation activities and performance.

Brynjolfsson and Saunders (2010) completed a comprehensive survey of ICT and innovation, and noted that the lower communication and replication costs provided by ICT can help firms innovate through new products. Bertschek et al. (2013) found that broadband exhibited a positive and significant impact on innovation activity in a sample of German firms through the period of expansion of digital subscriber lines (DSL) (2001–2003), and that its impact seemed to increase when they controlled for endogeneity. Polder et al. (2010) showed that ICT investment and usage constituted important drivers of innovation activity in the Dutch manufacturing and services sectors. Broadband was particularly relevant in the services sector, where it was found to be positively related to product, process, and organizational innovation, while in the manufacturing sector it was found to be significant only for product and organizational innovation. As for the LAC region, Santoleri (2013) provided evidence of the role of ICTs in enabling product and process innovation for a sample of Chilean firms. He also provided evidence that advanced ICT usage was needed to enhance the innovation-enabling role of the new technologies.

Regarding the impact of ICTs on productivity, several authors have found clear empirical evidence of a positive effect. In a seminal study, Brynjolfsson and Hitt (2003) explored the effect of computerization on productivity and output growth in a sample of US firms over the 1987–1994 period and found a positive relationship. This relationship has been confirmed over the years by several empirical studies in various contexts. For example, Hempell (2005) found significant evidence of the productivity effects of ICT using a generalized method of moments (GMM) estimator on panel data of German firms for 1994–1999. Arvanitis and Loukis (2009) and Kaiser and Bertschek (2004) confirmed this finding using data from Greece and Switzerland, and Germany, respectively. For the LAC region, Gutiérrez (2011) found a positive and significant effect of ICT investments on labor productivity in Colombian manufacturing enterprises.

However, the impact of ICT may be conditioned by certain characteristics of the internal context of a firm. In particular, some authors have highlighted the importance of complementary investments, pointing out that the productivity impact of ICT adoption may increase if combined with investment in human capital or internal restructuring (Brynjolfsson and Hitt 2000). Knowledge stock and skills are determinants of absorptive capacity, which may influence firm capabilities to make the most of new technologies (Benhabib and Spiegel 1994; Cohen and Levinthal 1990).

Organizational complements and intangible assets are considered crucial for ICT influence on productivity (Cardona et al. 2013). The economic impact of ICT may also depend on the sector of activity. In that sense, services-related firms may benefit more from ICT than companies in other sectors.[11]

External factors may also be important in determining impact. In fact, ICT effects can be larger if a firm has strong linkages with external organizations. Network externalities may also be present, whereby the benefits of having adopted a technology depend on the adoption decisions of other users. As for internet connection, the economic returns of connectivity should rise once the society achieves a certain threshold of connectivity penetration.

Clearly, the concept of ICTs includes a variety of different technologies, with different potential effects on firm performance. Recently, broadband internet connection has been indicated as one of the most effective ICTs because of its potential to enable a wide set of productivity-enhancing services. Some authors have argued that broadband has become a necessary part of the infrastructure for economic and social development, comparing it to historic advances such as railroads, roads, and electricity (Mack and Faggian 2013; Jordan and De León 2011).

In this section we contribute to the existing literature by empirically studying the impact of broadband adoption on firm performance in LAC, a region that has been understudied in relevant academic research. First we analyze the relationship of ICTs with innovation activities, and then we focus on their impact on firm productivity.

Broadband and Innovation

Empirical Model
To explore the link between broadband and innovation, we estimate the following equation, modeling the probability a firm will carry out an innovation activity:

$$\Pr\left[INNOVATION = 1\right] = f\left(\delta + \gamma\,Broadband + \beta_X X\right) \quad (4.2)$$

To measure innovation activity, we consider two binary variables: process innovation, which takes the value 1 if a firm has introduced a new or significantly improved process to produce or supply products over the previous three years; and product innovation, which takes the value 1 if the firm has introduced a new or significantly improved product (goods or services) over the previous three years. Broadband is a dummy variable that takes the value 1 if the firm has a high-speed internet connection on its premises.

We include control variable X to account for other factors that may influence innovation activity at the firm level. As in the case of technology diffusion, we use the percentage of workers with at least a bachelor's degree as a proxy for human capital (skilled human capital) and, as in Bertschek et al. (2013), we include investment to explain innovation. In this case, we approximate investment with a dummy variable that takes the value 1 if the firm has bought a fixed asset in the previous year, such as machinery, vehicles, equipment, land, or buildings.

We include four firm size variables (micro, small, medium, and large) since innovative activity may depend on the size of the enterprise (see also Chap. 2). Past research has found that big companies can amortize sunk costs related to innovation activity, exhibit more capacity for risk diversification, and have lower financial constraints (e.g. Acs and Audretsch 1988; Cohen and Klepper 1996). Moreover, we include exporter and FDI as control variables. It is possible that companies exposed to international markets face more pressure to innovate in order to remain competitive. FDI may also provide a channel for international knowledge spillovers, if the organizational structure and governance of the multinational companies allow it. In all estimations, we include country and three-digit sector dummy variables to control for unobserved industry- and country-specific effects.

In order to estimate the proposed equation, we first use a simple probit model. Nevertheless, this approach can provide biased results due to endogeneity (either deriving from reverse causality or unobservables). Given this, we complement the model with a bivariate recursive probit, instrumenting broadband access with two additional variables. The first instrument is the percentage of other firms that have adopted broadband in the same country and sector. This seems to be a suitable instrument, as individual firm performance is not expected to be related to industry averages (excluding the firm's own response), while these averages are expected to be positively related to a firm's decision to adopt broadband (see the "Data and Main Patterns of Internet Diffusion in LAC" section of this chapter). The second instrument is a variable that represents a firm's use of email. Email usage is supposed to be closely linked to broadband adoption, but not related to firm performance, because of its massive diffusion across all types of firms. Data analysis confirms these hypotheses.

Additionally, we extend the analysis by considering not only broadband adoption, but also the degree of exploitation of its potential. To do so, we run additional regressions including a dummy variable for the use of each of the following three internet activities: making purchases, delivering services to clients, and researching or developing ideas for new products and services. This information is collected through the survey only for the firms that have a broadband connection on their premises. Finally, we include an indicator of intensity of use, represented by a dummy variable taking the value 1 if a firm performs all three activities.

Estimation Results

Table 4.6 summarizes our estimation results for the determinants of innovation activities. As there is no direct interpretation of the coefficients of probit and biprobit models, we present average marginal effects, which represent the average percentage change in the probability of introducing a product or process innovation. Columns 1 through 4 display the results for product innovation, while columns 5 through 8 correspond to process innovation. For the biprobit estimations, the *Rho* term, which measures the correlation among the residuals of the innovation and broadband adoption equations, is negative and significant for all the specifications. This means that the biprobit model is probably more accurate and controls for the endogeneity caused by unobservables and for possible reverse causality.

The variable broadband shows a significant and positive impact on the probability of a firm introducing a product and a process innovation[12] in the specifications that do not consider different internet uses (columns 1, 3, 5, and 7).[13] In all these cases the significance level is at 1%. However, when we introduce the variables for different internet uses (columns 2, 4, 6, and 8), the coefficient and significance level of the broadband regressor decreases and some interesting results arise. First, as expected, internet use for research is clearly related to both product and process innovation. In all cases, the significance level is 1% and the average marginal effect is in the order of 11%.[14] Second, internet use to deliver services is not significant for product innovation but is positively correlated to process innovation. This result seems to confirm that the internet may promote innovation by enabling new distribution schemes. Third, internet use for purchases is not positively related to any innovation activity.

Table 4.6 Determinants of innovation

Variables	Product innovation				Process innovation			
	Probit		Biprobit		Probit		Biprobit	
	(1)	(2)	(3)	(4)	(5)	(6)	(7)	(8)
Broadband adoption	0.135*** (0.020)	-0.01 (0.030)	0.231*** (0.039)	0.086* (0.046)	0.128*** (0.021)	-0.026 (0.031)	0.268*** (0.042)	0.109** (0.050)
Internet use for purchases	n.a.	0.018 (0.020)	n.a.	0.014 (0.019)	n.a.	0.021 (0.020)	n.a.	0.021 (0.020)
Internet use to deliver services	n.a.	0.016 (0.020)	n.a.	0.012 (0.020)	n.a.	0.041** (0.021)	n.a.	0.037* (0.020)
Internet use for research	n.a.	0.119*** (0.020)	n.a.	0.110*** (0.020)	n.a.	0.110*** (0.021)	n.a.	0.106*** (0.021)
Internet for purchases, to deliver services, and for research	n.a.	0.057** (0.025)	n.a.	0.060*** (0.024)	n.a.	0.047* (0.025)	n.a.	0.045* (0.025)
Micro firm	-0.097*** (0.026)	-0.087*** (0.026)	-0.069*** (0.028)	-0.063** (0.028)	-0.071*** (0.027)	-0.061** (0.027)	-0.038 (0.028)	-0.032 (0.028)
Small firm	-0.041* (0.023)	-0.037* (0.023)	-0.034 (0.023)	-0.031 (0.022)	-0.072*** (0.023)	-0.069*** (0.023)	-0.068*** (0.023)	-0.066*** (0.023)
Medium firm	-0.041** (0.022)	-0.041* (0.022)	-0.040* (0.022)	-0.041* (0.022)	-0.069*** (0.022)	-0.069*** (0.022)	-0.074*** (0.022)	-0.075*** (0.022)
Skilled human capital	0.001*** (0.000)	0.001** (0.000)	0.001** (0.000)	0.001** (0.000)	0.001*** (0.000)	0.001*** (0.000)	0.001*** (0.000)	0.001** (0.000)
FDI	-0.002 (0.021)	0.008 (0.020)	-0.004 (0.020)	0.006 (0.020)	-0.036* (0.021)	-0.026 (0.021)	-0.037* (0.020)	-0.028 (0.020)

(continued)

Table 4.6 (continued)

Variables	Product innovation				Process innovation			
	Probit		Biprobit		Probit		Biprobit	
	(1)	(2)	(3)	(4)	(5)	(6)	(7)	(8)
Exporter	0.038**	0.031*	0.038**	0.031**	0.034**	0.027*	0.027*	0.021
	(0.016)	(0.016)	(0.016)	(0.016)	(0.016)	(0.016)	(0.016)	(0.016)
Investment	0.132***	0.122***	0.129***	0.120***	0.194***	0.185***	0.187***	0.179***
	(0.013)	(0.013)	(0.013)	(0.013)	(0.013)	(0.013)	(0.013)	(0.013)
Country dummies	Yes	Yes	Yes	Yes	Yes	Yes	Yes	Yes
Sector dummies	Yes	Yes	Yes	Yes	Yes	Yes	Yes	Yes
Log likelihood	-3636.74	-3574.01	-4973.88	-4915.17	-3720.49	-3661.42	-5054.89	-4999.6
Rho	n.a.	n.a.	-0.202**	-0.182**	n.a.	n.a.	-0.287***	-0.264***
			(0.069)	(0.069)			(0.073)	(0.075)
/Athrho	n.a.	n.a.	-0.205**	-0.184**	n.a.	n.a.	-0.295***	-0.270***
			(0.072)	(0.072)			(0.080)	(0.074)
Observations	5939	5939	5886	5886	5935	5935	5882	5882

Source: Authors' elaboration based on WBES data

Notes: Estimated marginal effects from the probit and biprobit regressions. Delta-method standard errors in parentheses. * Coefficient is statistically significant at the 10% level, ** at the 5% level, *** at the 1% level; no asterisk means the coefficient is not different from zero with statistical significance. n.a. = not applicable

As for the intensity indicator, in all cases it is positively related with innovation activity, which suggests that using broadband for a variety of activities is relevant beyond individual uses. In fact, firms that use the internet for all three activities increase their probability of innovating by approximately a further 5%.[15] Overall, these results seem to confirm the hypothesis that simple access to technology is not sufficient to improve performance, but that using technology adequately is necessary to exploit its potential fully.

Among control variables, being a large firm is positively associated with the probability of innovation. In fact, the micro, small, and medium firm coefficients are, in most cases, significant and negative. This shows that the baseline scenario (large firms) is the most propitious for both product and process innovation, confirming that size is an important determinant of innovation, as shown in Chap. 2. As for the coefficient associated with skilled human capital, it is always positive and significant, reflecting the importance of having internal skills to promote innovation. The coefficient of the exporter variable is also positive and significant in most cases, showing that companies competing in international markets have a higher propensity for innovation activity. Nevertheless, being foreign-owned does not seem to increase the probability of innovation in a firm, as the coefficients for FDI are either not significant or negative. A possible explanation for this is related to the fact that multinational enterprises usually concentrate R&D and innovation activities at headquarters and not in their subsidiaries abroad. Finally, the coefficient associated with investment is positive and significant at the 1% level.

Broadband and Productivity

Empirical Model
To analyze the impact of broadband on labor productivity, we use a model in which firms are supposed to produce according to a Cobb–Douglas production technology, with constant returns to scale on physical capital and labor:

$$\Upsilon = A K^{\alpha} L^{1-\alpha} \qquad (4.3)$$

where Υ represents output, K is physical capital stock, and L is labor. The term A represents total factor productivity (TFP), which may be affected by the availability of a broadband internet connection and by a vector of control variables X:

$$A = f\left(Broadband, X\right) \qquad (4.4)$$

Combining both expressions and applying logarithms to linearize the empirical specification:

$$\ln\left[\frac{Y}{L}\right] = \delta + \alpha \ln\left[\frac{K}{L}\right] + \gamma\, Broadband + \beta_X X \qquad (4.5)$$

Labor productivity is measured as sales per employee. Physical capital is approximated by the replacement value of machinery, vehicles, and equipment. Among controls X, we include some of the previously defined variables: firm size, skilled human capital, exporter, and FDI. We also include the previously defined product and process innovation dummy variables, considering that higher innovation activity is expected to increase productivity. In all estimations, we add country and three-digit sector dummy variables to control for unobserved effects. The unexplained part of the TFP is captured by the dummy variables and the constant term δ. As in the case of innovation activities, we run additional estimations considering the use of internet for specific activities and the intensity of use. We control for potential endogeneity by using an instrumental variable approach to complement the standard analysis. For that purpose, also in this case, the industry average of broadband adoption and email utilization at the firm level is used to instrument broadband.

Estimation Results

Table 4.7 summarizes the results of our estimations of the determinants of firm productivity. We present OLS results in columns 1 and 2, and the results for the instrumental variables in columns 3 and 4. To check the suitability of the instruments in the 2SLS estimation, we perform some hypothesis and robustness testing, which we also summarize in the table. Results of the Hansen test do not reject the exogeneity hypothesis, while the first-stage weak instrument test provides evidence of sufficient correlation between the instruments and the instrumented variable.

As for innovation activities, broadband has a positive and significant impact on the labor productivity of LAC firms, and its coefficient increases when we control for endogeneity. When we introduce internet

Table 4.7   Determinants of productivity

Variables	OLS estimations		2SLS estimations	
	(1)	(2)	(3)	(4)
Broadband adoption	0.306***	0.329***	0.551***	1.003***
	(0.047)	(0.072)	(0.112)	(0.294)
Internet use for purchases	n.a.	0.043	n.a.	−0.161*
		(0.044)		(0.096)
Internet use to deliver services	n.a.	−0.051	n.a.	−0.273***
		(0.045)		(0.104)
Internet use for research	n.a.	−0.059	n.a.	−0.329***
		(0.047)		(0.124)
Internet for purchases, to deliver services, and for research	n.a.	0.068	n.a.	0.352***
		(0.055)		(0.131)
Log (capital per worker)	0.193***	0.193***	0.192***	0.192***
	(0.011)	(0.011)	(0.011)	(0.011)
Investment	0.134***	0.131***	0.123***	0.126***
	(0.030)	(0.030)	(0.029)	(0.029)
Product innovation	0.056*	0.055*	0.049*	0.058*
	(0.030)	(0.030)	(0.030)	(0.030)
Process innovation	−0.044	−0.046	−0.051*	−0.042
	(0.028)	(0.028)	(0.028)	(0.028)
Micro firm	−0.525***	−0.514***	−0.468***	−0.449***
	(0.057)	(0.057)	(0.061)	(0.063)
Small firm	−0.356***	−0.352***	−0.340***	−0.329***
	(0.048)	(0.048)	(0.048)	(0.049)
Medium firm	−0.095**	−0.097**	−0.096**	−0.089*
	(0.046)	(0.046)	(0.045)	(0.046)
Skilled human capital	0.007***	0.007***	0.007***	0.007***
	(0.001)	(0.001)	(0.001)	(0.001)
FDI	0.295***	0.297***	0.303***	0.300***
	(0.050)	(0.050)	(0.049)	(0.048)
Exporter	0.208***	0.207***	0.201***	0.197***
	(0.034)	(0.034)	(0.034)	(0.034)
Constant	9.162***	9.150***	8.945***	8.825***
	(0.164)	(0.163)	(0.185)	(0.210)
Country dummies	Yes	Yes	Yes	Yes
Sector dummies	Yes	Yes	Yes	Yes
R^2	0.462	0.463	0.457	0.45
Observations	4215	4215	4189	4189
Hansen J			2.646	2.434
F-test weak instrument			204.728***	49.156***

Source: Authors' elaboration based on WBES data

Notes: Estimated coefficients from the regressions. Controls for sector and country fixed effects. Robust standard errors in parentheses. * Coefficient is statistically significant at the 10% level; ** at the 5% level; *** at the 1% level; no asterisk means the coefficient is not different from zero with statistical significance. n.a. = not applicable

use variables to the OLS estimation, broadband adoption remains positive and significant, while single activities and intensity do not appear to be relevant. For the instrumental variables estimation, we find a positive and significant coefficient for intensity of use, but a negative sign for individual uses. A possible explanation for these results may be related to the types of internet uses considered in the survey. On the one hand, such activities could have an impact on productivity only with a time lag. Since we are not working with time-series data, we cannot consider this. Also, the negative signs for some individual activities may be linked to the fact that these uses can generate short-term costs in terms of complementary investments, without immediate benefits. On the other hand—as the adoption indicator remains positive and highly significant in all estimations—the impact of broadband on productivity may be related to alternative uses, such as, for example, reducing internal communication costs, improving decision-making, developing new internal process or work practices, and firm restructuring. Finally, the positive and significant coefficient of the intensity indicator in the instrumental variable estimation confirms the importance of simultaneously using ICTs in various aspects of business activity in order to obtain productivity gains.

As expected, the coefficients for physical capital per worker and investment are positive and highly significant, as well as those for skilled human capital. The positive impact of exporter and FDI on productivity verifies the results in Chap. 9 ("International Linkages, Value-Added Trade, and Firm Productivity in Latin America and the Caribbean").[16] Results for innovation activity are also similar to those found in Chap. 2 ("Innovation Dynamics and Productivity").[17] Product innovation shows a positive and significant effect on productivity, while process innovation does not seem to be relevant. A possible explanation for the insignificance of process innovation may be a time lag necessary to translate these improvements into productivity gains. Another possibility is that part of the innovation effect is already captured by the broadband variable.

FINAL REMARKS

This chapter contributes to the empirical literature on technology diffusion and impact, identifying determinants of ICT adoption and exploring the link between broadband use, and innovation and productivity in LAC firms. We have analyzed both inter- and intra-firm diffusion patterns, finding that the ICT adoption behavior of LAC firms was characterized by a basic set of determinants that were quite robust across model estimations and different variable specifications. We found evidence of the presence of both epidemic and rank effects, where larger, older, skill-intensive, exporter, and urban firms were more likely to adopt ICTs. However, once ICTs were adopted, size and location lost importance in relation to intensity of use.

Additionally, we found robust empirical evidence for the positive relationship between broadband and firm performance. In particular, adopting broadband increased a firm's probability of innovating. This effect seemed mainly to be related to internet use in research and development and to the intensity of use, proxied by internet use for various activities. Further estimations provided evidence that broadband adoption and use were a source of productivity growth for LAC firms. These results are aligned with previous ICT literature in the developed world, which suggests that broadband plays an important role in enabling innovation and enhancing productivity.

The availability of novel empirical evidence specific to LAC may offer useful insights for policymakers in designing and implementing initiatives to foster productivity by increasing broadband connectivity. In fact, several countries in the region are investing considerable resources in initiatives such as the Plano Nacional de Banda Larga (National Broadband Plan) in Brazil or the Vive Digital (Live Digital) plan in Colombia.

However, our analysis was limited by data availability and should be complemented with future research. For example, the role of complementarities (e.g. human capital or organizational innovations) and network externalities in increasing the gains derived from ICT adoption remain largely understudied in the empirical literature on LAC. Further research could also look at the role of the national ICT industry. For example, the ability of a country to produce software adapted to the needs of local firms may play a role not only in decisions to adopt ICTs, but also on the impact of ICTs on firm performance once adopted. These extensions may provide a deeper understanding of the linkages between ICTs and firm performance, and on the characteristics that effective public policies should have.

Notes

1. Cathles et al. (2011) performed a time-distance analysis to explore the pace at which the Latin American region is filling the digital gap ascertained by the OECD, finding that it would take about 80 years to reach OECD levels of internet subscriptions.

2. For example, the 2009 Brazil survey included questions on broadband and ICT use in the services sector, but not in the manufacturing sector.
3. The higher percentage of firms using email compared to those having a broadband connection is explained by the fact that only a simple internet connection (not necessarily within the firm or broadband) is required for email.
4. Argentina, Bolivia, Chile, Colombia, Costa Rica, Dominican Republic, Ecuador, El Salvador, Guatemala, Honduras, Jamaica, Mexico, Nicaragua, Panama, Paraguay, Peru, Trinidad and Tobago, Uruguay, and Venezuela.
5. Of the observations, 11% are large firms (over 250 employees), 28% medium firms (51–250 employees), 39% small firms (11–50 employees), and 22% micro-firms (10 or less employees).
6. We could not test the stock and order models because of the lack of panel data.
7. See, for example, Chap. 8 of this book, where Presbitero and Rabellotti find that larger firms are more likely to request bank credit and less likely to be financially constrained.
8. Some studies have found a weak or insignificant correlation between size and ICT adoption, such as Lefebvre et al. (2005) and Love et al. (2005).
9. See for example, Arvanitis (2005); Bresnahan et al. (2002); Fabiani et al. (2005).
10. With the exception of the biprobit estimation in the services sector with broadband as independent variable.
11. Companies in the services sector tend to use ICTs more intensively. Additionally, Crandall et al. (2007) argued that the fact that individuals use broadband at home to connect to their offices or to telecommute makes ICTs more likely to be important in the services industries, such as finance, real estate, or miscellaneous business centers.
12. In Chap. 2, broadband access is found to be a significant determinant of product innovation and innovative sales, but not for process innovation. This inconsistency seems to be related to differences in the econometric approach and in the treatment of R&D as a control. However, overall, the results in Chap. 2 substantially confirm the important role .of broadband in explaining a firm's innovation performance.
13. It is interesting to notice that, once possible endogeneity between innovation and broadband is taken into account, the impact of broadband on innovation activity seems to be higher. This result is similar to what was found by Bertschek et al. (2013), and it may be explained by the fact that adopting broadband could induce a process of internal reorganization that may reduce the contribution of some existing practices to innovation activity.
14. To check the robustness of this result, we perform different estimations, adding alternative measures of R&D spending as controls. In all cases, internet use for research remains positive and significant.

15. The marginal effect for product innovation is slightly higher than for process innovation.
16. Although the magnitude of the coefficients is slightly different because of dissimilarities in the sample and control variables.
17. The difference in significance levels for product innovation compared with the results in Chap. 2 seems to be related to variances in the econometric approach and in the chosen control variables.

References

Acs, Z.J., and D. Audretsch. 1988. Innovation in Large and Small Firms: An Empirical Analysis. *American Economic Review* 78(4): 678–690.

Arvanitis, S. 2005. Computerization, Workplace Organization, Skilled Labour and Firm Productivity: Evidence for the Swiss Business Sector. *Economic of Innovation and New Technology* 4(4): 225–249.

Arvanitis, S., and E.N. Loukis. 2009. Information and Communication Technologies, Human Capital, Workplace Organization and Labour Productivity: A Comparative Study Based on Firm-Level Data for Greece and Switzerland. *Information Economics and Policy* 21(1): 43–61.

Atrostic, B.K., P. Boegh-Nielsen, K. Motohashi, and S. Nguyen. 2004. IT, Productivity and Growth in Enterprises: Evidence from New International Micro Data. In *The Economic Impact of ICT–Measurement, Evidence and Implications*, OECD (ed.). Paris: OECD.

Bartel, A.P., and N. Sicherman. 1999. Technological Change and Wages: An Interindustry Analysis. *Journal of Political Economy* 107(2): 285–325.

Bayo-Moriones, A., and F. Lera-Lopez. 2007. A Firm Level Analysis of Determinants of ICT Adoption in Spain. *Technovation* 27(6): 352–366.

Benhabib, J., and M. Spiegel. 1994. The Role of Human Capital in Economic Development: Evidence from Aggregate Cross-Country Data. *Journal of Monetary Economics* 34: 143–173.

Bertschek, I., D. Cerquera, and G.J. Klein. 2013. More Bits–More Bucks? Measuring the Impact of Broadband Internet on Firm Performance. *Information Economics and Policy* 25(3): 190–203.

Bresnahan, T.F., E. Brynjolfsson, and L.M. Hitt. 2002. Information Technology, Workplace Organization, and the Demand for Skilled Labor: Firm-Level Evidence. *Quarterly Journal of Economics* 117(1): 339–376.

Brynjolfsson, E., and L.M. Hitt. 2000. Beyond Computation: Information Technology, Organizational Transformation and Business Performance. *The Journal of Economic Perspectives* 14(4): 23–48.

Brynjolfsson, E., and L.M. Hitt. 2003. Computing Productivity: Firm-Level Evidence. *Review of Economics and Statistics* 85(4): 793–808.

Brynjolfsson, E., and A. Saunders. 2010. *Wired for Innovation*. Cambridge, MA: MIT Press.

Cardona, M., T. Kretschmer, and T. Strobel. 2013. ICT and Productivity: Conclusions from the Empirical Literature. *Information Economics and Policy* 25(3): 109–125.

Cathles, A., G. Crespi, and M. Grazzi. 2011. The Region's Place in the Digital World: A Tale of Three Divides. In *Development Connections. Unveiling the Impact of New Information Technologies*, A. Chong (ed.). Washington, DC: Inter-American Development Bank.

Chun, H. 2003. Information Technology and the Demand for Educated Workers: Disentangling the Impacts of Adoption Versus use. *Review of Economics and Statistics* 85: 1–8.

Cohen, W.M., and S. Klepper. 1996. Firm Size and the Nature of Innovation Within Industries: The Case of Process and Product R&D. *The Review of Economics and Statistics* 78(2): 232–243.

Cohen, W.M., and D. Levinthal. 1990. Absorptive Capacity: A new Perspective on Learning and Innovation. *Administrative Science Quarterly* 35(1): 128–152.

Colecchia, A., and P. Schreyer. 2002. ICT Investment and Economic Growth in the 1990s: Is the United States a Unique Case? A Comparative Study of Nine OECD Countries. *Review of Economic Dynamics* 5(2): 408–442.

Crandall, R.W., W. Lehr, and R. Litan. 2007. *The Effects of Broadband Deployment on Output and Employment: A Cross-Sectional Analysis of US Data*. Washington, DC: Brookings Institution Press.

Czernich, N., O. Falck, T. Kretschmer, and L. Woessmann. 2011. Broadband Infrastructure and Economic Growth. *The Economic Journal* 121(552): 505–532.

Fabiani, S., F. Schivardi, and S. Trento. 2005. ICT Adoption in Italian Manufacturing: Firm Level Evidence. *Industrial and Corporate Change* 14: 225–249.

Forman, C., and N. van Zeebroeck. 2012. From Wires to Partners: How the Internet has Fostered R&D Collaborations Within Firms. *Management Science* 58(8): 1549–1568.

Galliano, D., P. Roux, and M. Filippi. 2001. Organisational and Spatial Determinants of ICT Adoption: The Case of French Industrial Firms. *Environment and Planning A* 33(9): 1643–1663.

Gambardella, A., and S. Torrisi. 2001. Nuova industria o nuova economia? L'impatto dell'informatica sulla produttività dei settori manifatturieri in Italia. *Moneta e Credito* 54(213): 39–76.

Gilchrist, S., V. Gurbaxani, and R. Town. 2001. Productivity and the PC Revolution. *Working Paper*. Irvine, CA: Center for Research on Information Technology and Organizations, University of California.

Giunta, A., and F. Trivieri. 2007. Understanding the Determinants of Information Technology Adoption: Evidence from Italian Manufacturing Firms. *Applied Economics* 39: 1325–1334.

Greene, W.H. 2003. *Econometric Analysis*, 5th ed. Upper Saddle River, NJ: Prentice Hall.

Gutiérrez, L.H. 2011. ICT and Labor Productivity in Colombian Manufacturing Industry. In *ICT in Latin America: A Microdata Analysis*, ed. M. Balboni, S. Rovira, and S. Vergara. Santiago, Chile: United Nations.

Haller, S.A., and I. Siedschlag. 2011. Determinants of ICT Adoption: Evidence from Firm-Level Data. *Applied Economics* 43: 3775–3788.

Heckman, J. 1979. Sample Selection Bias as a Specification Error. *Econometrica* 47(1): 153–161.

Hempell, T. 2005. Does Experience Matter? Innovations and the Productivity of Information and Communication Technologies in German Services. *Economics of Innovation and New Technology* 14(4): 277–303.

Hollenstein, H. 2004. Determinants of the Adoption of Information and Communication Technologies: An Empirical Analysis Based on the Firm-Level Data for the Swiss Business Sector. *Structural Change and Economic Dynamics* 15(3): 315–342.

Jordan, V., and O. De León. 2011. Broadband and the Digital Revolution. In *Fast-Tracking the Digital Revolution: Broadband for Latin American and the Caribbean*, ed. V. Jordan, H. Galperín, and W. Peres. Santiago, Chile: United Nations.

Jorgenson, D.W. 2001. Information Technology and the US Economy. *American Economic Review* 91(1): 1–32.

Kaiser, U., and I. Bertschek. 2004. Productivity Effects of Organizational Change: Microeconometric Evidence. *Management Science* 50(3): 394–404.

Karlsson, C. 1995. Innovation Adoption, Innovation Networks and Agglomeration Economies. In *Technological Change, Economic Development and Space*, ed. C.S. Bertuglia, M.M. Fischer, and G. Preto. Berlin, Germany: Springer.

Karshenas, M., and P. Stoneman. 1995. Technological Diffusion. In *Handbook of the Economics of Innovation and Technological Change*, ed. P. Stoneman. Oxford: Blackwell.

Keller, W. 2004. International Technology Diffusion. *Journal of Economic Literature* 42: 752–782.

Lefebvre, L., E. Lefebvre, E. Elia, and H. Boek. 2005. Exploring B-to-B e-Commerce Adoption Trajectories in Manufacturing SMEs. *Technovation* 25: 1443–1456.

Love, P.E.D., Z. Irani, C. Standing, C. Lin, and J.M. Burn. 2005. The Enigma of Evaluation: Benefits, Costs and Risks of IT in Australian Small-Medium-Sized Enterprises. *Information and Management* 42: 947–964.

Lucchetti, R., and A. Sterlacchini. 2004. The Adoption of ICT Among SMEs: Evidence from an Italian Survey. *Small Business Economics* 23: 151–168.

Mack, E., and A. Faggian. 2013. Productivity and Broadband: The Human Factor. *International Regional Science Review* 36: 392–423.

Mansfield, E. 1963. Intra-Firm Rates of Diffusion of an Innovation. *Review of Economics and Statistics* 45: 348–359.

Narula, R., and A. Zanfei. 2005. Globalization of Innovation: The Role of Multinational Enterprises. In *The Oxford Handbook of Innovation*, ed. J. Fagerberg, D. Mowery, and R. Nelson. New York: Oxford University Press.

Oliner, S.D., and D. Sichel. 1994. Computers and Output Growth: How Big is the Puzzle? *Brookings Papers in Economic Activity* 2: 273–334.

Oliner, S.D., and D. Sichel. 2002. Information Technology and Productivity: Where Are We Now and Where Are We Going? *Federal Reserve Bank of Atlanta Review* 87(3): 15–44.

Polder, M., G. van Leeuwen, P. Mohnen, and W. Raymond. 2010. *Product, Process and Organizational Innovation: Drivers, Complementarity and Productivity Effects*. Maastricht, Netherlands: UNU-MERIT.

Santoleri, P. 2013. Diversity and Intensity of ICT Use Effects on Product Innovation: Evidence from Chilean Micro-Data. Paper presented at UNU-MERIT conference on *Micro Evidence on Innovation and Development*, Santiago de Chile.

Teo, T.S.H., and M. Tan. 1998. An Empirical Study of Adopters and Non-Adopters of the Internet in Singapore. *Information and Management* 34: 339–345.

Van de Ven, W.P.M., and B. Van Praag. 1981. The Demand for Deductibles in Private Health Insurance: A Probit Model With Sample Selection. *Journal of Econometrics* 17: 229–252.

CHAPTER 5

On-the-Job Training in Latin America and the Caribbean: Recent Evidence

Carolina González-Velosa, David Rosas, and Roberto Flores

The authors thank Rita Almeida, Gustavo Crespi, Matteo Grazzi, Carmen Pagés, Siobhan Pangerl, Carlo Pietrobelli, Graciana Rucci, Adam Szirmai, and Hong Tan for their valuable suggestions and comments, and Angela Zorro for her excellent research assistance. All errors are the sole responsibility of the authors.

One of the most urgent challenges faced by economies in Latin America and the Caribbean (LAC) is to increase the pace of their productivity growth, which is slow not only compared with developed countries but also with other developing and emerging economies (IDB 2013; OECD 2014). Sluggish productivity growth appears to be the main cause of the widening income gap between developed and LAC economies (IDB 2013; Pagés 2010; Daude and Fernández-Arias 2010).

As discussed in Chap. 1, increasing productivity in the region requires strategies that reallocate resources from less productive firms to more productive ones. Recent research, for example, recommends eliminating distortionary policies that artificially create incentives to invest in firms

---

C. González-Velosa • D. Rosas
Inter-American Development Bank
e-mail: cagonzalez@IADB.ORG • DAVIDRO@iadb.org

R. Flores
e-mail: floreslima@usa.net

© Inter-American Development Bank 2016
M. Grazzi and C. Pietrobelli (eds.), *Firm Innovation and Productivity in Latin America and the Caribbean*,
DOI 10.1057/978-1-349-58151-1_5

with low formality and productivity levels (e.g. IDB 2013; Pagés 2010; OECD 2014). However, efforts should also be made to increase within-firm efficiency through policies that improve production technologies and managerial processes and facilitate plant-level innovation. In this regard, a central issue concerns developing strategies that strengthen skill formation in the workforce. New evidence shows that a major obstacle faced by many firms in the region is the lack of adequate skills in the labor force. Enterprises have difficulties filling their vacancies and many individuals, especially younger people, cannot find jobs because of a mismatch between the skills learned in school and the skills demanded by the market (Bassi et al. 2012; Mourshad et al. 2011).

Thus, there is a clear need to reform the educational system to facilitate the transition of young people to the labor market. However, the agenda for change should not stop there, as human capital formation does not end with school. Approximately one-quarter of the human capital that individuals accumulate during their lives is achieved after the schooling process is completed (Heckman et al. 1998). Among the set of post-schooling investments, on-the-job training (OJT) can play an essential role. Employer-provided training is especially crucial to developing and updating skills in a context in which preferences and technologies change rapidly (Almeida et al. 2012). Through OJT, workers can be more productive, adapt more easily to technological change, make more efficient use of capital and machinery, and have a positive effect on the performance of their peers.

However, despite the potential of this type of investment, very little is known about OJT practices in LAC. Not only is there little evidence about the returns on OJT, but there is scant information on its basic characteristics, such as the frequency, content, and beneficiaries (Hunneus et al. 2011). This study aims to contribute to this literature by analyzing two business surveys, which, to our knowledge, are the only ones in LAC with comparable cross-country data on OJT practices: the Survey on Productivity and Human Resources Training in Establishments (EPFE by its Spanish acronym) and the World Bank Enterprise Surveys (WBES). Both surveys use a broad definition of OJT, encompassing all types of training offered by firms to their active workers.

Our contribution to the literature is threefold. First, we characterize OJT practices in the region by describing the basic characteristics of these investments. Both the EPFE and the WBES draw their samples from firms in registered directories, which restricts our analysis to the formal sector of the economy. Second, by examining correlates and determinants of the training decision, we provide suggestive evidence of the role of different market failures and constraints affecting OJT investments in LAC. Third, we provide additional evidence of the productivity effects of OJT practices in the region.

The rest of the chapter is organized as follows. We review the existing literature and then discuss the data and present stylized facts that characterize OJT in LAC. We present an analysis of the determinants of training investments among firms in the region, and then provide estimates of the wage and productivity effects of OJT. Finally, we make some concluding remarks.

Existing Literature

The literature on the impact of employer-provided training goes back to the seminal work of Becker (1964). This body of work states that, in a relatively flexible labor market, financing training and its effect on wages depends on the type of skills taught. *General training* enhances skills that are relevant not only to the firm in which the worker is employed but also to other firms. Since workers can increase productivity elsewhere, the market rewards this training with higher wages. In contrast, a worker's wage does not increase with training in *specific skills*, since such skills only increase productivity in the firm where he or she currently works.

Given that a worker with general skills may leave for another job at any time, the firm has no incentive to pay for training for these skills. Any productivity gains that the firm may benefit from will be offset by the higher wages that have to be paid to retain the worker. Therefore, general training is financed by workers indirectly through lower wages during the training period. Firms, on the other hand, have incentives to finance specific training as they may reap the benefits through larger productivity gains.[1]

Thus, in flexible labor markets, the rents from general training will be appropriated by the worker via higher wages, leaving firms with no incentive to invest in this kind of training. This appropriation problem may lead to investment in general skills training below the socially desirable level. This problem is the first of several market failures that could limit the decision to invest in OJT. Table 5.1 briefly enumerates market failures that affect OJT. A second market failure comes from credit constraints, which could limit the investments of employers who have difficulty accessing credit to finance OJT, even if such investments are profitable in the long run (see Chap. 8). Also, information problems can occur if employers do not have important information about key aspects of OJT, such as training techniques, training providers, benefits, and costs.

Table 5.1   Market failures that affect OJT

Restrictions to training supply	Appropriation problems	Firms do not have incentives to provide general (portable) skills training because they do not appropriate the rents of this training.
	Credit constraints	Firms have limited resources or credit to finance training, even if it is profitable in the long run.
	Information asymmetries and uncertainty	Firms have incomplete information or uncertainty about key aspects related to the benefits, costs, techniques, and providers of OJT.
Restrictions to training demand	Limits to the adoption of skill-intensive production technologies	Firms face barriers that limit the adoption of skill-intensive technologies, thereby reducing human capital requirements and, therefore, the demand for training (e.g., credit constraints, information asymmetries, lack of insurance, and externalities).
	Limits to the adoption of modern managerial practices	Credit constraints, lack of information, and labor regulations limit innovation in managerial practices and the adoption of high-performance workplace incentives that increase the productivity of training.

Source: Authors' elaboration

In addition to these three market failures, which limit the supply of employer-provided training, there are also failures that affect demand for OJT (Table 5.1). The first is barriers to technological adoption. Training demand is derived demand in that training requirements depend on production decisions. If a firm does not adopt innovative technologies that require more skilled personnel (for whatever reason), it will not need to invest in training. Thus, OJT investments are affected by a variety of market failures (credit, information, and externalities) that constrain adoption of more skill-intensive technologies and production systems. Similar considerations apply to possible constraints to the adoption of sound managerial practices. For example, credit constraints, lack of information, or labor regulations could limit a firm's ability to invest in modern managerial practices (e.g. performance incentives, profit sharing, analysis and feedback, mentoring, and employee participation in decision-making).[2]

Motivated by this framework, many researchers have tried to estimate the effects of employer-provided training. Most of the literature focuses on estimating private returns: studies that use firm data look at the effects on productivity, while studies that use employee data estimate wage effects. Very few studies directly compare results between general and specific training, given the difficulty of empirically observing the degree of specificity.

The current literature faces two important methodological challenges. First is the difficulty of measuring OJT. The definition of OJT can incorporate both formal training programs and informal learning-by-doing. Moreover, aspects such as duration or costs are difficult to calculate. Second, OJT can be associated with productivity and wages without reflecting a causal relationship. Other factors, such as the level of technological development or management skills, can make firms more productive. These same factors could be facilitating investment in OJT, creating a positive association between OJT and productivity that does not reflect a causal relationship. Likewise, the decision to invest in training a particular worker may be determined by attributes of the worker that impact productivity, such as, for example, educational attainment.

The vast majority of this literature uses data from developed countries and, despite the differences in the nature of the data and methodologies, studies generally show that OJT increases firm productivity and worker wages. However, there is no consensus on the magnitude of these effects. In order to address the endogeneity of the OJT decision, many studies use fixed effects or dynamic panel-data models which in most cases find large, positive impacts (e.g. Bartel 1994; Almeida and Carneiro 2008). A meta-analysis by Haelermans and Borghans (2012) reported that the average effect on wage returns of workers who received OJT is 2.6 % per course. Fewer studies exploit exogenous changes in the decision to estimate the effects of training and, in contrast, find relatively small impacts (e.g. Leuven and Oosterbeek 2004, 2008). However, as discussed by Bassanini et al. (2005), it is unclear whether the results from this group of studies are generalizable given that samples are small and specific.

In developing countries, the evidence is much scarcer, largely due to limitations on the availability and quality of data. Applying matching techniques on data from manufacturing firms in Kenya and Zambia, Rosholm et al. (2007) found very large positive effects: the average effect of receiving training in the year leading up to the survey was a 20 % increase in wages. Ibarrarán et al. (2009) estimated the impact of training with instrumental variables constructed from segments of firms with similar characteristics and, in general, found that training increased productivity. Finally, Rodríguez and Urzúa (2011) used data from administrative records to measure the impact on Chilean workers who received training as a result of the Chilean government's tax exemption program. They found that, in most cases, participation in the subsidy program had no positive impact on either the wages or the employment of participants. Only programs of longer duration produced marginal impacts, slightly above zero, but this type of course is only offered in 1% of cases. The authors also found no evidence of the effects of the program on hiring new workers.

Given the gaps in this literature, it is not surprising that there is practically no evidence regarding the social returns on OJT in LAC (Almeida et al. 2012). In fact, when it comes to social returns, even the literature for developed countries is lacking (Bassanini et al. 2005). This poses an important challenge for policy design.

DATA

We use the only two business surveys that, to the best of our knowledge, have cross-country comparable information on OJT in LAC. The first one is the WBES which has information about OJT for 12 countries in the region and longitudinal data for an important subset of countries.

The second one is the EPFE, which has been used in various countries in LAC with the support of the Inter-American Development Bank (IDB). This cross-sectional survey includes detailed questions about OJT that are not included in the WBES or other traditional business surveys, such as the components of OJT, its beneficiaries, and the sources of funding for training. At the time of writing, EPFE cross-sectional data was available for the Bahamas, Colombia, Honduras, Panama, and Uruguay from surveys collected between 2011 and 2013.[3] In every country except Colombia, surveys were representative at the national level. In Colombia, sampling was designed to make the survey representative at the sectoral level for three specific sectors: manufacturing, commerce, and services. Due to space limitations, the tables and graphs in this chapter refer only to the figures corresponding to the manufacturing sector. We discuss the results for the other sectors in the endnotes.

OJT IN LAC: PRACTICES, POLICIES, AND DETERMINANTS

Incidence and Intensity

Table 5.2 shows that, in almost all the sampled countries in LAC, at least a quarter of the surveyed firms offer some type of formal training to their full-time workers in a given year, and in many countries this share exceeds 50%.[4] However, training levels vary widely from country to country. As we discuss later in this chapter, this cross-country variation is likely associated with factors such as the size and technology level of the firms.

Table 5.2 Incidence and intensity of on-the-job training in LAC (sorted by incidence)

Country	Reference year	Incidence: proportion of firms that offer training (%)	Intensity: proportion of workers trained in manufacturing firms that offer training (%)
El Salvador	2010	60.4	54.1
Argentina	2010	58.1	61.2
Peru	2010	57.0	62.0
Colombia	2010	56.7	78.8
Ecuador	2010	56.4	65.0
Dominican Republic	2010	55.9	46.1
Bolivia	2010	54.1	43.8
Barbados	2010	53.1	n.a.
Brazil	2009	52.7	67.3
Paraguay	2010	51.7	61.0
Costa Rica	2010	48.9	71.0
Bahamas	2010	46.9	n.a.
Chile	2010	45.9	49.2
Mexico	2010	45.1	62.6
Guatemala	2010	43.6	67.7
Venezuela	2010	39.0	74.5
Nicaragua	2010	35.2	59.2
St. Kitts & Nevis	2010	35.0	n.a.
Saint Lucia	2010	34.2	n.a.
Honduras	2010	33.8	58.0
Uruguay	2010	32.3	38.1
Trinidad and Tobago	2010	31.5	42.1
Jamaica	2010	26.1	41.8
Dominica	2010	22.4	n.a.
Panama	2010	8.6	67.6

Source: Authors' elaboration based on WBES data

Notes: Calculation of the proportion of firms that train is based on the question: "During the [reference] fiscal year, did this establishment offer formal training programs for its full-time permanent employees?" Calculation of the proportion of workers trained in manufacturing firms is based on the question: "With respect to formal training programs for the [reference] fiscal year, what percentage of full-time permanent workers received formal training?" n.a. = not applicable

Because of the lack of information about the social returns on training, it is not possible to know if there is under-investment in OJT in LAC. However, we can see that the levels of OJT in the region are relatively high compared to countries with similar income levels. Figure 5.1 illustrates this point. The line shows the average incidence of training in a

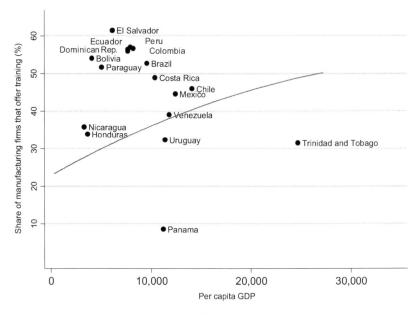

Fig. 5.1   Incidence of training in LAC and the rest of the world

Source: Authors' calculations based on WBES data

Notes: The line shows the average incidence of training in a set of 107 non-LAC countries

set of 107 non-LAC countries. The points, which represent the incidence of OJT in LAC countries, are mostly located above the line. Thus, the incidence of OJT in LAC is generally higher than in other countries with similar per capita income. The only exceptions are Trinidad and Tobago, Uruguay, and Panama.

However, measures of incidence do not differentiate between firms that train many workers and those that train a few. For this reason, we also consider *intensity* indicators, which measure the proportion of workers trained. Because of the design of the WBES, this indicator can only be calculated for the manufacturing sector, where firms that provide OJT programs typically train between 38 and 78 % of their workers (Table 5.2). The intensity of OJT can also be measured in terms of training duration. These figures, available only for the EPFE surveys conducted in Honduras and Uruguay, show that firms typically invest between 17 and 41 hours per year in training their workers. This is not

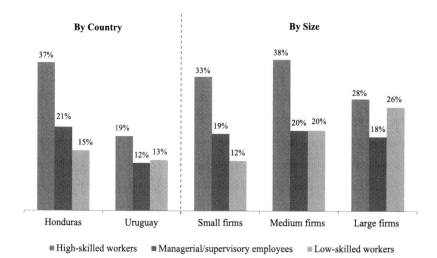

Fig. 5.2   Share of workers that received training by occupational category
Source: Authors' elaboration based on the EPFE
Notes: Small firms, 1 to 20 employees; medium firms, 21 to 100 employees; large firms, over 100 employees

very different from the levels seen in Europe.[5] However, this type of cross-country comparison should be considered with caution because of the differences in measurement and definitions.

Beneficiaries of OJT: High- vs Low-Skilled Workers

Evidence from developed countries consistently shows that high-skilled workers are not only more likely to be trained, but the training they receive is also more intensive (e.g. Bassanini et al. 2005; Bishop 1996; Heckman 2000; Frazis et al. 2000). This coincides with previous findings for LAC from Hunneus et al. (2011) and with the new findings we obtain from the EPFE, which show that low skilled workers in Honduras and Uruguay receive relatively shorter training.[6] Moreover, the share of workers that receives training is higher for skilled than for low skilled workers, especially in Honduras and in small firms (Fig. 5.2).

If OJT is differentially targeted to the higher skilled workers, these investments will only help to amplify the skill gaps in the workforce.

This is why some governments implement policies to stimulate training for workers with lower education levels. However, the literature that uses European data casts doubt on the cost-effectiveness of these efforts given how difficult it is to stimulate OJT for less skilled workers if the returns on these investments are very low (Bassanini et al. 2005). Recent evidence from Chile also points in this direction. A revision of the *franquicia tributaria*, a tax deduction for OJT, shows that firms mostly use it to train the more educated workers even though the value of the deduction declines with the worker's skill level (Ministry of Labor of Chile 2011). This highlights the importance of complementary efforts outside the workplace to increase the skills of the workforce, such as those aimed at building a lifelong training system.

Contents of OJT: General vs Specific

Results from the EPFE show that, when deciding the content of training, firms in LAC give priority to the technical skills that are relevant in the workers' current jobs and not to general skills.[7] This result is robust to restricting the sample for different countries or firm sizes (Fig. 5.3) and is consistent with Bassi et al. (2012) on Chile, Argentina, and Brazil.

This result is worth emphasizing for two reasons. First, as discussed earlier, even though training in specific skills can have a positive effect on productivity, it will likely have little impact on wages. This should be taken into account in the design of policies that target distributional goals. Second, recent evidence for LAC shows that socio-emotional or behavioral skills are the most highly valued by employers and the most difficult to find in the labor market (Bassi et al. 2012).[8] However, the fraction of firms that give priority to behavioral skills is much lower than the proportion that prioritizes specific skills. This is consistent with the results of the study by Bassi et al. (2012) in Argentina, Chile, and Brazil, which showed that even firms that have the greatest difficulties in fulfilling their requirements for socio-emotional skills tended to offer more training in specific skills.

The tendency to give more training in specific skills may result from a firm's lack of capacity (e.g. methodologies and technologies) to teach general skills. It may also reflect the disincentives that arise due to a lack of appropriation given that, as discussed below, most of the OJT in the region is financed by the employer.

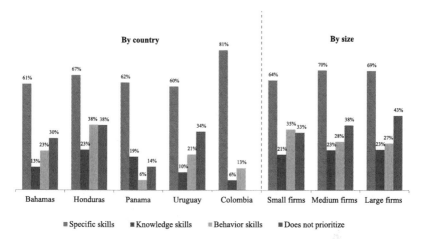

Fig. 5.3   Proportion of firms that train by prioritized skill

Source: Authors' calculations based on the EPFE

Notes: Figures calculated only for firms that train. Because respondents had the option of choosing more than one skill, the sum of the percentages in each category is not 100%. Data for Colombia shown in this figure are calculated with the sample of firms in the manufacturing sector. Firms in the commerce and services sectors in Colombia display the same pattern, with the majority prioritizing training in specific skills. The option "does not prioritize" was not included. Due to special confidentiality protocols by the statistics office in Colombia, the authors of this study were unable to aggregate the data from Colombia with that of other countries to build the indicators by firm size

Financing OJT

Results from the EPFE show that, to finance OJT, firms typically allocate a fraction of their operating costs, ranging from 2 to 4%, depending on the firm size. Moreover, since training usually takes place during working hours, firms generally also bear the extra costs in worker productivity as a result of hours missed.[9] Data from EPFE suggests that in LAC, OJT is mostly financed by the employers. Table 5.7 (in the Appendix) shows that, regardless of firm size or country, at least 70% of firms finance OJT with their own funds. Only a small percentage expects employees to use their personal funds or use public financing. However, due to the characteristics of the data, indirect financing by the employees through wage reductions cannot be ruled out.

Interestingly, in LAC, using public resources to finance OJT is no more frequent among small firms than among large- and medium-sized ones (see Table 5.7 in the Appendix). This result is consistent with the findings for other regions (Almeida et al. 2012) and also resonates with the literature on R&D incentives, which has documented that firms are more likely to apply for R&D tax credits if they are large and have the capacity for innovation.[10] To the extent that small firms face fewer credit restrictions and higher net returns, the subsidies might finance investments that would have happened anyway. Evidence of similar deadweight losses have also been documented in the literature that analyzes the effectiveness of incentives for R&D and innovation.[11]

In addition to subsidies and tax incentives (e.g. Chile and Uruguay), governments in LAC participate in the training market by directly providing free or low-cost training through public training institutes (e.g. SENA in Colombia or SENAI in Brazil). The evidence from the EPFE suggests that the role of these institutions in providing OJT is not significant: regardless of country and size, the share of firms that exclusively use external providers to deliver training is no greater than one-third. Moreover, the majority of firms that offered training with an external provider relied on a private institution (see Table 5.7 in the Appendix).

Results from the WBES also show that only a minority of firms in the region use public funding for their training initiatives. In this survey, respondents were asked: "During the last 3 years, did this establishment receive any public support (financial or otherwise) for training?" Despite the lack of specificity of the question, which could refer to any type of government support (e.g. public subsidies, technical support, or direct provision of training), of all the firms that trained, the percentage of firms that received public support was on average 18 (Fig. 5.4). Moreover, in 6 of the 11 countries, this percentage was less than 15. Chile is one exception, where over 60% of firms received public support. This is likely due to the high level of coverage of the *franquicia tributaria*.[12] Importantly, small firms use public support for training less than large enterprises, at only 13% receiving any kind of public support compared to 22% for large firms.

The low utilization of public instruments to promote OJT in LAC may be due to insufficient coverage. It may also reflect a lack of relevance, if these instruments do not target the market failures or barriers that firms face in the training decision. Unfortunately, the empirical literature does not shed light on this issue. As discussed previously, little is known about the market failures faced by employers in their decision to train, posing an important challenge in the design of policy instruments, whose relevance can only be assessed in terms of the ability to alleviate barriers to training

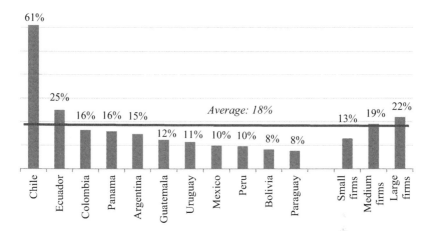

Fig. 5.4   Percentage of firms offering OJT that received public support

Source: Authors' calculations based on WBES data

Notes: Small firms, 1 to 20 employees; medium firms, 21 to 100 employees; large firms, over 100 employees

investments. Recent reviews of the literature on employer-provided training in the international context have reached a similar conclusion (Almeida et al. 2012; Bassanini et al. 2005).

Determinants of OJT in LAC

Below we provide suggestive evidence on the key factors that affect the decision to train in LAC. The market failures enumerated in Table 5.1 guide our conclusions, including restrictions that affect both supply and demand for training. Three pieces of evidence suggest that restrictions on demand might play a key role in OJT decisions in the region.

First, results from the EPFE show that the main reason employers do not train is that they do not believe it is necessary. Table 5.3 shows that, regardless of the country or firm size, the most frequent reason firms do not train in Bahamas, Honduras, and Colombia is that it is not necessary.[13] This finding resonates with previous evidence for Brazil and Central America.[14] While this result may be interpreted as evidence of lack of demand, it may also indicate that there is imperfect information about the returns on training. The next most cited reason for not offering training is the high cost (Table 5.3).

Table 5.3 Percentage of firms that do not train by reason not to provide training

	Bahamas	Honduras	Colombia	Less than 50 employees	50 + employees
Training was not useful; waste of time	6.7	8.3	10.0	8.2	9.5
High cost	16.4	30.3	26.0	28.8	35.6
Does not know / has not found training institutions	5.8	25.5	5.8	24.1	20.0
Trained staff can leave the firm	2.3	7.7	10.7	7.2	10.1
Not possible to measure the benefits of training	3.9	4.0	n.a	4.1	1.5
No need to provide training; staff is sufficiently well trained	72.8	62.4	34.5	63.0	67.3

Source: Authors' calculations based on EPFE

Notes: Each percentage measures the proportion of firms that did not train that chose each option as one of the two main reasons for not training. n.a. = not applicable

Second, firms that do not train claim to have fewer difficulties meeting their human capital requirements. This is shown by the EPFE data, which includes a question on whether human capital constraints are a major obstacle to firm productivity. Regardless of the country or firm size, the share of firms identifying human capital constraints as a major obstacle is higher among firms that train.[15] A similar conclusion emerges from an analysis of WBES data.[16] Table 5.4 shows that among firms that train, about one in three (37%) state that an inadequately educated workforce is a "major" or "very severe" obstacle. For firms that do not train, this proportion falls to just over one in four (29%).

Accordingly, limitations on human capital are a greater obstacle for the firms that train than for those that do not. This is likely associated with large differences in the production process, workforce characteristics, and personnel between these two groups of firms (Table 5.4). Firms that train are, on average, larger and older, have a higher probability of being in the manufacturing sector, and a higher probability of obtaining credit from financial institutions (see Chap. 8). They also have more links with foreign markets and face a greater number of competitors (see Chap. 9). There are

Table 5.4 Characteristics of firms that train vs. firms that do not train

	Train[a]	Do not train	P-Value (test differences)
General Attributes			
Age of firm (years)	28	22	0.000
Number of employees	215	67	0.000
Fraction of domestic ownership	83%	91%	0.000
Manufacturer	76%	53%	0.000
Credit with financial institutions	66%	48%	0.000
Competition			
Main product faced five or more competitors	38%	30%	0.000
Fraction of sales in domestic market	86%	93%	0.000
Innovation, Business Development, and Productivity			
Has ISO certificate	38%	13%	0.000
Spending on R&D	45%	12%	0.000
Introduced new products in the past 3 years	56%	26%	0.000
Improved processes in the past 3 years	52%	22%	0.000
Workforce Characteristics and Human Capital Requirements			
Fraction of permanent, full-time production workers that are skilled[b]	41%	45%	0.000
Fraction of production workers that are temporary	16%	15%	0.930
Lack of skills is major obstacle	37%	29%	0.000
Characteristics of Most Senior Manager			
Years experience of highest manager in the sector	22.9	21.4	0.065
Number of firms	7486	10,190	

Source: Authors' calculations based on WBES data

Notes: [a]The variable that indicates whether the firm trained or not is constructed from the question: "Over fiscal year X, did this establishment have formal training programs for its permanent, full-time employees?" where X is the reference year of the survey (2006 or 2010) [b]This indicator is built from a question in the WBES survey that asked: "How many permanent, full-time production workers are skilled? How many are unskilled?"

also differences with respect to practices of innovation and business development: firms that train also spend more on R&D and are more likely to have introduced new products and new or improved processes in recent years (see Chap. 2). Differences in the characteristics of the workforce are also present, such as the fraction of skilled workers and the experience of the most senior manager. Interestingly, there are no significant differences regarding the share of temporary workers, an attribute that in theory could affect the incentives to train if more temporary workers lead to a greater appropriation problem.[17]

Finally, the third result shows that the most important determinants of the training decision are the variables that measure innovation. To document this, we use WBES data for 11 LAC countries collected in 2006 and 2010 to estimate a probit model of the decision to train. We use a rich set of covariates that measure the characteristics of the firm and of the workers.[18] We also include dummy variables to control for country, year, and economic sector (manufacturing vs services). Separate estimates are made for the three subgroups of firms: small (less than 20 permanent employees), medium (over 20 to 100), and large (over 100).

The results are shown in Fig. 5.5. The location of the circles on the horizontal axis shows the marginal effects on the probability of training when the covariates are set at their average value. In the case of dummy

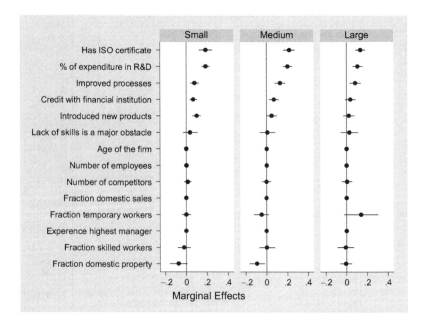

Fig. 5.5 Determinants of the decision to train in LAC

Source: Authors' calculations based on WBES data

Notes: This figure shows the results of probit models estimated with WBES data. The training variable is constructed from the question: "Over fiscal year X, did this establishment have formal training programs for its permanent, full-time employees?" where X is the reference year of the survey (2006 or 2010). Country dummy variables are also included

variables, the marginal effects measure the effect of changing the variable from 0 to 1. Horizontal bars show the 95% confidence intervals. The figure shows that, regardless of firm size, the most important determinants of the decision to train are those that measure innovation and technological development. For example, for small firms, the probability of training is associated with an increase of 18 percentage points if the firm has a quality certificate, 19 percentage points if R&D expenditures increase by 1%, and 10 percentage points if the firm has changed or improved its production processes in recent years. Interestingly, we find no difference in the marginal effects of the variables that measure innovations in products versus innovations in processes, even though the literature has stated that these may have differential effects on skill demand and on employment. Recent evidence for LAC has shown that product innovation may be more complementary to skilled than to unskilled labor (Crespi and E. Tacsir 2012).

Having credit with a commercial bank is also a significant determinant of training for small and medium firms (7 and 6 percentage points, respectively), suggesting liquidity constraints on OJT investments. Interestingly, the measures of the degree of competition (i.e. the number of competitors faced by the main product or product line in the market and the fraction of domestic sales) are not associated with training either, even though firms in more competitive markets could have greater incentives and need to invest in the human capital of their workers.

It is important to emphasize that the characteristics of the workforce, such as the proportion of skilled workers, do not seem to be associated with the decision to train. The same applies to the share of workers with a temporary contract, which is not statistically significant in any of the three models, even though this is a measure of turnover, which could lower a firm's incentives to provide training in general skills because of the appropriation problem. The study by Almeida and Aterido (2010) on small firms in developing countries also failed to find significant effects of worker turnover on OJT.

In summary, the three results presented in this section highlight the importance of the demand for skilled workers in the decision to train. The subset of firms that do not train may have fewer requirements for skilled workers, which could be associated with a lower degree of technological development. These results are consistent with the studies by Bassanini et al. (2005) for European countries and by Almeida and Aterido (2010) for developing countries.[19] However, due to the available data, we can only examine correlations between the decision to train and the firms' attributes, and no causal interpretation should be given due to endogeneity.

Nonetheless, even with these caveats, interesting conclusions emerge. First, the results highlight the importance of information problems that could be generating a misperception about the returns on OJT among firms in the region. Second, given that the demand for skilled workers seems to be playing a key role in the decision to train, public policies that attempt to create incentives for OJT mainly through subsidies may be insufficient. More comprehensive policies that not only facilitate the provision of training, but also aim to alleviate the constraints on technological adoption, may be required.

RETURNS ON OJT AMONG MANUFACTURING FIRMS IN LAC

As we noted earlier in this chapter, few studies provide empirical evidence about the productivity effects of OJT in LAC, probably due to the absence of adequate data. In this section, we make an effort to contribute to this literature. We take advantage of a longitudinal sample of manufacturing firms in 11 LAC countries for which OJT information was collected in 2006 and 2010. Using this data, we estimate the effect of OJT on total factor productivity (TFP).[20] Our empirical model is motivated by a simple conceptual framework. We assume a Cobb–Douglas production function to describe the technology of firm i:

$$Y_i = A_i K_i^{\alpha} E_i^{\beta} \qquad (5.1)$$

where Y_i is output, A_i is an efficiency parameter, K_i measures the capital stock, and E_i is a measure of effective work. Following Dearden et al. (2000) and Zwick (2006), we define effective work as the weighted sum of trained, L_{Ci}, and untrained, L_{Ni}, labor:

$$E_i = \gamma L_{Ci} + L_{Ni} \qquad (5.2)$$

where γ is greater than zero if the training has a positive impact on productivity. Substituting equation 5.2 in equation 5.1, and defining $H_i = \dfrac{L_{ci}}{L_i}$ as the proportion of workers in which the firms make human capital investments by training, gives:

$$Y_i = A_i K_i^{\alpha} \left(1 + (\gamma - 1) H_i \right)^{\beta} L_i^{\beta} \qquad (5.3)$$

Taking logs from equation 5.3 and with some algebra, we obtain the empirical model[21]:

$$y_{it} = \beta_h h_{it} + \beta_l l_{it} + \beta_k k_{it} + x_{it} + a_i + \varepsilon_{it} \qquad (5.4)$$

where y_{it} is the logarithm of output, h_{it} measures the intensity or incidence of training, l_{it} is the log of hours worked by permanent and temporary employees, and k_{it} is the logarithm of the value of the assets.[22] The term a_i is a fixed effect that measures time-invariant firm characteristics such as structural efficiency, administrative quality, and industrial relations, and ε_{it} is a time-varying error term. The subscript t denotes the years 2006 and 2010, for which longitudinal data were collected.

The objective is to estimate the parameter β_h. In this effort, we face two methodological challenges. First, time-invariant attributes of the firm, a_i, can have an impact on both productivity and training. For example, greater managerial capacity may lead to higher levels of productivity and increase OJT investments. Second, training, input allocation, and production decisions are affected simultaneously by unobservable productivity and demand shocks that vary over time, such as changes in work legislation or the introduction of a new product.

We therefore estimate equation 5.1 in two stages. In the first stage, the impact on the productivity of the production factors of capital and labor is calculated using the Levinsohn and Petrin (2003) technique. By using the cost of intermediate inputs to approximate unobservable productivity shocks, this technique, under certain assumptions, addresses the problem of endogeneity of the capital and labor inputs.[23] In the second stage, we estimate the impact of training on productivity using a methodology that combines firm-level fixed effects with a broad set of time-varying controls. The dependent variable is the measure of TFP, v_{it}, obtained as the residual of the production function estimated in the first stage with the Levinsohn and Petrin algorithm. The equation to estimate is described by:

$$v_{it} = \beta_h h_{it} + \beta_x x_{it} + \delta_i + \alpha_t + \mu_{it} \qquad (5.5)$$

where the term δ_i corresponds to a vector of firm-level fixed effects. With these fixed effects we can control for time-invariant unobserved factors that may be simultaneously correlated with productivity and training.

The term α_t is a year dummy that controls for confounding aggregate-level factors that may have simultaneously affected productivity and training, such as the national business cycle.

However, even including this set of controls, the estimate of β_h would be biased if the error term μ_{it} contains firm-specific time-varying shocks that simultaneously affect productivity and the decision to train. The lack of appropriate data to construct instrumental variables prevents us from implementing this identification strategy. Hence, in addition to using fixed effects, the estimate includes a series of exogenous variables at the firm level that vary over time. These variables, denoted as x_{it} in equation 5.2, are constructed from interactions between the dummy indicating the year and a rich set of predetermined 2006 variables, including the number of employees, economic subsector, existence of quality certificates, product and process innovation, expenditures in R&D, proportion of sales in the domestic market, existence of credit in the formal financial sector, an indicator of private and foreign ownership, share of skilled workers, share of temporary workers who are skilled, and the proportion of temporary employees. With this rich set of controls, we try to capture productivity shocks that can be associated with the training decisions.

Table 5.5 presents the estimates for equation 5.5, in which the dependent variable is the log of TFP. The endogenous variable of interest measures the intensity of training, calculated as the share of permanent workers who received training in the reference year. Column 1 reports the results of OLS models with no controls. Column 2 shows the results after adding firm-level fixed effects. Finally, column 3 shows the results after adding

Table 5.5 Estimates of the impact of training on productivity

	(1)	(2)	(3)
Intensity (share of trained workers)	0.009***	−0.001	−0.001
	(0.002)	(0.001)	(0.001)
Observations	1479	1479	1461
Fixed effects	No	Yes	Yes
Time-varying controls	No	No	Yes

Source: Authors' calculations based on WBES data

Notes: This table presents estimates of the effect of increasing the proportion of trained workers. Estimates were obtained using value added per worker as an alternative measure of productivity and, similarly, no statistically significant training effects were found. Standard errors are in parentheses.

* Coefficient is statistically significant at the 10% level, ** at the 5% level, *** at the 1% level; no asterisk means the coefficient is not different from zero with statistical significance

fixed effects and the complete vector of time-varying firm-level exogenous variables, x_{it}.

Column 1 shows a positive correlation between TFP and the intensity of training. A 1 percentage point increase in the proportion of skilled workers is associated with a 0.9% increase in productivity. As mentioned previously, this parameter cannot be interpreted as a causal estimate of the effect of training because of possible time-varying shocks and unobserved firm heterogeneity that simultaneously determine training and production decisions. Column 2 shows that, with firm-level fixed effects, the estimate has a much smaller magnitude and is not statistically significant, a result that confirms the importance of correcting for unobserved firm heterogeneity. Column 3 shows that these estimates remain stable after a rich set of time-varying controls are included.

Table 5.6 shows the results of an alternative version of equation 5.2 that models the heterogeneous effects of training. We consider four alternative

Table 5.6 Heterogeneous effects of training

Panel A: Size and Age of the Firm				
	(1)	(2)	(3)	(4)
Intensity	−0.001	−0.001	−0.001	−0.001
	(0.001)	(0.001)	(0.001)	(0.001)
Intensity × large firm	0.006*	0.007*	n.a.	n.a.
	(0.004)	(0.004)		
Intensity × improved processes	n.a.	n.a.	−0.003	0.002
			(0.002)	(0.002)
Panel B: Fraction of Female and Temporary Workers				
	(1)	(2)	(3)	(4)
Intensity	−0.001	−0.001	0	0
	(0.001)	(0.001)	(0.001)	(0.001)
Intensity × high fraction of skilled workers	0.000	0.001	n.a.	n.a.
	(0.003)	(0.004)		
Intensity × high fraction of temporary workers	n.a.	n.a.	−0.005	−0.006*
			(0.003)	(0.003)
Observations	1479	1461	1479	1461
Firm-level fixed effects	Yes	Yes	Yes	Yes
Time varying controls	No	Yes	No	Yes

Source: Authors' calculations based on WBES data

Notes: This table presents estimates of the effect of increasing the proportion of trained workers. Standard errors are in parentheses.

* Coefficient is statistically significant at the 10% level, ** at the 5% level, *** at the 1% level; no asterisk means the coefficient is not different from zero with statistical significance. n.a. = not applicable

sources of heterogeneity to examine if there are differential effects according to the characteristics of the firm (i.e. size and innovation) and characteristics of the workers (i.e. contractual stability and skill level).

Columns 1 and 2 of Panel A show the result of estimates that extend equation 5.2 with an interaction term between the intensity of training and a dummy variable indicating whether the firm had over 100 employees in the baseline year, 2006. Columns 3 and 4 of Panel A show the results of replicating the exercise with a dummy variable that indicates if the firm improved processes in the three years before the baseline. Columns 1 and 2 of Panel B show the result of models in which the interactions are constructed to indicate if in 2006 more than 60% of employees were temporary. Finally, in columns 3 and 4 of Panel B, the interactions show that in 2006 more than 75% of permanent employees were skilled. All models include firm-level fixed effects, but the time-varying controls are only included in the models presented in even-numbered columns.

The results show that the impact of training on productivity for firms with over 100 employees is positive. A 1 percentage point increase in the proportion of trained employees raises productivity by 0.6 or 0.7%, depending on the specification. The magnitude of this effect is similar to the estimated effect by Zwick (2006) for German firms. No differential effects are found for firms that innovate more or for firms that have more skilled workers, in spite of evidence suggesting the existence of complementarities between OJT, innovation, and the skill level of workers. The absence of these effects could be due to imprecise measurements, and we recommend that further research be done in this area. Finally, for firms with a high share of temporary workers, increases in training intensity seem to have a marginally significant negative effect on productivity, although this result is not robust to both specifications.

Our results suggest that training has a positive impact on productivity only for larger firms. This may be because, as firms grow, there are larger spillover productivity effects from trained workers to a greater number of untrained workers. Middleton et al. (1993) suggested an alternative explanation, stating that the existence of internal labor markets in large firms can result in higher returns from training because promotion opportunities make it more attractive for workers to stay in the firm, reducing the appropriation problem. A third possibility is that firm size is correlated with good managerial skills and internal labor markets that reward increased productivity by profit sharing and promotion (Lazear 1995). Finally, it is possible that larger firms provide a better quality of training due to the economies of scale of investing in training programs and technologies.

As a final caveat, we should mention two reasons why in these estimations there may be an attenuation of the true training effects. First, because of the characteristics of the data, we are only able to estimate the *contemporary* effects of training on productivity and wages. However, as we mentioned previously, most of the training takes place during working hours, which means that workers spend less time on production. There is, in fact, evidence from developed countries that the level of worker productivity falls during training (Bartel 1994; Dearden et al. 2000). Thus, the productivity impact of training could be low or negative in the immediate term and positive in the medium or long term. This could also explain the negative effects on the subset of firms with a high proportion of temporary workers.

Second, measurement errors in the training variable can attenuate the estimated effect. This problem can be particularly severe in the type of models we estimate, which have fixed effects and only two periods of observations per firm. Even so, positive productivity impacts are found in larger firms. Thus, further studies are needed to provide more robust evidence of these impacts as well studies that identify the conditions (i.e. characteristics of the firms, training, and workers) in which OJT is more productive, since this would certainly improve the targeting of policy interventions.

CONCLUSIONS

One of the most important challenges that LAC economies face is increasing the productivity of their workforces. In this effort, employer-provided training can play a key role by providing updated, relevant skills that are aligned with the demands of the market. In spite of their importance, little is known about the nature of the training investments made by firms in the region. This study aims to improve this knowledge.

We found that, in most countries in the region, between 30 and 50% of firms offer training to their workers through programs that are usually short, structured, and mostly targeted to the more skilled workers. Training content prioritized job-specific skills, something that was consistent with the fact that the majority of the training was financed with funds from the employer. Public subsidies for OJT were not often used and were more likely to be used by larger firms. Also, few firms seemed to use public institutions as external training providers.

We also presented evidence suggesting that, regardless of the firm size, the decision to train is determined by the firms' demand for skills, which, in turn, is associated with innovation and the adoption of more advanced production technologies. Finally, we assessed the effects of training on wages and productivity. Point estimates showed that a 1 percentage point increase in the proportion of trained employees raised productivity by 0.7%, but only in firms with more than 100 employees. We did not find evidence of wage effects from training. However, due to data limitations, our results should be interpreted with caution and may be a lower bound of the true effects.

Several policy recommendations emerge from these findings. First, the results are consistent with the view that providing training in general skills to low-skilled workers may have very low private returns for the firms. This highlights the importance of complementary policies to increase the skills of the workforce, such as developing lifelong vocational and educational training systems that allow workers to update their skills and reduce the skill gaps between individuals entering the workforce.

Our results also support the design of comprehensive interventions in which the instruments to promote OJT are part of a broader set of policies that foster technological transformation and innovation. Policies should take into account the coordination failure that may have caused some firms in the region to be caught in a low-technology low-skill trap. This means that some firms are not able to adopt skill-intensive productive technologies because of the lack of skilled workers and therefore do not invest in the human capital of their employees. Indeed, while this chapter shows that a lack of technology adoption limits human capital investments by firms, recent evidence shows that lack of skills impose serious constraints on the adoption of innovation in LAC (Hall and Maffioli 2008).

The results in this chapter also underscore the need for further research. First, there is a need to assess the magnitude of the private returns to OJT and how these are distributed between firms and workers. This implies making greater efforts in data collection, either by conducting longitudinal surveys or using administrative data. An effort should also be made to identify the complementary factors that make OJT productive, such as managerial decision-making. Suggestive evidence in this chapter indicates that OJT will have an impact on productivity if some of the attributes typical of larger firms are present. It is therefore important to identify the characteristics of the firms and personnel management practices required for training to be productive. Finally, an effort to identify the potential market failures that affect decisions about OJT is paramount to design evidence-based policies.

APPENDIX

Table 5.7   Providing and financing training services

	Bahamas	Honduras	Panama	Uruguay	Colombia	Small firms	Medium firms	Large firms
Percentage of firms that use at least one of the following sources to finance training								
Public sources	2%	24%	n.a.	7%	13%	14%	35%	19%
Private credit	n.a.	6%	n.a.	1%	2%	6%	3%	0%
Establishment funds	86%	81%	n.a.	87%	75%	78%	80%	94%
Employee personal funds	12%	4%	n.a.	4%	4%	4%	4%	5%
Other	5%	12%	n.a.	6%	7%	16%	6%	3%
Percentage of firms that use as a provider								
External provider	19%	37%	37%	30%	40%	28%	26%	35%
Internal provider	45%	27%	41%	29%	19%	55%	38%	74%
External and internal provider	36%	36%	22%	41%	41%	18%	36%	21%
Percentage of firms that use an external provider								
Public external providers	32%	35%	n.a.	32%	62%	21%	37%	46%
Private external providers	81%	84%	n.a.	87%	38%	74%	90%	81%

Source: Authors' calculations based on EPFE data

Notes: All statistics in the table are calculated for the subset of firms that train. The questionnaire allowed more than one choice of source of funding for the answer, so the percentages do not total 100%. The denominator is the number of firms that trained in the reference year. The percentages for Colombia are calculated using only manufacturing firms. Firms in the commerce and services sectors display very similar patterns: the majority of training is financed with establishment funds and external and internal providers are evenly distributed. Results are not presented due to space limitations but are available on request. Also, due to special confidentiality protocols by the statistics office in Colombia, the authors of this study were unable to aggregate the data from Colombia with that of other countries to build the indicators by firm size. n.a. = not available

Notes

1. However, in a market with frictions, the predictions are different. Given that market wages do not fully reflect increases in productivity, firms may have incentives to finance general skills training. It has been established that certain institutional aspects that characterize domestic labor markets, such as minimum wages, result in this type of friction (Acemoglu and Pischke 1998, 1999).
2. For evidence on the impact of modern workplace practices on productivity see Black and Lynch (2001). More recently, Lazear et al. (2012) provided evidence of the impact of the quality of bosses (supervisors or managers) on productivity.
3. The number of firms composing the sample in each country was: Bahamas, 505; Honduras, 658; Panama, 757; Colombia, 8071; and Uruguay, 636. For Panama, the sample used was significantly smaller than the sample surveyed because of problems with missing and inconsistent data.
4. These training levels are constructed with WBES data from a question in which respondents were asked: "Over [the last complete fiscal year], did this establishment have formal training programs for its permanent, full-time employees?"
5. In Scandinavian countries, which have the highest intensity levels in Europe, firms provide an average of 30 to 35 hours of training per employee per year (Bassanini et al. 2005).
6. On average, high- and low-skilled workers in Honduras receive 37 and 22 hours of training per year, respectively. In Uruguay, these figures are 23 and 17 hours.
7. The survey adopts the skills classification of Murnane and Levy (1996), which defined three categories: (i) *specific skills of the occupation*, defined as the techniques needed to develop a particular occupation that are not readily applicable to other occupations or industries (e.g. training in the use of certain equipment in the textile sector); (ii) *knowledge skills*, defined as the basic areas of knowledge of the curriculum in the formal education system: reading, writing, arithmetic, reasoning, and critical thinking; and (iii) *behavioral or socio-emotional skills*, related to responsibility, degree of commitment, ability to work in groups, persistence, and self-control.
8. The importance of socio-emotional skills in the working life of employees has been well documented in international literature (see Heckman et al. 2006). Given that socio-emotional skills appear to be malleable even after adolescence, the return on investing in development of such skills would be higher than investing in the development of cognitive skills (Cunha and Heckman 2010).
9. EFPE data shows that the share of firms that provide OJT during working hours are 67% in Honduras, 97% in Panama, and 91% in Uruguay.

10. See, for example, Ferrero Zucoloto (2010) for evidence from Brazil and Mercer-Blackman (2008) for evidence from Colombia.

11. See Chap. 2 and Ientile and Mairesse (2009) for a recent survey.

12. Since its origins in the 1970s, the *franquicia tributaria* has operated as a financial subsidy for the training that firms contract directly with private providers. This subsidy is notable for its extensive coverage and for its long run duration. According to information from Chile's National Training and Employement Service (Servicio Nacional de Capacitacion y Empleo, or SENCE), in 2011, 907,547 workers received OJT through this scheme, which represents 12% of the workforce employed in the country, and 24,885 firms that paid training costs via tax exemption during the same year. The delegation of training services to private providers that characterizes this system is unique in Latin America, where the state usually directly provides training services.

13. Unlike previous tables, firms in this table are grouped in two size categories. The reason for the change is that the number of firms that do not train, have over 100 employees, and answered the question on the reason for not training is very small.

14. Hunneus et al. (2011) found that, in Brazil, 63% of informal micro-enterprises did not train because they did not need training. Almeida et al. (2012) reported that almost 90% of firms in Central America did not provide formal training because informal OJT was sufficient.

15. A *t*-test shows that the differences between these proportions are statistically significant. These percentages cannot be constructed with the data for Panama and Colombia.

16. The relevant survey question is: "Is an inadequately educated workforce No Obstacle, a Minor Obstacle, a Major Obstacle, or a Very Severe Obstacle to the current operations of this establishment?"

17. We would have liked to compare the use of workplace personnel practices (e.g. performance incentives, mentoring, or evaluations) but, unfortunately, the WBES do not collect information on this. The EPFE do not provide a rich set of information on these features either.

18. Descriptive statistics of these variables are presented in Table 5.4, disaggregated by training category.

19. Almeida and Aterido (2010) used information from WBES in a sample of 99 developing countries and obtained results that point in the same direction. Their evidence suggested that the lower investment in training in small and medium firms was largely due to a lower expected return on training investments.

20. We choose a measure of TFP rather than sales per worker because arguably it is a more adequate proxy for productivity in commerce and services than in manufacturing. However, this may add noise to the outcome variable

given the plausible error in measurement of variables such as the value of capital stock. Therefore, we examine the sensitivity of our results to alternative outcomes.

21. We use the approximation $\ln\left(1 + x\right) = x$ and assume ($\gamma - 1$)H_i is small.

22. A. ll nominal variables were deflated at constant 2010 prices in local currency and then converted to US dollars.

23. More specifically, we estimate a Cobb–Douglas production function whose arguments are capital and labor, and which assumes that the error term incorporates a productivity shock observed by the firm but not by the econometrician. We approximate this shock by a function of the cost of the intermediate inputs. Levinsohn and Petrin (2003) showed that this results in a consistent estimate of the production function if three assumptions are met: (i) the productivity shock must follow a first order Markov process and be independent of other decisions of the firm; (ii) the productivity shock must be the only unobservable state variable that is part of the demand function and intermediate inputs; and (iii) the demand for inputs must be a strictly growing function of productivity, conditional on other state variables.

REFERENCES

Acemoglu, D., and J.S. Pischke. 1998. Why Do Firms Train? Theory and Evidence. *Quarterly Journal of Economics* 113(1): 79–119.

Acemoglu, D., and J.S. Pischke. 1999. The Structure of Wages and Investment in General Training. *Journal of Political Economy* 107(3): 539–572.

Almeida, R., and R. Aterido. 2010. The Investment in Job Training. Why Are SMEs Lagging So Much Behind? *World Bank Social Policy Working Paper No. 1004.* Washington, DC: The World Bank.

Almeida, R., and P. Carneiro. 2008. The Return to Firm Investments in Human Capital. Social Policy Working Paper No. 0822. Washington, DC: The World Bank.

Almeida, R., J. Behrman, and D. Robalino. 2012. *The Right Skills for the Job? Rethinking Training Policies for Workers.* Washington, DC: The World Bank.

Bartel, A.P. 1994. Productivity Gains from the Implementation of Employee Training Programs. *Industrial Relations* 33(4): 411–425.

Bassanini, A., A. Booth, G. Brunello, M. De Paola, and E. Leuven. 2005. Workplace Training in Europe. Discussion Document 1640. Bonn, Germany: IZA.

Bassi, M., M. Busso, S. Urzúa, and J. Vargas. 2012. *Desconectados: Habilidades, educación and empleo en América Latina.* Washington, DC: Inter-American Development Bank (IDB).

Becker, G. 1964. *Human Capital.* New York: Columbia University Press.

Bishop, J.H. 1996. What We Know About Employer-Provided Training: A Review of Literature. Cornell Center for Advanced Human Resource Studies (CAHRS) Working Paper Series. Ithaca, NY: Cornell University ILR School.

Black, S., and L. Lynch. 2001. How to Compete: The Impact of Workplace Practices on Productivity and Technology. *The Review of Economics and Statistics* 83(3): 434–445.

Crespi, G., and E. Tacsir. 2012. Effects of Innovation on Employment in Latin America. Technical Note IDB-TN-496. Washington, DC: IDB.

Cunha, F., and J.J. Heckman. 2010. Investing in Our Young People. Working Paper 16201. Cambridge, MA: The National Bureau of Economic Research (NBER).

Daude, C., and E. Fernández-Arias. 2010. On the Role of Productivity and Factor Accumulation in Economic Development in Latin America and the Caribbean. Working Document 155. Washington, DC: IDB.

Dearden, L., H. Reed, and J. van Reenen. 2000. Who Gains When Workers Train? Training and Corporate Productivity in a Panel of British Industries. Working Document 00/04. London, UK: The Institute of Fiscal Studies.

Ferrero Zucoloto, G. 2010. *Lei do Bem: Impactos nas atividades de P&D no Brasil.* Radar N. 6, Tecnologia. Brazil: *Produção e Comércio Exterior,* Instituto de *Pesquisa Econômica Aplicada* (IPEA).

Frazis, H., M. Gittleman, and M. Joyce. 2000. Correlates of Training: An Analysis Using Both Employer and Employee Characteristics. *Industrial and Labor Relations Review* 53(3): 443–462.

Haelermans, C., and L. Borghans. 2012. Wage Effects of On-the-Job Training: A Meta-Analysis. *British Journal of Industrial Relations* 50(3): 502–528.

Hall, B., and A. Maffioli. 2008. Evaluating the Impact of Technology Development Funds in Emerging Economies: Evidence from Latin America. Working Paper 13835. Cambridge, MA: NBER.

Heckman, J.J. 2000. Policies to Foster Human Capital. JCPR Working Document 154. Chicago, IL: Northwestern University/University of Chicago.

Heckman, J.J., L. Lochner, and C. Taber. 1998. *Tax Policy and Human Capital Formation.* Cambridge, MA: NBER.

Heckman, J.J., J. Stixrud, and S. Urzúa. 2006. The Effects of Cognitive and Noncognitive Abilities on Labor Market Outcomes and Social Behavior. *Journal of Labor Economics* 24(3): 411–482.

Hunneus, C., C. de Mendoza, and G. Rucci. 2011. *El estado del arte de la capacitación de los trabajadores en América Latina and el Caribe.* Technical Note 346. Washington, DC: IDB.

Ibarrarán, P., A. Maffioli, and R. Stucchi. 2009. SME's Policies and Firms' Productivity in Latin America. Discussion Document 4486. Bonn, Germany: IZA.

Ientile, D., and J. Mairesse. 2009. A Policy to Boost R&D: Does the R&D Tax Credit Work? *EIB Papers* 14(1):144–169. Luxembourg: European Investment Bank (EIB).

IDB. 2013. *Replantear las Reformas. Cómo América Latina and el Caribe puede escapar al menor Crecimiento mundial. Informe macroeconómico de América Latina and el Caribe.* Washington, DC: IDB.

Lazear, E. 1995. *Personnel Economics*. Cambridge, MA: MIT Press.

Lazear, E., K.L. Shaw, and C.T. Stanton. 2012. The Value of Bosses. Working Document 18317. Cambridge, MA: NBER.

Leuven, E., and H. Oosterbeek. 2004. Evaluating the Effect of Tax Deductions on Training. *Journal of Labor Economics* 22(2): 461–488.

Leuven, E., and H. Oosterbeek. 2008. An Alternative Approach to Estimate the Wage Returns to Private-Sector Training. *Journal of Applied Econometrics* 23: 423–434.

Levinsohn, J., and A. Petrin. 2003. Estimating Production Functions Using Inputs to Control for Unobservables. *Review of Economic Studies* 70: 317–341.

Mercer-Blackman, V. 2008. The Impact of Research and Development Tax Incentives on Colombia's Manufacturing Sector: What Difference Do They Make? Working Paper WP/08/178. Washington, DC: International Monetary Fund (IMF).

Middleton, J., A. Ziderman, and A. Van Adams. 1993. *Skills for Productivity: Vocational Education and Training in Developing Countries*. Washington, DC: The World Bank.

Mourshad, M., D. Farrell, and D. Barton. 2011. *From Education to Employment: Designing a System that Works*. New York: McKinsey and Company.

Murnane, R.J., and F. Levy. 1996. *Teaching the New Basic Skills. Principles for Educating Children to Thrive in a Changing Economy*. New York: Free Press.

Ministry of Labor of Chile. 2011. *Informe Final de la Comisión de Reforma al Sistema de Capacitación*. Santiago, Chile: Ministerio de Trabajo and Previsión Social.

OECD. 2014. Perspectivas Económicas de América Latina 2014. Logística and Competitividad para el Desarrollo. Paris, France: Organisation for Economic Co-operation and Development (OECD).

Pagés, C. (ed.). 2010. *La Era de la Productividad: cómo transformar las economías desde sus cimientos*. Washington, DC: IDB.

Rodríguez, J., and S. Urzúa. 2011. An Evaluation of Training Programs Financed By Public Funds in Chile. Mimeographed document.

Rosholm, M., H.S. Nielsen, and A. Dabalen. 2007. Evaluation of Training in African Enterprises. *Journal of Development Economics* 84: 310–329.

Zwick, T. 2006. The Impact of Training Intensity on Establishment Productivity. *Industrial Relations* 45(1): 26–46.

CHAPTER 6

Business Performance in Young Latin American Firms

Hugo Kantis, Juan Federico, Pablo Angelelli,
and Sabrina Ibarra García

Aggregate data on productivity growth provides only a partial view of the Latin American reality. Indeed, one of the most salient features of business structures in the region is the presence of a high degree of heterogeneity across firms. As far as productivity is concerned, a large base of micro and small firms with low levels of productivity coexists alongside a select group of

H. Kantis
Programa de Desarrollo Emprendedor (Prodem) y Universidad Nacional de
General Sarmiento, Argentina
e-mail: hkantis@gmail.com

J. Federico
Prodem (UNGS)
e-mail: juan.s.federico@gmail.com

P. Angelelli
Inter-American Development Bank
e-mail: PabloAn@IADB.ORG

S.I. García
Prodem (UNGS)
e-mail: saibarragarcia@yahoo.com.ar

© Inter-American Development Bank 2016
M. Grazzi and C. Pietrobelli (eds.), *Firm Innovation*
and Productivity in Latin America and the Caribbean,
DOI 10.1057/978-1-349-58151-1_6

167

large firms, including subsidiaries of transnational companies characterized by very high levels of productivity (Pagés 2010). As mentioned in Chap. 1, it is very important to understand the sources of this heterogeneity and to identify ways to reduce the productivity gap. One interesting dimension that deserves attention is firm age, in particular, the extent to which young firms can act as vehicles to reduce productivity gaps, since they are often considered a potential source of economic innovation, rejuvenation, and renewal. This expectation has motivated different studies in Europe and worldwide (Pellegrino et al. 2012; Schneider and Veugelers 2010; Ayyagari et al. 2011).

In Latin America, the study of young firms remains a nascent issue. Prior research has tried to understand the factors that affect the emergence of new dynamic firms by analyzing the entrepreneurial process and the characteristics of entrepreneurs (Kantis et al. 2002, 2005). Other studies used econometric methods to assess the influence of these characteristics on business growth (Federico et al. 2012; Capelleras and Kantis 2009). These studies mainly referred to the early phases of the business life cycle to demonstrate empirically the key role of entrepreneurial human capital (founders and their networks) in post-entry performance. However, they did not address the issues related to business performance that arise once firms outgrow the initial phase and move into the young firm stage.

In addition, the aforementioned studies were based on surveys conducted between 2001 and 2003. Since then, there have been many important changes in the region. For instance, most Latin American countries have experienced large economic growth periods leading to important changes not only at the economic level (e.g. new activities and new industries), but also at the social level (e.g. a larger middle class and access to education). In addition, following international trends, entrepreneurship and young growth-oriented firms have increasingly become part of the policy agenda in many Latin American countries (Kantis 2014; Kantis et al. 2012).

Interestingly, one of the unique cross-regional studies of the contribution of small and young firms to employment and job creation showed that, in Latin America, the contribution of young firms was below the median of the developing world (Ayyagari et al. 2011). Trying to shed some light on this result, a recent study affirmed that, in spite of what many people think, Latin America is characterized by a high level of entrepreneurship; however, these new firms tend to be smaller than in other regions and do not grow as much as similar firms in other regions (Lederman et al. 2014). Largely, this situation has been explained by the pre-eminence of informal micro-enterprises with low productivity levels and growth ambitions that characterize most countries in Latin America (CAF 2013).

Others argue that among the reasons young firms grow as slowly as they do is the lack of innovation. In fact, young firms in Latin America, defined as those that have been in business for ten years or less, tended to exhibit innovation rates slightly lower than mature firms (World Bank 2014). However, the same report remarked that there was an important degree of heterogeneity in terms of the innovative profiles of young firms. In fact, by grouping young firms according to their dynamism, these authors reported that such firms—defined as those selling to foreign markets, based on new products, or having created more employment than the median in their countries—exhibited significantly higher innovation rates than older firms and other young non-dynamic firms.

In this context, there is increasing consensus about the need to change the policy emphasis from supporting small firms to supporting startups and young firms because of their potential to innovate and close the productivity and growth gaps (Lederman et al. 2014; CAF 2013). However, fulfilling these expectations depends on how sustainable and profitable young firms' growth is in the long term. Therefore, there is a need to understand the main characteristics of young Latin American firms and their growth dynamics over time. This phase of organizational development is the least explored. It is the phase during which firms, having surpassed the startup hurdles, begin to face strategic and organizational challenges that can affect business performance (Garnsey 1998; Greiner 1972; Levie and Lichtenstein 2010).

This chapter offers new empirical evidence about the performance of young firms in Latin America by focusing on four research questions. The first three questions, which are addressed using statistical analysis, are (i) What are the main characteristics of young Latin American firms and their entrepreneurs? (ii) How well do these firms perform in terms of growth and productivity? (iii) How do young firms compare with mature companies? We seek to answer the fourth question—(iv) What are the principal characteristics associated with the performance of young firms?—by estimating different econometric models using a sub-sample of the firm population. Answering these questions should provide some inputs for policymakers interested in reducing the persistent Latin American productivity gap.

Conceptual Framework and Literature Review

Davidsson et al. (2006) argued that "firm growth is a complex phenomenon. It is not unidimensional and it is hard to predict and assess. Further, it can manifest itself in various ways, and consequently it can have differential effects on several different levels." Firm growth has been well studied, but the results of these studies vary widely. For instance, a review of 19 studies found that high-growth firms tended to be young (Henrekson and Johansson 2010), while a US-based study found that high-growth firms tended to be more mature (Acs et al. 2008).[1] Consequently, there is no unified, generally accepted theory of firm growth. Instead, different theoretical perspectives are combined in several integrated or holistic models (e.g. Baum et al. 2001; Chrisman et al. 1998; Storey 1994). These integrated approaches provide a more comprehensive view of firm growth than does an individual analysis of each variable (or set of variables) in isolation. We follow this approach to develop an integrated model of firm growth, where the following theoretical perspectives are combined: (i) entrepreneurial capabilities and firm resources, (ii) firm strategic behavior, and (iii) business regulations.

The rationale to include the characteristics of entrepreneurs is that, compared with large companies, young small and medium enterprises (SMEs) are characterized by a strong emotional connection between the owner and the firm (Chan and Foster 2001). Thus, certain characteristics of the entrepreneur strongly influence not only the type of firm that will be created, but also the way it will be managed (Bridge et al. 1998). The human capital of entrepreneurs may be seen as a unique resource (Álvarez and Busenitz 2001) that is formed through education and previous entrepreneurial experience (Brüderl et al. 1992). Higher education provides superior technical knowledge and contributes positively to developing individual learning capabilities to process new information and, likewise, recognize business opportunities (Shane 2000; Ucbasaran et al. 2008). Additionally, more educated entrepreneurs have the necessary skills, discipline, motivation, information, and self-confidence to attain higher growth rates in their businesses (Cooper et al. 1994). Previous working or entrepreneurial experiences also prove to be fruitful, as they provide information, knowledge, and abilities that allow the entrepreneur to efficiently solve new problems. Moreover, such experiences may contribute to the development of better technical and managerial skills, wider business networks, and access to specific, tacit knowledge about markets and customer needs (Shane 2000). Therefore, we expect the experience of the founder to have a positive effect on firm growth (e.g. Stuart and Abetti 1990; Colombo and Grilli 2005). The capabilities and characteristics of employees may also be relevant to firm performance, especially for young, growing companies.

Firm resources are relevant during the startup and young phases when firms need to achieve a threshold of scale and overcome what Stinchcombe (1965) called the "liability of newness." According to the resource-based view of a firm, resources are the primary driver of firm performance and greatly influence its strategy (Grant 1991). Although many resources may be identified as determinants of firm growth, one of the most studied and empirically examined has been financial capital (Cooper et al. 1994; Gilbert et al. 2006). A higher level of financial capital may allow entrepreneurs to use more aggressive growth strategies or more ambitious investment projects, which suggests there is a positive relationship between using external sources of financing (e.g. banks, governments, and venture capitalists) and business growth (Lee et al. 2001).

Additionally, financial capital may help young firms overcome their initial disadvantages and "mistakes" (Chrisman et al. 1998). Although most of the funding of young firms comes from entrepreneurs' own savings or money borrowed from relatives and friends, the amount of cash needed to accelerate growth processes usually exceeds these personal sources. Many young, growing firms rely on external sources of financing to accelerate their growth perspectives. However, smaller and younger firms tend to be at a disadvantage in securing bank credit compared to larger and older firms (see Chap. 8). Moreover, extensive research demonstrates the evolution of different sources of entrepreneurial finance throughout the life cycle of the business, for instance from friends and family during gestation to angel investors during the early stage and to venture capital for further expansion (Mason 1998; Gompers and Lerner 2004). In Latin America, these latter sources of entrepreneurial financing have recently begun to emerge but remain weakly developed (Kantis et al. 2005; Kantis 2010, 2014).

Strategic behavior is another factor that affects firm performance because it reflects the way entrepreneurs organize and assign resources to achieve business objectives. Innovation is one strategic behavior of particular importance. Innovative activities like R&D aimed at developing new products and processes or new business models may contribute to the emergence of new firms, the establishment of a sound competitive position, and/or improvements to the levels of productivity (Acs and Audretsch 2005; Audretsch and Keilbach 2007; Quince and Whittaker 2002).

Finally, from a broad systemic perspective, the emergence of dynamic young firms also depends on the institutional setting (Kantis et al. 2005; Kantis 2014; Acs et al. 2014). Regulations form part of this setting that can directly influence the performance of young firms by either restricting or enabling growth. The institutional setting also indirectly influences performance through its effect on the business environment for young firms (i.e. access to financing, human capital, and the stock of entrepreneurs willing to start new companies).

DATA AND RESEARCH METHODOLOGY

We base this study on a sample of young firms extracted from the World Bank Enterprise Surveys (WBES). We use the latest round of surveys, which were conducted in 2010. Young firms, our target group, are defined as those between four and ten years old.[2] Our sample includes only those countries with information on at least 30 young firms and with no missing values in the performance indicators (sales, employment, and productivity). After applying these filters, we end up with a final sample of 1074 young firms from Argentina, Brazil, Chile, Colombia, Costa Rica, Ecuador, Guatemala, Mexico, Panama, Paraguay, Peru, and Uruguay (see tables [6.8, 6.9, and 6.10] of independent variables and performance measures in the Appendix). To measure the business performance of young firms, we consider the following variables:

- **Average annual sales growth:** Using Haltiwanger's specification adopted by the World Bank, we compute sales growth as the average of the differences in sales between 2007 and 2009 divided by the average sales over that period (World Bank 2013).[3] We then divide this figure by the number of inter-annual periods (two) to obtain an average annual rate. The advantage of this specification is that, using average sales instead of initial sales controls for those cases where relative growth is large only because the initial base is too small, which could arguably be the case in many observations in the sample given our focus on young firms. The specific formula we use to calculate this variable is:

$$\mathrm{Sales\,Growth} = \frac{\left(\dfrac{\left(\mathrm{Sales}\,2009 - \mathrm{Sales}\,2007\right)}{\left(\mathrm{Sales}\,2009 + \mathrm{Sales}\,2007\right)/2}\right)}{2}$$

- **Average annual employment growth:** Using the same specification adopted above, we compute employment growth as the average of the differences in the number of full-time permanent workers between 2007 and 2009 divided by the average number of such workers over the same period of time. We then divide this figure by the number of inter-annual periods (two) to obtain the average annual employment growth rate.
- **Labor productivity:** We estimate labor productivity using the ratio of sales to the number of full-time permanent workers in 2009.

To answer our last research question about the main factors associated with the performance of young firms, we estimate different
econometric models for each of the aforementioned performance indicators. Independent variables refer to a set of dimensions associated with:
(i) the capabilities of entrepreneurs and firms, (ii) the adoption of innovations, (iii) financial constraints, (iv) market strategy, (v) the regulatory
framework, and (vi) firm characteristics. A complete description of these
variables is provided in Table 6.7 in the Appendix. The unit of analysis is
the firm and the model specification is the following:

$$y = \alpha + \beta 1 EXP + \beta 2 WKF + \beta 3 TRG + \beta 4 ASSIST + \beta 5 INNOV + \\ \beta 6 FIN + \beta 7 DIV + \beta 8 REG + \gamma AGE + \gamma 1 AGE^2 + \theta INSIZE + \\ \theta 1 INSIZE^2 + \lambda GEN + \phi LOC + \delta Sector + \delta 1 Country + \mu$$

We estimate all of these models first using ordinary least squares (OLS)
methods with robust standard errors. We limit model estimations to
manufacturing firms since only these firms were asked questions about
innovation practices and human resource capabilities. In addition, we
exclude Brazilian firms from our estimations since the survey did not
include data about innovation or information on technical assistance and
human resources.[4] The number of observations in the models declines to
444 firms as a result of these restrictions.[5]

We have a few caveats on the limitations of the data that could affect
our estimation results. First, the sample includes only surviving firms.
Survival and attrition bias is a question largely discussed in the literature
on firm growth (e.g. Nightingale and Coad 2013). This bias principally
affects the representativeness of our sample since it includes only a subset of young survivor firms. Hence, some caution should be taken when
trying to generalize the results of this study for the whole population.[6]
Also, our sample includes outliers and variables with a huge dispersion due
to extreme values,[7] which is expected given the heterogeneous nature of
the firm population under study. To deal with this, we report the median
instead of the mean as a summary measure.

Young Latin American Firms and Their Entrepreneurs: A Portrait Based on Descriptive Statistics

Almost one in five Latin American firms is young, meaning it is between
four and ten years old.[8] The majority of young firms in the region are
between eight and ten years old. Young firms in Chile, Ecuador, and

Panama tend to be older than the rest of the sample, while those in Uruguay and Costa Rica tend to be younger. Interestingly, in several countries, especially Argentina, Chile, and Peru, young firms tend to have a larger presence in knowledge-based sectors (i.e. technology services and engineering-intensive manufacturing) than the more mature companies, demonstrating a trend toward the diversification of the regional industrial structure.[9] Most of the entrepreneurs are male, although 40% of the young firms are either managed by a woman or have a woman among their founders.[10]

Looking at prior experience, the entrepreneurs in young firms tended to work as employees before starting their companies (75%); only one-third held managerial positions prior to working at the current firm. This finding is more frequent in Argentina (44%), Chile (42%), Guatemala (40%), and Paraguay (47%).[11] The Argentinean, Chilean, and Colombian entrepreneurs have the most experience in a similar industry (at least 20 years). Previous industry experience may positively influence business growth by allowing the entrepreneur to exploit competitive advantages derived from tacit knowledge, mainly by knowing both *how* and *who*. Entrepreneurs who were previously unemployed or that started their own company because of a lack of better job opportunities represent a limited proportion of the sample (3%). Of note, informal enterprises, where necessity entrepreneurship tends to dominate, are not included in the WBES.

In terms of firm size, half of the young Latin American firms in the sample employ between 10 and 49 full-time workers.[12] In other words, firms tend to be small, with a median number of full-time workers of around 18; however, there is significant dispersion across firms, with manufacturing firms (20 full-time workers) tending to be larger than services firms (17). These figures hide an important heterogeneity among countries. In Peru (seven full-time workers) and Panama (eight), the median sizes of young firms tend to be smaller; whereas in Chile (35) and Costa Rica (47), firms tend to be larger, though still smaller than mature firms.[13]

In general, most young firms tend to focus their sales in domestic markets. At the regional level, 84% do not export (compared to 75% of mature companies) and direct exports account for less than 5% of sales. Only in Costa Rica, Argentina, and Peru is there a relevant group of young active exporters (i.e. exporting 20% or more of their sales).[14] Young international new ventures or "born globals," as referred to in the literature, are not a generalized phenomenon in the region.[15]

Data on innovation-related activities indicate that almost 43% of the young firms in Latin America performed R&D activities between 2007 and 2009, in line with mature firms. Moreover, most of the ones we study introduced new products and/or processes during this period.[16] On the one hand, Argentina, Paraguay, and Uruguay had more young firms introducing new products. On the other hand, process innovations were more frequent among young firms in Chile, Colombia, and Peru. These findings align with the study presented in Chap. 2, which found that most firms in the region are actively introducing product and/or process innovations. While both young and mature firms innovate at similar rates, new products introduced by young firms constitute a larger proportion of sales compared to mature firms. New products account for at least 25% of sales in young firms compared to roughly 33% of sales in mature firms.

The Growth of Young Latin American Firms

Young Latin American firms usually begin operations as micro-enterprises. More than 40% have no more than five employees during the initial startup phase.[17] Young firms in certain countries, like Chile and Argentina, tend to start bigger than those in other countries (their median size is twice that for the region of six employees). Once in the market, these young firms do not just survive, but grow enough to become part of the SME segment. In fact, the median size in 2007, when these firms were about five years old, was 15 full-time workers—three times the initial size.[18] However, this initial growth tends to slow down in subsequent years; the increase in median firm size between 2007 and 2009 was just 20%. Interestingly, this performance cannot be attributed, at least predominantly, to the international crisis since the effect in most Latin American countries was small (World Bank 2010).

In addition, young firms, on the whole, perform better than mature companies. For instance, young firms in 9 out of 12 Latin American countries saw their sales growth outperform that of mature firms (5 vs 1.3%, respectively, using median values).[19]

Even in a context of lower dynamism, 28% of young Latin American firms grew in size (employment) at an annual average rate of 20% during the period surveyed.[20] In other words, a large number of young firms in our sample could be identified as high growth performers, despite the general finding of low firm-level growth.[21]

To capture the heterogeneity of the growth profiles of young firms, we propose a taxonomy that takes into account the different growth rates of past years and the final scale achieved. For the different thresholds for firm growth, we adopt the definitions of the OECD and the Global Entrepreneurship Monitor for moderate (annual average growth of 10%) and high growth (20%). The scale is calculated using a widely recognized size threshold based on employment. We define a micro-enterprise as a firm that has fewer than ten employees, while an SME has ten or more. By combining both variables (growth and final scale), we arrive at a taxonomy based on five categories (see Table 6.1 and Fig. 6.1).

Table 6.1 Taxonomy of young firms

		Average sales growth rate (2007–2009)		
		Low growth (10% or below)	Moderate growth (11% ≥ 19%)	High growth (20% or more)
Size (Employees in 2009)	Micro (1–9 employees)	Low-growth micro-enterprises		Micro-enterprises in transition
	SME (10+ employees)	Low-growth SMEs	Moderate-growth SMEs	High-growth SMEs

Source: Authors' elaboration

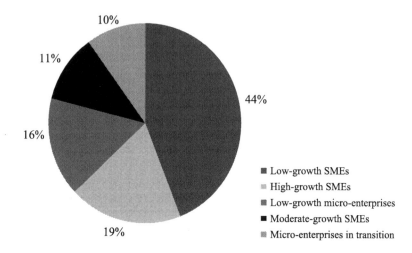

Fig. 6.1 Composition of the sample according to the taxonomy of the growth and scale of young firms

Source: Authors' elaboration based on WBES data

Using this taxonomy, Fig. 6.1 shows that low-growth SMEs make up the largest group (44%) within the subset of young firms. These are the firms that grew enough to become an SME, but stagnated in subsequent years. High-growth SMEs are the second largest group (19%), followed by moderate-growth SMEs (11%). Two distinct groups arise from the micro-enterprises: the first comprises micro-firms with low to negative growth rates (16% of firms), and the second those micro-enterprises experiencing high enough growth to be transitioning into the world of SMEs (10%). Overall, if we only consider those firms that experienced moderate to high growth rates during the 2007–2009 period (i.e. micro-enterprises in transition, moderate-growth SMEs, and high-growth SMEs), we see that growing firms represent 40% of the total sample of young firms.

One interesting feature of the high-growth SME segment is its important contribution to the sophistication of the regional business structure. For instance, these firms (29%) tend to be more concentrated in knowledge-intensive sectors, such as engineering-intensive manufacturing or technological services, than the rest of the young firms (21%) or the mature firms (21%).[22] To a lesser extent, the same is the case for micro-enterprises in transition (27% are in knowledge-intensive sectors), supporting the idea that they have potential to enlarge the base of growing and innovative SMEs.

THE PRODUCTIVITY OF YOUNG LATIN AMERICAN FIRMS

In terms of labor productivity, the results of our sample show that young firms' productivity levels are lower than those of mature firms. To calculate the productivity gap, we estimate the labor productivity for each firm using the logarithm of sales per employee in the previous fiscal year, with sales expressed in constant 2009 US dollars. Then, we compute the medians for these values and compare young and mature firms. We use the median instead of the mean because this measure is less sensitive to outliers and extreme values. At the regional level and considering all the sectors, the productivity gap between young and mature firms in 2009 was about 21% (Table 6.2). Three years earlier this difference was 27%, thus the gap was shrinking. By sector, the results are mixed. For services and manufacturing firms, the gap narrowed, while for commercial firms, the gap widened.

Overall, the progress made in reducing the productivity gap can be attributed to improving productivity in young firms, especially in the services

Table 6.2   Productivity gap between young and mature firms by sector (*median values*)

	Productivity gap (mature firms = 100)	
Sector	2007	2009
Manufacturing	73.7	79.4
Commerce	84.4	73.9
Services	70.3	81.1
Total	**72.8**	**79.2**

Source: Authors' elaboration based on WBES data

Table 6.3   Productivity growth between 2007 and 2009 by age and sector (median values)

Sector	Productivity growth: young firms (%)	Productivity growth: mature firms (%)
Manufacturing	1.4	–2.3
Commerce	–7.7	–1.1
Services	4.9	–2.3
Total	**2.1**	**–2.1**

Source: Authors' elaboration based on WBES data

sector. At the same time, mature firms experienced some setbacks in their productivity levels, which contributed to closing the gap (Table 6.3).

However, as mentioned, young firms are not a homogeneous group and comparing productivity levels according to the taxonomy of young firms reveals interesting results. For example, the levels of productivity among growing SMEs (moderate and high growth) are similar to those observed among mature firms. This situation is chiefly driven by the manufacturing sector, where young growing SMEs outperform mature firms. In addition, high-growth SMEs and micro-enterprises in transition show the biggest increases in productivity. Trends among moderate-growth SMEs are mixed: positive in commerce and services but negative in manufacturing (Table 6.4).

In sum, there is widespread heterogeneity among young firms. Between 2007 and 2009, their initial growth slowed. Despite this, the taxonomy proposed in this chapter shows that an important segment of young SMEs has continued growing and contributed to closing the productivity gap with mature firms. At the same time, a promising segment of rapidly growing micro-enterprises has been identified. The next section explores in depth the main factors associated with young manufacturing firms' growth and productivity.

Table 6.4 Productivity levels and growth according to the taxonomy of young firms by sector

Taxonomy of young firms	Productivity gap 2009 (mature firms = 100)				Productivity growth 2007–2009			
	Manufacturing	Commerce	Services	Total	Manufacturing	Commerce	Services	Total
Low-growth micro-enterprises	54.0	63.2	82.5	61.3	−8.1%	−35.2%	16.0%	−4.1%
Micro-enterprises in transition	62.9	91.0	76.0	67.8	69.1%	64.3%	21.6%	60.6%
Low-growth SMEs	73.6	87.8	84.6	77.2	−19.7%	−26.1%	−20.2%	−17.6%
Moderate-growth SMEs	110.3	105.0	76.9	102.9	−7.2%	3.5%	10.3%	−13.2%
High-growth SMEs	104.8	65.0	67.1	97.9	77.8%	84.8%	29.9%	76.8%
Total	**79.4**	**73.9**	**81.1**	**79.2**	**2.8%**	**−14.2%**	**10.2%**	**4.2%**

Source: Authors' elaboration based on WBES data

The Performance of Young Manufacturing Firms: Estimation Results[23]

In this section, we use OLS regression techniques to identify the main factors associated with the performance of young firms. We estimate four models using performance measures for labor productivity, sales growth, and employment growth as the dependent variables. We estimate additional models to check robustness.

Labor Productivity

Table 6.5 presents the OLS regression results for the two specifications using the logarithm of labor productivity levels as the dependent variable. Model 1 includes the main firm characteristics described earlier. Model 2 slightly adapts the first model by including a variable that captures the potential effect of firm dynamism on productivity levels by adding a dummy variable equal to one for high-growth firms and zero otherwise.[24]

Model 1 shows a positive and statistically significant association between workforce training and labor productivity for the sample of young manufacturing firms under study. There is a similar statistically significant relationship for hiring technical assistance (0.304). As we suggested earlier, these results propose that human capital variables (internal and external) can play an important role in boosting the productivity levels of young firms, which may help improve their competitive position in the market. In fact, as Model 2 shows, there is a positive and statistically significant relationship between the high growth status of young manufacturing firms and productivity levels. That is, productivity levels of high growth firms are, on average, 32 percentage points higher than their non-high growth counterparts.

Unsurprisingly, financial constraints are negatively associated with labor productivity in both models. The models show that young manufacturing firms that are either rationed or discouraged (financial constraint variable), on average, have labor productivity 25 percentage points lower, holding all else equal. However, the direction of causality could be the reverse, with less productive firms facing more difficulties accessing external resources.

Other variables, such as innovating and adopting diversification strategies, do not seem to be statistically associated with productivity. To some extent, this could be due to non-contemporaneous effects.[25] Finally, initial size has a slight positive effect on labor productivity, meaning firms that

Table 6.5 Regression outputs: labor productivity levels (in logs)

	Model 1	Model 2
Industry experience	0.0013	0.0009
	(0.0048)	(0.0047)
Workforce capabilities	0.0052*	0.0053*
	(0.0029)	(0.0029)
Workforce training	0.3302***	0.3223***
	(0.1039)	(0.1014)
Technical assistance	0.3037***	0.2734***
	(0.1036)	(0.103)
Innovation	0.105	0.103
	(0.1022)	(0.1019)
Financial constraint	−0.2480**	−0.2278**
	(0.0966)	(0.0974)
Diversification	−0.001	−0.0011
	(0.0017)	(0.0016)
Regulations	0.0237	0.0217
	(0.0511)	(0.0507)
Firm age	−0.0411	−0.0343
	(0.0324)	(0.0323)
Firm age squared	0.0074	0.0084
	(0.0126)	(0.0126)
Initial size	0.0027***	0.0031***
	(0.001)	(0.001)
Initial size squared	−0.0000**	−0.0000**
	(0.0000)	(0.0000)
Gender	−0.2367***	−0.2207**
	(0.0892)	(0.0884)
Location	0.0407	0.0418
	(0.1568)	(0.1562)
High growth (=1)	n.a.	0.3160**
		(0.1278)
Constant	10.1816***	10.1492***
	(0.267)	(0.267)
N	444	444
F-test	13.05***	12.36***
R²	0.3349	0.3463

Source: Authors' elaboration based on WBES data

Notes: * Coefficient is statistically significant at the 10% level, ** at the 5% level, *** at the 1% level; no asterisk means the coefficient is not different from zero with statistical significance. Robust standard errors are reported in parenthesis. Industry and country dummies are included but they are not reported here for the sake of simplicity. n.a. = not applicable

started out larger had higher productivity levels, although the magnitude of the effect is quite small. This finding may be due to minimum economies of scales.

Sales and Employment Growth

Previous studies in Latin America generally found a positive relationship between firm performance and entrepreneurial capabilities (Kantis et al. 2005; Federico et al. 2012). However, as discussed below, our estimations cannot confirm these results.

In the first model, the dependent variable is sales growth. The results of the OLS estimation show that, on the one hand, entrepreneurs' industry-specific experience has a slight positive association with sales growth; however, it is only significant at the 10% level and the magnitude is quite small. On the other hand, hiring technical assistance for quality control and/or certification has a positive relationship with sales growth and is statistically significant at the 1% level. Technical assistance is associated with a 9 percentage point increase in sales growth, all else being equal. In addition, the perception that regulations are an obstacle (e.g. taxation, trade and labor norms, and licenses and permits) has a negative effect on sales growth at a 5% significance level, although no such effect was found for employment growth. This result shows the negative influence that the regulatory framework may have on sales growth, although we note that obstacles are based on the subjective opinions of survey respondents.[26] Finally, neither workforce capabilities nor training were significant in the sales growth model.

The second model looks at employment growth. Those variables associated with the capabilities of entrepreneurs and firms (i.e. entrepreneurs' industry experience, workforce capabilities, and training) are all positively related with growth, but none are statistically significant. In turn, the results show that employment growth is negatively associated with firms that are credit constrained or discouraged, which may suggest the importance of access to external financing to expand the workforce. Financially constrained young manufacturing firms are associated with a larger decrease in employment growth than non-financially constrained firms (of about 6 percentage points), all else being equal. Young firms may need additional sources of financing to expand employment. Finally, we find a negative and highly statistically significant relationship between initial size and employment growth. This result, also observed in the sales growth model, suggests that young firms that begin operations with a smaller initial size tend to grow at a higher rate than those whose initial size was larger. In addition, we find evidence of a non-linear influence of initial size on growth. This could mean that smaller young firms need to grow at a greater rate in order to overcome their initial size disadvantages and to increase their chances of survival. However, the magnitude of these coefficients is small and they should be interpreted accordingly.

In sum, both the sales and employment growth models demonstrate low predictive power (R^2). However, a few significant findings emerge. One interesting result is that sales and employment growth are not affected by the same constraints.[27] This result is not necessarily obvious for policy-makers who tend to associate firm growth with job creation. For example, while technical assistance is found to be statistically associated with sales growth, the same relationship is not found for employment growth; regulations are found to have a negative and statistically significant effect on sales growth, but not on employment growth. Instead, in the employment growth model, access to external financing is the obstacle that has a negative and statistically significant effect on employment growth. One commonality between the two models is the negative association between initial firm size and growth. However, the low explanatory power of both models suggests that there might be other important variables associated with growth of young firms that are not accounted for here. Some of these variables could include entrepreneurial team characteristics, strategy implementation, entrepreneurial orientation, or the role of networks, which could not be included due to data limitations (Table 6.6).

Robustness Checks

We perform several sensitivity tests to examine further the empirical robustness of our results. We conduct these checks to observe whether a change in the key variables produces measurably different results (i.e. due to measurement error).[28] In the first test, we substitute firm productivity growth for the dependent variable firm productivity level. Using firm productivity growth, the results are qualitatively similar to those in the above models. Simple regressions show a positive association of both techni-

Table 6.6   Regression results: sales and employment growth

Dependent variable	Sales growth	Employment growth
Industry experience	0.0024*	0.0002
	(0.0013)	(0.0010)
Workforce capabilities	0.0006	0.0007
	(0.0008)	(0.0007)
Workforce training	0.0112	0.0137
	(0.0327)	(0.0236)
Technical assistance	0.0905***	0.0263
	(0.0319)	(0.0257)
Innovation	0.0002	–0.024
	(0.0308)	(0.0232)
Financial constraint	–0.038	–0.0558**
	(0.0286)	(0.0237)
Diversification	–0.0005	0.0001
	(0.0005)	(0.0004)
Regulations	–0.0304**	–0.0067
	(0.0151)	(0.0129)
Firm age	–0.0141	–0.0112
	(0.0091)	(0.0075)
Firm age squared	0.0069*	0.0021
	(0.0039)	(0.003)
Initial size	–0.0009***	–0.0008***
	(0.0002)	(0.0002)
Initial size squared	0.0000***	0.0000***
	(0.0000)	(0.0000)
Gender	–0.0702***	0.0116
	(0.0282)	(0.0233)
Location	–0.0021	0.0245
	(0.0371)	(0.0318)
Constant	0.082	0.0633
	(0.0667)	(0.0531)
N	444	444
F-test	2.56***	1.96***
R^2	0.1317	0.0810

Source: Authors' elaboration based on WBES data

Notes: * Coefficient is statistically significant at the 10% level, ** at the 5% level, *** at the 1% level; no asterisk means the coefficient is not different from zero with statistical significance. Robust standard errors are reported in parenthesis. Industry and country dummies are included but they are not reported here for the sake of simplicity

cal assistance and industry experience on firm productivity, although the association is only statistically significant for technical assistance at the 5% level. This is consistent with the positive relationships found in the above four models. We also do a second check with firm profitability. We find similar positive relationships between technical assistance and industry experience, and firm profitability, although neither association was significant. In addition, innovation is positively associated with firm profitability at the 10% level, whereby a firm's innovation increases firm profitability by 6.9 percentage points, all else being equal. This is the only model that shows innovation significantly affecting firm performance (albeit at a low level). On the whole, these results demonstrate that the direction of the main independent variables do not change when we use different measures of firm performance. In other words, the results are not sensitive to only one measure of firm performance.

CONCLUSIONS AND POLICY IMPLICATIONS

Young firms are receiving an increasing amount of attention worldwide. Their potential economic contribution has transformed them into relevant players whose importance for productivity growth should not be ignored. In Latin America, any strategy aimed at closing the productivity gap should consider young firms as part of the growing number of competitive SMEs. The key question is to what extent these young firms can contribute to reducing this gap.

To shed some light on their characteristics and performance, we analyzed a sample of young firms from selected Latin American countries. The findings demonstrated the heterogeneous nature of young firms. In particular, we observed that high- and moderate-growth SMEs, especially in the manufacturing sector, are more productive than mature firms, which could help close the productivity gap. Micro-enterprises in transition showed important increases in productivity, raising positive expectations for their potential in the future. We also found that most of the young firms we sampled managed to survive and grow enough within a five-year period to become part of the SME sector. This first stage of important growth tended to slow down during the last three years, although an important group of them continued to grow. In this general context of low growth rates, young firms tended to outperform more mature firms.

These results highlight the need to avoid generic and uniform strategies that assume a one-type-fits-all scenario. The key challenges in reducing the productivity gap and fostering a more innovative business sector require renewed focus on young firms. However, not all young firms are equally equipped to contribute to improved performance in the Latin American business sector. Instead, a more selective approach is needed. The results of this study tend to discourage those very restrictive niche policy targets (i.e. policies oriented toward fast-growing "gazelles"). The taxonomy of young firms developed in this chapter suggests adopting a broader strategic vision aimed at enlarging the competitive SME sector by segmenting the programs, setting objectives, and implementing instruments adjusted for each segment. In particular, high-growth young SMEs should be supported without diverting attention to moderate-growth SMEs and micro-enterprises in transition. This could be a promising route for both developing young firms in the region and for closing the productivity gap.

Conceptually, growth and productivity constitute pillars of the long-term competitiveness of young firms. In this chapter, we used econometric models to identify the main factors associated with the sales and employment growth of young firms, and productivity levels. According to the results of the regressions, one way to foster the growth of young firms is to support their access to and development of *know how* and *know who*. Indeed our research found that workforce training and technical assistance were positively associated with productivity in young manufacturing firms. Mentoring programs and networking activities that make access to know how and know who easier, and quality management technical assistance, are promising ways to achieve these goals.[29] The models also showed that those firms that started at a smaller scale tended to grow at higher rates. This result may suggest the need to grow in order to overcome the disadvantages associated with their limited scale during the initial stages of the business lifecycle. Furthermore, considering our sample only includes surviving firms, this implication is even more important. Entrepreneurship policies should focus not only on startups but also on young firms' needs to scale up in order to face the specific challenges present at each stage of development.

Another interesting result of this study was the importance of removing the financial and regulatory constraints facing young firms. In particular, we found that financial constraints hindered productivity and employment growth. This demonstrated that venture capital initiatives alone may not be enough for a young firm to grow and that other financial products are needed that provide working capital at a lower cost than equity. Nurturing the entire finance curve (i.e. covering all stages of firm development) should be a key policy objective. Additionally, we found that regulations negatively affect sales growth. The perceptions of tax rates and tax regulations as obstacles seemed to provide disincentives for young firm performance. There is a clear need to review the regulations and taxes that inhibit creating and developing growth-oriented SMEs. These policies should be rethought to set the right incentives for dynamic entrepreneurship.

Even with these findings, our models explained a relatively low percentage of the variation in firm performance, setting the stage for further research in this area. For example, the introduction of new processes or products did not have a significant impact on the performance of young firms. This brings to light the need to give greater attention to the effectiveness of innovation efforts by such firms. For instance, the issue could be rooted in a lack of capabilities to manage the implementation of such projects. In this case, training programs on innovation management, innovation clubs that share best practices, or partial subsidies of innovation certified consultants could be part of a future agenda. Therefore, one possible way to support innovation would be to subsidize part of the cost of highly qualified human resources engaged in innovative projects led by young firms.[30]

Overall, this chapter offers a first glimpse into young business performance. We derived clear policy implications from the results despite some data limitations. Further research is needed to deepen the understanding of the dynamics of young business performance and the contribution of young firms to economic development in the region.

APPENDIX

Table 6.7   Definition of independent variables

Dimension	Variable	Definition	Type
Capabilities of entrepreneurs and firms	Entrepreneurs' industry experience	Years of previous experience in the same industry of the top management	Continuous
	Workforce capabilities	Proportion of the workforce with at least a Bachelor's degree	Continuous
	Workforce training	Dummy variable that equals 1 if the firm has implemented some training activities	Binary
	Technical assistance	Dummy variable that equals 1 if the firm has hired some type of external technical services*	Binary
Innovation	Product and process innovation	Dummy variable that assumes value 1 if the firm has introduced some product and/or process innovation over the last three years	Binary
Financial resources	Financial constraints	A dummy variable that assumes value 1 in the case of firms that were rationed from banks or were discouraged from applying to a line of credit	Binary
Market strategy	Diversification	The mathematical complement of the percentage of sales corresponding to the main product	Continuous

Table 6.7 (continued)

Dimension	Variable	Definition	Type
Regulations	Regulations	Latent variable reflecting the importance of certain regulatory and taxation obstacles to firms' operations**	Continuous
Firm characteristics	Firm age	Years since the firm began operations (centered at the median value)	Continuous
	Firm age squared	Squared term of firm age	Continuous
	Initial firm size	Number of full-time workers at the beginning (centered at the median value)	Continuous
	Initial size squared	Squared term of initial firm size	Continuous
	Gender	A dummy variable with value 1 if the firm has at least one female owner and/or the top manager is female	Binary
	Location	A dummy variable with value 1 if the firm is located in a capital city or in a city with a population of more than 1 million individuals	Binary
Control variables	Industry sector	Sector dummies using ECLAC's taxonomy of manufacturing activities in (i) labor intensive, (ii) natural resources intensive, (iii) engineering intensive, and (iv) food and beverages***	Binary
	Country dummies		Binary

Notes: *We tested different types or areas of technical assistance and chose to report only the one corresponding to quality certification and quality management. ** To build the "regulations" variable, we conducted a Principal Components Factor Analysis on different interrelated scale variables. We asked the respondents to what extent (from 1 to 5) each of the following issues were an obstacle for their operations: (i) customs and trade regulations, (ii) tax rates, (iii) tax administration, (iv) labor regulations, (v) licenses and permits. The Cronbach Alpha for this construct was 0.751. *** We also used the OECD's taxonomy of technological level, and the results were the same as using ECLAC's taxonomy

Table 6.8 Performance measures: descriptive statistics by firm age (full sample)

		Initial size (no. employees)	Employees		Sales (USD 000)*		Sales growth	Employment growth	Productivity level 2009**	Productivity growth
			2007	2009	2007	2009				
Mature firms	Mean	22	90	96	8394	4,870,000	0.017	0.034	88,149	-0.014
	Median	6	30	31	1099	19,500	0.013	0.01	35,973	-0.02
	Standard deviation	84.2	228.6	210.4	30,700	34,100,000	0.255	0.19	873,594	0.269
	Coefficient variation	3.9	2.5	2.2	3.7	7.0	14.8	5.6	9.9	-19.8
	N	4217	4677	4677	4677	4677	4677	4677	4677	4677
Young firms	Mean	21	46	49	3516	2,200,000	0.069	0.083	75,546	-0.007
	Median	6	15	18	457	5800	0.056	0.081	28,355	-0.019
	Standard deviation	80.4	150.4	108.2	17,300	26,900,000	0.308	0.234	321,042	0.319
	Coefficient variation	3.8	3.3	2.2	4.9	12.2	4.4	2.8	4.2	-42.9
	N	1049	1074	1074	1074	1074	1074	1074	1074	1074
Total	Mean	22	82	87	7483	4,370,000	0.027	0.043	85,796	-0.012
	Median	6	25	28	919.2	16,000	0.020	0.024	34,710	-0.02
	Standard. deviation	83.4	216.8	196.3	28,700	32,900,000	0.266	0.200	799,924	0.279
	Coefficient variation	3.8	2.6	2.3	3.8	7.5	9.9	4.6	9.3	-22.4
	N	5266	5751	5751	5751	5751	5751	5751	5751	5751

Source: Authors' elaboration based on WBES data

Notes: * Expressed in constant 2009 US dollars. ** Estimated as the logarithm of sales over full-time permanent workers' ratio in 2009

Table 6.9   Performance measures: descriptive statistics by sector (only young firms)

		Initial size (no. employees)	Employees		Sales (USD 000)*		Sales growth	Employment growth	Productivity level 2009**	Productivity growth
			2007	2009	2007	2009				
Manufacturing	Mean	23.1	49.4	52.0	3435	1,360,000	0.064	0.078	70,244	−0.008
	Median	7.0	16.0	20.0	457.2	5000	0.060	0.080	26,630	−0.014
	Standard deviation	92.5	168.6	114.7	14,300	9,850,000	0.317	0.235	371,028	0.321
	Coefficient variation	4.0	3.4	2.2	4.2	7.3	5.0	3.0	5.3	−41.3
	N	722	738	738	738	738	738	738	738	738
Commerce	Mean	13.1	34.9	36.7	2978	1,630,000	0.064	0.100	105,774	−0.036
	Median	5.0	10.0	13.0	517.9	15,100	0.049	0.077	49,107	−0.04
	Standard deviation	28.0	105.1	75.1	6381	5,930,000	0.250	0.211	178,317	0.278
	Coefficient variation	2.1	3.0	2.0	2.1	3.6	3.9	2.1	1.7	−7.7
	N	190	194	194	194	194	194	194	194	194
Services	Mean	22.4	44.2	50.0	4701	7,380,000	0.102	0.085	62,214	0.033
	Median	6.0	15.0	17.0	341.2	6000	0.051	0.091	24,615	0.016
	Standard deviation	57.1	90.2	111.2	33,900	70,300,000	0.330	0.259	140,674	0.356
	Coefficient variation	2.5	2.0	2.2	7.2	9.5	3.2	3.0	2.3	10.7
	N	136	141	141	141	141	141	141	141	141

(continued)

Table 6.9 (continued)

Total		Initial size (no. employees)	Employees		Sales (USD 000)*		Sales growth growth	Employment growth	Productivity level 2009**	Productivity growth
			2007	2009	2007	2009				
	Mean	21.2	46.1	49.0	3519	2,200,000	0.069	0.083	75,613	-0.008
	Median	6.0	15.0	18.0	459	5800	0.056	0.081	28,485	-0.02
	Standard deviation	80.4	150.4	108.2	17,300	26,900,000	0.308	0.234	321,185	0.319
	Coefficient variation	3.8	3.3	2.2	4.9	12.2	4.5	2.8	4.2	-42.5
	N	1048	1073	1073	1073	1073	1073	1073	1073	1073

Source: Authors' elaboration based on WBES data

Notes: * Expressed in constant 2009 US dollars. ** Estimated as the logarithm of sales over full-time permanent workers' ratio in 2009

Table 6.10   Performance measures: descriptive statistics by country (only young firms)

Country	Variable	Mean	Median	Standard deviation	Coefficient variation	N
Argentina	Initial size (no. of employees)	31.8	11.0	69.0	2.2	60
	Employees 2007	62.3	25.0	103.0	1.7	63
	Employees 2009	63.1	20.0	102.4	1.7	63
	Sales 2007 (USD 000)*	8639	1235	23,500	2.7	63
	Sales 2009 (USD 000)	30,200	5880	69,200	2.3	63
	Sales growth	0.011	0.01	0.314	29.4	63
	Employment growth	0.024	0.029	0.197	8.2	63
	Productivity level 2009**	106,364	57,757	113,084	1.1	63
	Productivity growth	−0.007	−0.044	0.304	−41.1	63
Brazil	Initial size (no. of employees)	20	7	73	3.7	242
	Employees 2007	42	16	104	2.4	245
	Employees 2009	32	12	84	2.6	245
	Sales 2007 (USD 000)*	2098	276	8158	3.9	245
	Sales 2009 (USD 000)	4373	700	16,000	3.6	245
	Sales growth	0.110	0.109	0.416	3.8	245
	Employment growth	0.163	0.167	0.277	1.7	245
	Productivity level 2009**	65,879	20,051	222,574	3.4	245
	Productivity growth	−0.034	−0.04	0.442	−12.8	245

(*continued*)

Table 6.10 (continued)

Country	Variable	Mean	Median	Standard deviation	Coefficient variation	N
Chile	Initial size (no. of employees)	24.8	12.0	27.7	1.1	50
	Employees 2007	58.9	30.0	95.2	1.6	51
	Employees 2009	55.0	30.0	77.6	1.4	51
	Sales 2007 (USD 000)*	3928	1839	5304	1.4	51
	Sales 2009 (USD 000)	2,250,000	1,350,000	2,960,000	1.3	51
	Sales growth	0.073	0.046	0.216	3	51
	Employment growth	0.048	0.045	0.201	4.2	51
	Productivity level 2009**	96,949	48,983	161,911	1.7	51
	Productivity growth	0.031	0.019	0.202	6.5	51
Colombia	Initial size (no. of employees)	16.9	5.0	48.7	2.9	154
	Employees 2007	35.0	14.5	73.6	2.1	158
	Employees 2009	36.4	12.0	79.2	2.2	158
	Sales 2007 (USD 000)*	6063	402	38,800	6.4	158
	Sales 2009 (USD 000)	9,320,000	890,000	66,900,000	7.2	158
	Sales growth	0.041	0.054	0.312	7.6	158
	Employment growth	0.045	0.054	0.248	5.5	158
	Productivity level 2009**	49,870	28,675	79,859	1.6	158
	Productivity growth	−0.009	−0.028	0.314	−35.3	158

Table 6.10 (continued)

Country	Variable	Mean	Median	Standard deviation	Coefficient variation	N
Costa Rica	Initial size (no. of employees)	18.0	6.0	27.8	1.5	42
	Employees 2007	62.0	21.5	111.3	1.8	42
	Employees 2009	59.0	21.0	108.7	1.8	42
	Sales 2007 (USD 000)*	3018	799	6304	2.1	42
	Sales 2009 (USD 000)	1,810,000	400,000	3,670,000	2	42
	Sales growth	−0.03	−0.059	0.212	−7.1	42
	Employment growth	0.049	0.011	0.203	4.1	42
	Productivity level 2009**	57,551	37,768	86,848	1.5	42
	Productivity growth	−0.075	−0.097	0.234	−3.1	42
Ecuador	Initial size (no. of employees)	10.3	6.5	13.8	1.3	44
	Employees 2007	31.7	14.0	50.9	1.6	46
	Employees 2009	29.7	12.5	49.7	1.7	46
	Sales 2007 (USD 000)*	2674	581	6507	2.4	46
	Sales 2009 (USD 000)	2693	640	6454	2.4	46
	Sales growth	0.098	0.047	0.253	2.6	46
	Employment growth	0.078	0.063	0.191	2.4	46
	Productivity level 2009**	90,228	50,455	96,157	1.1	46
	Productivity growth	0.027	0.035	0.276	10.4	46

(*continued*)

Table 6.10 (continued)

Country	Variable	Mean	Median	Standard deviation	Coefficient variation	N
Guatemala	Initial size (no. of employees)	24.6	6.0	52.2	2.1	35
	Employees 2007	62.4	17.0	116.6	1.9	36
	Employees 2009	76.4	12.5	206.7	2.7	36
	Sales 2007 (USD 000)*	1943	212	4053	2.1	36
	Sales 2009 (USD 000)	14,600	1744	26,600	1.8	36
	Sales growth	0.028	-0.003	0.176	6.3	36
	Employment growth	0.022	0.000	0.224	10.2	36
	Productivity level 2009**	25,587	18,379	32,556	1.3	36
	Productivity growth	0.009	−0.014	0.242	27.7	36
Mexico	Initial size (no. of employees)	15.8	6.0	29.5	1.9	164
	Employees 2007	41.7	14.0	84.9	2	168
	Employees 2009	60.8	13.0	315.4	5.2	168
	Sales 2007 (USD 000)*	2375	258	8468	3.6	168
	Sales 2009 (USD 000)	37,400	4000	118,000	3.2	168
	Sales growth	0.053	0.037	0.257	4.9	168
	Employment growth	0.041	0.000	0.194	4.7	168
	Productivity level 2009**	42,727	22,200	93,979	2.2	168
	Productivity growth	0.017	0.001	0.251	14.6	168

Table 6.10 (continued)

Country	Variable	Mean	Median	Standard deviation	Coefficient variation	N
Panama	Initial size (no. of employees)	9.5	5.5	14.3	1.5	28
	Employees 2007	30.8	15.0	40.1	1.3	31
	Employees 2009	26.5	10.0	34.4	1.3	31
	Sales 2007 (USD 000)*	4237	161	8815	2.1	31
	Sales 2009 (USD 000)	14,000	500	45,100	3.2	31
	Sales growth	0.118	0.057	0.306	2.6	31
	Employment growth	0.100	0.080	0.124	1.2	31
	Productivity level 2009**	503,186	17,556	1,672,237	3.3	31
	Productivity growth	0.029	−0.034	0.346	12.1	31
Paraguay	Initial size (no. of employees)	20.2	6.5	25.6	1.3	34
	Employees 2007	54.1	20.0	86.1	1.6	34
	Employees 2009	32.4	17.0	52.0	1.6	34
	Sales 2007 (USD 000)*	3540	381	7355	2.1	34
	Sales 2009 (USD 000)	20,000,000	2,250,000	38,200,000	1.9	34
	Sales growth	0.066	0.051	0.182	2.8	34
	Employment growth	0.124	0.127	0.252	2	34
	Productivity level 2009**	69,941	23,905	105,981	1.5	34
	Productivity growth	−0.064	−0.041	0.250	−3.9	34

(*continued*)

Table 6.10 (continued)

Country	Variable	Mean	Median	Standard deviation	Coefficient variation	N
Peru	Initial size (no. of employees)	22.3	6.0	60.7	2.7	141
	Employees 2007	77.3	22.0	187.0	2.4	145
	Employees 2009	56.8	19.0	100.2	1.8	145
	Sales 2007 (USD 000)*	3039	683	6881	2.3	145
	Sales 2009 (USD 000)	11,000	2800	24,000	2.2	145
	Sales growth	0.077	0.105	0.274	3.6	145
	Employment growth	0.091	0.091	0.233	2.6	145
	Productivity level 2009**	57,786	28,097	110,905	1.9	145
	Productivity growth	−0.014	−0.002	0.268	−19.4	145
Uruguay	Initial size (no. of employees)	52.9	8.0	268.5	5.1	55
	Employees 2007	43.8	20.0	49.4	1.1	55
	Employees 2009	38.4	20.0	43.2	1.1	55
	Sales 2007 (USD 000)*	2696	1104	5866	2.2	55
	Sales 2009 (USD 000)	72,700	31,400	143,000	2	55
	Sales growth	0.115	0.096	0.217	1.9	55
	Employment growth	0.072	0.067	0.174	2.4	55
	Productivity level 2009**	80,884	41,602	129,612	1.6	55
	Productivity growth	0.050	0.044	0.227	4.5	55

Table 6.10 (continued)

Country	Variable	Mean	Median	Standard deviation	Coefficient variation	N
Total	Initial size (no. of employees)	21.2	6.0	80.4	3.8	1049
	Employees 2007	48.9	18.0	108.2	2.2	1074
	Employees 2009	46.1	15.0	150.4	3.3	1074
	Sales 2007 (USD 000)*	3516	457	17,300	4.9	1074
	Sales 2009 (USD 000)	2,200,000	5800	26,900,000	12.2	1074
	Sales growth	0.069	0.056	0.308	4.4	1074
	Employment growth	0.083	0.081	0.234	2.8	1074
	Productivity level 2009**	75,546	28,355	321,042	4.2	1074
	Productivity growth	−0.007	−0.019	0.319	−42.9	1074

Source: Authors' elaboration based on WBES data

Notes: * Expressed in constant 2009 US dollars. ** Estimated as the logarithm of sales over full-time permanent workers' ratio in 2009

NOTES

1. Empirical evidence about high-growth firms is still inconclusive and presents a number of methodological and statistical limitations, as recently highlighted by Nightingale and Coad (2013).
2. For some descriptive analyses, we also include a control group of mature firms (i.e. firms older than ten years).
3. All sales values are expressed in constant 2009 US dollars.
4. To account for the possible differential effect of certain variables on firm performance according to its dynamics, we run some auxiliary quartile regressions. Where appropriate, we include the results from these estimations in endnotes.
5. In addition, the models omit any firms that did not respond to innovation and/or human resources questions and therefore have missing information for these variables.
6. We recognize the possibility of endogeneity, which could bias our estimations. Unfortunately, in the case of young firms, there are not enough observations to build a panel, which is why we are forced to focus on cross-sectional data. Additionally, data limitations would reduce the number of valid instruments that could be used to control for potential endogeneity.
7. This situation would affect mean analyses since they are sensitive to the presence of extreme values.
8. This figure refers to the proportion of young firms of the full sample (see Table 6.8 in the Appendix). The proportion of young firms in the total sample is higher in Panama, at 27%, and in Peru, at 25%. On the contrary, Chile and Argentina have the lowest proportion of young firms (10%).
9. In Argentina, 38% of young firms are in knowledge-based sectors vs 31% mature firms; Chile, 33 vs 25%; Colombia, 23 vs 19%; Ecuador, 9 vs 6%; Panama, 13 vs 6%; Paraguay, 12 vs 7%; Peru, 25 vs 17%.
10. The presence of female entrepreneurs is lower in services than in manufacturing activities (38 vs 26%). In Paraguay and Colombia, the presence of female entrepreneurs or managers is higher than in the remaining countries, reaching 50%. On the contrary, in Chile, the percentage of women owners or managers is just above 20.
11. Unfortunately, the WBES do not ask about previous entrepreneurial experience, so it is not possible to track serial or habitual entrepreneurs.
12. According to the WBES definition, permanent, full-time employees are paid employees that are contracted for a term of one or more fiscal years and/or have a guaranteed renewal of their employment contract and that work for eight or more hours per day.
13. See more on the size distribution of firms among countries in the Appendix.
14. In Costa Rica, 27% are young active exporters; in Peru, 19%; and in Argentina, 17%.

15. "Born globals" are companies that conduct international business at or near the time of the firm's founding.
16. Innovation data is only available for manufacturing firms. The WBES of Brazil does not include the innovation section.
17. The initial startup phase refers to the number of full-time workers employed when the firm first started operations; the median is six full-time workers, but with a high degree of dispersion.
18. One key feature to note here is that firm heterogeneity, measured by the coefficient of variation, tends to diminish with time, although it is still important. The coefficient of variation of employment size is 3.78 at startup, 3.26 in 2007, and 2.21 in 2009.
19. We obtain the same results when we compare employment growth between young and mature firms (8 and 1%, respectively).
20. The annual average growth rate was particularly fast in Brazil (36%), Colombia (21%), and Peru (26%).
21. Looking at sales growth, the general overview is similar both in terms of average growth and the existence of a relevant proportion that grew their sales at an annual rate higher than 20% on average (25%).
22. Engineering-intensive manufacturing includes metal-mechanic, automotive industry, electrical, and electronic equipment. Technological services include, for example, software development.
23. Only manufacturing firms are included in the models because data about innovation and capabilities is only available for this sector. The innovation module was not included in the 2009 survey wave in Brazil, which is, therefore, excluded from the econometric analysis.
24. As in the previous section, we define high-growth firms as those young firms that are SMEs (i.e. ten or more employees in 2009) and experienced high-growth rates in sales between 2007 and 2009. We acknowledge that this estimator could be biased because of the potential endogeneity between the growth and productivity variables.
25. In addition, we view these results cautiously since we are only measuring labor productivity, which could be less influenced by such strategies.
26. In fact, it could be the case that those firms with poorer performance are those more prone to report external obstacles, precisely because of their situation. This would be a sign of potential bias due to endogeneity.
27. To check statistically the difference between the two sets of regressors, we run a test on the difference between the two joint sets of coefficients, finding it significantly different from 0. Then, we test the difference between the most relevant single coefficients in the two regressions. In this case, the results show that the coefficients for experience, technical assistance, and gender are statistically different in the two equations, but we cannot reject the null hypothesis of zero difference for financial constraint and regulation.

28. We also run the same regressions on a sample of older firms and the results are quite similar. The only change worth mentioning is that managers' previous work experience affects productivity and sales growth in young firms, while for older firms the signs are the opposite. This result makes sense since young firms' knowledge base and social capital (networks)—critical issues when it comes to firm performance—would depend heavily on entrepreneurs' previous industry experience. In older firms, formal and professional management and operation structures would already be in place, so the relationship between managers' industry experience and performance would be less clear.

29. Some institutions, such as Endeavor or Enablis, are examples of such programs. The Chilean government's new entrepreneurship policy includes a mentoring program. For earlier stages, business accelerators, such as Wayra or Nextplabs, both with operations at the regional level, should also be mentioned.

30. To some extent, the instrument Proyectos de Innovación de Amplia Cobertura implemented by the National Agency of Research and Innovation in Uruguay could be considered an example of this type of idea (see www.anii.org.uy). Other initiatives in this vein include the ANR Recursos Humanos Altamente Calificados executed by the National Agency of Science and Technology in Argentina (see http://www.mincyt.gob.ar).

REFERENCES

Acs, Z.J., and D.B. Audretsch. 2005. *Entrepreneurship, Innovation, and Technological Change*. Hanover, MA: Now Publishers.

Acs, Z.J., S. Desai, and J. Hessels. 2008. Entrepreneurship, Economic Development and Institutions. *Small Business Economics* 31(3): 219–234.

Acs, Z.J., L. Szerb, and E. Autio. 2014. *Global Entrepreneurship and Development Index 2014*. Washington, DC: Global Entrepreneurship and Development Institute. Available at http://thegedi.org/global-entrepreneurship-and-development-index/.

Álvarez, S., and L. Busenitz. 2001. The Entrepreneurship of Resource-Based Theory. *Journal of Management* 27(6): 755–775.

Audretsch, D., and M. Keilbach. 2007. The Theory of Knowledge Spillover Entrepreneurship. *Journal of Management Studies* 44(7): 1242–1254.

Ayyagari, M., A. Demirguc-Kunt, and V. Maksimovic. 2011. Small vs. Young Firms Across the World: Contribution to Employment, Job Creation, and Growth. Policy Research Working Paper 5631. Washington, DC: The World Bank.

Baum, J.R., E.A. Locke, and K.G. Smith. 2001. A Multidimensional Model of Venture Growth. *Academy of Management Journal* 44(2): 292–303.

Bridge, S., K. O'Neill, and S. Cromie. 1998. *Understanding Enterprise, Entrepreneurship and Small Business*. London: Palgrave Macmillan.

Brüderl, J., P. Preisendörfer, and R. Zieger. 1992. Survival Chances of Newly Founded Business Organizations. *American Sociological Review* 57(2): 227–242.

CAF. 2013. *Emprendimientos en América Latina. Desde la subsistencia hacia la transformación productiva*. Caracas: CAF Development Bank of Latin America (CAF).

Capelleras, J.L., and H. Kantis. 2009. *Nuevas empresas en América Latina: factores que favorecen su rápido crecimiento*. Barcelona: University of Barcelona, Office of Publications.

Chan, S., and M. Foster. 2001. Strategy Formulation in Small Business, the Hong Kong Experience. *International Small Business Journal* 19(3): 56–71.

Chrisman, J., A. Bauerschmidt, and C. Hofer. 1998. The Determinants of New Venture Performance: An Extended Model. *Entrepreneurship Theory and Practice* 23(Fall): 5–29.

Colombo, M., and L. Grilli. 2005. Founder's Human Capital and the Growth of new Technology-Based Firms: A Competence-Based View. *Research Policy* 34(6): 795–816.

Cooper, A., F.J. Gimeno-Gascon, and C. Woo. 1994. Initial Human and Financial Capital as Predictors of New Venture Performance. *Journal of Business Venturing* 9(5): 371–396.

Davidsson, P., F. Delmar, and J. Wiklund. 2006. *Entrepreneurship and the Growth of Firms*. Cheltenham, UK: Edward Elgar Publishing.

Federico, J., R. Rabetino, and H. Kantis. 2012. Comparing Young SMEs' Growth Determinants Across Regions. *Journal of Small Business and Enterprise Development* 19(4): 575–588.

Garnsey, E. 1998. A Theory of the Early Growth of the Firm. *Industrial and Corporate Change* 7(3): 523–556.

Gilbert, B., P. McDougall, and D. Audretsch. 2006. New Venture Growth: A Review and Extension. *Journal of Management* 32(6): 926–950.

Gompers, P.A., and J. Lerner. 2004. *The Venture Capital Cycle*. Cambridge, MA: MIT Press.

Grant, R. 1991. The Resource-Based Theory of Competitive Advantage: Implications for Strategy Formulation. *California Management Review* 33(3): 114–135.

Greiner, L.E. 1972. Evolution and Revolution as Organizations Grow. *Harvard Business Review* 50(4): 37–46.

Henrekson, M., and D. Johansson. 2010. Gazelles as Job Creators: A Survey and Interpretation of the Evidence. *Small Business Economics* 35(2): 227–244.

Kantis, H. 2010. *Aportes para el diseño de políticas integrales de desarrollo emprendedor en América Latina*. Washington, DC: Inter-American Development Bank (IDB).

Kantis, H. (ed.). 2014. ¿Emprendimientos dinámicos en América del Sur?: la clave es el (eco)sistema. Montevideo, Uruguay: Mercosur Economic Research Network.

Kantis, H., P. Angelelli, and V. Moori Koenig. 2005. Developing Entrepreneurship: Latin America and World Wide Experience. Washington, DC: IDB.

Kantis, H., J. Federico, and C. Menéndez. 2012. Políticas de fomento al emprendimiento dinámico en América Latina: tendencias y desafíos. Working paper. Caracas: CAF.

Kantis, H., M. Ishida, and M. Komori. 2002. Entrepreneurship in Emerging Economies: The Creation and Development of New Firms in Latin America and East Asia. Washington, DC: IDB.

Lederman, D., J. Messina, S. Pienknagura, and J. Rigolini. 2014. Latin American Entrepreneurs: Many Firms but Little Innovation. Washington, DC: The World Bank.

Lee, C., K. Lee, and J.M. Pennings. 2001. Internal Capabilities, External Networks, and Performance: A Study on Technology-Based Ventures. Strategic Management Journal 22(6/7): 615–640.

Levie, J., and B. Lichtenstein. 2010. A Terminal Assessment of Stages Theory: Introducing a Dynamic States Approach to Entrepreneurship. Entrepreneurship Theory and Practice 34(2): 317–350.

Mason, C. 1998. El financiamiento y las pequeñas y medianas empresas. In Desarrollo y gestión de PYMEs: Aportes para un debate necesario, H. Kantis (ed.). Buenos Aires, Argentina: National University of General Sarmiento (known by its Spanish acronym UNGS).

Nightingale, P., and A. Coad. 2013. Muppets and Gazelles: Political and Methodological Biases in Entrepreneurship Research. Working Paper Series 2013-03. Brighton, UK: Science Policy Research Unit or the University of Sussex (SPRU).

Pagés, C. (ed.). 2010. The Age of Productivity: Transforming Economies from the Bottom Up. London, UK: Palgrave Macmillan.

Pellegrino, G., M. Piva, and M. Vivarelli. 2012. Young Firms and Innovation: A Microeconometric Analysis. Structural Change and Economic Dynamics 23(4): 329–340.

Quince, T., and H. Whittaker. 2002. Close Encounters: Evidence of the Potential Benefits of Proximity to Local Industrial Clusters. Cambridge, UK: ESRC Centre for Business Research, University of Cambridge.

Schneider, C., and R. Veugelers. 2010. On Young Highly Innovative Companies: Why They Matter and How (Not) to Policy Support Them. Industrial and Corporate Change 19(4): 969–1007.

Shane, S. 2000. Prior Knowledge and the Discovery of Entrepreneurial Opportunities. Organization Science 11(4): 448–469.

Stinchcombe, A. 1965. Social Structure and Organizations. In Handbook of Organizations, ed. J. March. Chicago, IL: Rand McNally.

Storey, D. 1994. Understanding the Small Business Sector. London, UK: Routledge.

Stuart, R., and P. Abetti. 1990. Impact of Entrepreneurial and Management Experience on Early Performance. *Journal of Business Venturing* 5(3): 151–162.

Ucbasaran, D., P. Westhead, and M. Wright. 2008. Opportunity Identification and Pursuit: Does an entrepreneur's Human Capital Matter. *Small Business Economics* 30(2): 153–173.

World Bank. 2010. *The World Bank Annual Report 2010*. Washington, DC: The World Bank Group.

World Bank. 2013. *World Bank Enterprise Surveys (WBES). Indicator Descriptions*. Washington, DC: The World Bank Group.

World Bank. 2014. *Innovating in the Manufacturing Sector in Latin America and the Caribbean*. Latin America and the Caribbean Series Note No. 9. Washington, DC: The World Bank Group.

CHAPTER 7

Different Obstacles for Different Productivity Levels? An Analysis of Caribbean Firms

Alison Cathles and Siobhan Pangerl

Much of the literature relating firm characteristics to productivity and growth in Latin America and the Caribbean (LAC) either lumps Caribbean countries into one observation or tends to overlook them altogether. This is not because researchers want to exclude the Caribbean, but because the data deficit that often poses a challenge for the LAC region is even more extreme when it comes to Caribbean countries. Only a small fraction of over 100 identified indicators affecting growth are available for these countries. Further, limited availability of household data or fewer observations on firms is often prohibitive for standard methodological analysis of economic growth (Ruprah et al. 2014).

So, is an independent analysis of Caribbean firms even needed? The simple answer is yes. Small population size, geographical characteristics,

A. Cathles
UNU-MERIT
e-mail: cathles@merit.unu.edu

S. Pangerl
Inter-American Development Bank
e-mail: siobhanp@IADB.ORG

© Inter-American Development Bank 2016   207
M. Grazzi and C. Pietrobelli (eds.), *Firm Innovation and Productivity in Latin America and the Caribbean*,
DOI 10.1057/978-1-349-58151-1_7

and main economic activities set Caribbean economies apart from most Latin American economies. As with Latin America, there is stark heterogeneity among and within Caribbean countries. Even though size may be a defining factor, it is lower productivity levels that define the declining growth of Caribbean economies relative to other small-sized economies (Ruprah et al. 2014). Increasingly, understanding macroeconomic trends requires an understanding of firm dynamics at a micro-level and productivity levels within and across industries (Syverson 2011). Therefore, Caribbean policymakers need this type of micro-data, analysis, and dissemination of information tailored to the region at their disposal. Recent firm-level data from the World Bank Enterprise Surveys (WBES) and the Productivity, Technology, and Innovation in the Caribbean (PROTEQin) Survey offer new opportunities to understand better the characteristics of Caribbean firms at different levels of productivity and the challenges or obstacles that they face in their daily operations.

The primary objective of this chapter is to fill a void in the literature about firms in the Caribbean through a comprehensive analysis of different firm characteristics and productivity. These firm-level characteristics are discussed at length in this book, but they are not directly applied to the Caribbean context.[1]

In the next section, we briefly contextualize the Caribbean economies within which firms are operating. Then we examine some of the basic firm characteristics that are frequently empirically linked with productivity, such as firm size, sector, age, exporter status, and use of information and communication technologies (ICT). We then deepen the analysis by specifically focusing on human capital, looking at both management and employees. The following section shows our analysis of firm-level labor productivity in relation to the main characteristics of firms (firm size, sector, age, exporter status, and ICT usage). Then we investigate the obstacles reported by the firms surveyed, specifically looking at the correlation and variation between obstacles and firm performance. Most of the analysis draws on the most recent wave of the WBES, which was carried out for the first time in 14 Caribbean countries in 2010.[2] We complement the analysis with data from the PROTEQin, which was conducted for the first time in 2013 in five Caribbean countries (Barbados, Belize, Jamaica, Guyana, and Suriname).

Overall, the results from the Caribbean micro-data tell a familiar story about firms with lower productivity levels—they tend to be smaller, to export less, and to have less human capital and technological inputs—but they also tend to report different obstacles to their current operations. If private-sector-led growth is expected to bolster the economy, then documentation and dissemination of the characteristics of this sector and the bottlenecks that lower and higher productivity firms are facing seems to be a necessary first condition for apt policymaking.

LANDSCAPE OF THE CARIBBEAN ECONOMIES

This chapter uses data from 14 Caribbean economies. Table 7.1 shows that all of the Caribbean economies discussed in this chapter meet the definition of a small economy[3] (except the Dominican Republic) based on having a population of less than three million people. The majority of the economies have a population of less than one million people. The econ-

Table 7.1 Brief characterization of Caribbean economies

Country name	GDP per capita, PPP (2012)	Total population (2012)	Largest industry (value of annual output)	No. of cargo ports	Island	No. of firms (WBES)
Antigua & Barbuda	20,385	89,069	Tourism-based	1	Yes	151
Bahamas	22,705	371,960	Tourism-based	2	Yes	148
Barbados	15,299	283,221	Tourism-based	1	Yes	150
Belize	8313	324,060	Garment production	1	No	149
Dominica	9829	71,684	Soap	2	Yes	150
Dominican Republic	11,016	10,276,621	Tourism-based	7	Part of one	360
Grenada	10,975	105,483	Food and beverages	1	Yes	153
Guyana	6054	795,369	Bauxite	2	No	162
Jamaica	8521	2,707,805	Tourism-based	6	Yes	375
St. Kitts & Nevis	20,100	53,584	Tourism-based	1	Yes	150
Saint Lucia	10,359	180,870	Tourism-based	2	Yes	150
St. Vincent & the Grenadines	10,039	109,373	Tourism-based	2	Yes	154
Suriname	15,174	534,541	Bauxite and gold mining	5	No	152
Trinidad and Tobago	29,086	1,337,439	Petroleum	6	Yes	366
Average	14,132	1,231,506		3		
Median	10,995	303,641		2		

Sources: Adapted from Ruprah et al. 2014. Data for no. of firms is from the WBES; data for GDP and population are from WDI; data for no. of ports is from CargoRouter.com; largest industry data is from the CIA Factbook; and island category is from Ruprah et al. 2014, except the Dominican Republic

Notes: The number of firms used in the two sections of this chapter on characteristics follow a preliminary cleaning of the data. GDP per capita are in constant 2011 PPP

omy with the smallest population is St. Kitts & Nevis, with a population of less than 54,000 (2012). In 2012, Trinidad and Tobago was reported to have the highest GDP per capita ($29,086 in purchasing power parity [PPP]) and Guyana had the lowest ($6053 PPP). The median GDP per capita was almost $11,000 in 2012, with a mean of $14,132 (in PPP terms).

The majority of the countries are islands where tourism is the largest industry. The number of ports is included in Table 7.1 to demonstrate the interconnectedness of the region to world trade networks, with the vast majority[4] of the trade being transported by sea (Kaluza et al. 2010). Naturally, these economies face a small domestic market and can be at a disadvantage in global markets, although size does not have to be a binding constraint. Low productivity levels in the private sector in the region compared with similar small economies is a pressing concern for the future of the Caribbean (Ruprah et al. 2014).

Box 7.1. Recent developments in data collection in the Caribbean The release of the 2010 WBES was a starting point for comparable firm-level data in the Caribbean. However, from the outset, researchers recognized the need for subsequent surveys in order to analyze the evolution of firms in the region. Fortunately, not too long after the first WBES was conducted, the region implemented the first wave of pseudo-follow-up surveys—the PROTEQin. This survey was commissioned by the Inter-American Development Bank (IDB), with funding from the Compete Caribbean Program, a regional private sector development and technical assistance initiative financed by the IDB; the United Kingdom Department for International Development; and Canada's Department of Foreign Affairs, and Trade and Development. The survey was executed in partnership with the Caribbean Development Bank.[5] Administered between 2013 and 2014, the PROTEQin is a critical development in terms of data collection in the Caribbean and targeted establishments that were covered by the 2010 WBES in five economies: Barbados, Belize, Jamaica, Guyana, and Suriname. This decision allowed researchers a first opportunity to use panel data in analyzing firm-related issues in the Caribbean.[6]

The PROTEQin expands the scope of the WBES while also incorporating more detailed questions related to labor, productivity, technology and innovation for 727 firms. The dataset provides updated information on how firm characteristics and performance have evolved since the 2010 WBES. For this reason, we intersperse findings from the PROTEQin where possible to provide more recent information for selected countries and to check the robustness of the WBES data.

Principal Characteristics of the Firms in the Caribbean

The dominating characteristics of the firms surveyed in the Caribbean are that they tend to be micro or small, concentrated in the services sectors, mature, and non-exporters. The documentation of the proportions of WBES firms with these attributes in each of the countries illustrates the heterogeneity between Caribbean countries and serves as a starting point for the rest of the chapter, establishing the particular features of the firms that are often linked to productivity in the literature.

The majority of firms are small (11 to 50 employees) or micro (10 employees or less). Figure 7.1 shows that 54% of the firms in St. Vincent & the Grenadines are micro and 38% are small for a total of 92%; a little over 6% of the firms are medium and just a shade over 1% are large. Very few large firms exist in any of the Caribbean countries. The Dominican Republic is the only country where more than 10% of the firms in the WBES are large enterprises. As we expect, typically countries with very small populations have a relatively greater percentage of micro and small firms. These countries appear on the left side of the graph, but there are some exceptions. For example, Barbados has a smaller population than Belize but a greater proportion of medium firms.

In a recently published note that maps the enterprises in LAC based on WBES data, there tend to be even more small and medium enterprises (SMEs) in the Caribbean than in the rest of LAC (94% versus 90%) and more firms are in the services sector (Francis et al. 2014).[7] Although favorable views of SMEs contend that they spur competition and are a good source of employment, this argument only holds if the SMEs are productive, which implies that they are competitive and innovative (Pagés 2010).

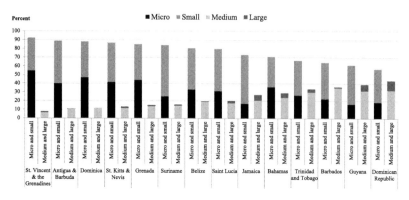

Fig. 7.1   Caribbean firms by size (number of employees)

Source: Authors' elaboration based on WBES data

Notes: firm size is based on the number of full-time, permanent employees in the previous fiscal year. The number of employees per size category is micro (≤10), small (>10 and ≤50), medium (>50 and ≤250), and large (>250)

In fact, research using the global WBES found that, while small firms may have the largest shares of job creation and sales growth, large firms tend to display higher productivity growth (Ayyagari et al. 2011). Chapter 3 showed that large firms are more likely to invest in innovation and that those that do are more productive.

In most countries in the Caribbean, there is a greater proportion of firms in the services sector; however in Suriname, for example, firms are split roughly evenly between the services and manufacturing sectors. In the WBES, the firms self-classify as either being in manufacturing or in services. The corresponding workforce within the countries may be even more heavily concentrated in the services sector. In the LAC region, over 60% of the workforce is in services; in the Organization of East Caribbean States, the number is over 80% (Caribbean Knowledge Series 2013).

As discussed in Chap. 1, and in line with recent research on productivity growth, it is the services sector that drags down overall productivity levels in LAC (Pagés 2010). Several studies have looked at the differences in productivity and innovation in the two sectors (Arias Ortiz et al. 2014; Crespi et al. 2014, for Latin America only; Arias Ortiz et al. 2012; IDB 2011a). These studies found that the allocative efficiency in the services sector tends to be much lower than in manufacturing. Knowing the sectoral composition of the firms in each country is a key element for analyzing the productivity of firms.

In addition to being small and largely in the services sector, Caribbean firms also tend to be older. Very few new firms (defined as less than three years old) exist, whereas mature firms (defined as those in existence for over ten years) are much more prevalent. Mature firms represent the majority, except in Dominica, where the proportion of such firms dips below 50%. In general, the LAC region tends to have a smaller proportion of young firms compared with other developing regions (Francis et al. 2014). The implications of age and productivity could go in either direction. Young firms are often seen as being a potential source of newness and innovation; however, mature firms may be seen as having stood the test of time.

The next important question relates to how connected these firms are. Given that firms tend to be smaller and older, have they adopted ICTs to connect to domestic or international markets? Are they internationally engaged? Figure 7.2 shows that cellphones and email are widely used in everyday business practices. More sophisticated ICTs, such as owning a website, which often requires some basic programming knowledge, are much less pervasive. There is a lot of heterogeneity within the Caribbean with regard to ICT, as there is throughout LAC, where evidence suggests that

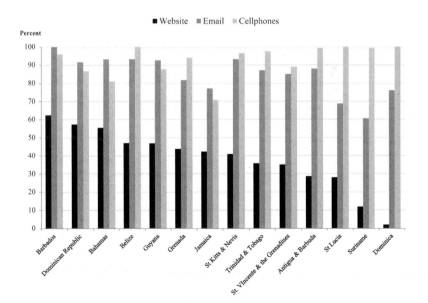

Fig. 7.2   ICT usage in the Caribbean

Source: Authors' elaboration based on WBES data

within-country differences are as notable as between-country differences (IDB 2011b). The low levels of website ownership by tourism-based economies suggest that there is room for gains by attracting new clients who are not being reached by conventional hotel and restaurant search methods.

The PROTEQin provides updated information about ICT penetration in select Caribbean countries. Firms were asked the same series of questions about email, websites, and cellphones for business operations. The improvements in these indicators vary by country. Countries like Barbados and Belize, which already showed relatively high levels in 2010, saw slight improvements in websites (Barbados and Belize) and cellphones (Barbados). With a 4% improvement over 2010 in cellphone usage, Barbados reached 100% penetration in both cellphone and email usage to communicate with clients. Suriname and Jamaica showed significant improvements in ICT usage between the two survey periods. For example, in Jamaica, cellphone use increased by 24%. Suriname saw sizeable increases in both website usage (28%) and email usage (18%). Guyana is the only country that showed declines in ICT penetration in both website and email usage. On the whole, for cellphone penetration, the PROTEQin shows improvement over the WBES 2010 average, with all five countries above 90%.[8] To meet regional averages, Jamaica, Guyana, and Suriname need to improve email usage. Use of firm websites was by far the weakest area for the selected countries, with Barbados being the only one to outperform the 2010 regional average. Despite these gaps, the large improvements between 2010 and 2013 in some of the underperforming countries, like Jamaica and Suriname, should not be overlooked.

In terms of international linkages, the WBES data shows that most Caribbean firms are non-exporters (Fig. 7.3a); therefore, a very small proportion of sales are derived from either indirect or direct exports (Fig. 7.3b). In general, exporting is thought to be positively linked with productivity. A recent survey of micro-econometric studies from 33 developed and developing countries summarizes corroborative evidence from 1995 to 2004 (Wagner 2005). The author claimed that most of the differences were due to pre-entry self-selection into export markets rather than gains in productivity post-entry into the market (Wagner 2005).[9] In addition to whether or not a firm is exporting, the average proportion of sales earned from exports ranges from 3% in Grenada to 16% in Dominica. Across the Caribbean, a very small average proportion of sales are being generated from indirect export sales.

Given the dominating characteristics of the firms covered in this section (small, old, and in the services sector), if policymakers want to help firms become more internationally engaged and connected through technology,

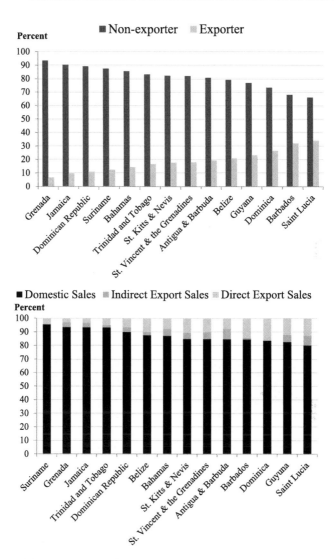

Fig. 7.3   (a) Export status; (b) domestic, indirect, and direct sales

Source: Authors' elaboration based on WBES data

preparatory work along the supply chain is needed on the pre-entry side. For example, in the Caribbean, even fewer firms are engaged in indirect export sales than are in direct export sales.

Principal Characteristics of Human Capital in the Caribbean

Every firm is made up of its people. Just as aggregate productivity is the combination of the productivity of individual firms, each individual firm's productivity is the sum of the productivity of its workers. In this section, we delve into the characteristics of human capital in Caribbean firms, from managers down to workers. Unobservable factors such as the skills of the workforce and managerial capability are often more responsible for the variation in firm performance than are observable firm attributes such as size, age, and international linkages (Jensen and McGuckin 1997). A better understanding of the knowledge, capabilities, and background of the workforce is important, as both the observable and unobservable characteristics of a firm must be included in a complete analysis of firm growth (Laursen et al. 1999).

Entrepreneurs in the Caribbean

We begin with an analysis of the entrepreneurs (firm owners or managers) in the Caribbean. Recently, some scholars have attributed entrepreneurship with the commercialization of new knowledge and consider it a third driver of economic growth (Vivarelli 2013).[10] Although the economic literature has long been fascinated with entrepreneurship, not all characterizations describe entrepreneurs as agents of change and economic growth (Wennekers and Thurik 1999).[11] Although new businesses may contribute to job creation, in order to contribute to productivity, businesses must also grow into their potential (Wagner 2014).

Figure 7.4 shows that firms in the Caribbean are not often created to introduce a new product or idea. Coupled with the fact that firms tend to be mature, this suggests that the majority are not responsible for commercializing new knowledge that would position them as drivers of economic growth. Figure 7.4a shows whether the firm was established out of necessity; the responses vary widely across countries. Figure 7.4b shows what type of opportunity motivated the firm's creation. For example, more than 80% of the firms interviewed in Suriname reported that the business was started because of a lack of better employment opportunities. In contrast, none of the firms in Dominica responded that this was the case.[12]

Figure 7.4b shows that fewer firms were created to develop a completely new product or idea than to replicate or modify an existing product or idea. The results are similar for both Caribbean countries and Latin American countries (see Chap. 6). These findings are consistent

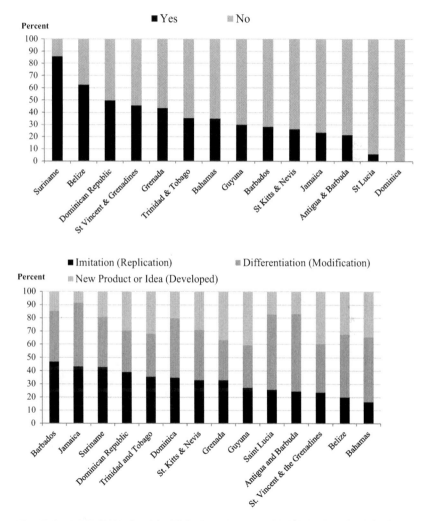

Fig. 7.4 (a) Was the firm established Due to necessity? (b) what type of opportunity motivated the firm's creation?

Source: Authors' elaboration based on WBES data

with general theories about the dominant nature of innovative business activities in less developed countries (Abramovitz 1989). Data analysis for LAC suggests the same, although studies are largely concentrated on Latin America (Pagés 2010); however, it may not be so different in the Caribbean.

The previous experience of top managers varies widely throughout the Caribbean. In Fig. 7.5 a significant number of countries have some top managers that transitioned from being unemployed into the position. In Suriname, for example, over 10% of those surveyed transitioned from being unemployed to being employed as a top manager, but this does not seem to be the general trend. On the whole, the top manager tends to have previously held a managerial position that may have provided the impetus to start a new business, especially given that the majority of firms are created to either imitate or replicate existing products or services.

In sum, Caribbean firms tend to replicate, imitate, or differentiate products or services that exist in the market. Further, very few of the firms surveyed are considered high-growth ones. The role of the entrepreneur in transforming an economy rests on the match between available market opportunities and entrepreneurial talent (Naudé 2008).[13] So,

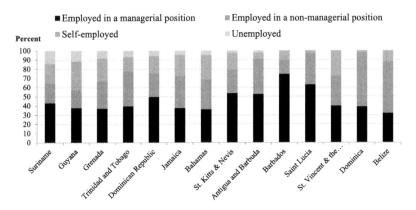

Fig. 7.5 Previous occupation of the Top manager

Source: Authors' elaboration based on WBES data

Notes: Questions about employment in a managerial versus non-managerial position were differentiated in the questionnaire by whether the firm was owned by the respondents' family, but were combined in this figure to reflect only the previous position

if most of the entrepreneurs in the Caribbean are not commercializing new knowledge, they may be absorbing technology from elsewhere, which requires social capacity to imitate and differentiate—skills also associated with gains in productivity. These skills relate to a broad variety of factors within economies, including but not limited to the general level of education of the workforce, the technical competence of workers, and the amount of technical training provided to workers.

The Caribbean Workforce

Since 1960, there has been a lot of progress in the Caribbean in terms of attaining primary and secondary education. The region's average years of schooling for the adult population are now on par with the rest of Latin America and approaching Organisation for Economic Co-operation and Development (OECD) averages. The same is not true of transition from secondary to tertiary education. In the firms surveyed, the average percentage of workers with at least a bachelor's degree ranges from 2 in Grenada to 20 in the Dominican Republic.[14] In addition, pass rates for math and English tests are often below 50%. These signs point to a deeper issue of whether there is a match between skills taught in school and those demanded by employers in the workplace (Caribbean Knowledge Series 2013) (Fig. 7.6).

Finding workers with the right skillset is a major issue in the Caribbean, where over 35% of firm owners report having unfilled vacancies. An inadequately educated workforce is one of the most often cited obstacles to firm growth in the region (see "Obstacles to Firm Operation in the Caribbean" below). The "right" skills, however, differ by country. On the one hand, in Grenada, Barbados, and Antigua and Barbuda, workers with technical skills are more difficult to find. On the other hand, in Guyana and the Dominican Republic, employers have a slightly harder time finding workers with social skills.

An interesting finding from the PROTEQin data is the variation in the difficulty of finding certain skills by job type (i.e. managerial versus professional). For example, the PROTEQin asks firm owners to rate the difficulty of finding candidates with appropriate skills by different positions within the firm. Figure 7.7 displays the percentage of firm owners who responded that certain skills were very difficult or almost impossible to find in candidates.[15] The findings are notable. Adequate job-related skills tend to be the most difficult attributes to find in candidates for both managerial

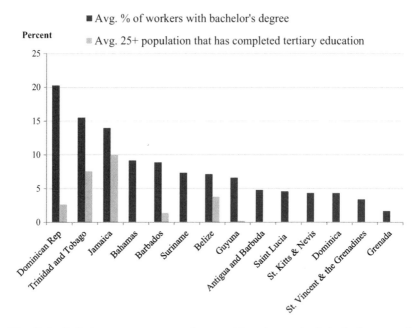

Fig. 7.6 Full-time permanent employees with at least a bachelor's degree and population over age 25 that has completed tertiary education (%)

Source: Authors' elaboration based on WBES data and Barro and Lee [2010]

and professional positions. On average, almost 30% of firm owners in this subsample found core skills to be very difficult or almost impossible to find when hiring professionals compared to one-fifth when hiring managers. These results show that, in the Caribbean, there is a lack of adequate skills not only for lower-level workers, but also when seeking capable managers.

When firms were asked in the PROTEQin to identify the importance of various factors causing skill shortages, 52% cited worker emigration as important, very important, or critical. Considering in the Caribbean net migration is among the highest in the world and that outflows are predominantly migrants with a tertiary education (Nurse and Jones 2009),[16] it could even be surprising that *only* 52% of firms cited worker emigration as such an important factor. It is possible that the diaspora has come to be seen in the Caribbean as a unique source of human capital that provides links to external markets and international customer bases, transfers

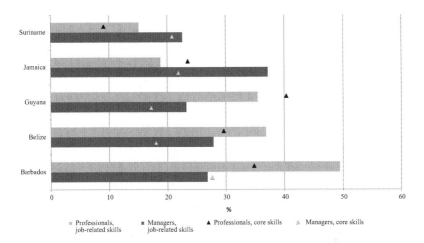

Fig. 7.7   Difficulty finding skills by job type (respondents who cited very difficult or almost impossible)

Source: PROTEQin

Notes: The bars represent the difficulty in finding job-related skills among professionals [*light gray*] and managers [*dark gray*]; the triangles represent the level of difficulty in finding core skills among professionals [*dark gray*] and managers [*light gray*]

industry-specific knowledge, and acts as sources of investment.[17] Evidence from a recent report suggested around 40% of the diasporic entrepreneurs surveyed,[18] [19] indicated that they earned some form of revenue from clients in the diaspora. In addition, interviews with large iconic firms in the Caribbean (Suriname, Jamaica, and Guyana) and diasporic firms outside the Caribbean (e.g. New York) revealed these large iconic firms have designed business strategies to target the diasporic customer base (Nurse and Kirton 2014) who then also influence consumer taste in the international markets where they have migrated. While the majority of firms responding to the PROTEQin acknowledged that emigration may deplete *local* human capital resources, causing skill shortages, they more frequently cited the quality of education or a shortage in the number of local professionals trained by local institutions.,[20] [21] They also noted that emigration of workers may provide intangible inputs to local business development, especially through their potential link to an international network and potential customer base outside the country.

Box 7.2. Education and skills in the Caribbean The PROTEQ in was a first attempt to deepen the micro-data available for the region, and one of the most important areas was education and skill development. The PROTEQin data breaks out education levels of the workforce beyond that included in the WBES. With such a detailed classification, researchers can readily assess the differences in education levels across countries. A cursory analysis finds similar patterns for Barbados, Belize, Jamaica, and Guyana and Suriname. For example, about 80% of managers in Barbados, Belize, and Jamaica have completed some sort of tertiary education, compared to around 50% for Guyana and Suriname. Education levels for skilled workers follow a similar pattern as for managers. For less skilled jobs, such as plant and machine operators, firms in Barbados, Belize, and Jamaica tend to employ workers with less education than firms in Guyana and Suriname. Over half of the plant and machine operators in Barbados, Belize, and Jamaica have only completed primary education compared to 29% in Guyana and 22% in Suriname.

Despite managers and skilled workers having relatively high levels of educational attainment in Barbados, Belize, and Jamaica, over 60% of firms in those countries cite a lack of a strong educational background as a major or severe obstacle to productivity. This may be an indication of a mismatch between the skills students are learning in school and the skills desired by the employers in these countries rather than a reflection of low educational attainment. These workforce constraints are less of an issue in Guyana and Suriname, where only around 30% of firms cited lack of educational background as a major or severe obstacle. This does not mean that it is not an important issue for firm productivity, just that there are likely other, more pressing, obstacles in the firm manager's mind.

FIRM PRODUCTIVITY IN THE CARIBBEAN

How do the firm characteristics presented above relate to firm performance? Table 7.2 presents the results of an analysis of firm characteristics disaggregated by productivity levels. First, we calculate the average firm labor productivity (sales/employees) for the main product ISIC code in each country. Then, we determine whether the individual firm is above or

Table 7.2   Firm characteristics by productivity level

Firm characteristics	Full sample			Manufacturing			Services		
	N	Mean	S.D.	N	Mean	S.D.	N	Mean	S.D.
Firm size (2009) (No. of full-time permanent employees)	2380	51	111	822	66.5	150.7	1558	42.8	82.4
Higher productivity	1150	59.5	138	474	73.4	177.3	676	49.7	100.3
Lower productivity	1230	43	78.3	348	57	103.4	882	37.5	65
Firm size (2007) (No. of full-time permanent employees)	2292	49.6	128	798	66.9	185	1494	40.4	80.6
Higher productivity	1109	59.5	167	462	77.8	229.2	647	46.5	99.2
Lower productivity	1183	40.4	73	336	51.8	93.6	847	35.8	62.4
Firm age (years)	2340	21.5	20.4	815	24.2	23.8	1525	20.1	18.1
Higher productivity	1136	23.3	22.5	472	26	26.6	664	21.4	18.8
Lower productivity	1204	19.9	18	343	21.7	19.1	861	19.1	17.5
Foreign ownership (≥10%)	2380	15.5	36.2	822	15.7	36.4	1558	15.4	36.1
Higher productivity	1150	18.1	38.5	474	17.1	37.7	676	18.8	39.1
Lower productivity	1230	13.1	33.7	348	13.8	34.5	882	12.8	33.4
Exports (≥10% direct)	2380	17.1	37.7	822	26.6	44.2	1558	12.1	32.6
Higher productivity	1150	19.5	39.6	474	29.5	45.7	676	12.4	33
Lower productivity	1230	14.9	35.6	348	22.7	42	882	11.8	32.3
Motive for firm creation: New product or idea	893	29.1	45.5	285	34.4	47.6	608	26.6	44.2
Higher productivity	388	29.4	45.6	161	35.4	48	227	25.1	43.5
Lower productivity	505	28.9	45.4	124	33.1	47.2	381	27.6	44.7
Motive for firm creation: Modification	893	38.3	48.6	285	34.7	47.7	608	40	49
Higher productivity	388	39.2	48.9	161	34.2	47.6	227	42.7	49.6
Lower productivity	505	37.6	48.5	124	35.5	48	381	38.3	48.7
Motive for firm creation: Replication	893	32.6	46.9	285	30.9	46.3	608	33.4	47.2
Higher productivity	388	31.4	46.5	161	30.4	46.2	227	32.2	46.8
Lower productivity	505	33.5	47.2	124	31.5	46.6	381	34.1	47.5
Managerial years of experience	2347	18.1	11.4	812	18.5	11.2	1535	17.8	11.5
Higher productivity	1134	18.4	11.5	469	19	11.6	665	17.9	11.4
Lower productivity	1213	17.8	11.4	343	17.8	10.8	870	17.8	11.6

(*continued*)

Table 7.2   (continued)

Firm characteristics	Full sample			Manufacturing			Services		
	N	Mean	S.D.	N	Mean	S.D.	N	Mean	S.D.
Full-time workers with at least a bachelor's degree (%)	2284	9.7	16	794	8.5	12.6	1490	10.3	17.5
Higher productivity	1102	9.7	16.2	458	8.6	13	644	10.6	18.1
Lower productivity	1182	9.6	15.8	336	8.4	12.1	846	10.1	17
Internationally recognized quality certification	2299	16.8	37.4	798	18.5	38.9	1501	15.9	36.6
Higher productivity	1113	17.9	38.3	459	19	39.2	654	17.1	37.7
Lower productivity	1186	15.9	36.5	339	18	38.5	847	15	35.7
Website	2370	38.2	48.6	819	35.9	48	1551	39.4	48.9
Higher productivity	1146	43.2	49.6	472	38.6	48.7	674	46.4	49.9
Lower productivity	1224	33.5	47.2	347	32.3	46.8	877	34	47.4
Use of foreign technology	2380	5	21.7	822	14.1	34.8	1558	0.1	3.6
Higher productivity	1150	6.4	24.5	474	15.2	35.9	676	0.3	5.4
Lower productivity	1230	3.6	18.6	348	12.6	33.3	882	0	0

Source: Authors' elaboration based on WBES data

below the average. Then, we analyze the relationship between different firm characteristics and higher performing firms versus lower performing firms. We repeat the exercise for the subsamples of firms in the manufacturing and services sectors.

Table 7.2 shows different patterns for higher and lower productivity levels in relation to various characteristics of firms. Relatively higher productivity firms tended to be larger at the end of 2009 and to have more employees in 2007. The pattern is the same for manufacturing and services, but the average size of manufacturing firms appears to be larger than services. The higher productivity firms are also generally older, have a greater proportion of sales from direct exports, and have more than 10% foreign ownership. In manufacturing, the higher productivity firms are older, on average, than services firms. In the services sector, higher productivity firms have a greater concentration of foreign ownership. In addition, the proportion of higher productivity firms with direct exports is greater in manufacturing than in services.

Human capital patterns are as we might expect. Managers of relatively higher productivity firms tend to have slightly more years of experience, on average. Interestingly, the proportion of full-time permanent employees with at least a bachelor's degree is the highest in the relatively higher productivity firms in the services sector.

For technological absorption capacity and usage, different patterns emerge for manufacturing and services based on having a website, using foreign technology, or having an internationally recognized certification. First, a very small proportion of firms in the services sector use technology licensed from a foreign company. Second, a greater proportion of firms in manufacturing have an internationally recognized quality certification (19 versus 16% in services). Third, a greater proportion of services firms have their own website, which is likely consistent with how critical it is to share information with clients. As mentioned earlier, for firms in services, such as hotels and restaurants, online advertising is becoming increasingly important. Across the board, a greater proportion of higher productivity firms have a website, use foreign technology, or have an internationally recognized certification.

As a robustness check, we conduct a similar analysis using the PROTEQin data. We find many of the same results using the much smaller subset of data.[22] However, we note a few interesting deviations. First, firms in the five countries are generally slightly older than in the Caribbean as a whole. The average age of low-productivity firms in this subsample is four years older than the average age of low-productivity firms in the 14 Caribbean countries surveyed for the 2010 WBES. The differences are even starker on a sectoral basis, where firms that maintain higher productivity levels are, on average, ten years older than low-productivity firms in the manufacturing sector (the gap is six years in the services sector). In other words, the most productive manufacturing firms tend to be the oldest in this subsample and unproductive services firms tend to be the youngest. In terms of exports, the PROTEQin data shows a much wider gap between the percentage of exporting firms above and below-average productivity levels (33% of above-average manufacturing firms export versus 18% of below-average firms). Interestingly, the reverse is true for services, with a larger percentage of low-productivity firms exporting (11%); only 8% of services firms with average or above-average productivity levels are exporters. This may signify that services firms are beginning to export before they have the required internal capacities, thus hindering their productivity.

Obstacles to Firm Operation in the Caribbean

The WBES asks firm owners a series of questions about their perceived obstacles to current operations. The goal of these questions is to identify particular aspects of the business environment that are constraining firms. Subjective measures of the perceptions of obstacles have been found to be highly correlated with objective measures for the Caribbean specifically (Ruprah and Sierra 2013) and worldwide (Hallward-Driemeier and Aterido 2009). Therefore, in this chapter, we do not question the validity of a particular obstacle being seen as the biggest one, rather we take the firms at their word. Figure 7.8 presents the frequency with which interviewed firms in selected Caribbean countries reported each of the 15 identified obstacles in the survey.

Caribbean firms identify different obstacles as the biggest, which assumes that the most frequently reported obstacle in a country is the one considered to be the most constraining for the majority of firms. For example, in the Bahamas, the highest percentage of firms (34%) reports lack of an educated workforce as their biggest obstacle; whereas, in Barbados the highest percentage (28%) identify access to finance as their biggest obstacle to operations. In Jamaica, 34% of firms identified tax rates as their biggest obstacle. A recent, in-depth analysis by Nugent and Schmid (2014) confirmed that Jamaica's tax system has long been an issue in the country.

The 2013 PROTEQin data also enabled us to analyze whether the perceptions of primary obstacles have changed for the five PROTEQin countries since the 2010 WBES. Table 7.3 shows that, for the most part, the

Table 7.3 Top obstacle(s) cited by firms, 2010 vs 2013

	2010	*2013*
Barbados	Access to finance (28%)	Electricity (21%)
Belize	Inadequately educated workforce (17%)	Inadequately educated workforce (14%); Crime, theft, and disorder (14%)
Guyana	Inadequately educated workforce (18%)	Electricity (15%)
Jamaica	Tax rates (34%)	Tax rates (33%)
Suriname	Inadequately educated workforce (30%)	Inadequately educated workforce (11%)

Sources: 2010 data from WBES; 2013 from PROTEQin

main constraints on firm growth remain unchanged in Belize and Jamaica. While the same holds true in Suriname, the severity of the obstacle (an inadequately trained workforce) decreased by almost two-thirds from 2010, and firms began to cite a wider array of obstacles in 2013. In Barbados, electricity replaced access to finance as the biggest obstacle, and in Guyana, electricity replaced an inadequately trained workforce. Overall, access to finance, a trained workforce, electricity, and tax rates were consistently cited by firms as primary, secondary, or tertiary obstacles to firm growth in 2010 and 2013. Possible explanations for the shifts in the relative importance between particular top obstacles may stem from other changes that the firms in the group surveyed have experienced in the three-year period.

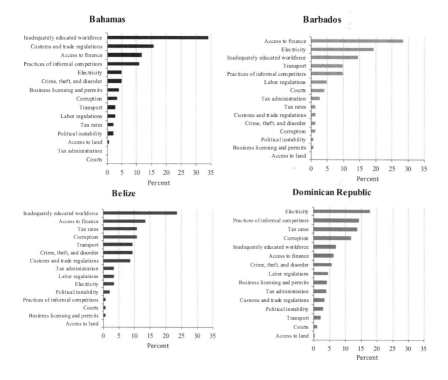

Fig. 7.8   The biggest obstacles by country

Source: Authors' elaboration based on WBES data

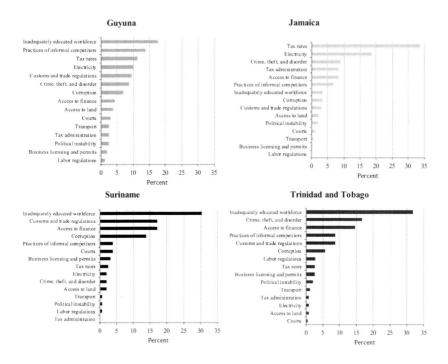

Fig. 7.8   Continued

Are Obstacles Different for Firms in Different Productivity Quintiles?

The biggest obstacles identified in Figure 7.8 are for all of the firms in a given country. Hallward-Driemeier and Aterido (2009) found that firm characteristics had an impact on the relative importance of obstacles and highlighted the need to look at differences within countries based on firm characteristics. In this vein, we separate firms by labor productivity quintiles to explore whether firms with different levels of labor productivity in the Caribbean identify different primary obstacles to operations.

First we divide the firms evenly into five productivity quintiles where one is the lowest productivity quintile and five is the highest. Table 7.4 visually presents the frequency with which the biggest obstacle is identified by a particular quintile of productivity. In the Bahamas and Barbados,

Table 7.4 The biggest obstacle by productivity quintile

Country	Productivity quintile (1=low; 5=high)	Access to finance	Access to land	Business licensing and permits	Corruption	Crime, theft, and disorder	Customs and trade regulations	Electricity	Inadequately educated workforce	Practices of competitors in informal sector	Tax rates	Transport
Bahamas	1	30										
	2								30			
	3						26		26			
	4								35			
	5								39			
Barbados	1	43										
	2							27	33			
	3											
	4	36										
	5								35			
Belize	1	24							24			
	2								46			
	3								34			
	4											
	5											
Dominican Republic	1							14				
	2							20				
	3							31				
	4							19				21
	5									20		

(continued)

Table 7.4 (continued)

Country	Productivity quintile (1=low; 5=high)	Access to finance	Access to land and	Business licensing and permits	Corruption	Crime, theft, and disorder	Customs and trade regulations	Electricity	Inadequately educated workforce	Practices of competitors in informal sector	Tax rates	Transport
Guyana	1								25			
	2								31			
	3		15					15		15		
	4					15		15	15		15	
	5									22		
Jamaica	1										28	
	2										38	
	3										25	
	4										30	
	5										42	
Suriname	1				23				23			
	2	32							32			
	3				25				32			
	4								41			
	5											
Trinidad and Tobago	1								30			
	2								27			
	3								44			
	4								33			
	5								31			

Source: Author's own elaboration based on WBES data

Notes: Productivity is measured by the firm's sales for the last fiscal year deflated to 2009 US dollars and divided by the total number of permanent full-time employees plus the total number of temporary full-time employees (adjusting for the number of months). The quintiles are divided evenly within each country, so there are roughly the same number of firms in each quintile. Quintile 1 represents the lowest productivity firms and Quintile 5 represents the highest productivity firms in each country. For each quintile, the number represents the percentage of firms declaring the corresponding category as the biggest obstacle

the majority of firms in the lowest productivity quintile identify access to finance as their biggest obstacle.[23] In the Bahamas, as the productivity quintiles increase, the majority of firms identify an inadequately educated workforce as their biggest obstacle. It is possible that these shifts in identified obstacles reflect increases in exposure to a wider gamut of obstacles as a firm becomes more productive and is faced with more challenges to growth. In the Bahamas, for example, the medium productivity quintile displays an even split between firms that report customs and trade and an inadequately educated workforce as the biggest obstacles. A possible explanation for this could be that these medium productivity firms are at the stage when they are just beginning to export. The relatively lower productivity firms may not be attempting to export yet and thus are not affected by such regulations, while higher productivity firms may already have mastered the red tape and no longer see that as an obstacle. In other countries, such as Jamaica and Trinidad and Tobago, the dominance of a particular obstacle does not differ by productivity quintile. This suggests that the country's business environment may have a feature that affects all businesses and may trump the degree to which the biggest obstacles change according to firms' characteristics.

Econometric Model

Within economies and within industries, some firms are simply more efficient than others. Using the same measured inputs, high-productivity firms (in the 90th percentile) outperform low-productivity firms by 2:1. In India and China, the ratio has been found to be as high as 5:1. Further, within-industry dispersion has been found to be on the rise in the United Kingdom (Syverson 2011). Recent publications about innovation and productivity in the LAC region found that firm-level productivity is heterogeneous even within specific economic sectors (log productivity differences between the 90th and 10th percentile were found to be 2.66 log points in services and 2.53 log points in manufacturing). Theory often attributes this to market frictions that can be exacerbated by weaknesses in the institutional environment (Arias Ortiz et al. 2014). The following analysis uses quantile regression techniques following the methodology described in Goedhuys and Sleuwaegen (2009). This methodology is relevant given that the distribution of the dependent variable, labor productivity, is skewed.[24, 25]

Our interest is in the relationship between perceived obstacles to operation and productivity changes among the different quantiles of the distribution. Since a large number of observations are needed for this type of analysis, we pool the responses of all the firms in all 14 Caribbean countries surveyed for the 2010 WBES. We then list-wise delete the variables with missing values, leaving 2047 observations. The basic model closely follows variables[26] included in recent work assessing the determinants of productivity in the LAC region using WBES data (Arias Ortiz et al. 2014). We test the model using least squares (LS) and quantile regression techniques.

The basic model is:

$$\log \textit{of Labor Productivity}$$
$$= \alpha + \beta 1 \textit{Firm Size} + \beta 2 \textit{Age} + \beta 3 \textit{Foreign Ownership} + \beta 4 \textit{Export}$$
$$+ \beta 5 \textit{Website} + \beta 6 \textit{Human Capital} + \beta 7 \textit{Biggest Obstacle Finance}$$
$$+ \beta 8 \textit{Biggest Obstacle Edu WF} + \delta \textit{Country Dummies}$$
$$+ \delta 1 \textit{Sector Dummies} + \mu$$

where the dependent variable is the log of labor productivity as measured by the firm's total annual sales at the end of the previous fiscal year (in 2009)[27] divided by the number of permanent and temporary[28] full-time employees at the end of the same previous fiscal year. The firm size is the log of the firm's response to the number of full-time permanent employees three fiscal years previously (in 2007). Age is a dummy variable that takes the value of 1 if the firm is less than ten years of age. Foreign ownership is a dummy variable that takes the value of 1 if the firm reports that more than 10% is owned[29] by foreign individuals, companies, or organizations. Export is a dummy variable that takes the value of 1 if the firm reports more than 10% of its sales are direct exports. Website is a dummy variable that takes the value of 1 if the firm reports having a website. Human capital is a continuous variable for the percentage of the firm's employees that are reported to have at least a university degree. Biggest obstacle finance is a dummy variable that takes the value of 1 if the firm reports access to finance as its biggest obstacle. Biggest obstacle edu WF is a dummy variable that takes a value of 1 if the firm reports an inadequately educated workforce as its biggest obstacle. We include these two obstacles because they were the most frequently cited in the sample, at 342 for finance and 316[30] for workforce education. We include country dummies to account for country-specific effects, such as the number of ports indi-

Table 7.5 Relating obstacles to different productivity quantiles

	LS	Q10	Q25	Q50	Q75	Q90
Biggest obstacle = Access to finance	-0.208***	-0.183*	-0.07	-0.097	-0.193***	-0.235**
	(-4.03)	(-2.11)	(-1.27)	(-1.87)	(-3.61)	(-2.79)
Biggest obstacle = Inadequately educated workforce	-0.102	0.028	0.014	-0.011	-0.1	-0.193*
	(-1.89)	(0.35)	(0.39)	(-0.20)	(-1.59)	(-2.14)
Employment (2007), log	0.089***	0.052	0.118***	0.076***	0.075**	0.116**
	(5.00)	(1.71)	(6.43)	(3.68)	(3.14)	(3.03)
Young firm (<10 years)	-0.026	0.09	0.027	-0.043	-0.052	-0.016
	(-0.63)	(1.84)	(0.62)	(-0.91)	(-1.11)	(-0.21)
Foreign ownership (>10%)	0.093	-0.058	-0.065	0.068	0.07	0.13
	(1.76)	(-0.78)	(-0.91)	(0.94)	(1.08)	(1.04)
Exports (>10% direct)	0.024	-0.139	-0.069	0.015	0.048	0.271*
	(0.45)	(-1.50)	(-0.88)	(0.27)	(0.61)	(1.96)
Firm has its own website	0.203***	0.207**	0.128**	0.162**	0.249***	0.254**
	(4.76)	(3.10)	(2.90)	(3.10)	(4.28)	(2.78)
Full-time employees with at least a bachelor's degree (%)	0.005***	0.004**	0.002	0.004	0.006*	0.011***
	(3.88)	(2.85)	(1.92)	(1.64)	(2.20)	(3.64)
Constant	10.336***	9.431***	9.846***	10.409***	10.755***	10.979***
	(106.53)	(66.25)	(58.31)	(100.09)	(87.72)	(53.54)
Observations	2047	2047	2047	2047	2047	2047
Adjusted or pseudo R-squared	0.17	0.13	0.11	0.1	0.13	0.14

Source: Authors' elaboration based on WBES data

Notes: Country and sector dummies were used. The reference country was Antigua and Barbuda and the reference sector was low-tech manufacturing. Sectors included construction, low-tech manufacturing, medium-high-tech manufacturing, wholesale/retail, hotels/restaurants, transport and IT.

t statistics in parentheses; *$p < 0.05$, **$p < 0.01$, ***$p < 0.001$

cated in Table 7.1. We include sector dummies to control for differences in productivity among the different sectors, as recent literature suggests is appropriate (Arias Ortiz et al. 2014; Chap. 2 of this book) (Table 7.5).

The results of the LS regression are in line with the results found by Arias Ortiz et al. (2014). In 2007, firm size, whether or not the firm had a website, and human capital were statistically significant. On the other hand, the age of the firm, foreign ownership, and exporter were not statistically significant. This could be due to the fact that firms in the Caribbean tend to be older, on average, than in the rest of LAC. Also, as shown in Chap. 3, there are relatively small proportions of firms in each country that are foreign-owned and similarly relatively small proportions of firms that export. The access to finance obstacle is highly significant and negatively correlated with productivity. The inadequately educated workforce obstacle is not statistically significant, but this changes if the human capital variable is dropped from the equation, at which point it becomes statistically significant. In Table 7.7 (in the Appendix) we present results for just the manufacturing sector, where we include capital per worker. The access to finance obstacle remains significant in the LS regression, but loses significance in the quantile regression analysis. By restricting the sample to manufacturing firms with available data on capital, the number of observations drops to 600 firms, which limits the statistical power. We therefore present it more as a robustness check. We note that some of the other variables respond as expected. Exporter becomes statistically significant and having a website loses significance, which would be consistent with the different nature of business in manufacturing versus services firms.

The estimates for the different quantiles above and in the Appendix are the result of a simultaneous quantile regression that was bootstrapped at the standard 100 repetitions. This means that, while the coefficients and the pseudo R-squared do not change when the regression is run again, the standard errors can change slightly and some of the variables that are on the cusp of significance can change. This can also affect whether the differences between the quantiles are statistically significant.[31]

The results from the analysis should be taken as preliminary evidence that not only do the firm characteristics vary as you move from lower to higher productivity levels, but also that these characteristics may affect performance to varying degrees, depending on where the firms lie in the distribution of labor productivity. One interpretation could be that there are firms in the lowest productivity category in which variables such as lack of access to finance are truly prohibitive. However, there are also slightly more productive firms that remain in the lower half of the productivity distribution. Despite reporting access to finance as an obstacle, these firms do not actually perform differently from their counterparts in the same part of the distribution who do not report this as their biggest obstacle. As firms move into higher productivity quantiles, those firms reporting access to finance as their biggest obstacle are indeed under-performing relative to the other firms in their performance quantile who do not report access to finance as their biggest obstacle. The preliminary results corroborate the notion that the characteristics of a firm and the obstacles it faces can indeed vary by and relate differently to productivity.

CONCLUSION

The goal of this chapter was to better understand the firms in the Caribbean using micro-data from the WBES and PROTEQin. Since the data deficit has been acknowledged as a challenge for evidenced-based policymaking in the Caribbean, our descriptive data presents firm characteristics from several perspectives. We sought to distinguish whether, after calibrating by main product (or sector) and country, the relatively higher or lower productivity firms show different patterns with respect to the key characteristics linked to productivity. They do. The story of productivity in the Caribbean appears to be consistent with findings outside the region. Therefore, this chapter should serve as a point of departure for further research to gain a deeper understanding of how the characteristics of the private sector in the Caribbean countries exacerbate (or perhaps do not exacerbate) stagnated growth. Preliminary evidence suggests that there is variation in the obstacles identified by relatively higher or lower productivity firms and, perhaps more importantly, individual obstacles such as access to finance associate differently with productivity performance.

This is an original contribution that has rich policy implications for those in the region who wish to tailor or nuance policies to different types of firms in their economies. If policymakers are interested in moving relatively lower productivity firms into the higher productivity realms, they should zero in on the particular obstacles that the relatively lower productivity firms face. If, on the other hand, policymakers are concerned about how to support their relatively higher productivity firms, they should focus on the subset of obstacles reported by those firms.

APPENDIX

Table 7.6   Caribbean PROTEQin firm characteristics: high and low productivity

Firm characteristics	Full sample			Manufacturing			Services		
	N	Mean	S.D.	N	Mean	S.D.	N	Mean	S.D.
Firm size last FY, 2012 (No. of full-time, permanent employees)	648	65.1	141.2	279	77.0	162.1	369	56.1	122.6
High productivity	224	86.3	145.4	98	109.9	175.4	126	67.8	114.2
Low productivity	424	53.9	137.8	181	59.1	152.0	243	50.0	126.5
Firm size, 2011 (No. of full-time, permanent employees)	648	62.7	137.0	279	74.5	162.1	369	53.8	114.0
High productivity	224	84.6	148.9	98	107.6	182.9	126	66.7	113.3
Low productivity	424	51.1	129.1	181	56.6	147.0	243	47.1	114.1
Firm age (years)	621	25.8	19.8	272	27.7	19.9	349	24.4	19.6
High productivity	216	30.7	22.7	95	33.9	23.8	121	28.2	21.6
Low productivity	405	23.2	17.6	177	24.3	16.6	228	22.3	18.3
Foreign ownership (≥10%)	648	13.1	33.8	279	13.6	34.4	369	12.7	33.4
High productivity	224	19.2	39.5	98	18.4	38.9	126	19.8	40.0
Low productivity	424	9.9	29.9	181	11.0	31.4	243	9.1	28.8
Exports (≥10% direct)	648	15.6	36.3	279	23.3	42.3	369	9.8	29.7
High productivity	224	19.2	39.5	98	33.7	47.5	126	7.9	27.1
Low productivity	424	13.7	34.4	181	17.7	38.3	243	10.7	31.0
Managerial years of experience	634	18.8	10.4	272	19.9	11.0	362	17.9	9.9
High productivity	220	19.2	9.6	96	20.0	9.7	124	18.7	9.5
Low productivity	414	18.5	10.9	176	19.8	11.7	238	17.5	10.1

(continued)

DIFFERENT OBSTACLES FOR DIFFERENT PRODUCTIVITY LEVELS? ...   237

Table 7.6 (continued)

Firm characteristics	Full sample			Manufacturing			Services		
	N	Mean	S.D.	N	Mean	S.D.	N	Mean	S.D.
Internationally recognized quality certificate (%)	648	25.5	43.6	279	27.6	44.8	369	23.8	42.7
High productivity	224	29.0	45.5	98	30.6	46.3	126	27.8	45.0
Low productivity	424	23.6	42.5	181	26.0	44.0	243	21.8	41.4
Has a website	648	45.4	49.8	279	40.1	49.1	369	49.3	50.1
High productivity	224	61.2	48.8	98	58.2	49.6	126	63.5	48.3
Low productivity	424	37.0	48.3	181	30.4	46.1	243	42.0	49.5
Source of working capital: Internal (%)	644	62.2	27.4	275	60.3	26.5	369	63.7	27.9
High productivity	222	61.9	25.4	96	60.8	22.9	126	62.8	27.2
Low productivity	422	62.4	28.4	179	60.0	28.4	243	64.1	28.4
Source of working capital: Banks (%)	644	18.0	21.3	275	18.3	19.5	369	17.8	22.6
High productivity	222	18.8	19.7	96	18.0	16.4	126	19.4	21.9
Low productivity	422	17.6	22.1	179	18.5	21.1	243	16.9	22.9

Source: Authors' elaboration using PROTEQin data

Table 7.7 Relating obstacles to different productivity quantiles (manufacturing only)

	LS	Q10	Q25	Q50	Q75	Q90
Biggest obstacle = Access to finance	-0.241**	-0.047	-0.114	-0.135	-0.093	-0.13
	(-2.75)	(-0.34)	(-1.23)	(-1.52)	(-0.74)	(-0.93)
Biggest obstacle = Inadequately educated workforce	-0.212**	-0.017	-0.082	-0.164*	-0.112	-0.147
	(-2.60)	(-0.10)	(-0.95)	(-2.04)	(-1.16)	(-0.97)
Employment (2007), log	0.080*	0.084	0.077*	0.034	0.038	0.123*
	(-2.58)	(-1.35)	(-2.10)	(-0.99)	(-0.84)	(-2.16)
Capital per worker	0	0.002	0	0	-0.001	-0.001
	(-0.15)	(-0.25)		(-0.05)	(-0.10)	(-0.08)
Young firm (<10 years)	0.011	0.197*	0.005	-0.148*	-0.011	0.021
	(-0.15)	(-1.99)	(-0.07)	(-1.99)	(-0.11)	(-0.2)
Foreign ownership (>10%)	0.025	-0.224	-0.177	0.022	0.118	0.143
	(-0.27)	(-1.20)	(-1.35)	(-0.21)	(-0.81)	(-0.72)
Exports (>10% direct)	0.164*	-0.099	0.013	0.12	0.304	0.455*
	(-2.09)	(-0.93)	(-0.15)	(-1.62)	(-1.96)	(-2.52)
Firm has its own website	0.046	0.148	0.097	-0.008	-0.067	-0.008
	(-0.64)	(-1.22)	(-1.27)	(-0.10)	(-0.56)	(-0.06)
Full-time employees with at least a bachelors degree (%)	0.007*	0.006	0.005	0.007	0.009	0.008
	(-2.47)	(-1.32)	(-1.18)	(-1.51)	(-1.78)	(-1.28)
Constant	10.239***	9.210***	9.740***	10.441***	10.693***	10.891***
	(-55.51)	(-40.75)	(-31.64)	(-45.64)	(-46.32)	(-45.06)
Observations	600	600	600	600	600	600
Adjusted or pseudo R-squared	0.19	0.2	0.15	0.09	0.13	0.22

Source: Authors' elaboration based on WBES data

Notes: Country and sector dummies were used. The reference country was Antigua & Barbuda and the reference sector was low-tech manufacturing. Included sectors: low-tech manufacturing, medium-high-tech manufacturing, medium-high-tech manufacturing; t statistics in parentheses; $*p<0.05$, $**p<0.01$, $***p<0.001$. Medium-high-tech manufacturing sectors were found to be statistically significant at the 99% level in the LS regression and at the 95% level in all of the quantiles presented except the 75th, where it was not statistically significant. We also tried adding Manager Experience to the regressions since some of the other models have included that variable; the results are very similar without having any significance specifically for that variable. We cannot include Broadband because the WBES data in the Caribbean did not ask questions about broadband. We included the variable about owning a website as a proxy for ICT connectivity and sophistication

NOTES

1. An exception is Chap. 3, which analyses product and process innovations as drivers of firm performance in the Caribbean.
2. There are specific WBES questionnaires for the Caribbean (manufacturing and services) that contain minor differences from the WBES questionnaires used in Latin America. For example, the Caribbean questionnaires do not ask firms about high-speed broadband connections.
3. Measures of small economies can be based on population, GDP, or land area, which have been found to be highly correlated (Ruprah et al. 2014). To be consistent with other recent publications about the Caribbean, the same definition of small economy has been adopted.
4. In 2006, 90 %.
5. For more information, see www.competecaribbean.org
6. In some instances, firms that were not included in the 2010 round of WBES were added in the 2013 survey.
7. Francis et al. (2014) used slightly different country groupings for the Caribbean. In their note, they used small countries: Antigua and Barbuda, The Bahamas, Barbados, Belize, Dominica, Grenada, Guyana, Suriname, St. Kitts & Nevis, Saint Lucia, and St. Vincent & the Grenadines.
8. The regional average for LAC cellphone usage was 88 % (2010 WBES). In 2010, Jamaica and Guyana were both below this threshold but well surpassed it in the 2013 PROTEQin.
9. The article describes self-selection as more productive or more ambitious, and forward-looking firms as those preparing themselves to opt into markets with foreign competition. This is in contrast to the post-entry learning-by-exporting perspective: once you are an exporter, you must increase your productivity to survive the competition, but you also benefit from the positive externalities offered by involvement with international suppliers and competitors.
10. Building on growth theorists who attribute growth to human capital and R&D, these recent scholars postulate that entrepreneurship links investment in new knowledge (R&D) and economic growth (Vivarelli 2013).
11. See Szirmai et al. (2011) for a recent study of entrepreneurship as it relates to innovation and economic development.
12. An important consideration regarding whether a firm was created due to lack of a better opportunity is that the WBES excludes firms that are smaller than five employees. A concentration of firms that are started for lack of better employment may exist in firms that were excluded from the survey.
13. Here the author's literal phrase "structural transformation" is interpreted as transformation.
14. The proportion of the population that has completed tertiary education— a broader measure than a bachelor's degree—is 10 % or less. However, in

the Barro and Lee dataset (1950–2010), this variable is only available for five of the surveyed countries, supporting what is mentioned at the outset of this chapter, namely that when it comes to commonly used indicators, many of the Caribbean countries suffer from a deficit of data.

15. The questions are based on a five-point scale from "not difficult" to "almost impossible."

16. Biene et al. (2008) offered empirical evidence that brain drain is detrimental.

17. For example, Gibson and McKenzie (2011) raised questions about the existence of brain gain and proposed ideas to frame the empirical analysis of a series of understudied aspects of the impact of highly skilled migration.

18. Diasporic entrepreneurs are defined as entrepreneurs who are tapping into the Caribbean or diaspora markets.

19. A total of 67 diasporic firms responded to an online survey. The sample was mainly gathered from Compete Caribbean's registered database of entrepreneurs that responded to the open call for the Caribbean Idea Marketplace (CIM).

20. Of the firms surveyed by PROTEQin 79% cited the quality of education as a factor ranging from important to critical in causing skill shortages and almost 77% cited a shortage in the number of local professionals trained by local institutions.

21. A shortage in local professionals trained by local institutions could also be affected by people who migrate away from the Caribbean to pursue educational opportunities elsewhere (Thomas-Hope 2002).

22. See Table 7.6 in the Appendix for complete results.

23. Hallward-Driemeier and Aterido (2009) pointed out that endogeneity remains a concern with the obstacle of access to finance. In other words, it may be precisely because these firms have low productivity that they experience access to finance as their biggest obstacle. That does not mean that they are not objectively experiencing this obstacle.

24. Goedhuys and Sleuwaegen (2009) confronted a skewed distribution of their dependent variable and, as they describe, classical regression approaches are a location shift where the covariates are conditioned to the mean and are interpreted as being associated with a shift in the mean, but not in the shape or distribution of the dependent variable. They used quantile regression because they were interested in the factors that stretched the tail of distribution and had a strong effect where the high-growth firms were located.

25. Since the mean could be distorted by outliers in the tail of the distribution.

26. This model differs from some of the other approaches used in other chapters of this book because of the necessity to focus on the services sector,

which is extremely relevant in the Caribbean. Therefore, we choose to closely follow Arias Ortiz et al. (2014)), who used an approach readily applicable to our analysis. For example, we initially do not include capital per worker in our model because capital is not available in the survey for the services sector. In order to check how the results would differ, we perform the same analysis for the manufacturing sector only. The results are presented in Table 7.7 in the Appendix.

27. Standardized in the dataset by deflating all responses to 2009 US dollars.
28. Correcting for the number of months of the year during which the temporary employees were working.
29. In the sample there were 12 observations of the 2047 that were categorized in the dataset as state-owned enterprises; these 12 observations were included as domestically owned (and took a value of zero).
30. The next most frequently cited biggest obstacle (by 238 firms) was electricity.
31. In this case, the following variables are statistically different at the 95% level among the quantiles: employment in 2007 (size of the firm), full-time employees with at least a bachelor's degree, and exports. The biggest obstacle being access to finance was significantly different at the 90% level.

REFERENCES

Abramovitz, M. 1989. *Thinking About Growth and Other Essays on Economic Growth and Welfare in Studies in Economic History and Policy: The United States in the Twentieth Century.* L. Galambos and R. Gallman (eds.). Cambridge: Cambridge University Press.

Arias Ortiz, E.A., G. Crespi, E. Tacsir, F. Vargas, and P. Zuniga. 2012. Innovation for Economic Performance: The Case of Latin American and Caribbean Firms. *Technical Note IDB-TN-494.* Washington, DC: IDB.

Arias Ortiz, E., G. Crespi, A. Rasteletti, and F. Vargas. 2014. Innovation and Productivity in Services in Latin America and the Caribbean. Discussion Paper: IDB-DP-346. Washington, DC: IDB.

Ayyagari, M., A. Demirguc-Kent, and V. Maksimovic. 2011. Small vs. Young Firms Across The World: Contribution to Employment, Job Creation and Growth. Policy Research Working Paper 5631. Washington, DC: The World Bank.

Barro, R., and J.W. Lee. 2010. A New Data Set of Educational Attainment in the World, 1950–2010. *Journal of Development Economics* 104: 184–198.

Biene, M., F. Docquier, and H. Rapoport. 2008. Brain Drain and Human Capital Formation in Developing Countries: Winners and Losers. *The Economic Journal* 118(April): 631–652.

Caribbean Knowledge Series. 2013. Quality Education Counts for Skills and Growth. LAC 78597. Washington, DC: The World Bank.

Crespi, G., E. Tacsir, and F. Vargas. 2014. Innovation and Productivity in Services: Evidence from Latin America. Technical Note IDB-TN-690. Washington, DC: IDB.

Francis, D., J.L. Rodriguez Meza, and J. Yang. 2014. Mapping Enterprises in Latin American and the Caribbean. Latin America and the Caribbean Series, Note 1, Rev. 8/2014. Washington, DC, and Christ Church, Barbados: The World Bank Group, IDB, and Compete Caribbean.

Gibson, J., and D. McKenzie. 2011. Eight Questions about Brain Drain. Policy Research Working Paper 5668. Washington, DC: The World Bank.

Goedhuys, M., and L. Sleuwaegen. 2009. High-Growth Entrepreneurial Firms in Africa: A Quantile Regression Approach. Research Paper 2009(11). Helsinki, Finland: United Nations University World Institute for Development Economics Research (UNU-Wider).

Hallward-Driemeier, M., and R. Aterido. 2009. Comparing Apples with ... Apples. How to Make (More) Sense of Subjective Rankings of Constraints to Business. Policy Research Working Paper 5054. Washington, DC: The World Bank.

IDB. 2011a. Innovation in Services: The Hard Case for Latin America and the Caribbean. Discussion Paper IDB-DP-203. Washington, DC: IDB.

IDB. 2011b. The Region's Place in the Digital World: A Tale of Three Divides. In *Development Connections: Unveiling the Impact of New Information Technologies*, ed. A. Chong. Washington, DC: IDB and Palgrave Macmillan.

Jensen, J.B., and R.H. McGuckin. 1997. Firm Performance and Evolution: Empirical Regularities in the U.S. Microdata. *Industrial and Corporate Change* 6(1): 25–47.

Kaluza, P., A. Kolzsch, M. Gastner, and B. Blasiu. 2010. The Complex Network of Global Cargo Ship Movements. *Journal of the Royal Society Interface* 7(48): 1093–1103.

Laursen, K., V. Mahnke, and P. Vejrup-Hansen. 1999. *Firm Growth from a Knowledge Structure Perspective*. Frederiksberg, Denmark: Department of Industrial Economics and Strategy, Copenhagen Business School.

Naudé, W. 2008. Entrepreneurship in Economic Development. Research paper/ UNUWIDER2008/20.

Nugent, S., and J.P. Schmid. 2014. The Business Climate in Jamaica: What Does the Enterprise Survey Have to Say? Policy Brief No. IDB-PB-211. Washington, DC: IDB.

Nurse, K., and J. Jones. 2009. Brain Drain and Caribbean-EU Labour Mobility. Cave Hill, Barbados: Shridath Ramphal Centre for International Trade Law, Policy and Services, UWI.

Nurse, K., and C. Kirton. 2014. *Caribbean Diasporic Entrepreneurship: Analytical Report*. Washington, DC: IDB.

Pagés, C. (ed.). 2010. *The Age of Productivity: Transforming Economies from the Bottom Up*. Washington, DC: IDB and Palgrave Macmillan.

Ruprah, I., and R. Sierra. 2013. Laments of the Caribbean Businessperson Are Based on Facts? Policy Brief No. IDB-PB-205. Washington, DC: IDB.

Ruprah, I., K. Melgarejo, and R. Sierra. 2014. Is There a Caribbean Sclerosis? Stagnating Economic Growth in the Caribbean. Monograph 178. Washington, DC: IDB.

Syverson, C. 2011. What Determines Productivity? *Journal of Economic Literature* 49(2): 326–365.

Szirmai, A., W.A. Naudé, and M. Goedhuys. 2011. *Entrepreneurship, Innovation, and Economic Development*. Oxford: Oxford University Press.

Thomas-Hope, E. 2002. Skilled Labour Migration from Developing Countries: Study on the Caribbean Region. International Migration Papers 50. Geneva: International Migration Programme, International Labour Organization.

Vivarelli, M. 2013. Is Entrepreneurship Necessarily Good? Microeconomic Evidence from Developed and Developing Countries. *Industrial and Corporate Change* 22(6): 1453–1495.

Wagner, J. 2005. Exports and Productivity: A Survey of the Evidence from Firm Level Data. Working Paper Series in Economics 4:1860–5508. Lüneburg, Germany: Lüneburg University.

Wagner, R. 2014. Promoting Entrepreneurship: The Start-Up and Scale-Up of High-Productivity Firms. In *Development in the Americas: Rethinking Productive Development: Sound Policies and Institutions for Economic Transformation*, ed. G. Crespi, E. Fernández-Arias, and E. Stein. Washington, DC: IDB and Palgrave Macmillan.

Wennekers, S., and R. Thurik. 1999. Linking Entrepreneurship and Economic Growth. *Small Business Economics* 13(1): 27–56.

OPEN

CHAPTER 8

Credit Access in Latin American Enterprises

Andrea F. Presbitero and Roberta Rabellotti

The views expressed herein are those of the authors and should not be attributed to the IMF, its Executive Board, or its management. We thank Gustavo Crespi, Matteo Grazzi, Siobhan Pangerl, Carlo Pietrobelli, Joan Prats, Eddy Szirmai, and the participants at the IDB workshop "Determinants of Firm Performance in LAC: What Does the Micro Evidence Tell Us?" for useful comments on an earlier draft.

Access to bank credit is often indicated as one of the main constraints impairing firm growth, productivity, innovation, and export capacity, particularly as it affects small- and medium-sized enterprises (SMEs). As most of the literature on small business lending is focused on the United States and Europe (Berger and Udell 2002; Berger et al. 2005; Beck and Demirgüç-Kunt 2006), results are not easily applicable to emerging and developing countries because of significant differences in firm size distributions and characteristics as well as in institutional, macroeconomic, and financial structures.

A. F. Presbitero
IMF and MoFiR
e-mail: APresbitero@imf.org

R. Rabellotti
University of Pavia, Italy
e-mail: roberta.rabellotti@gmail.com

© Inter-American Development Bank 2016
M. Grazzi and C. Pietrobelli (eds.), *Firm Innovation and Productivity in Latin America and the Caribbean*,
DOI 10.1057/978-1-349-58151-1_8

245

The extent to which firms may be financially constrained varies across countries according to both micro and macro-factors. Based on the World Bank Enterprise Surveys (WBES), which provide cross-country comparable firm-level data, several studies investigate the existence of common micro-determinants in financing constraints (for example, see Beck et al. [2006], and for a recent comprehensive survey, Ayyagari et al. 2012). The data has also been used to study how different institutional frameworks and credit market structures affect access to credit (Beck et al. 2004, 2011; Clarke et al. 2006).

Among the few studies of Latin America, Galindo and Schiantarelli (2003) undertook a number of country case studies to assess how the characteristics of firms and credit markets shape access to external finance. In another study, Stallings (2006) reported that access to finance is a key problem for SMEs in Latin America, with significant variations across countries. The Organisation for Economic Co-operation and Development (OECD) recently described a similar picture and argued that, notwithstanding improvements in the depth of the financial systems in the region, a significant proportion of Latin American SMEs still had limited access to finance (OECD 2013).

Some recent literature has shown that the lack of adequate access to finance is an important constraint to productivity growth at the firm level (De Mel et al. 2008; Banerjee and Duflo 2014), profoundly undermining aggregate output growth. The focus of this book is on the sources of and constraints on productivity growth at the firm level. The book shows how economic growth largely depends on the dynamics of productivity. It is therefore important to investigate the extent and the determinants of financing constraints in Latin America and the Caribbean (LAC). We want to clarify from the beginning that the link between access to finance and productivity is complex because it can go in two directions. Further, the link can be indirect given that, for instance, the lack of credit could hamper innovation and foreign competitiveness, which impact productivity. In fact, the evidence collected in this book suggests that there are several other factors that deeply affect productivity and are related to access to credit. For example, innovation (see Chap. 2) and the limited openness to exports, foreign investments, and global value chains (see Chap. 9) affect productivity.

In this chapter, we aim to uncover the possible heterogeneities in financing constraints across both firms and countries, and to explain them according to differences in the micro-characteristics, as well as the institutional, macroeconomic, and financial settings at the country level. The empirical analysis uses the comprehensive data from the WBES for 31 countries in LAC, providing information about the sources of finance and access to credit for firms with five or more employees.[1] This data is matched with macroeconomic data on credit market structure and the institutional setting.

We address the following research questions:

1. Regarding the extent of financing constraints on firms: What is the share of firms that lack access to bank financing? How do firms finance themselves in the short and long term? How diffuse are different forms of credit?

2. Regarding the characteristics of financially constrained firms: Which firms are more likely to be financially constrained? To address this issue, we focus on the differences across several characteristics at the firm level—productivity, size, age, ownership structure, gender of the owner, location, and financial structure.

3. Regarding the role of external factors: Do differences in macroeconomic, financial, and institutional variables (income levels, presence of credit registries, financial development, presence of foreign banks, market competition) across countries help explain the variability in access to finance?

In the next section, we review the literature on credit market structure and financing constraints on firms. Then we describe the main characteristics of the banking systems in the region and provide an overview of the financing structure. Then we look at firms' access to bank financing in LAC. We examine firm-specific characteristics and country-specific credit market features associated with financing constraints. Finally, we provide some conclusions.

THE LITERATURE

Credit Market Structure and Financing Constraints on Firms

Credit markets are characterized by asymmetric information between borrowers and lenders, imperfect screening and monitoring technologies, and a paucity of collateral that can be pledged; therefore, financial constraints emerge as an equilibrium phenomenon (Jaffee and Russell 1976; Stiglitz and Weiss 1981). This phenomenon implies that firms that are more informationally opaque are more likely to be financially constrained, given that they cannot communicate their creditworthiness to lenders. This problem is particularly binding for small and young firms that cannot overcome the information asymmetry by pledging collateral, and for firms in countries where there are no credit registries, which is the case in many LAC countries (see "Credit Markets in LAC" below).

On the lender side, banks use imperfect screening technologies and rely as much as possible on transactional lending schemes, addressing the informational opacity of potential borrowers using *hard*, codified information. Lending technologies may overcome informational asymmetries by using soft (non-codified, difficult to summarize numerically) information, but this requires building a long-term lending relationship.

Therefore, the pervasiveness of financing constraints depends not only on firm characteristics, but also on the structure of the local credit markets in which they operate. The degree of market concentration, the proximity between lenders and borrowers, and the types of banks operating locally affect firms' access to credit. In fact, different banks may apply different lending technologies and may adopt different organizational structures (Berger et al. 2005; Beck et al. 2011). Moreover, the bank–borrower distance and the degree of market competition also affect the collection and transmission of soft information and lenders' market power (Petersen and Rajan 1995; Degryse and Ongena 2005; Cetorelli and Strahan 2006).

Among these factors, the growing importance of foreign-owned banks in a number of emerging and developing countries has sparked a broad discussion about their effect on market competition and credit availability (Claessens and Van Horen 2014). On the one hand, the size of the bank and the distance that separates its decision-making center from local firms could reduce the capacity and willingness of foreign banks to engage in SME lending and induce them to choose borrowers selectively, especially in developing countries (Mian 2006; Detragiache et al. 2008). On the other hand, some people argue that foreign multiservice banks are more efficient, especially in developing and emerging markets. They believe that foreign banks have a comparative advantage in offering a wide range of products and services by using new technologies, business models, and risk management systems. On this basis, their presence could be associated with reducing financing constraints on firms (de la Torre et al. 2010). In addition, foreign bank penetration could increase credit availability because it increases market competition and exerts competitive pressures on domestic banks. Domestic banks could be forced to reorient their lending activity to informationally opaque borrowers, with whom they have a relative advantage compared to foreign competitors (Dell'Ariccia and Marquez 2004).[2]

Finally, the literature stresses the role that the institutional setting and the legal infrastructure can play in easing access to finance. The efficiency of the legal system, the enforcement of contracts, and mechanisms that enable information sharing among lenders can attenuate adverse selection and moral hazard, improving credit availability (Beck et al. 2006; Pagano and Jappelli 1993; Padilla and Pagano 1997).

Empirical Evidence

In this section we selectively review the extensive literature on the micro-determinants of financing constraints and credit market structures. We pay special attention to the empirical studies with a global perspective, using firm-level data—especially the WBES—specifically focusing on LAC.

Firm-Level Characteristics

The literature has consistently shown that older, larger, more productive, and foreign-owned firms are less likely to encounter financing obstacles. Beck et al. (2006) and Cole and Dietrich (2014) used the WBES database to show that there was a robust correlation around the world (including the LAC region) between firm size and access to finance and that SMEs were more likely to face credit constraints. Kuntchev et al. (2013) also found that internationalized and more productive firms were less likely to suffer from difficulties in accessing credit, with the latter association being stronger for larger firms. Specifically using WBES data for Argentina, Brazil, Chile, and Mexico, Makler et al. (2013) supported the standard hypothesis that smaller and younger firms are disadvantaged when it comes to securing bank credit compared to larger and older enterprises.

Based on surveys conducted in Argentina, Colombia, Costa Rica, Ecuador, Mexico, and Uruguay investigating the determinants of financing constraints on firms, Galindo and Schiantarelli (2003) found empirical evidence supporting theoretical predictions about the importance of asymmetric information.[3] The severity of financing constraints did not only depend on observable firm balance sheet characteristics (i.e. hard [quantifiable] information), but also on the strength of the bank–firm relationship, on the firm's credit history, and on the firm's characteristics, which, on average, were correlated with creditworthiness. Furthermore, they confirmed that financing constraints were less binding for larger firms and for those that were foreign-owned or belonged to a business group.

Credit Market Structure

An important strand of the literature on bank credit investigates how financial development, market competition, and foreign bank presence affect firm access to finance. In a seminal contribution, Beck et al. (2004) combined firm-level data from 74 countries to show that market concentration was positively associated with financing obstacles, especially in developing countries. However, this negative effect of market concentration was mitigated in countries with a large presence of foreign banks and where credit registries facilitated information sharing, while it was magnified in countries with high government interference and a dominant presence of state-owned banks.

Clarke et al. (2006) did not confirm the widespread concerns that foreign banks reduce credit availability for SMEs. The authors found that, in countries with a strong presence of foreign-owned banks, access to bank credit was perceived as less constraining on enterprises, including SMEs. In a similar vein, focusing on Argentina, Chile, Colombia, and Peru and using bank-level data, Clarke et al. (2005) showed that the effect of foreign presence on small business lending was heterogeneous but, on average, small firms were more likely to take advantage of the presence of foreign banks when these institutions had a significant local presence.

Claessens and Van Horen (2014) collected the most comprehensive dataset on foreign bank presence and documented the sharp expansion of foreign banks since the mid-1990s, especially in emerging and developing countries. Their country-level data showed that foreign bank presence was negatively related to private credit in developing countries, especially in countries where foreign banks had a low market share, high costs of contract enforcement, and low credit information.

Finally, there is a large strand of evidence supporting the importance of credit registries for business lending. Djankov et al. (2007) found that private and public registries were associated with more private credit, especially in poor countries. Similarly, Jappelli and Pagano (2002) used aggregate data to show that bank lending was higher in countries where lenders shared information, regardless of the private or public nature of the information sharing mechanism.

Credit Markets in LAC

Since the mid-1990s, there has been a structural change in credit markets around the world. Financial liberalization has contributed to a general contraction of the role played by state-owned banks and to increasing penetration of foreign banks in domestic credit markets. LAC is no exception. After the financial crises in the 1990s, banking systems in LAC underwent significant changes. Deregulation and the opening of the financial markets to foreign competition helped increase competitive pressures and led to an intense process of bank restructuring, privatization, and consolidation (Cardim De Carvalho et al. 2012).

A recent study by the World Bank (2012) benchmarked financial development in the LAC-7 countries[4] against countries at comparable levels of economic development and advanced countries. The authors found that, since the early 2000s, there was a general deepening of the domestic financial systems in the region. However, there were still significant gaps and, in general, there had not been a convergence toward the indexes of financial maturity observed in more developed countries. More developed credit markets emerged in certain countries within the region, especially the offshore centers in the Caribbean (World Bank 2012; Čihák et al. 2012; Cardim De Carvalho et al. 2012; Didier and Schmukler 2014).

A useful view of financial development across LAC is provided by the ratio between bank credit and GDP, a measure of financial depth calculated on the basis of the Global Financial Development Database. On average, this ratio is 40%, ranging from very low values in Argentina, Mexico, Peru, and Uruguay—similar to what we find in much poorer countries such as Tanzania, Ghana, and Mozambique[5]—to high ratios in Chile (64%) and some of the Caribbean countries, especially in the offshore centers (e.g. The Bahamas, Barbados, and Panama), which are the clear outliers.

Other indicators can be used to investigate the structure of domestic credit markets: the number of bank branches per 100,000 adults, which is a standard measure of the development of and access to credit markets; the degree of competition, as measured by the share of the banking assets of the three largest national banks over total banking assets; and the presence of foreign banks, measured as the share of the total number of banks operating in the country. All these three indicators are from the Global Financial Development Database.

The number of bank branches can be considered a prerequisite for financial inclusion, facilitating access to financial services for individuals and firms. According to the World Bank (2012), the median number of branches (13) and ATMs (37) per 100,000 adults in the LAC-7 is lower than in Eastern European countries (22 branches and 54 ATMs) and in the G7 economies (24 and 118), but it is similar to the Asian economies

(11 and 34). Based on the Global Financial Development Database and considering Latin America as a whole, the median number is 20 branches per 100,000 adults, with very large differences among countries. Of the LAC-7, only Brazil and Peru have a number of branches above the median in the region; some small Caribbean island countries are also above the median.

In contrast to what has happened in other regions since the 2000s, credit markets in the LAC-7 countries have become more concentrated (Didier and Schmukler 2014). The share of bank assets held by the three largest banks represents credit concentration. Of the LAC-7, the most concentrated banking sector is in Peru and the least is in Argentina (based on the Global Financial Development Database). In the rest of the region, concentration is relatively high, especially in many small Caribbean countries, such as Suriname, Guyana, Barbados, Antigua, Belize, Trinidad and Tobago, and Jamaica.

LAC's financial systems show a very high penetration of foreign banks. The ratio of foreign banks to total banks has increased sharply since 1995 (28%), reaching 42% in 2009, similar to Eastern Europe (47%) and much higher than East Asia (24%) and the OECD countries (24%). Considering the share of assets held by foreign banks, the differences between LAC (29%), East Asia (4%), and OECD countries (11%) are even larger (Claessens and Van Horen 2014). Of the LAC-7, Mexico and Peru have a large presence of foreign banks, and Brazil and Colombia have a smaller presence.

Finally, the region is also characterized by a certain degree of heterogeneity in the presence of credit registries, which had been established in about half of the countries by 2010.[6]

Firm Financing in LAC

In this section we present some facts about the financing structure in LAC and access to bank financing by firms, exploring a set of well-defined firm characteristics:

- **Size:** Micro (10 or less employees), small (11 to 50), medium (51 to 250), and large (more than 250).
- **Productivity:** The logarithm of labor productivity; low and high productivity defined as below and above the median.
- **Age:** New (three years or less since inception), young (four to ten years) and mature (older than ten years).

- **Degree of internationalization:**
  - *Foreign-owned enterprises*: 10 % or more of the firm is owned by foreign private individuals or companies.
  - *Exporters*: Direct exports account for 10 % or more of annual sales.
- **Female owned:** At least one woman among the firm's owners.
- **Sector:** *Services* or *manufacturing*.[7]

Financing Structure

The WBES provide information about the sources of finance for working capital expenditures in a subsample of 13,676 firms. Table 8.1 presents the differences across some firm characteristics and across countries.[8] The table clearly shows that firms primarily finance their working capital through internal sources (58 %), followed by trade credit (21 %), with bank credit (17 %) being the third source.

Table 8.1 also shows the significant degree of variability in the use of bank credit across the different firm characteristics. Its use is limited for micro[9] and new firms, while it is the second source of financing (after internal funds) for large firms. The difficulty that small firms have accessing bank credit is statistically significant, confirming the findings of the OECD (2013), which found that less than 15 % of lending in the region goes to smaller firms even though they provide almost 80 % of jobs.

More productive firms rely less on internal funding to finance working capital and tend to use more bank and trade credit. Exporters are significantly more likely to use bank credit than non-exporting firms (possibly because they tend to be larger), while foreign-owned firms rely significantly less on bank credit than do domestic firms. Foreign firms mainly finance their working capital internally, possibly because of availability of resources in multinationals. There are no significant differences in financing between male-owned businesses and those with a female owner. Across sectors, manufacturing firms on average are more dependent on internal financing and less on trade credit than services enterprises, but there is no significant difference in accessing bank credit.

Access to Banking Products

In LAC, 90 % of the firms in the sample have a bank account, similar to Europe and Central Asia but somewhat higher than in Asia and Africa. However, there is a certain degree of variability in the use of banking

Table 8.1 Financing structure by firm characteristics and countries (% of working capital)

	Internal funds	Banks	Other financial institutions	Trade credit	Other (e.g. money lenders, friends)
Whole sample	57.52	17.01	1.66	21.35	2.45
Size					
Micro	62.04	12.63	1.71	19.95	3.67
Small	57.44	16.35	1.71	21.88	2.62
Medium	55.84	19.40	1.57	21.54	1.64
Large	51.66	23.80	1.55	21.96	1.03
Productivity					
Low	58.31	16.15	1.77	20.43	3.34
High	54.58	18.99	1.56	23.26	1.61
Age					
New	60.34	13.63	1.58	19.28	5.18
Young	59.31	15.92	1.89	19.66	3.22
Mature	56.99	17.40	1.61	21.84	2.17
Ownership					
Domestic	57.22	17.06	1.64	21.55	2.53
Foreign	62.24	14.46	1.33	19.96	2.00
Gender					
No female ownership	58.06	16.65	1.60	21.25	2.44
At least one female owner	57.12	16.99	1.60	21.71	2.58
Internationalization					
Exporter	52.30	20.54	1.41	23.36	2.40
Non-exporter	58.44	16.37	1.71	21.02	2.46
Sector					
Manufacturing	61.26	16.17	1.45	18.91	2.21
Services	55.12	17.56	1.79	22.92	2.61
Country					
Antigua and Barbuda	69.80	14.37	0.00	12.90	2.93
Argentina	*58.09*	*11.76*	*1.15*	*26.81*	*2.19*
Bahamas	64.72	13.54	1.27	19.42	1.06
Barbados	69.78	14.94	0.36	13.53	1.40
Belize	62.24	19.50	0.13	15.64	2.48
Bolivia	62.14	15.94	2.24	16.52	3.17
Brazil	*50.79*	*23.82*	*2.81*	*20.32*	*2.26*
Chile	*54.33*	*19.02*	*1.51*	*23.24*	*1.90*
Colombia	*38.08*	*21.25*	*1.42*	*35.13*	*4.12*
Costa Rica	74.56	11.77	1.39	11.00	1.28

(continued)

Table 8.1   (continued)

	Internal funds	Banks	Other financial institutions	Trade credit	Other (e.g. money lenders, friends)
Dominica	77.08	9.36	0.00	12.26	1.30
Dominican Republic	48.18	22.17	1.52	26.51	1.61
Ecuador	49.49	18.67	1.48	26.83	3.53
El Salvador	46.32	21.61	2.24	25.70	4.13
Grenada	51.85	19.72	2.10	21.03	5.30
Guatemala	60.15	10.98	1.96	24.07	2.84
Guyana	48.82	19.97	0.38	24.63	6.19
Honduras	69.11	16.01	1.34	11.07	2.48
Jamaica	63.88	14.99	0.24	20.05	0.85
Mexico	*61.61*	*9.14*	*1.38*	*24.89*	*2.99*
Nicaragua	75.47	12.52	0.83	10.29	0.89
Panama	89.05	3.75	1.88	3.63	1.68
Paraguay	62.71	15.94	3.94	15.87	1.54
Peru	*41.77*	*29.29*	*2.29*	*23.87*	*2.78*
St. Kitts & Nevis	54.07	20.72	0.39	21.28	3.54
Saint Lucia	73.23	12.18	0.00	12.89	1.70
St. Vincent & the Grenadines	63.66	25.67	1.02	8.97	0.68
Suriname	56.22	17.93	1.58	21.35	2.93
Trinidad and Tobago	50.37	26.64	2.79	18.51	1.69
Uruguay	67.88	8.52	1.01	20.64	1.95
Venezuela	*57.94*	*15.28*	*1.66*	*22.92*	*2.20*

Source: Authors' elaboration based on WBES data

Note: The countries in italics are part of the LAC-7

products (Table 8.2). For instance, almost 18% of micro-enterprises have neither savings nor a checking account. From a country perspective, while almost all firms sampled in Argentina, Brazil, Chile, and Colombia have a banking account, only 61% of Mexican firms have one.

Access to bank credit (overdraft, line of credit, or loan) is less widespread and more heterogeneous. On average, less than two-thirds of all firms surveyed have an overdraft facility, with this instrument being less frequent among micro (46%), new (52%), and non-exporter (62%) firms. In addition, only 54% of LAC firms have a line of credit or a loan, and the diffusion of these instruments is again significantly different across firm size, age, and export status. Access to bank credit is also highly heterogeneous across countries: in Mexico only 24% of firms have an overdraft

Table 8.2   Access to bank finance by firm characteristics and countries (%)

	Checking/ savings account	Overdraft	Line of credit/loan
Whole sample	90.68	63.62	54.18
Size			
Micro	82.34	46.19	37.75
Small	91.69	64.78	53.90
Medium	92.62	73.91	65.11
Large	94.34	81.78	76.26
Productivity			
Low	86.29	55.42	49.13
High	94.58	74.15	61.95
Age			
New	85.93	51.56	40.02
Young	88.47	58.15	49.08
Mature	90.23	65.74	56.41
Ownership			
Domestic	88.64	61.96	54.97
Foreign	94.18	71.59	51.47
Gender			
No female ownership	88.47	62.39	53.56
At least one female owner	90.71	64.12	56.58
Internationalization			
Exporter	94.75	74.10	65.63
Non-exporter	88.76	61.76	52.19
Sector			
Manufacturing	92.21	65.94	51.25
Services	88.14	62.30	55.94
Country			
Antigua and Barbuda	100.00	63.89	48.55
Argentina	98.48	76.00	49.95
Bahamas	97.28	60.00	34.27
Barbados	99.32	82.88	55.10
Belize	100.00	71.72	45.27
Bolivia	93.28	48.86	55.70
Brazil	97.87	82.89	65.54
Chile	96.22	86.60	75.42
Colombia	98.07	86.00	70.89
Costa Rica	96.16	38.28	59.23
Dominica	100.00	49.32	41.38
Dominican Republic	99.16	83.66	64.12

(continued)

Table 8.2 (continued)

	Checking/ savings account	Overdraft	Line of credit/loan
Ecuador	98.85	87.47	59.64
El Salvador	92.23	57.63	60.74
Grenada	98.68	57.53	49.66
Guatemala	70.87	52.76	46.36
Guyana	100.00	66.04	50.94
Honduras	87.63	56.34	52.19
Jamaica	99.19	69.72	29.94
Mexico	60.53	23.83	30.73
Nicaragua	79.46	33.51	43.41
Panama	86.26	58.92	41.77
Paraguay	87.78	67.78	52.18
Peru	94.26	69.92	75.83
St. Kitts & Nevis	100.00	60.54	49.66
Saint Lucia	100.00	53.42	40.00
St. Vincent & the Grenadines	98.68	60.26	58.94
Suriname	100.00	76.32	44.74
Trinidad and Tobago	99.72	78.85	61.10
Uruguay	89.47	62.62	52.66
Venezuela	97.33	38.89	30.94

Source: Authors' elaboration based on WBES data

Note: The countries in italics are part of the LAC-7

and only 30% have a line of credit or a loan. These shares are much higher in Brazil, Colombia, and Chile, while Argentinian firms are somewhat in the middle. In the Caribbean, there is almost universal access to a bank account, even if loans and overdraft facilities are far less diffused (see, for instance, Barbados and Jamaica in Table 8.2).

Financing Constraints

The surveys collect information about loan applications and their outcomes for the previous fiscal year. In contrast to most of the literature on access to finance as an obstacle to business activities (Beck et al. 2006), we exploit the richness of information about loan applications to measure demand for credit and the extent of credit availability across firms and countries (Cole and Dietrich 2014). In particular, we define the following binary indicators:

- **Loan Demand:** Dummy identifying firms that applied for a bank loan or a line of credit.
- **Loan Denial:** Dummy identifying firms that applied for a bank loan or a line of credit but whose request was denied.
- **Constrained:** Dummy identifying the borrowers whose loan applications were denied and those who decided not to apply because interest rates and collateral requirements were too high, the size of the loan and the maturity insufficient, or in general, they believed that the loan would not be approved (Hansen and Rand 2014; Presbitero et al. 2014).
- **Discouraged:** Dummy identifying the firms that did not apply for credit because the procedures were too complex, interest rates and collateral requirements were too high, the size of the loan and the maturity were insufficient, or in general, they believed that the loan would not be approved (Kon and Storey 2003).

For Latin American firms, Table 8.3 confirms the common patterns observed in the literature: demand for bank credit is more likely to come from larger, older firms that export. This pattern is reflected in a higher share of discouraged borrowers in smaller, younger, domestic companies, which are also more likely to be financially constrained.[10] By contrast, the gender of the owner and the sector are not clearly different. In particular, firms with at least one female owner are more likely to request credit and to perceive access to finance as an obstacle than other firms, but the shares of denied, discouraged, and constrained firms are not statistically different.

We also observe that labor productivity is statistically associated with better access to credit. Demand for credit is more likely to come from highly productive firms, which are also less likely to be constrained, regardless of the definition adopted (i.e. discouraged borrowers or firms with a denied loan application, see Fig. 8.1), than low-productivity firms. While we do not identify any causal impact between higher productivity and better access to finance, the finding suggests that lower productivity and financing constraints are linked, since low-productivity firms are also more likely to be financially constrained and therefore cannot invest to improve their performance. There is wide empirical evidence confirming that SMEs' lack of finance negatively affects productivity (De Mel et al. 2008; Banerjee and Duflo 2014).

Access to finance is also extremely heterogeneous across LAC countries, as shown in Fig. 8.2. A first difference is LAC-7 countries being significantly less financially constrained than the rest of the sample. Second, large differ-

Table 8.3 Financing constraints by firm characteristics and countries (%)

	Constrained	Loan demand	Discouraged	Loan denial
Whole sample	17.01	42.59	19.7	14.04
Size				
Micro	23.47	29.97	27.36	24.56
Small	18.31	41.58	20.88	15.79
Medium	11.47	50.89	13.54	8.95
Large	6.37	62.73	7.80	4.65
Productivity				
Low	20.37	37.84	23.38	17.65
High	13.18	49.72	15.3	9.78
Age				
New	20.55	35.24	23.30	23.81
Young	19.73	38.99	22.13	16.90
Mature	16.07	43.96	18.84	12.96
Ownership				
Domestic	17.47	42.76	20.36	13.93
Foreign	13.25	39.24	15.89	14.50
Gender				
No female ownership	17.05	41.62	20.07	14.23
At least one female owner	17.40	44.06	19.78	13.75
Internationalization				
Exporter	13.20	51.74	15.64	8.90
Non-exporter	17.72	40.99	20.43	15.23
Sector				
Manufacturing	17.24	43.99	19.85	13.25
Services	16.59	40.12	19.43	15.58
Country				
Antigua and Barbuda	26.85	22.15	31.54	12.90
Argentina	*25.85*	*42.00*	*29.96*	*14.53*
Bahamas	11.89	13.99	40.56	25.00
Barbados	18.06	18.06	25.00	38.46
Belize	36.91	11.41	41.61	17.65
Bolivia	17.67	41.16	23.71	13.91
Brazil	*15.36*	*53.85*	*13.25*	*11.90*
Chile	*8.16*	*59.35*	*9.84*	*7.86*
Colombia	*11.91*	*62.16*	*14.51*	*7.64*
Costa Rica	10.62	34.17	21.62	9.60
Dominica	41.33	24.00	38.00	38.89
Dominican Republic	12.85	42.18	13.13	12.00

(continued)

Table 8.3   (continued)

	Constrained	Loan demand	Discouraged	Loan denial
Ecuador	15.61	57.07	10.65	16.51
El Salvador	13.09	43.66	19.88	9.43
Grenada	15.75	30.82	21.23	26.67
Guatemala	17.37	32.73	18.71	20.88
Guyana	15.82	31.65	18.35	16.00
Honduras	18.57	42.44	21.35	16.93
Jamaica	26.93	23.84	34.98	42.67
Mexico	*19.58*	*23.13*	*22.70*	*22.59*
Nicaragua	20.15	37.24	17.73	25.43
Panama	13.63	28.79	13.30	31.03
Paraguay	17.64	45.27	18.81	15.13
Peru	*13.21*	*67.76*	*12.71*	*8.07*
St. Kitts & Nevis	21.68	33.57	25.87	29.79
Saint Lucia	39.33	24.00	31.33	52.78
St. Vincent & the Grenadines	18.79	34.23	20.13	13.73
Suriname	21.71	23.68	36.18	8.33
Trinidad and Tobago	27.48	25.78	38.81	19.78
Uruguay	16.40	35.42	24.51	11.69
Venezuela	*11.47*	*42.20*	*20.18*	*15.56*

Source: Authors' elaboration based on WBES data

Note: The countries in italics are part of the LAC-7

ences are also present within the LAC-7. In Argentina, access to finance is a relevant problem, with 25% of firms financially constrained compared to the LAC-7 average of 15%. In Mexico, the share of constrained firms is 23%, while in Chile, Colombia, and Peru, the share of firms whose loan applications were denied and the share of financially constrained firms are among the lowest in the region. Among the remaining countries, the Caribbean is, on average, the region where access to finance is a most pressing problem.

To investigate the correlation between credit market structure and firm financing constraints at the country level, we plot the country-average residuals of a simple linear regression in which the variable "constrained" is a function of a standard set of firm-specific characteristics divided by a specific measure of credit market structure (see "Credit Markets in LAC" above). By doing this, we purge all individual-specific effects that may impact access to credit (e.g. some countries may have a large share of micro-firms, resulting in an aggregate share of financially constrained firms), and we can better assess the association between credit market

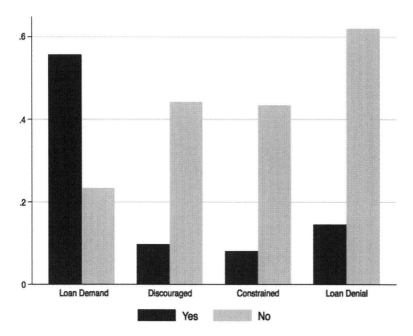

Fig. 8.1   Financing constraints and labor productivity

Source: Authors' elaboration based on WBES data

Notes: For each category of firms, we report the logarithm of labor productivity (minus 10 to improve the readability of the figure). The differences between firms with and without access to finance are statistically significant at the 95 % level of confidence. YES means that the firm requested a bank loan (loan demand) or suffers from financial constraints (discouraged, constrained, loan denial)

structure and access to finance. Figure 8.3 shows that countries with more bank branches per capita (Fig. 8.3a) and with less concentrated credit markets (Fig. 8.3b) have a smaller share of financially constrained firms. In contrast, the presence of foreign banks appears to be positively correlated with financing constraints (Fig. 8.3c). Figure 8.3d shows that financially constrained firms are not significantly correlated with the strength of the rule of law.[11]

Considering the average values of the four access-to-credit variables to the presence of a public credit registry in the country, we observe that the existence of credit registries is associated with higher demand for credit and with lower financing constraints, which is consistent with the theoretical predictions that an institutional setting that facilitates information sharing can make a difference in terms of credit access.

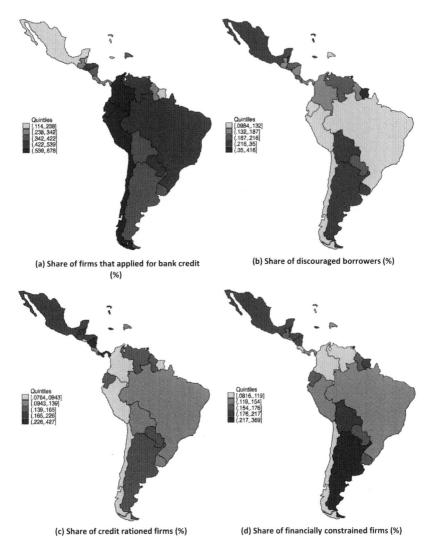

(a) Share of firms that applied for bank credit (%)

(b) Share of discouraged borrowers (%)

(c) Share of credit rationed firms (%)

(d) Share of financially constrained firms (%)

Fig. 8.2   Access to finance across the LAC region

Source: Authors' elaboration based on WBES data

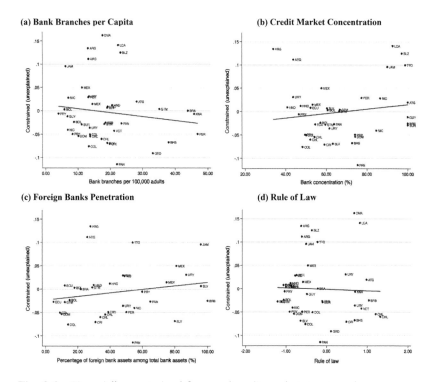

Fig. 8.3   Financially constrained firms and credit market structure, by country

Source: Authors' elaboration based on WBES data, Global Financial Development Database, and Worldwide Governance Indicators (Kaufman et al. 2010)

Notes: The vertical axis presents the OLS residuals from a firm-level regression in which the variable "constrained" is a linear function of a set of firm-level characteristics

Determinants of Firm Financing Constraints

Empirical Models

In this section, we investigate the association between firm-specific characteristics and country-specific credit market features with firm financing constraints, estimating the following model:

$$\Pr\left(OUTCOME\right)_{ijt} = \mathrm{f}\left(FIRM_{it}, COUNTRY_{jt}\right) \qquad (8.1)$$

where *outcome* is one of the two binary indicators identifying whether the *i*-th firm located in country *j* in year *t* is, alternatively, financially constrained or discouraged. *Firm* is a vector of firm-specific characteristics, including labor productivity (measured by the logarithm of labor productivity),[12] size (measured by a categorical variable based on the number of employees and by a dummy for plants belonging to a large firm), age, location, legal status, the tenure of the top manager, and a set of dummies for foreign ownership, exporting capacity (more than 10% of production), gender of the firm (at least one woman among the owners), and the possession of a quality certification. *Country* is a set of country-level (time varying) variables that measure the extent that differences in the credit market structure, legal infrastructure, and economic development affect access to credit. The focus of the analysis is on the credit market structure, which is measured by (i) the number of branches per capita (bank penetration), (ii) the share of the three largest banks' assets over total commercial bank assets (credit market concentration), and (iii) the share of foreign bank assets over total bank assets (foreign bank presence). To minimize the possibility that the credit market structure variables pick up other macroeconomic and institutional effects, we include a measure of rule of law, a dummy for the presence of a credit registry, the log of GDP per capita, the GDP growth rate, and the share of the agricultural value added in total GDP.[13] When we consider firms whose loan applications have been denied, the *outcome* variable is censored, because we only look at the bank decision to grant credit for the subsample of firms that applied for a bank loan or a line of credit. Hence, we estimate the following binary selection model as per Heckman (1979):

$$\Pr\left(LOAN\ DEMAND\right)_{ijt} = f\left(FIRM_{it}, SALES\ GROWTH_{it}, COUNTRY_{jt}\right)$$

$$\Pr\left(LOAN\ DENIAL\right)_{ijt} = f\left(FIRM_{it}, COUNTRY_{jt}\right) \tag{8.2}$$

where *loan demand* is the dummy variable identifying the i-th firm in country j that has applied for bank credit in year t, and *loan denial* is the binary indicator for the same firm, whose application has been denied by the bank. The set of explanatory variables used in the two-equation model is the same as the one discussed for equation 8.1. The sole exception is the variable *sales growth*, which measures the annual change in sales; we include it as an excluding restriction because it is expected to influence demand for credit, being a proxy for the firm's level of economic activity.

We estimate equations 8.1 and 8.2 using a sample of data collected between 2006 and 2010 in 30 LAC countries (see Table 8.9 in the Appendix). We include a large set of dummies to control as much as possible for the unobserved firm-level heterogeneity that may affect credit market outcomes. In particular, we include dummies to control for the possibility of year- and industry-specific shocks. Given that, in the first set of regressions, we do not include any country-specific variables, we add country fixed effects and interact them by year and by a dummy for sector (manufacturing or services) to allow for sector-specific fixed effects varying by country and over time.[14] Finally, to deal with possible serial correlation across firms interviewed in each survey, we cluster the standard errors at the country-year level.

THE RELATIVE ROLE OF FIRM-LEVEL AND COUNTRY-LEVEL CHARACTERISTICS

Tables 8.4 and 8.5 present the estimates for equations 8.1 and 8.2, including firm-specific control variables and checking for unobserved heterogeneity with country, year, and industry dummies. To check whether significant differences emerge, for each model we present the results for the whole sample, for the LAC-7, and for the remaining countries.

Considering firm-level characteristics, our results confirm the existing evidence (Brown et al. 2011; Cole and Dietrich 2014) that shows smaller and less productive firms are less likely to apply for credit and more likely to be financially constrained. Foreign-owned firms and exporters are also less likely to apply for bank credit than domestically oriented ones, while there is no robust evidence that they are more likely to be financially constrained.[15] Firms with a quality certification are less likely to be discouraged from applying for a bank loan.

Moreover, we assess the relative importance of firm- and country-specific factors in explaining the variability of firm financing constraints, estimating a linear probability model and comparing the R-squared when (i) using only firm-specific factors (used in the regressions reported in Tables 8.4 and 8.5), and (ii) including country fixed effects. In line with the previous evidence using the WBES (Beck et al. 2004, 2006), our results (Table 8.6) show that the firm-level variables explain only a small fraction of the variance of the dependent variables, irrespective of the measure of financing constraints adopted. The inclusion of country fixed effects does not dramatically improve the fit of the model in absolute terms. However, the increase in the explanatory power of the model is quite relevant in relative terms, as the R squared increases by 55 to 80%, depending on the measure of financing constraints.

Table 8.4 Constrained and discouraged borrowers

Dependent variable	Constrained			Discouraged		
Sample	All	LAC-7	Others	All	LAC-7	Others
	(1)	(2)	(3)	(4)	(5)	(6)
Labor productivity	-0.107***	-0.096***	-0.123***	-0.115***	-0.134***	-0.094***
	(0.021)	(0.029)	(0.024)	(0.013)	(0.025)	(0.014)
Firm size (Reference: *Micro*)						
Small	-0.131***	-0.149**	-0.116***	-0.144***	-0.140*	-0.149***
	(0.038)	(0.074)	(0.038)	(0.037)	(0.072)	(0.035)
Medium	-0.387***	-0.434***	-0.339***	-0.373***	-0.391***	-0.352***
	(0.055)	(0.091)	(0.069)	(0.048)	(0.086)	(0.059)
Large	-0.689***	-0.681***	-0.765***	-0.763***	-0.731***	-0.802***
	(0.071)	(0.101)	(0.117)	(0.085)	(0.122)	(0.109)
Large establishment	-0.157***	-0.144**	-0.181***	-0.069	-0.094	-0.041
	(0.036)	(0.056)	(0.050)	(0.044)	(0.066)	(0.054)
Exporter	0.060	0.079	0.049	0.076**	0.101	0.054
	(0.037)	(0.053)	(0.053)	(0.037)	(0.069)	(0.037)
Firm age (Reference: *New*)						
Young	0.028	-0.019	0.076	0.030	-0.041	0.096
	(0.070)	(0.111)	(0.087)	(0.069)	(0.078)	(0.110)
Mature	-0.078	-0.124	-0.026	-0.057	-0.147	0.030
	(0.071)	(0.106)	(0.093)	(0.078)	(0.091)	(0.120)
Foreign ownership	0.071	0.172*	0.013	0.081**	0.112	0.064*
	(0.056)	(0.092)	(0.067)	(0.033)	(0.072)	(0.038)
Female ownership	-0.005	0.004	-0.014	-0.043*	0.003	-0.088**
	(0.029)	(0.027)	(0.050)	(0.024)	(0.023)	(0.037)
Top manager tenure	0.016	0.091**	-0.051	-0.001	0.043	-0.042
	(0.031)	(0.043)	(0.038)	(0.030)	(0.046)	(0.035)

(continued)

Table 8.4 (continued)

Dependent variable	Constrained			Discouraged		
Sample	All	LAC-7	Others	All	LAC-7	Others
	(1)	(2)	(3)	(4)	(5)	(6)
Quality certification	-0.057	-0.072	-0.043	-0.117***	-0.131***	-0.097
	(0.044)	(0.052)	(0.063)	(0.040)	(0.046)	(0.062)
Location size (Reference: Capital)						
Over 1 million	-0.027	-0.046	0.039	0.025	0.027	0.022
	(0.060)	(0.078)	(0.093)	(0.058)	(0.074)	(0.098)
Between 250,000 and 1 million	-0.018	-0.003	-0.033	0.076*	0.115**	0.035
	(0.055)	(0.067)	(0.096)	(0.043)	(0.050)	(0.066)
Between 50,000 and 250,000	-0.012	0.053	-0.046	-0.011	0.085**	-0.056
	(0.053)	(0.060)	(0.066)	(0.059)	(0.042)	(0.075)
Less than 50,000	-0.118**	-0.290***	-0.075	0.008	-0.114**	0.035
	(0.054)	(0.058)	(0.062)	(0.069)	(0.051)	(0.081)
Observations	16,200	8243	7957	16,200	8243	7957

Source: Authors' elaboration based on WBES data

Notes: Each regression includes country * year * manufacturing sector dummies, sector and legal status dummies, and a constant. Standard errors (in parentheses) are clustered at the country-year level. * Coefficient is statistically significant at the 10% level; ** at the 5% level; *** at the 1% level; no asterisk means the coefficient is not different from zero with statistical significance

Table 8.5 Credit rationed borrowers

Sample	All		LAC-7		Others	
Dependent variable	Constrained	Demand	Constrained	Demand	Constrained	Demand
	(1)	(2)	(3)	(4)	(5)	(6)
Sales growth	n.a.	-0.039	n.a.	-0.057	n.a.	0.001
		(0.053)		(0.085)		(0.057)
Labor productivity	-0.117***	0.086***	-0.074**	0.084***	-0.169**	0.082***
	(0.039)	(0.015)	(0.030)	(0.022)	(0.074)	(0.021)
Firm size (Reference: _Micro_)						
Small	-0.230**	0.255***	-0.187*	0.249***	-0.261	0.260***
	(0.111)	(0.036)	(0.097)	(0.053)	(0.266)	(0.051)
Medium	-0.583***	0.511***	-0.466**	0.551***	-0.688*	0.472***
	(0.188)	(0.046)	(0.183)	(0.051)	(0.418)	(0.081)
Large	-0.780***	0.855***	-0.492***	0.899***	-1.266**	0.779***
	(0.241)	(0.059)	(0.162)	(0.083)	(0.639)	(0.079)
Large establishment	-0.110**	-0.018	-0.088	0.003	-0.142	-0.056
	(0.054)	(0.041)	(0.064)	(0.061)	(0.103)	(0.051)
Exporter	0.003	-0.144***	0.009	-0.172***	-0.001	-0.116**
	(0.069)	(0.034)	(0.064)	(0.045)	(0.146)	(0.055)
Firm age (Reference: _New_)						
Young	0.035	-0.015	-0.190	0.066	0.259	-0.079
	(0.245)	(0.105)	(0.311)	(0.160)	(0.316)	(0.137)
Mature	-0.038	-0.034	-0.216	0.068	0.148	-0.119
	(0.232)	(0.109)	(0.297)	(0.165)	(0.316)	(0.139)
Foreign ownership	0.210	-0.277***	0.249	-0.333***	0.179	-0.238***
	(0.135)	(0.051)	(0.189)	(0.070)	(0.267)	(0.073)
Female ownership	-0.054	0.052*	-0.077	0.008	-0.047	0.099***
	(0.063)	(0.028)	(0.076)	(0.043)	(0.131)	(0.033)

(continued)

Table 8.5 (continued)

Sample	All		LAC-7		Others	
Dependent variable	Constrained	Demand	Constrained	Demand	Constrained	Demand
	(1)	(2)	(3)	(4)	(5)	(6)
Top manager tenure	-0.017	0.015	0.024	0.010	-0.067	0.021
	(0.046)	(0.025)	(0.072)	(0.037)	(0.060)	(0.035)
Quality certification	0.018	0.058	-0.019	0.048	0.070	0.055
	(0.065)	(0.044)	(0.060)	(0.068)	(0.133)	(0.050)
Location size (Reference: *Capital*)						
Over 1 million	-0.154***	-0.072**	-0.132***	-0.049	-0.219	-0.107
	(0.050)	(0.033)	(0.043)	(0.032)	(0.142)	(0.079)
Between 250,000 and 1 million	-0.125	-0.077	-0.099	-0.100	-0.212	-0.026
	(0.080)	(0.067)	(0.072)	(0.093)	(0.169)	(0.094)
Between 50,000 and 250,000	-0.023	-0.018	0.075	0.010	-0.038	-0.044
	(0.077)	(0.051)	(0.089)	(0.070)	(0.141)	(0.077)
Less than 50,000	-0.059	-0.111	-0.248***	-0.156	0.043	-0.115
	(0.127)	(0.070)	(0.082)	(0.097)	(0.164)	(0.092)
Observations	13,835	n.a.	7195	n.a.	6640	n.a.
Censored	7814	n.a.	3613	n.a.	4201	n.a.

Source: Authors' elaboration based on WBES data

Notes: Each regression includes country * manufacturing sector dummies, year, industry, and legal status dummies, and a constant. Standard errors (in parentheses) are clustered at the country-year level. * Coefficient is statistically significant at the 10% level; ** at the 5% level; *** at the 1% level; no asterisk means the coefficient is not different from zero with statistical significance. n.a. = not applicable

Table 8.6 The relative importance of firm and country-specific effects

Dependent variable	Constrained		Discouraged		Loan denial	
	(1)	(2)	(3)	(4)	(5)	(6)
Observations	16,200	16,200	16,200	16,200	6958	6958
R-squared	0.034	0.061	0.041	0.069	0.064	0.099
Industry × year FE	Yes	Yes	Yes	Yes	Yes	Yes
Country FE	No	Yes	No	Yes	No	Yes
F-test (p-value)	n.a.	0.000		0.000		0.000

Source: Authors' elaboration based on WBES data

Notes: For each dependent variable, we estimate two linear probability models, including the standard set of firm-level control variables (see Table 8.4, in addition there are industry * year dummies), with and without the country fixed effects. The bottom row reports the p-value of an F-test for the joint significance of the country dummies. n.a. = not applicable

This exercise points to two important considerations for interpreting our findings. First, a lot of the variability in financing constraints is due to unobservable heterogeneity at the firm level. Second, country-specific factors can potentially explain about 40% of the "explained part" of the variability in financing constraints. Even if the role of unknown and unmeasured firm-specific factors is dominant, there is still a significant wrole for policy at the country level to ease financing constraints on firms. Therefore, in what follows, we try to assess whether some specific structural characteristics of the credit markets are more likely to be associated with better access to bank credit.

ROLE OF CREDIT MARKET STRUCTURE

Adding country-specific controls to our estimations of equations 8.1 and 8.2 indicates that the macroeconomic and institutional settings are significant predictors of access to credit. Financing constraints seem to be worse in richer countries but less prohibitive in countries experiencing faster GDP growth. Moreover, contract enforcements, property rights, and the quality of the legal system, as measured by the rule of law indicator, are associated with stronger demand for bank credit and a lower share of financially constrained and discouraged borrowers (Beck et al. 2006). The presence of credit registries is associated with less access to bank credit, which is apparently counter-intuitive with the descriptive evidence. Of note, the positive association between credit registries and better access to finance becomes negative once firm characteristics are taken

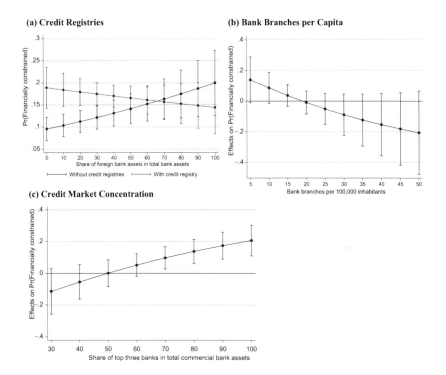

Fig. 8.4   The heterogeneous effect of foreign banks on financing constraints

Source: Authors' elaboration based on WBES data, Global Financial Development Database and Credit Reporting Database (Bruhn et al. 2013)

Notes: Panel (a) plots the estimated probability that a firm is financially constrained for different shares of foreign bank assets in total bank assets, disaggregating between countries with and without a credit registry. Panels (b) and (c) plot the effects of the share of foreign bank assets in total bank assets on the probability that a firm is financially constrained, for different values of the number of bank branches per 100,000 adults (panel b), and the share of top three banks in total commercial bank assets (panel c). The vertical lines represent the 95% confidence intervals. The diagrams are based on the estimates reported in Table 8.8, respectively columns 1, 2, and 3

into account, confirming the relevance of the heterogeneity of firms in different countries

The results for the credit variables lend support to the descriptive evidence (see Figs. 8.4) and to the hypothesis that the credit market structure is not neutral with respect to financing constraints on firms (Table 8.7).

Bank penetration, measured by the number of branches per capita, is significantly correlated with a lower probability that borrowers are

Table 8.7   The role of credit market structure

Dependent variable	Constrained	Discouraged	Loan denial	Loan demand
	(1)	(2)	(3)	(4)
Agriculture (% GDP)	0.663	1.380	−0.468	−3.859
	(1.931)	(2.059)	(2.269)	(2.919)
GDP	0.328***	0.341**	0.116	−0.597***
	(0.115)	(0.147)	(0.215)	(0.208)
GDP growth	−0.016	−0.038***	−0.009	0.052**
	(0.016)	(0.012)	(0.027)	(0.026)
Rule of law	−0.327***	−0.275***	−0.136	0.285***
	(0.069)	(0.079)	(0.095)	(0.087)
Credit register	0.188*	0.196**	0.028	−0.062
	(0.114)	(0.097)	(0.079)	(0.145)
Bank branches	−0.991***	−0.690*	−0.654	0.848
	(0.383)	(0.393)	(0.505)	(0.656)
Bank concentration	−0.377	−0.534*	−0.059	−0.291
	(0.316)	(0.291)	(0.300)	(0.354)
Foreign banks	0.133	0.136	0.130	−0.372
	(0.160)	(0.157)	(0.257)	(0.263)
Observations	11,909	11,909	11,899	11,899

Source: Authors' elaboration based on WBES data, Global Financial Development Database, Worldwide Governance Indicators (Kaufman et al. 2010), and Credit Reporting Database (Bruhn et al. 2013)

Notes: Each regression includes all firm-level characteristics as in the baseline (Table 8.4), year, sector and legal status dummies and a constant. Standard errors (in parentheses) are clustered at the country-year level. * Coefficient is statistically significant at the 10% level; ** at the 5% level; *** at the 1% level; no asterisk means the coefficient is not different from zero with statistical significance

financially constrained (Column 1) and discouraged (Column 2). This finding is consistent with the hypothesis that physical proximity in credit markets helps mitigate informational asymmetries between lenders and borrowers. Controlling for the degree of competition, a larger number of branches per capita reduces the average distance between firms and banks and a smaller distance reduces informational asymmetries and facilitates the screening and monitoring activities of banks.

Market concentration shows a negative correlation with the measures of financing constraints, even if the coefficient is significant only when explaining the probability that a firm is discouraged from demanding credit. In other words, more concentrated markets seem to favor access to finance, in line with the hypothesis that a certain degree of market power is necessary for banks to invest in a lending relationship, especially with informational opaque firms (Petersen and Rajan 1995). Finally, the positive coefficients for foreign banks suggest that their larger presence is associated with a higher probability that domestic borrowers are financially constrained (Gormley 2010), but it is not statistically significant. Given the relevance of foreign banks in a number of countries in Latin America and the Caribbean, the next section focuses on their role in assessing whether the non-significant average effect could mask a non-linearity.

ROLE OF FOREIGN BANKS

To shed light on how the presence of foreign banks affects access to credit, we inspect the possibility that their effect could differ across markets depending on the degree of domestic competition and on some institutional features. Thus, we interact the share of foreign banks with (i) a dummy that signals the existence of a public credit registry, (ii) the number of bank branches per capita, and (iii) a measure of market concentration.

The results reported in Table 8.8 show that the correlation between foreign banks and financing constraints depends on the development and institutional setting of national credit markets. The association between foreign banks and the share of financially constrained and denied borrowers turns from positive to negative moving from countries without a public credit registry to those with one (columns 1 and 4). Moreover, in countries where there are public credit registries, a larger share of foreign banks is associated with a higher likelihood that firms demand bank credit and a lower probability that their loan applications are denied (columns 7 and 8).

We also find that the correlation between foreign bank presence and financing constraints turns from positive to negative as the number of branches per capita in the country increases and the degree of market concentration decreases. While Brown et al. (2011) found that foreign banks were associated with a larger share of discouraged borrowers, we find that this correlation holds exclusively in countries lacking credit registries and in concentrated credit markets. Hence, foreign banks seem to have a detrimental effect on access to credit in less developed and more concentrated markets, but they are indeed beneficial in more competitive and financially developed ones.

To assess the economic relevance of these effects, Fig. 8.4 plots the results of columns 1 through 3 of Table 8.8, considering the differentiated effects of foreign bank penetration on the probability that the average firm is financially constrained. Figure 8.4a shows that foreign banks are associated with more binding financing constraints only in countries that do not have a credit registry. In the other countries, there is no evidence that a larger presence of foreign banks penalizes local firms, consistent with what was recently shown by Claessens and Van Horen (2014). Figures 8.4b and 8.4c

Table 8.8 The differentiated effect of foreign banks on financing constraints

Dependent variable	Constrained		Discouraged			
	(1)	(2)	(3)	(4)	(5)	(6)
Agriculture (% GDP)	1.692	-0.043	0.343	2.104	1.095	1.074
	(2.274)	(2.231)	(2.109)	(2.168)	(2.239)	(2.162)
GDP	0.286**	0.270*	0.287***	0.314**	0.317*	0.302**
	(0.114)	(0.144)	(0.093)	(0.154)	(0.172)	(0.136)
GDP growth	-0.021	-0.006	-0.008	-0.042***	-0.034***	-0.031***
	(0.013)	(0.012)	(0.013)	(0.010)	(0.010)	(0.009)
Rule of law	-0.266***	-0.313***	-0.322***	-0.235**	-0.270***	-0.270***
	(0.080)	(0.076)	(0.060)	(0.104)	(0.099)	(0.088)
Credit register	0.451***	0.197	0.218	0.363***	0.199*	0.223*
	(0.106)	(0.128)	(0.138)	(0.120)	(0.109)	(0.114)
Bank branches	-0.652**	0.776	-0.950***	-0.459	0.014	-0.652*
	(0.287)	(1.109)	(0.338)	(0.340)	(1.232)	(0.371)
Bank concentration	-0.579**	-0.391	-1.499***	-0.677**	-0.539*	-1.540***
	(0.295)	(0.291)	(0.532)	(0.274)	(0.278)	(0.456)
Foreign banks	0.493***	0.748*	-1.116**	0.370**	0.382	-0.956*
	(0.169)	(0.420)	(0.473)	(0.172)	(0.424)	(0.519)
Foreign banks × Credit register	-0.683***			-0.443*		
	(0.238)			(0.230)		
Foreign banks × Bank branches		-3.942*			-1.572	
		(2.346)			(2.424)	
Foreign banks × Bank concentration			2.239***			1.968**
			(0.724)			(0.781)
Observations	11,909	11,909	11,909	11,909	11,909	11,909

(continued)

Table 8.8 (continued)

Dependent variable: Prob(LOAN:)	Denial	Demand	Denial	Demand	Denial	Demand
	(7)	(8)	(9)	(10)	(11)	(12)
Agriculture (% GDP)	1.280	-6.909***	-1.186	-2.102	-0.473	-4.047
	(2.773)	(2.145)	(1.816)	(3.680)	(2.479)	(3.381)
GDP	0.136	-0.493***	0.116	-0.460*	0.127	-0.616**
	(0.172)	(0.132)	(0.160)	(0.244)	(0.239)	(0.264)
GDP growth	-0.024	0.066***	0.002	0.029	-0.008	0.056*
	(0.025)	(0.017)	(0.016)	(0.027)	(0.032)	(0.031)
Rule of law	-0.103*	0.122*	-0.167*	0.260***	-0.149	0.286***
	(0.063)	(0.068)	(0.085)	(0.073)	(0.109)	(0.089)
Credit register	0.470**	-0.788***	0.047	-0.077	0.062	-0.042
	(0.210)	(0.115)	(0.081)	(0.166)	(0.089)	(0.171)
Bank branches	-0.222	-0.158	3.378	-3.266	-0.701	0.854
	(0.614)	(0.369)	(2.753)	(2.252)	(0.568)	(0.571)
Bank concentration	-0.272	0.270	-0.093	-0.264	-0.873	-0.935
	(0.243)	(0.207)	(0.261)	(0.385)	(0.551)	(0.711)
Foreign banks	0.756*	-1.380***	1.614	-1.818**	-0.836**	-1.113**
	(0.405)	(0.140)	(1.080)	(0.763)	(0.421)	(0.541)
Foreign banks × Credit register	-1.123*	1.959***				
	(0.584)	(0.242)				
Foreign banks × Bank branches			-8.993	9.199**		
			(6.117)	(4.681)		

(continued)

Table 8.8 (continued)

Dependent variable	Constrained		Discouraged			
	(1)	(2)	(3)	(4)	(5)	(6)
Foreign banks × Bank concentration					1.747**	1.319
					(0.753)	(0.915)
Observations	11,899		11,899		11,899	

Source: Authors' elaboration based on WBES data, Global Financial Development Database, Worldwide Governance Indicators (Kaufman et al. 2010), and Credit Reporting Database (Bruhn et al. 2013)

Notes: Each regression includes all firm-level characteristics as in the baseline (Table 8.4), year, sector, and legal status dummies, and a constant. Standard errors (in parentheses) are clustered at the country-year level. * Coefficient is statistically significant at the 10 % level; ** at the 5 % level; *** at the 1 % level; no asterisk means the coefficient is not different from zero with statistical significance. n.a. = not applicable

show that the average partial effect of foreign banks on the probability of being credit constrained decreases from positive (and statistically significant) to negative as the number of per capita branches increases. By contrast, the same average partial effect increases with the share of bank assets held by the three largest banks and moves from negative to positive (with statistically significant values) when the asset share of the top three banks is above 60%.

CONCLUSIONS

In this chapter, we provided a thorough analysis of firm credit access in LAC countries based on the data available in the WBES. We also aimed to explore the role played by heterogeneity in micro-firm characteristics and in macro-institutional credit market structures. Three main sets of issues were addressed: (i) financing constraints on firms and the types of credit accessed; (ii) the characteristics of the financially constrained firms; and (iii) the role of the differences across countries in terms of their financial development and credit market structure. We found access to bank credit among LAC firms to be very heterogeneous with a lot of variety according to firm characteristics such as size, productivity, and informational transparency. Demand for bank credit was more likely to come from larger, older, and less export-oriented firms, and consequently these firms were less likely to be discouraged or constrained. Labor productivity was also positively associated with higher demand for credit and better access to finance. Even if we were unable to identify the causality of the relationship, this was an important result, signaling the existence of a trap between low productivity and financing constraint that needs to be addressed using policies designed to strengthen economic growth in the region.

In addition to individual firms' characteristics, we also found the structure of the credit market to be important for explaining the heterogeneity in credit access. In particular, we found that a high degree of bank penetration and competition were significantly correlated with a lower probability of borrowers being financially constrained. Interestingly, we found that the presence of foreign banks had a differentiated effect on financing constraints: foreign bank penetration had a negative effect on access to credit in less developed and more concentrated markets, while it had a positive influence in more competitive and financially developed markets.

Some interesting policy implications can be drawn from our findings. In LAC there is a widely acknowledged low productivity trap, which slows economic growth (IDB 2010). Improving access to credit should help escape this trap. Our empirical results underline the importance of improving the functioning of the domestic market structures. Interventions aimed at increasing the degree of bank penetration and the competition in financial markets should positively impact firms' access to credit and their productivity. From this point of view, the large heterogeneity in LAC financial markets opens up a crucial space for intervention aimed at increasing productivity in many countries in the region.

APPENDIX

Table 8.9   Number of observations, 2006 and 2010

Country	Year	Number of observations	Country	Year	Number of observations
Antigua and Barbuda	2010	128	Guyana	2010	127
Argentina		*1417*	Honduras		*533*
	2006	553		2006	308
	2010	864		2010	225
Bahamas	2010	102	Jamaica	2010	235
Barbados	2010	121	Mexico		*2135*
Belize	2010	144		2006	885
Bolivia		*474*		2010	1250
	2006	292	Nicaragua		*641*
	2010	182		2006	378
Brazil	2009	1043		2010	263
Chile		*1274*	Panama		*340*
	2006	519		2006	171
	2010	755		2010	169
Colombia		*1309*	Paraguay		*564*
	2006	572		2006	283
	2010	737		2010	281
Costa Rica	2010	384	Peru		*1065*
Dominica	2010	140		2006	314
Dominican Republic	2010	304		2010	751
Ecuador		*605*	St. Kitts and Nevis	2010	111
	2006	289	St. Lucia	2010	139
	2010	316	St. Vincent and the Grenadines	2010	116
El Salvador		*760*	Suriname	2010	148
	2006	514	Trinidad and Tobago	2010	280
	2010	246	Uruguay		*689*
Grenada	2010	113		2006	263
Guatemala		*759*		2010	426
	2006	385			
	2010	374			

Source: Authors' elaboration based on WBES data

Notes

1. The exclusion of micro-enterprises and of the informal sector could represent a relevant issue in some countries, especially given that micro and informal firms are more likely to be financially constrained and to be less productive. Bruhn and McKenzie (2014) provided a broad and accessible discussion on some important issues about informal firms in developing countries, including access to finance.

2. Similar considerations hold when discussing the entry of large banks and the competitive pressure on small banks to orient their lending activity toward SMEs. Moreover, the literature has also stressed the importance of state-owned banks, but this is beyond the scope of this chapter. A detailed discussion about the role of state-owned banks in developing countries is presented in Micco et al. (2007). Some recent works suggest that state-owned banks could have played a pivotal counter-cyclical role in Latin America during the recent global crisis (Cull and Martínez Pería 2013).

3. These studies are collected in a volume edited by Pagano (2001).

4. The LAC-7 countries are Argentina, Brazil, Chile, Colombia, Mexico, Peru, and Venezuela. Combined, they account for 90% of Latin America's GDP.

5. For a recent analysis of the development of the financial systems around the world, see World Bank (2013).

6. A credit registry is defined as an entity managed by the public sector (central bank or superintendent of banks) that collects information on the creditworthiness of borrowers and shares this information with banks and other regulated financial institutions (Bruhn et al. 2013).

7. The WBES provides a more detailed two-digit disaggregation. For the purpose of this descriptive analysis, we limit the disaggregation to services and manufacturing.

8. Tables 8.1, 8.2, and 8.3 do not report the t-test statistics for the differences in the values across firm characteristics. However, the statistical significance of the main results (at the usual 90% level of confidence) is always indicated in the text.

9. In developing countries, micro-firms typically address their requests for credit to micro-finance institutions (Hulme and Arun 2009).

10. This pattern is confirmed—to a similar extent—considering the subjective indicator of access to finance as an obstacle to business activity, which is not reported here.

11. We measure the rule of law using one of the Worldwide Governance Indicators published by the World Bank (Kaufman et al. 2010). Specifically, the rule of law captures perceptions of the extent to which agents have confidence in and abide by the rules of society, and in particular the quality

of contract enforcement, property rights, the police, and the courts, as well as the likelihood of crime and violence.

12. Given that the measure of labor productivity is not available for quite a substantial number of firms, to check the robustness of our findings, we also estimate equation 8.1 on a larger sample of firms, excluding labor productivity. The results are broadly unchanged.

13. When we control for these variables, we cannot add country-fixed effects to equation 8.1 because we only have a survey repeated over time for a few countries.

14. We are not able to go beyond this degree of granularity in modeling the unobserved heterogeneity because using country * year * industry dummies would make a number of cells without variation in the dependent variable. For the same reasons, when estimating equation 8.2, we only have country * manufacturing dummies and, separately, year dummies. See the notes in the tables presenting the results of the regression tests for details.

15. We also control for innovation at the firm level and find no significant correlation between different measures of innovation (R&D spending, or the introduction of process or product innovations) and firm financing constraints. This regression is not included because data availability significantly reduces the sample size. In addition, there are no significant differences in terms of access to credit across sectors, especially separating manufacturing from market and non-market services.

References

Ayyagari, M., A. Demirgüç-Kunt, and V. Maksimovic. 2012. Financing of Firms in Developing Countries. Policy Research Working Paper, No. 6036. Washington, DC: The World Bank.

Banerjee, A., and E. Duflo. 2014. Do Firms Want to Borrow More? Testing Credit Constraints Using a Direct Lending Program. *The Review of Economic Studies* 81: 572–607.

Beck, T., and A. Demirgüç-Kunt. 2006. Small and Medium-Size Enterprises: Access to Finance as a Growth Constraint. *Journal of Banking & Finance* 30(11): 2931–2943.

Beck, T., A. Demirgüç-Kunt, L. Laeven, and V. Maksimovic. 2006. The Determinants of Financing Obstacles. *Journal of International Money and Finance* 25(6): 932–952.

Beck, T., A. Demirgüç-Kunt, and V. Maksimovic. 2004. Bank Competition and Access to Finance: International Evidence. *Journal of Money, Credit, and Banking* 36(3): 627–648.

Beck, T., A. Demirgüç-Kunt, and M.S. Martínez Pería. 2011. Bank Financing for SMEs: Evidence Across Countries and Bank Ownership Types. *Journal of Financial Services Research* 39(1–2): 35–54.

Berger, A.N., N.H. Miller, M.A. Petersen, R.G. Rajan, and J.C. Stein. 2005. Does Function Follow Organizational Form? Evidence from the Lending Practices of Large and Small Banks. *Journal of Financial Economics* 76: 237–269.

Berger, A.N., and G.F. Udell. 2002. Small Business Credit Availability and Relationship Lending: The Importance of Bank Organisational Structure. *Economic Journal* 112: F32–F53.

Brown, M., S. Ongena, A. Popov, and P. Yesin. 2011. Who Needs Credit and Who Gets Credit in Eastern Europe? *Economic Policy* 26: 93–130.

Bruhn, M., S. Farazi, and M. Kanz. 2013. Bank Competition, Concentration, and Credit Reporting. Policy Research Working Paper, No. 6442. Washington, DC: The World Bank.

Bruhn, M., and D. McKenzie. 2014. Entry Regulation and the Formalization of Microenterprises in Developing Countries. *The World Bank Research Observer* 29(2): 186–201.

Cardim De Carvalho, F.J., L.F. De Paula, and J. Williams. 2012. Banking in Latin America. In *The Oxford Handbook of Banking*, ed. A.N. Berger, P. Molyneux, and J.O.S. Wilson. Oxford: Oxford University Press.

Cetorelli, N., and P.E. Strahan. 2006. Finance as a Barrier to Entry: Bank Competition and Industry Structure in Local U.S. Markets. *Journal of Finance* 61(1): 437–461.

Čihák, M., A. Demirgüç-Kunt, E. Feyen, and R. Levine. 2012. Benchmarking Financial Systems Around the World. Policy Research Working Paper, No. 6175. Washington, DC: The World Bank.

Claessens, S., and N. Van Horen. 2014. Foreign Banks: Trends and Impact. *Journal of Money, Credit, and Banking* 46(s1): 295–326.

Clarke, G., R.J. Cull, and M.S. Martínez Pería. 2006. Foreign Bank Participation and Access to Credit Across Firms in Developing Countries. *Journal of Comparative Economics* 34(4): 774–795.

Clarke, G., R.J. Cull, M.S. Martínez Pería, and S.M. Sanchez. 2005. Bank Lending to Small Businesses in Latin America: Does Bank Origin Matter? *Journal of Money, Credit, and Banking* 37(1): 83–118.

Cole, R.A., and A. Dietrich. 2014 (unpublished). SME Credit Availability around the World: Evidence from the World Bank's Enterprise Survey. Chicago, IL: DePaul University.

Cull, R., and M.S. Martínez Pería. 2013. Bank Ownership and Lending Patterns During the 2008–2009 Financial Crisis: Evidence from Latin America and Eastern Europe. *Journal of Banking & Finance* 37(12): 4861–4878.

De la Torre, A., M.S. Martínez Pería, and S.L. Schmukler. 2010. Bank Involvement With SMEs: Beyond Relationship Lending. *Journal of Banking & Finance* 34(9): 2280–2293.

De Mel, S., D. McKenzie, and C. Woodruff. 2008. Returns to Capital in Microenterprises: Evidence from a Field Experiment. *The Quarterly Journal of Economics* 124(4): 1329–1372.

Degryse, H., and S. Ongena. 2005. Distance, Lending Relationships, and Competition. *Journal of Finance* 60(1): 231–266.

Dell'Ariccia, G., and R. Marquez. 2004. Information and Bank Credit Allocation. *Journal of Financial Economics* 72(1): 185–214.

Detragiache, E., T. Tressel, and P. Gupta. 2008. Foreign Banks in Poor Countries: Theory and Evidence. *Journal of Finance* 63(5): 2123–2160.

Didier, T., and S.L. Schmukler. 2014. *Emerging Issues in Financial Development: Lessons from Latin America*. Washington, DC: The World Bank.

Djankov, S., C. McLiesh, and A. Shleifer. 2007. Private Credit in 129 Countries. *Journal of Financial Economics* 84(2): 299–329.

Galindo, A.J., and F. Schiantarelli, eds. 2003. *Credit Constraints and Investment in Latin America*. Washington, DC: Inter-American Development Bank (IDB).

Gormley, T.A. 2010. The Impact of Foreign Bank Entry in Emerging Markets: Evidence from India. *Journal of Financial Intermediation* 19(1): 26–51.

Hansen, H., and J. Rand. 2014. The Myth of Female Credit Discrimination in African Manufacturing. *Journal of Development Studies* 50(1): 81–96.

Heckman, J.J. 1979. Sample Selection Bias as a Specification Error. *Econometrica* 47(1): 153–161.

Hulme, D., and T. Arun. 2009. *Microfinance—A Reader*. Routledge Studies in Development Economics. London: Routledge.

IDB. 2010. *The Age of Productivity: Transforming Economies from the Bottom-Up*. Washington, DC: IDB.

Jaffee, D.M., and T. Russell. 1976. Imperfect Information, Uncertainty, and Credit Rationing. *The Quarterly Journal of Economics* 90(4): 651–666.

Jappelli, T., and M. Pagano. 2002. Information Sharing, Lending and Defaults: Cross-Country Evidence. *Journal of Banking & Finance* 26(10): 2017–2045.

Kaufman, D., A. Kraay, and M. Mastruzzi. 2010. The Worldwide Governance Indicators: Methodology and Analytical Issues. Policy Research Working Paper, No. 5430. Washington, DC: The World Bank.

Kon, Y., and D.J. Storey. 2003. A Theory of Discouraged Borrowers. *Small Business Economics* 21: 37–49.

Kuntchev, V., R. Ramalho, J. Rodriguez-Meza, and J.S. Yang. 2013. What Have We Learned from the Enterprise Survey Regarding Access to Finance by SMEs? Policy Research Working Paper, No. 6670. Washington, DC: The World Bank.

Makler, H., W.L. Ness, and A.E. Tschoegl. 2013. Inequalities in Firms' Access to Credit in Latin America. *Global Economic Journal* 13(3–4): 283–318.

Mian, A. 2006. Distance Constraints: The Limits of Foreign Lending in Poor Economies. *Journal of Finance* 61(3): 1465–1505.

Micco, A., U. Panizza, and M. Yanez. 2007. Bank Ownership and Performance. Does Politics Matter? *Journal of Banking & Finance* 31(1): 219–241.

OECD. 2013. *Latin American Economic Outlook 2013—SME Policies for Structural Change*. Paris: OECD–ECLAC.

Padilla, A.J., and M. Pagano. 1997. Endogenous Communication Among Lenders and Entrepreneurial Incentives. *Review of Financial Studies* 10(1): 205–236.

Pagano, M. 2001. *Defusing Default: Incentives and Institutions*. Washington, DC: Development Centre of the OECD and IDB.

Pagano, M., and T. Jappelli. 1993. Information Sharing in Credit Markets. *Journal of Finance* 48(5): 1693–1718.

Petersen, M.A., and R.G. Rajan. 1995. The Effect of Credit Market Competition on Lending Relationships. *The Quarterly Journal of Economics* 110(2): 407–443.

Presbitero, A.F., R. Rabellotti, and C. Piras. 2014. Barking Up the Wrong Tree? Measuring Gender Gaps in Firm Access to Finance. *Journal of Development Studies* 50(10): 1430–1444.

Stallings, B. 2006. *Finance for Development—Latin America in Comparative Perspective*. Washington, DC: Brookings Institution Press.

Stiglitz, J.E., and A. Weiss. 1981. Credit Rationing in Markets With Imperfect Information. *American Economic Review* 71(3): 393–410.

World Bank. 2012. *Financial Development in Latin America and the Caribbean—The Road Ahead*. Washington, DC: The World Bank.

World Bank. 2013. *Global Financial Development Report 2013*. Washington, DC: The World Bank.

OPEN

CHAPTER 9

International Linkages, Value-Added Trade, and Firm Productivity in Latin America and the Caribbean

Pierluigi Montalbano, Silvia Nenci, and Carlo Pietrobelli

One of the key issues in the current empirical debate on the determinants of firm performance is the influence of international linkages. The aim of this chapter is to study the causal relationship between international linkages and firm performance in Latin America and the Caribbean (LAC). The notion of international linkages adopted in this analysis includes two different dimensions: participation in international trade and inward Foreign Direct Investment (FDI). To this end, we take advantage of recent firm-level data provided by the World Bank Enterprise Survey (WBES). Moreover, by matching WBES firm-level data with the new Trade in Value Added (TiVA) dataset by the Organisation for Economic Co-operation and Development (OECD) and the World Trade Organization (WTO),

P. Montalbano
Sapienza University, Rome and University of Sussex
e-mail: pierluigi.montalbano@uniroma1.it

S. Nenci
University Roma Tre
e-mail: silvia.nenci@uniroma3.it

C. Pietrobelli
Inter-American Development Bank and University Roma Tre
e-mail: carlop@iadb.org

© Inter-American Development Bank 2016
M. Grazzi and C. Pietrobelli (eds.), *Firm Innovation and Productivity in Latin America and the Caribbean*,
DOI 10.1057/978-1-349-58151-1_9

we provide a richer picture of the relationship between firm performance and country/industry involvement in international production networks in the LAC region. In particular, this chapter addresses the following research questions:

1. Are firms characterized by international linkages more productive than firms that are not?
2. Are firms that belong to industries more involved in global value chains (GVCs) even more productive?

To empirically derive the causal relationship between firms performance and their international linkages we provide:

1. A static analysis of productivity premiums associated with participation in international trade and inward FDI.
2. A version of the standard Cobb–Douglas output function expanded to a firm's international linkages.
3. A further expanded version of the above relationship including indicators of value added trade as well as the degree and type of industry involvement in GVCs.

In carrying out the empirical exercises, we control for heterogeneity among firms by country, industry, and survey waves, and for endogeneity bias by using instrumental variables and control function techniques.

Our empirical outcomes confirm a positive causal relationship between participation in international activities and firm performance in LAC. Focusing on four big LAC countries (Argentina, Brazil, Chile, and Mexico), we show that the extent of involvement in GVCs matters as well. More specifically, we highlight the key role of both trade in value added and GVC position, with a positive impact of upstreamness on firm performance. These empirical results also appear relevant for policymaking.

In the next section, we review the literature on international linkages and firm productivity, and then we describe how to trace a country's production of value-added as well as their level of integration in global markets. Next we report some stylized facts about the main characteristics of LAC firms related to internationalization and the relevant GVC indicators. The next section presents the empirical analysis, and finally we provide some conclusions.

International Linkages and Firm Productivity: Review of the Literature

Participation in international trade can be an important source of information, knowledge spillovers, technology transfers, technical assistance, competitive pressures, and other productivity advantages for firms, leading to significant performance improvements (Grossman and Helpman 1991; Clerides et al. 1998; Verhoogen 2007; Fafchamps et al. 2008; Bernard et al. 2003). At the same time, firms with FDI and/or multinational firms may generate a total cost reduction through low-priced production factors. All of these factors may generate a positive learning effect of global activities. This "learning-by-exporting" hypothesis has spurred a large number of empirical studies that seek to assess the causal effect of exporting at the firm level.[1] However, there is no consensus among scholars on whether such a learning effect exists or what specific factors may be behind it. While a comprehensive survey by Wagner (2007) indicated that the evidence on this learning effect was mixed and unclear, a significant positive effect of the export experience on firm productivity has been found in several studies.[2] The meta-analysis conducted by Martins and Yang (2009) indicated that the impact of exporting on productivity was higher for developing than for developed economies. Most importantly, the direction of causality between openness and firm performance is controversial (see Greenaway and Kneller 2007).

Firm productivity and sunk costs play important roles in how firms select international activities. These costs tend to discourage less productive firms from international linkages; therefore, firms generally self-select to participate in global markets. This selection mechanism according to the level of productivity is called the "selection effect" in exporting. Melitz (2003), who showed that exporting firms had relatively higher productivity, has provided the theoretical benchmark for the above selection mechanism, while the pioneering empirical work by Bernard and Jensen (1999) on US firms has been followed by many scholars. López (2005), Greenaway and Kneller (2007), and Wagner (2007) have done surveys on the topic. Most of the studies on the selection effect found that more productive producers self-select into the export market (Clerides et al. 1998; Álvarez and López 2005; Hayakawa et al. 2012).

Identifying the learning effects of FDI is also important. On the one hand, the performance of domestic firms may improve with FDI, particularly inward FDI in the form of cross-border mergers and acquisitions (M&A). Fostered by superior know-how, human capital, and organization of foreign firms, local firms with FDI could strengthen their local advantages (i.e. experience in the local market and knowledge of the local institutional environment) and enhance their productivity (see UNCTAD's *World Investment Reports* from various years). On the other hand, Helpman et al. (2004) theoretically showed that investing firms have relatively high productivity. Several studies have empirically tested this proposition (see Greenaway and Kneller 2007, for a survey within this literature).[3] Studies do not necessarily detect a positive causal effect of investing on firm productivity. While Barba Navaretti and Castellani (2004) and Kimura and Kiyota (2006) found significant positive impacts, Aitken and Harrison (1999), Hijzen et al. (2007), and Ito (2007) detected a small or non-positive effect. Hijzen et al. (2006) and Barba Navaretti et al. (2006) further explored a possible qualitative difference in learning related to two types of FDI: horizontal (many plants doing the same activities in a number of countries to put production near consumers) and vertical (different stages of production in different countries). For French firms, they found positively significant enhancements in productivity from horizontal FDI but not from vertical FDI. Other papers have focused specifically on the impact of M&A on firm performance, and most have found a significant positive impact.[4]

TRADE IN VALUED ADDED AND GVCS: DEFINITION AND MEASUREMENT

The increasing international fragmentation of production that has occurred in recent decades has challenged the conventional wisdom on how we look at and interpret trade. Traditional measures of trade record gross flows of goods and services each and every time they cross borders, leading to a multiple counting of trade, which may lead to misguided empirical analyses (Cattaneo et al. 2013; OECD–WTO 2012). Furthermore, since these days a large number of countries have developed comparative advantages in specific parts of the value chains and not necessarily on final goods, standard trade statistics are becoming much less informative.

Tracing Trade in Value Added

The relevance of this issue is confirmed by the many initiatives and efforts that try to address the measurement of trade flows in the context of the fragmentation of world production and try to estimate the so-called trade in value added. Value added reflects the value that is added by industries in producing goods and services. It is equivalent to the difference between industry output and the sum of its intermediate inputs. Looking at trade from a value added perspective reveals better how upstream domestic industries contribute to exports, as well as how much (and how) firms participate in GVCs (OECD–WTO 2012). The overall perspective is shifting from exports to imports. In a world of international fragmentation, access to efficient imports matters as much as access to markets (Ahmad 2013).

A new literature has emerged regarding tracing the value added of a country's trade flows by combining input–output tables with bilateral trade statistics and proposing new indicators.[5] In addition, advanced research on constructing appropriate databases is also being conducted by the WTO and the OECD. However, the interpretation of these indicators and results for individual countries in the temporal, geographic, and industry dimensions are still in progress and pose new challenges to scholars and policy experts. In this chapter, we use data from the OECD-WTO TiVA database, which aims to track global production networks and value chains better.[6] This dataset presents three clear advantages with respect to its main counterpart, the World Input-Output Database (WIOD). First, the TiVA covers four big LAC countries instead of two. Second, it presents a set of ready-to-use trade in value added decompositions and GVC indicators. Third, it links the OECD Inter-Country Input-Output (ICIO) tables using the Bilateral Trade Database in goods by Industry and End-use category (BTDIxE) and estimates of bilateral trade flows in services.[7]

Trade in Value Added and GVC Indicators

Our aim is to go beyond the information provided by standard trade statistics. Specifically, we gather a set of TiVA indicators to map country trade relations and describe the competitiveness of country industries by looking at their production of value added and their level of integration in global markets. These indicators are (i) the decomposition of the value added embodied in national exports, (ii) the participation in GVCs, and (iii) the position in GVCs.

We follow the decomposition of the value added embodied in national gross exports proposed by Koopman et al. (2011). According to this methodology, gross exports can be decomposed into the following components (see Fig. 9.1):

- (1a) *Direct domestic value-added embodied in exports of goods and services (DVA)*, which reflects the direct contribution made by an industry in producing a final or intermediate good or service for export (i.e. value added exported in final goods or in intermediates absorbed by direct importers).

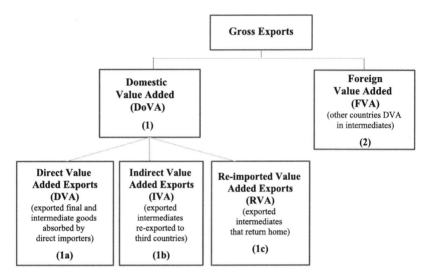

Fig. 9.1 Gross export decomposition in value added
Source: Adapted from Koopman et al. 2011

- (1b) *Indirect domestic value added embodied in intermediate exports (IVA)*, which reflects the indirect contribution of domestic supplier industries of intermediate goods or services used in the exports of other countries (i.e. value added exported in intermediates re-exported to third countries).
- (1c) *Re-imported domestic value added embodied in gross exports (RVA)*, which reflects the domestic value added that was exported in goods and services used to produce the intermediate imports of goods and services used by the industry (i.e. exported intermediates that return home).
- (2) *Foreign value-added embodied in gross exports (FVA)*, which reflects the foreign value added content of intermediate imports embodied in gross exports (i.e. other countries domestic value added in intermediates used in exports).

In Fig. 9.1, components 1a, 1b, and 1c represent the value of exports that is created domestically (i.e. the domestic value added, or DoVA), while component 2 shows the value of exports created abroad. Only components 1b, 1c, and 2 can be thus considered part of the GVC framework.

By combining these value-added components it is possible to assess both the level of participation and whether a country (or industry) is located upstream or downstream in the global production chain. Thus, a first indicator, namely the *GVC participation index*, takes into account the IVA and the FVA to summarize the importance of global production chains in country (or industry) exports. The higher (or lower) the value of the index, the larger (or smaller) is the participation of a country in GVCs. It is worth noting that a high IVA component shows the importance of domestic production in GVCs, while a high FVA component reveals that the country/industry is deeply embedded in GVCs but only captures a small part of the value added.

To complete information on international integration into global markets, we present a second index that characterizes the position of country (or industry) exporters in GVCs: the *GVC position indicator*. This measures the level of involvement of a country (or industry) in vertically fragmented production. It is determined by the extent to which the country (or industry) is upstream or downstream in the GVCs, depending on its specialization (Koopman et al. 2011). A country lies upstream either if it produces inputs and raw materials for others, or it provides manufactured intermediates or both; a country lies downstream if it uses a large portion of intermediates from other countries to produce final goods for export (i.e. it is a downstream processor or assembler adding inputs and value toward the end of the production process). The position indicator is given by the ratio of the IVA exports and the FVA exports. Since at the global level IVA and FVA equal each other, the average IVA/FVA ratio is equal to 1. Therefore, a ratio larger than 1 indicates the country lies upstream, while a ratio lower than 1 means the country lies downstream in the GVCs.[8] Since two countries can have identical GVC position index values in a given sector but very different degrees of GVC participation, it is important to look at both of these indicators to obtain a correct picture of the degree of integration of a country in GVCs (Koopman et al. 2011).

FIRM CHARACTERISTICS IN LAC AND TRADE IN VALUED ADDED PERFORMANCE: A DESCRIPTIVE ANALYSIS

Enterprise-level data offers crucial information to understand the drivers of productivity and competitiveness, as aggregate performance depends strongly on firm-level factors such as size, ownership, and technological capacity. For our empirical exercise, we use a subset of the WBES database specifically focused on firms in LAC countries. This subset provides information on the characteristics of firms across various dimensions, including size, ownership, trading status, and performance, and collects data for 14,657 firms and 31 LAC countries.[9] Table 9.6 in the Appendix presents information about the international linkages we analyze (exports, imports, and foreign-owned firms) for the whole LAC sample by country and survey year. In addition, in order to provide a richer picture of the phenomena we analyze (and to combine different levels of aggregation) and to map out sources and components of trade in value added, we use the OECD-WTO TiVA dataset by industry (see "Trade in Valued-Added and GVCs" above). We focus specifically on the following countries for which TiVA and WBES data are both available for the same fiscal year: Argentina, Brazil, Chile, and Mexico.[10] Looking at all of the data on firms and industries, we can draw a picture of the current international linkages of the four LAC countries as well as trade in value added components and GVC characteristics.

Table 9.1 presents a descriptive analysis of the characteristics of the firms' international linkages (WBES) and GVC indicators (TiVA) for the four LAC countries.[11] The WBES subsample includes 5120 firms across the four countries. The first five columns of Table 9.1 (WBES data) show that, overall, almost 15% of these firms declare themselves to be exporters[12] and their export intensity is on average more than 33% of their total sales.[13] Only 8.5% are foreign-owned firms, but on average foreign investors own a significant share (85.4%). The level of firm internationalization is heterogeneous across these four countries. With regards to international trade, Argentina has the highest number of exporting firms (over 27%), followed by Chile (17%), Mexico (15%), and Brazil (7%). Chile shows the highest export intensity (42%), followed by Mexico (36%), Argentina (33%), and Brazil (30%). With regards to FDI, Chile and Argentina have the highest number of foreign-owned firms (both around 13%), while Brazil has the lowest (4%). The foreign ownership share of these firms is high, ranging from about 83% in Mexico to nearly 90% in Argentina.

Concerning trade in value added components, columns 6 to 9 in Table 9.1 (TiVA data) present the main components of the decomposition of the overall gross exports described in Fig. 9.1 by country (IVA and FVA). The last two columns provide some perspective on the role and position in GVCs by country, using the indicators of GVC participation and position illustrated in the "Trade in Valued-Added and GVCs" section above.

The reported decomposition components show some degree of heterogeneity among the countries. Specifically, Chile has the highest IVA value, suggesting it provides relatively higher domestic added value inputs

Table 9.1 Firms' international linkages and TiVA indicators for four LAC countries (2010)

| | WBES | | | | | TiVA data | | | |
| | Internationalization of firms | | | | | Gross export decomposition in value-added components*** | | GVC indicators | |
Country	No. of firms	No. of exporters*	Export intensity**	No. of foreign owned firms	% foreign ownership	IVA (%)	FVA (%)	GVC participation (a)	GVC position (b)
Argentina	1010	276	33.30 (24.30)	129	89.68 (22.44)	22.53	12.08	34.61	1.86
Mexico	1421	216	35.49 (27.18)	126	83.08 (26.99)	11.46	30.33	41.79	0.38
Chile	897	150	41.80 (30.23)	116	83.13 (27.83)	33.75	18.46	52.21	1.83
Brazil	1792	126	30.33 (27.01)	66	85.55 (27.34)	27.17	9.03	36.20	3.01

Source: Authors' elaboration based on WBES and TiVA data

Notes: Export intensity and foreign ownership are sample means. Standard deviations are reported in parentheses

* Only direct exporters (above 10% of total sales)

** Ratio of exports to total sales

***Following Iossifov (2014), the IVA measure is obtained from the TiVA variable EXGR_FVA for its trade partners (i.e. value-added from country embodied in trade partners total exports, in % of country total exports). The FVA measure is obtained from the EXGR_FVA variable for the country (i.e. value-added from trade partners embodied in country total exports, in % of country total exports)

(a) GVC participation (in % of country total exports) = IVA + FVA

(b) GVC position = IVA/FVA

to other countries' exports. This is followed by Brazil and Argentina, with Mexico having the lowest value, which is in line with its relative specialization in processing foreign inputs. On the other hand, Argentina and Brazil show, on average, a lower level of FVA, suggesting they contribute to their gross exports mainly with domestic value added, relying less on imported inputs. This can be related to the fact that these countries are, on average, more involved in exporting goods in which the main source of inputs comes from the primary domestic sector (Blyde 2014). We note that Brazil shows the smallest share of FVA—only 9% of the value added incorporated in the Brazilian exports comes from other countries. On the other hand, Chile and Mexico show a relatively higher level of FVA, suggesting a relevant presence of foreign inputs in their overall exports. It is worth noting that about 30% of the value of Mexican processing exports comes from abroad. This heterogeneity is associated to some extent with the country dimension (Cattaneo et al. 2013), but also with differences in the patterns of specialization: a relative specialization in producing primary goods requires, on average, less imported inputs than manufacturing them.

Figure 9.2 presents the international comparison of the value added decomposition for selected industrialized, emerging, and developing/ transition economies,[14] as well as the sample of LAC countries. Other than Mexico, the LAC countries show a relatively high level of IVA but generally lower FVA (i.e. a lower content of intermediate inputs coming from abroad). This confirms the relative specialization of LAC countries within GVCs in exports of primary goods. In Table 9.7 in the Appendix, we provide the details of the main value added components of gross exports for the countries in Fig. 9.2.

Figure 9.3 provides an international comparison of the GVC participation and GVC position indicators. The figure shows that Chile's GVC participation is substantial, Mexico's is somewhat lower, and Argentina's and Brazil's are below the selected world counterparts, except for South Africa. This heterogeneity may be attributed to a size effect (i.e. larger economies tend to have a relatively higher degree of self-sufficiency in producing inputs for exports: Brazil and Argentina) and/or patterns of specialization (relatively high specialization in manufacturing can justify a higher degree of global participation: Chile and Mexico). This empirical evidence is consistent with similar analyses of LAC integration into the global production network (see UNCTAD 2013; Blyde 2014).

As stated in the "Trade in Valued-Added and Global Value Chains" section above, the GVC position index reflects where countries fit in the value chain. A country can be upstream or downstream, depending on its

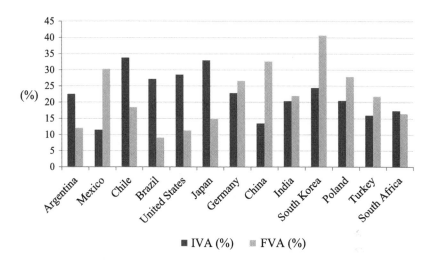

Fig. 9.2 Trade in value-added components: IVA and FVA
Source: Authors' calculation based on OECD-WTO TiVA data

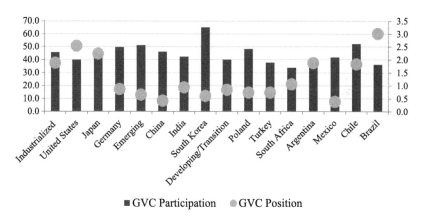

Fig. 9.3 GVC indicators: international comparison
Source: Authors' calculation based on OECD-WTO TiVA data

specialization. Upstream countries produce inputs and/or raw materials used at the beginning of the production process and do not rely on foreign inputs for their exports. Downstream countries assemble products and provide relatively less intermediates to the exports of other countries.

The higher the value of the index (higher than 1), the more upstream the country's exporters are in GVCs. In general, the sample of LAC countries is upstream (i.e. away from the final customer) in GVCs more than their international counterparts; however, again, there is a degree of heterogeneity. Brazil is the most upstream and has the highest GVC position in our international comparison. This is consistent with the fact that Brazil, more specialized in natural resources, mainly provides inputs to other countries' exports and does not rely much on other countries' inputs. Thus, Brazil is positioned more at the beginning of the GVCs. On the opposite side is Mexico, which is located more at the end of GVCs and acts as a final producer, using inputs provided by upstream countries in the form of *maquila* (factory) processing operations (Contreras et al. 2012; De La Cruz et al. 2011; Dussel Peters 2003) and does not provide many intermediates to other countries' exports.

Figure 9.4 presents the comparison of the GVC position indicator by industry for the four big LAC countries. We provide an international comparison with the selected counterparts in Table 9.8 in the Appendix. The indicator used for the industry analysis is obtained from TiVA data, as proposed by Fally (2012) and Antràs et al. (2012).[15] In line with the literature, industries such as mining and quarrying, wood, paper, paper products,

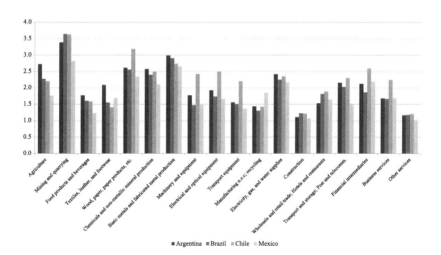

Fig. 9.4   GVC industry position index
Source: Authors' calculation based on OECD-WTO TiVA data

printing and publishing, chemicals and non-metallic mineral products, and basic metals and fabricated metal products are at the highest level of upstreamness since they provide raw materials and inputs for the beginning of the value chain. Among those industries, the big LAC countries (except Mexico) show relatively high specialization, with a degree higher than 2. Brazil has the highest index of upstreamness in mining and quarrying, with a value higher than 3.5. Concerning services, Fig. 9.4 shows that the most upstream services are, on average, telecommunications and financial. Of the LAC countries, Chile is positioned more upstream in the value chain in all the services sectors, while Mexico, in line with the result at the aggregate level is, on average, the most downstream, with the relevant exception of financial intermediates.

THE ECONOMETRIC ANALYSIS

The aim of our empirical exercise is to investigate whether LAC firms characterized by international linkages have higher productivity than other LAC firms. Specifically, we want a more in-depth assessment of whether there is a causal relationship between the degree and type of involvement in international production networks and firm performance in the LAC region.

We start by presenting static differences in firm productivity premia between exporters and non-exporters, and foreign-owned[16] and domestic enterprises. First we pool data for the entire sample of LAC countries included in the WBES. Productivity premia are measured as the coefficients for export and inward FDI dummies in a regression of the form:

$$\theta_i = \alpha_1 + \alpha_2 d_i + \eta_c + \eta_j + \varepsilon_i \tag{9.1}$$

where θ_i is the log of firm labor productivity,[17] d_i is a set of dummies for exporting firms and firms characterized by foreign ownership (i.e. our proxy of inward FDI); η_c and η_j are dummies for country and industry, respectively, to control for bias due to unobserved factors; ε_i is the error term. Table 9.2 confirms the expected positive relationship between international linkages and firm productivity based on firm-level data. These findings are in line with the theoretical predictions that low-productivity firms stay in the domestic market, while firms with higher productivity export and/or engage in FDI (Helpman et al. 2004).

Table 9.2   Export and FDI premiums

Dependent variable: (ln) labor productivity

Exporter	0.177***	—	0.144***
	(0.019)	—	(0.020)
Inward FDI	—	0.218***	0.170***
	—	(0.026)	(0.027)
Constant	1.705***	1.715***	1.654***
	(0.186)	(0.204)	(0.196)
Country dummies[a]	Yes	Yes	Yes
Industry dummies	Yes	Yes	Yes
Observations	11,505	11,158	11,150
R²	0.052	0.051	0.056

Sources: Authors' elaboration based on WBES and TiVA data

Notes: *** Coefficient is statistically significant at the 1% level; no asterisk means the coefficient is not different from zero with statistical significance. Robust standard errors in parentheses. n.a. = not applicable

[a]Includes dummies for different survey rounds for the same country

So far we have presented stylized facts, which cannot yet allow any causal interpretation. Taking advantage of the availability of the set of firm-level covariates provided by the WBES, we can test the above relationship by presenting a version of the standard constant returns to scale Cobb–Douglas production function with labor, capital, and knowledge expanded to international linkages as follows:

$$\theta_i = \beta_1 + \beta_2 k_i + \beta_3 z_i + \beta_4 d_i + \eta_c + \eta_j + \varepsilon_i \qquad (9.2)$$

Equation 9.2 adds the following explanatory variables (all variables are in logs) to equation 9.1: k_i for firm "capital intensity" and z_i for a bundle of firm-level observables (human capital, employment, firm size, and technological innovation). As in Farole and Winkler (2012), the latter variable is a dummy that controls whether firms use technology licensed from a foreign-owned company (excluding office software), their own internationally recognized quality certification (e.g. ISO), or use a firm website and/or email to communicate with clients and suppliers. To avoid bias due to unobservable factors,[18] we control for the geographical location and industry of the firms. A full description of the above variables is provided in Table 9.9 in the Appendix.

Table 9.3 shows the regression results of the base model. It is organized in ten columns. The first five columns report the estimates for

Table 9.3 Base model

Dependent variable: (ln) labor productivity	Export dummy					Export values				
	(1) All firms	(2) Micro-firms	(3) Small firms	(4) Medium firms	(5) Large firms	(6) All firms	(7) Micro-firms	(8) Small firms	(9) Medium firms	(10) Large firms
(ln) K intensity	0.110***	0.0907***	0.106***	0.151***	0.138***	0.0495***	0.193***	0.00681	0.0942***	0.0412
	(0.00820)	(0.0191)	(0.0126)	(0.0132)	(0.0216)	(0.0126)	(0.0531)	(0.0288)	(0.0141)	(0.0261)
(ln) Human K	−0.344***	−0.168***	−0.143***	−0.162***	−0.259***	−0.388***	0.0478	−0.185***	−0.218***	−0.218***
	(0.0127)	(0.0409)	(0.0198)	(0.0214)	(0.0312)	(0.0209)	(0.158)	(0.0386)	(0.0270)	(0.0349)
(ln) Employment	0.551***	0.725***	0.659***	0.654***	0.710***	0.105***	0.388***	0.187***	0.256***	0.295***
	(0.0121)	(0.0357)	(0.0202)	(0.0242)	(0.0391)	(0.0257)	(0.135)	(0.0656)	(0.0331)	(0.0496)
Technology	0.112***	0.0706	0.191***	0.238*	−0.695***	−0.287	−0.787*	−0.276	n.a.	−1.162***
	(0.0390)	(0.0626)	(0.0551)	(0.135)	(0.203)	(0.178)	(0.426)	(0.258)		(0.258)
Exporter	0.0567**	0.180	0.0996**	0.136***	−0.0243	n.a.	n.a.	n.a.	n.a.	n.a.
	(0.0275)	(0.128)	(0.0446)	(0.0382)	(0.0638)					
Inward FDI	0.0496	0.106	0.244***	0.109*	0.0397	n.a.	n.a.	n.a.	n.a.	n.a.
	(0.0402)	(0.162)	(0.0886)	(0.0557)	(0.0702)					
(ln) Export value	n.a.	n.a.	n.a.	n.a.	n.a.	0.424***	0.486***	0.466***	0.451***	0.429***
						(0.0181)	(0.0817)	(0.0299)	(0.0223)	(0.0442)
Constant	4.217***	2.345***	3.243***	3.426***	3.337***	2.795***	−1.006	2.765***	−0.219	2.334***
	(0.232)	(0.412)	(0.899)	(0.448)	(0.534)	(0.484)	(1.183)	(0.798)	(0.453)	(0.654)
Country dummies	Yes	Yes	Yes	Yes	Yes	Yes	Yes	Yes	Yes	Yes

(continued)

Table 9.3 (continued)

Dependent variable: (ln) labor productivity	Export dummy					Export values				
	(1)	(2)	(3)	(4)	(5)	(6)	(7)	(8)	(9)	(10)
	All firms	Micro-firms	Small firms	Medium firms	Large firms	All firms	Micro-firms	Small firms	Medium firms	Large firms
Industry dummies	Yes	Yes	Yes	Yes	Yes	Yes	Yes	Yes	Yes	Yes
Observations	6438	1084	2892	1864	598	1422	51	401	650	320
R^2	0.543	0.568	0.558	0.558	0.719	0.664	0.954	0.722	0.747	0.810

Sources: Authors' elaboration based on WBES and TiVA data

Notes: * Coefficient is statistically significant at the 10% level; ** at the 5% level; *** at the 1% level; no asterisk means the coefficient is not different from zero with statistical significance. Robust standard errors in parentheses. Country dummies include dummies for different survey rounds for the same country. n.a. = not applicable

equation 9.2. Columns 6 to 10 report the same estimates for the subsample of exporting firms by substituting the dummy variable for exports with a continuous variable (i.e. the value of sales exported directly). Also in this case, we use pooled data for the entire LAC dataset. The signs of the relationship between labor productivity and the set of firm-level explanatory variables are significant and consistent with the theory. A positive coefficient is estimated for the relationship between labor productivity, capital intensity, employment, and innovation, while a negative coefficient is estimated for unskilled workers (a proxy of human capital). Also in this case, on average and all else being equal, our findings are consistent with the view that exporter and/or foreign-owned firms (i.e. characterized by inward FDI) show higher productivity. To look more in depth at firm heterogeneity, we also carried out separate regressions by firm size (distinguishing micro, small, medium, and large firms). On average and all else being equal, the subsample of exporting firms (columns 6 to 10) confirms the positive relationship between the level of gross exports and productivity for all of the size categories.

Because of the lack of panel data, our base model cannot avoid further bias due to unobserved characteristics that are correlated with firm characteristics and productivity. To this end, we provide additional empirical estimates for the subsample of exporting firms located in the LAC region by controlling for endogeneity bias in the relationship between firm productivity and the value of their gross exports with excluded instruments. More specifically, from the WBES dataset we select some additional explanatory firm-level variables that are supposed to be correlated with gross exports but not with domestic productivity: average time to clear imports from customs (days), and days to obtain import license. We use these variables as proxies for international trade obstacles that are negatively correlated with export flows but do not depend on firm productivity.[19]

Table 9.4 provides estimates for an instrumental variable (IV-2SLS) and a control function (CF) for the pooled data (the first stage estimates are not reported in the table). The IV results are robust and significant. Moreover, the Hansen's J statistics of over-identifying restrictions—which is consistent in the presence of heteroskedasticity—does not reject the null hypothesis that our instruments are valid. However, the Angrist-Pischke (AP) F-statistic of weak identification is significant only at the 5% level. Since the IV inconsistency increases with the number of instruments used, we opt for more parsimonious behavior by using only one instrument, the average time to clear imports from customs. Further, we apply a CF

Table 9.4   Instrumental variables 2SLS and CF (sample restricted to exporting firms)

Dependent variable: (ln) labor productivity	(1) IV	(2) CF	(3) Small firms	(4) Medium firms	(5) Large firms
(ln) K intensity	−0.0130	0.0881***	0.0137	0.130***	0.0980***
	(0.0518)	(0.0118)	(0.0449)	(0.0185)	(0.0138)
(ln) Human K	−0.439***	−0.364***	−0.214***	−0.247***	−0.231***
	(0.0458)	(0.0180)	(0.0488)	(0.0297)	(0.00948)
(ln) Employment	−0.0921	0.273***	0.435***	0.361***	0.499***
	(0.200)	(0.0250)	(0.0597)	(0.0268)	(0.0579)
Technology	−0.338*	0.288	1.403***	0.0675	−0.435
	(0.203)	(0.218)	(0.151)	(0.315)	(0.294)
(ln) Export value	0.653***	0.426**	0.921	0.338**	0.364***
	(0.213)	(0.169)	(0.819)	(0.137)	(0.0305)
ρ	n.a.	−0.231	−0.701	−0.113	−0.220***
		(0.168)	(0.796)	(0.135)	(0.0447)
Constant	−2.141	0.584	−9.649	1.128	−2.224
	(2.524)	(3.066)	(12.07)	(2.540)	(1.524)
Country dummies	Yes	Yes	Yes	Yes	Yes
Industry dummies	Yes	Yes	Yes	Yes	Yes
Observations	518	1389	345	671	358
R^2	0.397	0.588	0.631	0.659	0.748
Instruments	2	1	1	1	1
Hansen J (prob > z)	0.14	n.a.	n.a.	n.a.	n.a.
AP (prob > F)	0.05	n.a.	n.a.	n.a.	n.a.

Sources: Authors' elaboration based on WBES and TiVA data

Notes: * Coefficient is statistically significant at the 10% level; ** at the 5% level; *** at the 1% level; no asterisk means the coefficient is not different from zero with statistical significance. Robust standard errors in parentheses. Country dummies include dummies for different survey rounds for the same country. n.a. = not applicable

approach that controls for the endogeneity bias by directly adding the estimated residual of the first stage equation to the main regression providing an unbiased CF estimator that is generally more precise than the IV estimator (Wooldridge 2010). The significance of the CF estimates confirms the above evidence of a relationship between trade and firm-level productivity for the full sample and by firm size (with the exception of small firms)[20] as well as the absence of reverse causality.[21]

Finally, we provide a more detailed investigation of the linkages between firm-level exports and productivity and specifically address our second research question, which is related to the effect of firm involvement in GVCs (participation and position) on firm productivity. Thus, we present a further empirical test of equation 9.2 for the subsample of exporting firms by controlling for the decomposition of the value added embodied in national exports as well as the GVC indicators at the industry level. This further test assumes that firm performance in value added trade is heterogeneous across industries but homogeneous within them. We acknowledge this is a strong assumption. However, it is consistent with the high level of aggregation of TiVA industry data that supports the hypothesis of firm heterogeneity across industries. It is also consistent with detailed investigations at the industry level that show a very low degree of firm heterogeneity across sector functions in the LAC region (Gereffi et al. 2005; Pietrobelli and Rabellotti 2011). However, we empirically test this assumption by applying a Levine test (i.e. similar to the standard ANOVA test but less sensitive to the violation of normality assumption) to a set of firm characteristics. The outcomes of the Levine test confirm, on average, that we can reject the null hypothesis that the "within variances" of the set of firm-level characteristics across industries are equal (with a probability below 0.05). This strongly supports the assumption of intra-industry firm homogeneity across ISIC industries and, thus, the relative homogeneity in value added trade across industries.

Before presenting this further empirical test, it is worth recalling that FVA (foreign value-added embodied in total exports) and IVA (indirect domestic value-added embodied in intermediate exports used in other countries' exports) are the key value-added components of total exports. Moreover, the ratio between these two components provides a measure of country/industry relative upstreamness/downstreamness (i.e. the GVC position index). Since the GVC participation index is a linear combination of IVA and FVA, the parameters associated with these components of gross exports are jointly considered indicators of GVC participation.

Table 9.5 presents the results of the value added and GVC estimates. Unfortunately, due to data constraints, we can run the latter test only for a restricted sample of exporting firms from the four LAC countries for which TiVA data are available (Argentina, Brazil, Chile, and Mexico).[22] The results are fully consistent with the theory and with the results of the previous empirical exercises (the coefficients of the base model are all significant and show the expected signs): firms' international linkages are positively correlated with productivity. There appears to be an additional and heterogeneous impact on firm productivity in clustering firms by trade in value added (specifically in value added embodied in foreign intermediate imports) once the causal impact of gross exports is controlled for. These estimates confirm

Table 9.5 Value-added and GVC estimates (§)

Dependent variable: (ln) labor productivity	(1) Gross	(2) GVC
(ln) K intensity	0.0815*	0.0843*
	(0.0396)	(0.0406)
(ln) Human K	−0.412***	−0.415***
	(0.0309)	(0.0302)
(ln) Employment	0.177***	0.179***
	(0.0322)	(0.0292)
Technology	—	—
(ln) Export value	0.434***	0.432***
	(0.0382)	(0.0371)
IVA	n.a.	−0.0537
		(0.101)
FVA	n.a.	0.0355**
		(0.0149)
GVC position	n.a.	0.0376**
		(0.0161)
Constant	0.897	1.273*
	(0.621)	(0.560)
Country dummies	Yes	Yes
Industry dummies	Yes	Yes
Observations	392	390
R^2	0.649	0.650

Sources: Authors' elaboration based on WBES and TiVA data

Notes: *Coefficient is statistically significant at the 10% level; **at the 5% level; ***at the 1% level; no asterisk means the coefficient is not different from zero with statistical significance. Robust standard errors in parentheses. Country dummies include dummies for different survey rounds for the same country. n.a. = not applicable

(§) Sample restricted to exporting countries and four LAC countries: Argentina, Mexico, Chile, and Brazil

that international trade participation has a positive effect on productivity at the firm level and suggest it is not independent of the decomposition of the added value of gross exports by industry. Furthermore, the robust and positive relationship between firm-level productivity and the industry GVC position suggests that the position of the industry in the GVC matters as well: the higher the industry upstreamness in the GVC, the greater the impact of its international linkages on firm productivity. In other words, firms operating in the industries that get added value from exporting intermediates and primary goods used in other countries' exports tend to be more productive than firms operating in industries whose value added comes primarily from imported inputs.

CONCLUSIONS

In this chapter, we have addressed two key research questions:

1. Are firms characterized by international linkages more productive than firms that are not?
2. Are firms that belong to industries more involved in GVCs even more productive?

Our empirical analysis provides a rich picture of the relationship between firm performance and country/industry involvement in international production networks in the LAC region by combining the WBES firm-level data and the OECD-WTO TiVA data.

First, we estimated the productivity premiums associated with participation in trade and the presence of inward FDI, while controlling for firm heterogeneity by using dummies for country, sector, and survey waves. Second, we analyzed the relationship between firm international linkages and productivity by using a standard output function with constant returns to scale Cobb–Douglas technology with labor, capital, and knowledge, presenting both OLS, IV, and CF estimates. Third, we ran a final test of the same equation expanded to account for TIVA-based indicators of value-added trade and industry involvement in global production networks.

Our empirical analysis confirmed a positive causal relationship between international activities and firm performance in the LAC region. Furthermore, focusing on four big LAC countries (Argentina, Brazil, Chile, and Mexico), we showed that the level of involvement in GVCs matters as well. More specifically, our empirical analysis highlighted the key role of both trade in value added and GVC position, with a positive impact of upstreamness on firm performance. Firms operating in the industries exporting intermediates and primary goods used in other countries' exports tend to be more productive than firms operating in industries whose value-added comes primarily from imported inputs.

We suggest that research into constraints preventing a country from fuller engagement in GVCs would be a natural next step to our research. We also believe it will be important to propose adequate criteria to prioritize different constraints depending on whether a country tries to go upstream or to integrate downstream, or to broaden the variety of its exports and opportunities to attract greater GVC participation. Research to assess feasible changes in the business or policy environment in relation to the above factors is alsonecessary.

Appendix

Table 9.6 The LAC sample: exporting, importing, and foreign-owned firms by country

Country	Year	Total firms	Exporting	Importing	Foreign	Exp & foreign	Exp & imp
Antigua and Barbuda	2010	151	29	21	15	3	5
Argentina	2006	975	281	329	139	71	122
	2010	1010	276	441	130	78	162
Bahamas	2010	148	21	28	33	10	6
Barbados	2010	150	48	60	29	15	33
Belize	2010	149	31	46	19	9	7
Bolivia	2006	608	74	271	80	14	42
	2010	340	33	84	45	6	17
Brazil	2003	1642	—	381	—	—	—
	2009	1792	126	355	68	22	41
Chile	2006	984	129	393	74	26	66
	2010	899	150	448	118	55	99
Colombia	2006	980	102	288	29	8	40
	2010	845	151	384	77	35	100
Costa Rica	2005	343	—	145	—	—	—
	2010	525	94	216	85	39	63
Dominica	2010	150	40	9	35	8	4
Dominican Republic	2010	360	39	87	57	13	28
Ecuador	2006	599	72	247	80	15	41
	2010	360	21	84	62	5	13
El Salvador	2006	679	158	294	85	36	109
	2010	332	72	87	57	15	47
Grenada	2010	153	10	20	26	2	4
Guatemala	2006	520	106	207	56	21	63
	2010	547	119	212	68	23	87
Guyana	2010	162	37	51	41	16	19
Honduras	2006	433	52	135	62	17	28
	2010	334	25	86	38	8	15
Jamaica	2010	375	36	81	52	9	16
Mexico	2006	1420	133	269	123	50	84
	2010	1436	216	526	127	58	137
Nicaragua	2006	470	42	212	45	10	24
	2010	320	21	68	36	8	10
Panama	2006	587	77	169	71	18	24
	2010	362	10	31	69	5	2
Paraguay	2006	604	73	292	68	20	41
	2010	348	37	82	38	13	20
Peru	2006	536	101	217	65	24	55
	2010	882	203	455	100	45	124

(*continued*)

Table 9.6   (continued)

Country	Year	Total firms	Exporting	Importing	Foreign	Exp & foreign	Exp & imp
St. Kitts & Nevis	2010	150	26	28	31	8	11
Saint Lucia	2010	150	51	31	28	13	11
St. Vincent & the Grenadines	2010	154	26	36	24	9	12
Suriname	2010	152	19	36	9	2	5
Trinidad and Tobago	2010	366	61	88	47	14	33
Uruguay	2006	605	99	275	77	20	65
	2010	585	110	261	63	25	67
Venezuela	2006	500	15	—	—	—	—
	2010	251	1	41	27	—	—
Total		26,423	3653	8607	2708	921	2002

Source: Authors' elaboration based on WBES data

Table 9.7   Gross export decomposition in value-added and GVC indicators in selected countries (2009)

Countries	Gross export decomposition in value added components*		GVCs indicators	
	IVA (%)	FVA (%)	GVC participation (a)	GVC position (b)
Industrialized				
United States	28.53	11.29	39.82	2.53
Japan	32.94	14.79	47.73	2.23
Germany	22.82	26.64	49.46	0.86
Emerging				
China	13.42	32.63	46.05	0.41
India	20.34	21.92	42.27	0.93
South Korea	24.38	40.64	65.03	0.60
Developing/ Transition				
Poland	20.45	27.89	48.34	0.73
Turkey	15.93	21.79	37.72	0.73
South Africa	17.33	16.49	33.82	1.05

Source: TiVA (2009)

Notes: *Following Iossifov (2014), the IVA measure is obtained from the TiVA variable EXGR_FVA for its trade partners (i.e. value-added from country embodied in trade partners' total exports, in % of country total exports). The FVA measure is obtained from the EXGR_FVA variable for the country (i.e. value-added from trade partners embodied in country total exports, in % of country total exports)
(a) GVC participation (in % of country total exports) = IVA + FVA
(b) GVC position = IVA/FVA

Table 9.8 International comparison of GVC industry position index (2009)

Position index	Germany	Japan	United States	China	India	Korea	Poland	Turkey	South Africa	Argentina	Brazil	Chile	Mexico
Agriculture	2.0	2.3	2.4	3.1	1.6	2.2	2.1	1.7	1.6	2.7	2.3	2.2	1.8
Mining and quarrying	3.0	3.3	2.4	4.4	3.8	4.1	3.0	2.6	2.8	3.4	3.6	3.6	2.8
Food products and beverages	1.3	1.6	1.5	2.6	1.3	1.8	1.6	1.3	1.3	1.8	1.6	1.6	1.2
Textiles, leather, and footwear	1.5	2.0	1.7	2.5	1.6	2.4	1.4	1.9	1.7	2.1	1.6	1.4	1.7
Wood, paper, paper products, printing, and publications	2.5	3.1	2.1	3.6	2.6	3.1	2.5	2.5	2.8	2.6	2.6	3.2	2.3
Chemicals and non-metallic mineral production	2.6	2.9	2.3	3.4	2.7	3.5	2.4	2.3	2.2	2.6	2.4	2.5	2.1
Basic metals and fabricated metal production	3.0	3.5	2.7	3.5	2.6	3.7	2.8	2.4	2.4	3.0	2.9	2.7	2.7
Machinery and equipment	2.0	1.7	1.7	2.3	1.7	2.3	1.9	1.4	0.0	1.8	1.5	2.4	1.5
Electrical and optical equipment	2.2	2.2	1.9	2.6	1.9	3.1	1.8	1.7	2.2	1.9	1.7	2.5	1.7
Transport equipment	1.9	2.4	1.8	2.3	1.6	2.3	1.6	1.2	1.7	1.6	1.5	2.2	1.4
Manufacturing n.e.c; Recycling	1.5	2.8	1.5	2.5	1.9	3.0	1.8	1.4	1.7	1.4	1.3	1.4	1.9
Electricity, gas, and water supplies	2.3	2.4	1.7	4.1	2.8	3.1	2.2	2.5	2.2	2.4	2.3	2.4	2.2

(continued)

Table 9.8 (continued)

Position index	Germany	Japan	United States	China	India	Korea	Poland	Turkey	South Africa	Argentina	Brazil	Chile	Mexico
Construction	1.5	1.3	1.3	1.1	1.2	1.1	1.7	1.2	1.6	1.1	1.2	1.2	1.1
Wholesale and retail trade; Hotels and restaurants	1.7	1.8	1.4	2.6	2.1	2.1	2.0	1.9	1.9	1.5	1.8	1.9	1.6
Transport and storage; Post and telecommunications	2.4	2.1	2.0	3.0	2.2	2.6	2.2	2.0	2.5	2.2	2.0	2.3	1.5
Financial intermediaries	2.2	2.5	2.1	3.3	2.5	2.3	1.8	2.2	2.4	2.1	1.9	2.6	2.2
Business services	2.2	1.8	1.9	2.2	1.6	2.3	2.0	1.6	2.2	1.7	1.7	2.3	1.7
Other services	1.2	1.2	1.1	1.5	1.1	1.1	1.2	1.1	1.3	1.2	1.2	1.2	1.0

Source: TiVA (2009)

Table 9.9 Variables used in the analysis

Variable name	Definition
Dependent variable	
Labor productivity	Sales per worker (2010 US dollars)
Covariates	
Exporter	Firm with at least 10% of its annual sales derived from direct exports.
Inward FDI	Firm with at least 10% of ownership held by private foreign investors.
K intensity	Capital stock per worker.
Human K	Number of full-time unskilled workers at end of the surveyed fiscal year.
Employment	Number of permanent and temporary full-time workers.
Firm size	Micro (<10 employees), small (≥10 to 50), medium (>50 to 250), large (>250).
Technology innovation	Technology = 1 if firms use technology licensed from a foreign-owned company (excluding office software), own internationally recognized quality certification (e.g. ISO), and use firm website and/or use email to communicate with clients and suppliers. Technology = 0 otherwise.
Export value	Sales exported directly (% of sales).
Excluded Instruments	
Average time to clear imports from customs (days).	
Days to obtain import license.	

Source: Authors' elaboration

NOTES

1. The learning effect has not been fully examined theoretically in the literature. The major exceptio n is Clerides et al. (1998).
2. See Girma et al. (2004) for UK firms; Van Biesebroeck (2005) for sub-Saharan African countries; Fernandez and Isgut (2005) for Colombia; Álvarez and López (2005) for Chile; De Loecker (2007) for Slovenia; Lileeva and Trefler (2007) and Serti and Tomasi (2008) for Italy; and Park et al. (2010) for China.
3. Papers analyzing the learning effect in investing for multinational enterprises include, among others, Aitken and Harrison (1999) for Venezuela; Murakami (2005), Kimura and Kiyota (2006), Hijzen et al. (2007), and Ito (2007) for Japan; Barba Navaretti and Castellani (2004) for Italy; and Hijzen et al. (2006) and Barba Navaretti et al. (2006) for France.
4. Arnold and Javorcik (2005) and Petkova (2008) for Indonesia; Conyon et al. (2002), Girma (2005), Girma et al. (2007), and Harris and Robinson (2002) for the United Kingdom; Bertrand and Zitouna (2008) for France; Salis (2008) for Slovenia; Piscitello and Rabbiosi (2005) for Italy; Fukao et al. (2006) for Japan; and Chen (2011) for the United States.

5. Hummels et al. (2001); Johnson and Noguera (2012a), (2012b); Miroudot and Ragousssis (2009); Koopman et al. (2011), (2014); De La Cruz et al. (2011); Stehrer (2013).

6. The World Input-Output Database (WIOD) is a related but separate data initiative funded by the European Commission and developed by the University of Groningen, based on individual countries' supply-and-use tables (Timmer et al. 2014). Another source of data, characterized by a further level of detail, is the Global Trade Analysis Project (GTAP), which is not grounded in official national I/O and does not distinguish trade flows between intermediate and final consumption.

7. The current TiVA version provides 39 indicators for 57 countries (34 OECD countries plus 23 other economies, including Argentina, Brazil, China, India, Indonesia, the Russian Federation, and South Africa) with a breakdown into 18 industries. As for the WBES, the industry classification is based on the ISIC Rev. 3.1. The time coverage includes the years 1995, 2000, 2005, 2008, and 2009.

8. We note a caveat in this decomposition at the industry level. While the value added embedded in a given imported intermediate could travel across many sectors before it is exported, the adopted decomposition traces only the direct and indirect effects.

9. The WBES uses a stratified random sampling method where the strata are business sector, location, and firm size (for additional details on the WBES dataset see Chap. 1). We take this into account in our empirical exercises by using a full set of industry and country dummies.

10. We use the firm-level data from the 2010 WBES survey for Argentina, Chile, and Mexico since the information collected in the surveys refers to characteristics of the firm to the last completed fiscal year (2009), and the 2009 WBES survey for Brazil.

11. Further details on this analysis by industry for each of the four LAC countries are available from the authors on request.

12. Exporters are only those firms that directly export more than 10% of total sales.

13. Because of the adopted threshold of 10% of exports on total sales, the registered export intensity is slightly higher than that reported in similar analyses (see, among others, Lederman 2010, 2013).

14. For the industrialized economies, we selected the United States, Japan, and Germany; for the emerging economies, we selected China, India, and South Korea; and for the developing/transitioning economies, we selected Poland, Turkey, and South Africa.

15. For a given industry, the index measures how many stages of production are left before the goods or services produced by this industry reach final consumers. High index values are associated with industries that are more involved in upstream activities, while lower values correspond with

industries specialized in downstream activities and, therefore, closer to final consumption.

16. As is common in the literature, we consider a firm to be foreign-owned only if the foreign ownership is 10% or higher.

17. Although labor productivity is a quite imperfect measure of firm productivity, our cross-sectional dataset does not allow us to calculate total factor productivity using standard methodologies.

18. For instance, country dummies capture the heterogeneity in price differences across countries.

19. It can be argued that better performing firms are more likely to prepare trade documents and shipments better and thereby spend less time in customs or in getting a license. However, in our case, the weak correlation between firm labor productivity and the above instruments confirms that these trade obstacles are more related to causes that are external to firms (e.g. procedures, institutional efficiency, etc.).

20. The number of micro-firms is not sufficient to carry out these empirical analyses for the subsample of exporting firms.

21. The lack of significance of the ρ coefficient is normally considered a reliable test for the absence of endogeneity bias. This assumption is not rejected in all of our estimates with the relevant exception of the subsample of large firms.

22. Moreover, in this exercise we cannot further test the hypothesis of absence of endogeneity due to reverse causality. The positive outcomes of the tests in the previous empirical exercises make us confident that this condition holds even when it is not directly testable.

References

Ahmad, N. 2013. Measuring Trade in Value Added, and Beyond. Paper prepared for the Conference on Measuring the Effects of Globalization, February 28–March 1 in Washington, DC.

Aitken, B.J., and A.E. Harrison. 1999. Do Domestic Firms Benefit from Direct Foreign Investment? Evidence from Venezuela. *American Economic Review* 89(3): 605–618.

Álvarez, R., and R. López. 2005. Exporting and Performance: Evidence from Chilean Plants. *Canadian Journal of Economics* 38(4): 1384–1400.

Antràs, P., D. Chor, T. Fally, and R. Hillberry. 2012. Measuring the Upstreamness of Production and Trade Flows. *American Economic Review* 102(3): 412–416.

Arnold, J.M., and B. Javorcik. 2005. Gifted Kids or Pushy Parents? Foreign Acquisitions and Plant Performance in Indonesia. Discussion Paper 5065. Washington, DC: Centre for Economic Policy Research (CEPR).

Barba Navaretti, B., and D. Castellani. 2004. Investments Abroad and Performance at Home: Evidence from Italian Multinationals. Discussion Paper 4284. Washington, DC: CEPR.

Barba Navaretti, B., D. Castellani, and A.C. Disdier. 2006. How Does Investing in Cheap Labour Countries Affect Performance at Home? France and Italy. Discussion Paper 5765. Washington, DC: CEPR.

Bernard, A.B., and J.B. Jensen. 1999. Exceptional Exporter Performance: Cause, Effect, or Both? *Journal of International Economics* 47: 1–25.

Bernard, A., J. Eaton, B. Jensen, and S. Kortum. 2003. Plants and Productivity in International Trade. *American Economic Review* 93(4): 1268–1290.

Bertrand, O., and H. Zitouna. 2008. Domestic Versus Cross-Border Acquisitions: Which Impact on the Target Firms' Performance? *Applied Economics* 40(17): 2221–2238.

Blyde, J.S. (ed.). 2014. *Synchronized Factories: Latin America and the Caribbean in the Era of Global Value Chains.* Washington, DC: Inter-American Development Bank and Springer Open.

Cattaneo, O., G. Gereffi, S. Miroudot, and D. Taglioni. 2013. Joining, Upgrading and Being Competitive in Global Value Chains: A Strategic Framework. Policy Research Working Paper 6406. Washington, DC: The World Bank.

Chen, W. 2011. The Effect of Investor Origin on Firm Performance: Domestic and Foreign Direct Investment in the United States. *Journal of International Economics* 83(2): 219–228.

Clerides, S.K., S. Lach, and J. Tybout. 1998. Is Learning by Exporting Important? Micro-Dynamic Evidence from Colombia, Mexico, and Morocco. *Quarterly Journal of Economics* 113(3): 903–947.

Contreras, O.F., J. Carrillo, and J. Alonso. 2012. Local Entrepreneurship Within Global Value Chains: A Case Study in the Mexican Automotive Industry. *World Development* 40(5): 1013–1023.

Conyon, M.J., S. Girma, S. Thompson, and P.W. Wright. 2002. The Productivity and Wage Effects of Foreign Acquisition in the United Kingdom. *Journal of Industrial Economics* 50(1): 85–102.

De La Cruz, J., R. Koopman, and Z. Wang. 2011. Estimating Foreign Value-Added in Mexico's Manufacturing Exports. Working Paper No. 2011-04. Washington, DC: U.S. International Trade Commission.

De Loecker, J. 2007. Do Exports Generate Higher Productivity? Evidence from Slovenia. *Journal of International Economics* 73(1): 69–98.

Dussel Peters, E. 2003. Ser maquila o no ser maquila, ¿es ésa la pregunta? *Comercio Exterior* 53(4): 328–336.

Fafchamps, M., S. El Hamine, and A. Zeufack. 2008. Learning to Export: Evidence from Moroccan Manufacturing. *Journal of African Economies* 17(2): 305–355.

Fally, T. 2012. *Production Staging: Measurement and Facts.* Boulder, CO: University of Colorado.

Farole, T., and D. Winkler. 2012. Foreign Firm Characteristics, Absorptive Capacity and the Institutional Framework. The Role of Mediating Factors for FDI Spillovers in Low- and Middle-Income Countries. Policy Research Working Paper 6265. Washington, DC: The World Bank.

Fernandez, A., and A. Isgut. 2005. Learning-by-Doing, Learning-by-Exporting, and Productivity: Evidence from Colombia. Policy Research Working Paper 3544. Washington, DC: The World Bank.

Fukao, K., K. Ito, H.U. Kwon, and M. Takizawa. 2006. Cross-Border Acquisitions and Target Firms' Performance: Evidence from Japanese Firm-Level Data. Working Paper 12422. Cambridge, MA: The National Bureau of Economic Research (NBER).

Gereffi, G., J. Humphrey, and T. Sturgeon. 2005. The Governance of Global Value Chains. *Review of International Political Economy* 12(1): 78–104.

Girma, S. 2005. Technology Transfer from Acquisition FDI and the Absorptive Capacity of Domestic Firms: An Empirical Investigation. *Open Economies Review* 16(2): 175–187.

Girma, S., D. Greenaway, and R. Kneller. 2004. Does Exporting Increase Productivity? A Microeconometric Analysis of Matched Firms. *Review of International Economics* 12(5): 855–866.

Girma, S., R. Kneller, and M. Pisu. 2007. Do Exporters Have Anything to Learn from Foreign Multinationals? *European Economic Review* 51(4): 993–1010.

Greenaway, D., and R. Kneller. 2007. Firm Heterogeneity, Exporting and Foreign Direct Investment. *Economic Journal* 117(517): 134–161.

Grossman, G., and E. Helpman. 1991. *Innovation and Growth in the World Economy.* Cambridge, MA: MIT Press.

Harris, R., and C. Robinson. 2002. The Effect of Foreign Acquisitions on Total Factor Productivity: Plant-Level Evidence from UK Manufacturing, 1987–1992. *The Review of Economics and Statistics* 84(3): 562–568.

Hayakawa, K., T. Machikita, and F. Kimura. 2012. Globalization and Productivity: A Survey of Firm-Level Analysis. *Journal of Economic Surveys* 26(2): 332–350.

Helpman, E., M.J. Melitz, and S.R. Yeaple. 2004. Export versus FDI With Heterogeneous Firms. *American Economic Review* 94(1): 300–316.

Hijzen, A., T. Inui, and Y. Todo. 2007. The Effects of Multinational Production on Domestic Performance: Evidence from Japanese Firms. Discussion Paper 07-E-006. Tokyo: Research Institute of Economy, Trade and Industry (RIETI).

Hijzen, A., S. Jean, and T. Mayer. 2006. *The Effects at Home of Initiating Production Abroad: Evidence from Matched French Firms. Mimeo.* Paris: Centre d'Etudes Prospectives et d'Informations Internationales.

Hummels, D., J. Ishii, and K. Yi. 2001. The Nature and Growth of Vertical Specialization in World Trade. *Journal of International Economics* 54(1): 75–96.

Iossifov, P. 2014. Cross-Border Production Chains and Business Cycle Co-movement Between Central and Eastern European Countries and Euro Area Member States. Working Paper Series no. 1628. Washington, DC: European Central Bank.

Ito, Y. 2007. Choice for FDI and Post-FDI Productivity. Discussion Paper 07-E-049. Tokyo: RIETI.

Johnson, R.C., and G. Noguera. 2012a. Accounting for Intermediates: Production Sharing and Trade in Value Added. *Journal of International Economics* 86: 224–236.

Johnson, R.C., and G. Noguera. 2012b. Fragmentation and Trade in Value Added Over Four Decades. Working paper 18186. Cambridge, MA: NBER.

Kimura, F., and K. Kiyota. 2006. Exports, FDI, and Productivity: Dynamic Evidence from Japanese Firms. *Review of World Economics* 142(4): 695–719.

Koopman, R., W. Powers, Z. Wang, and S.J. Wei. 2011. Give Credit to Where Credit Is Due: Tracing Value Added in Global Production Chains. Working Papers Series 16426. Cambridge, MA: NBER.

Koopman, R., Z. Wang, and S.J. Wei. 2014. Tracing Value-Added and Double Counting in Gross Exports. *American Economic Review* 104(2): 459–494.

Lederman, D. 2010. An International Multilevel Analysis of Product Innovation. *Journal of International Business Studies* 41(4): 606–619.

Lederman, D. 2013. International Trade and Inclusive Growth: A Primer. *Indian Growth and Development Review* 6(1): 88–112.

Lileeva, A., and D. Trefler. 2007. Improved Access to Foreign Markets Raises Plant-Level Productivity for Some Plants. Working Paper 13297. Cambridge, MA: NBER.

López, R. 2005. Trade and Growth: Reconciling the Macroeconomic and Microeconomic Evidence. *Journal of Economic Surveys* 19(4): 623–648.

Martins, P.S., and Y. Yang. 2009. The Impact of Exporting on Firm Productivity: A Meta-Analysis of the Learning-by-Exporting Hypothesis. *Review of World Economics* 145: 431–445.

Melitz, M. 2003. The Impact of Trade on Intra-Industry Reallocations and Aggregate Industry Productivity. *Econometrica* 71(6): 1695–1725.

Miroudot, S., and A. Ragoussis. 2009. Vertical Trade, Trade Costs and FDI. Trade Policy Working Paper 89. Paris: OECD.

Murakami, Y. 2005. Are Multinational Enterprises More Productive? A Test of the Selection Hypothesis. *Journal of Asian Economics* 16(2): 327–339.

OECD–WTO. 2012. Trade in Value-Added: Concepts, Methodologies, and Challenges. Joint OECD–WTO Note. Washington, DC: OECD–WTO. http://www.oecd.org

Park, A., D. Yang, X. Shi, and Y. Jiang. 2010. Exporting and Firm Performance: Chinese Exporters and the Asian Financial Crisis. *The Review of Economics and Statistics* 92(4): 822–842.

Petkova, N. 2008. *Does Foreign Ownership Lead to Higher Firm Productivity?* *Mimeo.* Eugene, OR: University of Oregon, Department of Finance.

Pietrobelli, C., and R. Rabellotti. 2011. Global Value Chains Meet Innovation Systems: Are There Learning Opportunities for Developing Countries? *World Development* 39(7): 1261–1269.

Piscitello, L., and L. Rabbiosi. 2005. The Impact of Inward FDI on Local Companies' Labour Productivity: Evidence from the Italian Case. *International Journal of the Economics of Business* 12(1): 35–51.

Salis, S. 2008. Foreign Acquisition and Firm Productivity: Evidence from Slovenia. *The World Economy* 31(8): 1030–1048.

Serti, F., and C. Tomasi. 2008. Self-Selection and Post-Entry Effects of Exports: Evidence from Italian Manufacturing Firms. *Review of World Economics* 144(4): 660–694.

Stehrer, R. 2013. Accounting Relations in Bilateral Value Added Trade. Working Paper. Vienna: The Vienna Institute for International Economic Studies (WIIW).

Timmer, M.P., E. Dietzenbacher, B. Los, R. Stehrer, and G.J. de Vries. 2014. The World Input-Output Database: Contents, Concepts and Applications. Research Memorandum 144. Groningen, The Netherlands: Groningen Growth and Development Centre (GGDC).

UNCTAD. 2013. *World Investment Report 2013: Global Value Chains: Investment and Trade for Development.* New York and Geneva: United Nations.

Van Biesebroeck, J. 2005. Exporting Raises Productivity in Sub-Saharan African Manufacturing Plants. *Journal of International Economics* 67(2): 373–391.

Verhoogen, E. A. 2007. Trade, quality upgrading and wage inequality in the Mexican manufacturing sector. Discussion Paper 2913. Bonn, Germany: IZA.

Wagner, J. 2007. Exports and Productivity: A Survey of the Evidence from Firm-Level Data. *World Economy* 30(1): 60–82.

Wooldridge, J.M. 2010. *Econometric Analysis of Cross Section and Panel Data.* Cambridge, MA: MIT Press.

CHAPTER 10

Innovation and Productivity in Latin American and Caribbean Firms: Conclusions

Matteo Grazzi, Carlo Pietrobelli, and Adam Szirmai

We began this book with two central questions: What is behind the weak performance in Latin America and the Caribbean (LAC)? Why have other regions been able to develop so much more rapidly than LAC? This book goes beyond traditional macroeconomic analyses, investigating the factors preventing faster productivity growth based on the study of firm dynamics in the region. One common argument is that productivity gains may be the result of the reallocation of resources from less productive sectors and firms to more productive ones due to competition and (Schumpeterian) processes of creation and destruction. However, another important source of productivity growth is related to firm improvements in terms of better organization and production methods, new products, learning, and capability development.

M. Grazzi
Inter-American Development Bank
e-mail: matteog@iadb.org

C. Pietrobelli
Inter-American Development Bank and University Roma Tre
e-mail: carlop@iadb.org

A. Szirmai
UNU-MERIT
e-mail: szirmai@merit.unu.edu

© Inter-American Development Bank 2016
M. Grazzi and C. Pietrobelli (eds.), *Firm Innovation and Productivity in Latin America and the Caribbean*,
DOI 10.1057/978-1-349-58151-1_10

317

This book provides original evidence on the determinants of firm productivity in LAC based on quantitative analysis, using data from the latest round of the World Bank Enterprise Surveys (WBES) and, in most chapters, other data sources.

In Chap. 1, we detected signals of strong heterogeneity in productivity performance among firms, even firms belonging to the same sector. Also, as suggested in much of the literature, the productivity gap between the most and the least productive firms is much wider in emerging than in advanced economies. Therefore, we argue for the need to seek out explanations that explicitly take into account this heterogeneity. Throughout the book, we show that differences in the business environment, more or less friendly to entrepreneurial activities, are important in setting the stage for business operations, though we only offer a partial explanation of enterprise behavior and ensuing performance. In order to obtain a more complete picture, we have focused on firm-level dynamics.

Innovation is one of the main focuses of this book, and we confirm the general result that it matters for firm productivity. On average, we have found that the labor productivity of innovative firms in Latin America is 50% higher than that of non-innovative firms (Chap. 2). We substantially validate this result by applying the same model in the Caribbean (Chap. 3), where the estimated elasticity is 63%. However, differences in the magnitude of effects in each region indicate that innovation dynamics are very sensitive to the innovation systems where they are located.

The mechanisms that lead to innovation, as well as its impact on performance, vary largely depending on firm capabilities. The same decision to invest in knowledge, as well as the relationship between R&D, innovation outputs, and productivity performance, are significantly correlated with firm characteristics and decisions. On the one hand, some factors, such as size, market diversification, and fixed investment, are important determinants of innovation outputs beyond their influence through R&D investment. On the other hand, we find human capital to be relevant to the intensity of investment in R&D but not to innovation performance, suggesting a complex relationship between human capital and innovation.

Among the various complementary assets that may influence the relationship between innovation investment, innovation results, and productivity dynamics, a key element is human capital, as well as efforts to create and strengthen it through on-the-job training. Results in Chap. 5 show that—regardless of size—the decision to train workers is determined by the firm's demand for skills, which in turn is associated with various measures of innovation and technological development, such as R&D expenditures, improved processes, ISO certificates, and new products.

Another factor that is certainly related to the complex link between innovation and productivity is access to and use of technology, in particular information and communication technologies (ICTs). This relationship is not as simple and linear as expected. In the modern economy, ICTs are often indicated as a key factor in enabling the development of new processes and new work practices. In Chap. 4, we have clearly shown that broadband is an important component of the innovation process, but also that access alone only offers a potential avenue to more innovation. Indeed, broadband needs to be used correctly for its full benefits to be derived. Firms can use it for very different purposes: purchasing, delivering services, or researching. First and foremost, internet use to perform research is positively and significantly related to innovation, not other kinds of internet use. Second, the broader the variety of activities for which broadband is used, the greater the impact on innovation, on top of the overall effects of internet use for research purposes. We also find that the combined use of broadband for various activities has an additional direct positive effect on labor productivity, reinforcing the conclusion that technology needs to be used adequately to exploit its full potential.

Along this line of interpretation, the evidence presented throughout this book suggests that firm performance is the result of processes of cumulative causation and multiple mutually reinforcing factors. Innovation clearly plays a positive and significant role in productivity, but so do other dimensions and complementary assets. Among these factors, it is worth mentioning firm age, access to credit markets, and openness to international relations through, for example, exports, foreign direct investments, and participation in global value chains (GVCs). Because of all of these dimensions, inter-firm differences in productivity and in other aspects of performance are continuing to increase.

The result is that multiple equilibria appear to emerge within the same sectors, and different factors play different roles in the different sets of firms. For example, in Chap. 2, we show that the impact of innovation on productivity is remarkably different across productivity quartiles, being much higher for more productive firms. In other words, innovation has much larger effects on the firms that are already more productive. At the upper end of the distribution (the top 10% in terms of productivity), the increase in productivity due to innovation is much larger than in the lower quartiles (an increase of no less than 65% versus 29 to 34% in the first three quartiles).

Interestingly, the difference in coefficients between the bottom and the top of the distribution is also observed with respect to human capital. In fact, while the premium for having a more educated workforce is 17% for firms at the bottom end of the distribution, it grows to almost 77%

for firms at the top. This result is consistent with the results in Chap. 5 on the relationship between on-the-job training and productivity in LAC. In fact, we find training to have a significant positive effect only for large manufacturing firms: a 1% increase in the proportion of trained employees would raise productivity by 0.7%, but only in firms with more than 100 employees. If we consider that larger firms tend to have a more skilled workforce and that skilled workers receive much more training than unskilled workers, diverging productivity trajectories are bound to emerge.

Our analysis of the dynamics of young firms in the region suggests that firm age may be an additional source of productivity differences (Chap. 6). Generally, young firms are considered a potential engine of economic innovation, rejuvenation, and renewal. However, though they tend to have dynamic growth performance, they appear to be less productive than more mature firms. Their productivity in 2009 was, on average, more than 20% lower than that of mature firms. Looking at the main factors associated with the productivity performance of young firms, it is noteworthy how the introduction of innovations and the adoption of diversification strategies do not seem to affect productivity significantly. Again, the returns on innovation do not seem to be the same for all firms.

Does it follow that in LAC generally "old is beautiful"? Being in the market for many years probably helps in many ways, such as doing more innovation and benefitting more from it, more intensively using new technologies, and having a better trained workforce. We have no information and could not control for competition in markets and market functioning, but we believe we can safely assume that in some markets in LAC, entry and exit do not occur smoothly, and substantial rents and monopolistic niches remain.

This hypothesis seems to be confirmed by our analysis of performance relative to access to finance in the region (Chap. 8). Demand for bank credit is more likely to come from older, larger, and more export-oriented firms, which are consequently less likely to be discouraged and financially constrained. But higher foreign bank penetration and competition are significantly correlated with a lower probability of borrowers being financially constrained. Also, better access to finance is clearly associated with higher productivity.

In an analysis specific to the Caribbean, Chap. 7 has shown that—among firms that report access to finance as the principal obstacle to their operations—only those that record very low or very high productivity underperform with respect to those that do not consider it their main problem. On the contrary, for firms in other parts of the productivity distribution, there is no evidence of significant differences in performance between enterprises reporting and not reporting credit access as their main obstacle. These findings suggest a low-productivity–financing constraints trap, where low-productivity firms cannot find resources in the financial markets to invest in productivity enhancements. At the opposite end of the distribution, the result relative to the most productive firms can perhaps be related to difficulties finding financing for more sophisticated (and riskier) innovation-related activities essential to their performance.

Credit access is also affected by features of the banking sector, and bank penetration (i.e. the number of branches per capita) is significantly correlated with a lower probability that borrowers are financially constrained or discouraged from asking for financing. The limited distribution of banks in the territory prevents firms from exploiting the opportunity offered by physical proximity to credit markets to mitigate informational asymmetries between lenders and borrowers. When the degree of competition is controlled for, a larger number of branches per capita reduces the average distance between firms and banks, and this in turn reduces informational asymmetries and facilitates the screening and monitoring activities of the banks. Interestingly, the openness to foreign banks can have both positive and negative effects on financing constraints depending on the level of development of the financial markets. Foreign bank penetration has a negative effect on access to credit in less developed and more concentrated markets, while it has a positive influence in more competitive and financially developed markets.

This characteristic of openness of an economy to foreign actors and markets—in this case to foreign banks—and its effect on firm productivity is a notable example of a more general phenomenon. Thus, another important determinant of differences in performance is the linkages that firms themselves have with international markets. This relationship is complex and multifold. The standard result that low-productivity firms stay in the domestic market while those with higher productivity compete successfully in international markets is confirmed by the results of several chapters in the book. However, while firms that are partly (or fully) foreign-owned tend to be more productive, they do not invest more in R&D, they do not use ICTs more intensively, and they are not more innovative. Multinational corporations do not carry out their R&D activities (or even their more knowledge-intensive activities) in LAC, and this poses urgent questions about the approach that countries should follow toward foreign investors.

Chapter 9 confirms the result of positive productivity premiums associated with the participation in trade and inward foreign direct investment, while controlling for firm heterogeneity by using dummies for country and sector. We test this hypothesis for a large sample of LAC countries, using firm-level data. Furthermore, in addition to confirming a well-established result in the literature, we add a new element to the analysis of firm participation in international markets that needs to be considered and better understood: the nature of firm integration in GVCs. Integration has at least two important dimensions: participation in GVCs as such, and position along the chain, whether more upstream (closer to primary resource processing and manufacturing) or downstream (closer to the market, in the assembly and commercial phases of the chain). Focusing on four big Latin American countries (Argentina, Brazil, Chile, and Mexico), Chap. 9 has shown that the actual level of involvement in GVCs matters for the productivity of firms in these countries. Moreover, the key role of the GVC position is highlighted, with a positive impact of upstreamness on firm performance. This means that firms operating in the industries exporting intermediates and primary goods used in other countries' exports tend to be, all else being equal, more productive than firms operating in industries whose value-added comes primarily from imported inputs. Being upstream in a GVC has a positive impact on firm productivity, and firms in resource production and processing in the Latin American countries considered appear to be more productive than those in downstream assembly.

So, what are the policy insights offered by the studies in this book? Although the book does not primarily address policy-related questions, the authors still offer useful considerations for policymaking. All chapters suggest that achieving efficiency improvements within firms often requires detailed microeconomic policies that address the factors hindering firm-level innovation, technology, management and organization improvements, and technical human capital development.

However, our evidence reveals that, in Latin America, few firms get access to public policy programs, even if—once access is granted—it appears to have a positive impact on innovation decisions, such as investing in R&D. Moreover, we find positive and significant spillover relationships between R&D performed by other firms in the same sector and country and the economic performance of a firm, and this further strengthens the justification for public policies to foster innovation.

The inter-firm heterogeneity in productivity performance that we have shown and analyzed in the book calls for specific policies for specific kinds of firms. For example, the lower returns on innovation investment at the bottom of the productivity distribution presented in Chap. 2 suggest that the constraints on innovation for these firms are not primarily financial. These firms are innovating (i.e. they have the financial resources to innovate), but innovation does not have much impact on their productivity. This has to do with some firm characteristics, for instance the lack of complementary assets (e.g. capital, technical skills, and infrastructure) or the lack of an adequate system to protect and promote innovation (e.g. rules governing the appropriability of the results from innovation and intellectual property rights regimes). Therefore, public programs should be tailored to distinct firm needs. Detailed research and impact evaluations should provide more information on what kind of tools need to be employed in each case. However, the need for a *balanced* policy mix with different policies for different kinds of firms is clear from the notable heterogeneity that we document in this book. For the numerous low-productivity firms, information asymmetries and externalities would call for technology extension services, technical training, and easier access to common knowledge and technology. On the other hand, a variety of tools are available for the few higher productivity firms, such as facilitating and promoting university–industry collaborations, contract research with specialized technology centers, and advanced technical human capital formation—and the choice will depend on the context and on rigorous analyses.

Very few firms access public training programs, and many find their workers to be adequately trained. The policy implication is that it does not make much sense to subsidize on-the-job training in the absence of demand, when demand is limited by the absence of innovative skill-intensive technologies. Thus, rather than directly subsidizing on-the-job training, public policy should promote increased innovativeness, which would raise demand for skilled labor and training.

The evidence we find regarding young firms also suggests that generic and uniform strategies that assume a one-type-fits-all strategy should be avoided, since not all young firms are equipped to grow and increase their productivity. A broader strategic vision aimed at enlarging the competitive enterprise sector by segmenting the programs, setting objectives, and implementing instruments adjusted for each segment should be preferred. Moreover our research finds that workforce training and technical assistance are positively associated with productivity in young manufacturing firms. Mentoring programs and networking activities can help access to *know how* and *know who*, and to quality technical assistance for management. Public resources are not used much, not even by small firms, thus currently they do not represent a factor in balancing the gap. Governments provide some training opportunities, but these are not used much.

However, the data on access to publicly supported programs do not assess the quality and design of these policies and programs. In other words, it is not clear whether these programs address the right problems, whether their design is coherent with a correct diagnosis of the factors hindering enterprise performance in LAC, or indeed, whether the quality of policy design is responsible for much of the success and failure of many policies in the region.

For many years, the priority given to macroeconomic reforms has shifted interest away from the microeconomic dimension in LAC, leading many governments to place microeconomic concerns further down the policy agenda. Therefore, while the consensus on the appropriate macro-economic policies is widespread, the variety and the ongoing experimentation with many different microeconomic policies reveal that the issue is far from being settled. A better understanding of the factors that foster firm performance is increasingly important for policy design and implementation. This book offers new insights here.

The book also points to further research in several areas that could not be analyzed here. The list is long and far from being complete, but it would include more analyses focused on the services sector and on different subsectors (e.g. high- versus low-tech manufacturing), complementary research on the informal sector that is so relevant in Latin America, deeper analyses of GVCs and the constraints on their integration, and the role of complementarities in factors affecting performance (e.g. human capital, organizational innovations, and ICT adoption). New methods could be used to address the issue of dispersion and heterogeneity in productivity (e.g. quantile regressions), as well as panel data to add a time dimension to these analyses.

INDEX

Note: Page numbers followed by f, t, n refer to figures, tables and notes

technological adoption.
See information and
communication technologies
(ICTs); innovation activities
Teece, D., 7
Tekin, R.B., 39
Teo, T.S.H., 110
Thomas-Hope, E., 240n21
Thurik, R., 216
Timmer, M.P., 311n6
TiVA. *See* Trade in Value Added
(TiVA)
Tobit model, 43–44, 53, 91–93
Tomasi, C., 310n2
Torrisi, S., 111
total factor productivity (TFP), 14
LAC relative to comparison
countries, 2–4, 2*t*
LAC relative to United States,
3–4, 3*f*
as measure of performance, 14
tourism-based economies, 209*t*, 210,
213–214
trade. *See* international linkages
Trade in Value Added (TiVA), 14,
285, 288–297, 290*f*, 293*t*,
295–296*f*
training. *See* on-the-job training (OJT)
Trefler, D., 310n2
Trinidad and Tobago
banking products, access to, 257*t*
credit access and financing
constraints, 252, 260*t*
economy, characterization of,
209*t*, 210
education and skill levels,
worker, 220*f*
entrepreneurship in, 217–218*f*
financing structure in, 255*t*
firm operation, obstacles to, 228*f*,
230*t*, 231

firms surveyed, 11*t*
ICT usage in, 213*f*
informal sector firms, 12
innovation activities, 9*t*, 78–80*t*, 79,
94*t*, 96*t*
on-the-job training, 143*t*, 144, 144*f*
sales, export *vs.* non-export, 215*f*
size of firms, 212*f*
Trivieri, F., 110, 111

U
Ucbasaran, D., 170
Udell, G.F., 245
UNCTAD, 288, 294
United States
growth accounting in, LAC *vs.*,
1–2, 2*t*
internet diffusion and use in,
104–107, 105*f*, 107*f*
TFP performance in, 2*t*, 3–4, 3*f*,
32n2
Uruguay
banking products, access to, 257*t*
banking systems in, 251
credit access and financing
constraints, 249, 260*t*
credit markets in, 251
financing structure in, 255*t*
firms surveyed, 11*t*
innovation activities, 41
on-the-job training, 143*t*, 144–145,
144*f*, 145*f*, 147*t*, 161*t*
productivity performance, 4, 4*f*
young firms, 174, 175, 198*t*
Urzúa, S., 141

V
Van Biesebroeck, J., 310n2
Van de Ven, W.P.M., 116

Made in the USA
Middletown, DE
26 October 2022

13570048R00208